Social Catholicism for the Twenty-First Century?

— Volume 2 —

"This is that rare volume combining scholarly erudition with inspiring visions (and many heroes) of social justice. Each essay in this book serves as a reminder that Catholic social teaching, while solidly principle-based, is never reducible to ideology or abstractions. Rather, it is an adaptable resource capable of nurturing our practice of charity and our commitment to social justice. The reader will emerge from this volume with a thousand ideas for living out a renewed social Catholicism for our times."

—THOMAS MASSARO, SJ, professor of
moral theology, Fordham University

"This volume provides essential historical and theological context for an appreciation of the renewed focus on social Catholicism and the controversies that the pontificate of Pope Francis has sparked especially in North America. This book is essential for all those who want to comprehend the potential of social Catholicism in the context of the crisis of the liberal order and the disruption of globalization."

—MASSIMO FAGGIOLI, professor of historical
theology, Villanova University

"As strange as it is to call these very current and forward-looking volumes a recovery, the essays compiled in *Social Catholicism for the Twenty-First Century?* in fact do recover some of the priority of practical reason for social questions in the moral tradition. The effort is timely and much needed. Murphy has gathered a splendid group of scholars in these volumes whose essays offer much for students of Catholic social thought to think about."

—STEVEN P. MILLIES, professor of public
theology, Catholic Theological Union

"The antiliberal and antidemocratic drift of some contemporary conservativism has found an unforeseen expression in the re-emergence of Catholic integralism—a tradition that resists the postwar evolution of Catholic social doctrine as the papal and conciliar magisterium moved toward a reconciliation with constitutional democracy and a strong affirmation of human dignity and rights against totalitarian threats. Partly in response to these developments, William Murphy has brought together in these volumes a forceful reaffirmation of social Catholicism that is both timely and welcome. These two volumes will be essential reading not only for scholars and students, but also for bishops, policymakers and advocates."

—J. AUGUSTINE DI NOIA, OP, archbishop

Social Catholicism for the Twenty-First Century?

— Volume 2 —

New Hope for Ecclesial and Societal Renewal

Edited with an Introduction by
WILLIAM F. MURPHY JR.

☙PICKWICK *Publications* · Eugene, Oregon

SOCIAL CATHOLICISM FOR THE TWENTY-FIRST CENTURY?— VOLUME 2
New Hope for Ecclesial and Societal Renewal

Copyright © 2024 Wipf and Stock Publishers. All rights reserved. Except for brief quotations in critical publications or reviews, no part of this book may be reproduced in any manner without prior written permission from the publisher. Write: Permissions, Wipf and Stock Publishers, 199 W. 8th Ave., Suite 3, Eugene, OR 97401.

Pickwick Publications
An Imprint of Wipf and Stock Publishers
199 W. 8th Ave., Suite 3
Eugene, OR 97401

www.wipfandstock.com

PAPERBACK ISBN: 978-1-6667-8862-4
HARDCOVER ISBN: 978-1-6667-8863-1
EBOOK ISBN: 978-1-6667-8864-8

Cataloguing-in-Publication data:

Names: Murphy, William F., Jr., editor.

Title: Social Catholicism for the twenty-first century?—volume 2 : new hope for ecclesial and societal renewal / edited by William F. Murphy Jr.

Description: Eugene, OR : Pickwick Publications, 2024 | Includes bibliographical references and index(es).

Identifiers: ISBN 978-1-6667-8862-4 (paperback) | ISBN 978-1-6667-8863-1 (hardcover) | ISBN 978-1-6667-8864-8 (ebook)

Subjects: LCSH: Catholic Church—Doctrines. | Church and social problems—Catholic Church. | Christian sociology—Catholic Church—History—20th century. | Capitalism—Religious aspects—Catholic Church. | Economics—Religious aspects—Catholic Church. | Christianity and politics.

Classification: BX1753 .S6250 2024 (paperback) | BX1753 .S6250 (ebook)

VERSION NUMBER 09/09/24

Scripture quotations marked (NRSV) are from the New Revised Standard Version Bible, copyright © 1989 the Division of Christian Education of the National Council of the Churches of Christ in the United States of America. Used by permission. All rights reserved.

Scripture quotations (NAB) in this work are taken from the New American Bible, revised edition© 2010, 1991, 1986, 1970 Confraternity of Christian Doctrine, Washington, D.C. and are used by permission of the copyright owner. All Rights Reserved. No part of the New American Bible may be reproduced in any form without permission in writing from the copyright owner.

This book is dedicated to those who exemplify the hunger and thirst for justice that Jesus proclaimed to be blessed, and for those who bring hope and healing to a wounded world.

We know that all things work together for good for those who love God, who are called according to his purpose.... If God is for us, who is against us?... For I am convinced that neither death, nor life, nor angels, nor rulers, nor things present, nor things to come, nor powers nor height, nor depth, nor anything else in all creation will be able to separate us from the love of God in Christ Jesus our Lord.

(Romans 8:28, 31, 38–39)

Contents

Lists of Tables | ix
Contributors to Volume 2 | xi
Acknowledgments | xv

14 Introduction: New Hope for Ecclesial and Societal Renewal | 1
   —William. F. Murphy Jr., Initiative for Social Catholicism

15 Integral Human Development in the Digital Age:
   Social Catholicism and Christian Humanism | 16
   —Roshnee Ossewaarde-Lowtoo,
      Tilburg University

16 After Moyn: Historians, the Catholic
   Church, and Human Rights | 40
   —Peter Cajka, University of Notre Dame

17 Christendom and the Marian Path of the Church | 62
   —Frederick C. Bauerschmidt, Loyola University Maryland

18 After Neoliberalism | 82
   —Joseph E. Stiglitz, Columbia University

19 Biophilic Markets | 86
   —Eric D. Beinhocker, Oxford University

20 Toward a New Economics | 94
   —Anthony M. Annett, Fordham University
      and Sustainable Development Solutions Network

Contents

21 A New Vision for the Economy:
   Social Catholicism in the Twenty-First Century | 113
   —Matthew A. Shadle, Independent Scholar

22 Reimagining the World from the Peripheries:
   The Social Vision of Pope Francis | 146
   —Clemens Sedmak, University of Notre Dame

23 Social Catholicism and Race | 168
   —Rev. Martin Zielinski (†), University of St. Mary
   of the Lake / Mundelein Seminary

24 Mediating the Common Good: Social Movements
   in the Ecology of Social Catholicism | 196
   —Kevin Ahern, Manhattan College

25 The Worker's Paradise: Eternal Life, Economic Eschatology,
   and Good Work as the Keys to Social Catholicism | 223
   —David Cloutier, The Catholic University of America

26 #SocialCatholic: Social Media, the Internet, and the
   Social Catholic Vision of a Better World | 251
   —James F. Caccamo, St. Joseph's University

27 Cooperating Beyond Borders: Catholic Social
   Teaching and the Global Human Family | 282
   —Maryann Cusimano Love, Catholic University of America

28 Bridging the Divide: Pastoral Leadership in a
   Time of Tribalism and Polarization | 303
   —Thomas J. Hennen, Diocese of Davenport, IA

29 The Future of Catholic Social Teaching | 321
   —John A. Coleman, SJ, Institute for Advanced Catholic Studies

30 Epilogue: After Populism and Polarization—
   A Better Kind of Politics | 340
   —Paul Vallely

Subject Index | 371
Author Index | 391

Lists of Tables

Table 1. Assumptions of Neoclassical Economics vs. Catholic Social Teaching | 100

Contributors to Volume 2

Kevin Ahern, Professor of Religious Studies at Manhattan College (Bronx, NY) and director of the Dorothy Day Center for Social Catholicism. He is the editor of several books and the author of *Structures of Grace: Catholic Organizations Serving the Global Common Good* and serves in leadership of several national and international organizations. From 2016–21, he was president of the International Catholic Movement for Intellectual and Cultural Affairs (ICMICA-Pax Romana).

Anthony M. Annett, Gabelli Fellow, Fordham University, and Senior Advisor, Sustainable Development Solutions Network. He spent sixteen years at the International Monetary Fund in Washington, DC, as an economist in a variety of countries and regions and as a speechwriter to two successive Managing Directors. He recently published *Cathonomics: How Catholic Tradition Can Create a More Just Economy*. Other publications include "Our Common Responsibility for Our Common Home: The Activist Vision of *Laudato Si'*," and "The Economic Vision of Pope Francis."

Frederick C. Bauerschmidt, Professor of Theology at Loyola University Maryland. His recent publications include *The Love That Is God: An Invitation to Christian Faith*, "Against Bourgeois Religion: Remembering Johann Baptist Metz," and *Thomas Aquinas: Faith, Reason and Following Christ*.

Eric D. Beinhocker, Professor of Public Policy Practice at the Blavatnik School of Government, University of Oxford. He is also the Executive Director of the Institute for New Economic Thinking at the Oxford Martin School. He was previously a partner at McKinsey & Company with leadership roles in their Strategy Practice, in their Climate Change and Sustainability Practice, and of the McKinsey Global Institute. His recent publications include "Is It Time to Reboot Welfare Economics? Overview," and "Are Financial Regulations Impairing the Transition to Net Zero?"

James F. Caccamo, Professor of Theology and Associate Dean of Students and Experiential Learning in the College of Arts and Sciences at Saint Joseph's University in Philadelphia, PA. Recent publications include "The Catholic Tradition and Posthumanism: A Matter of How to Be Human."

Peter Cajka, Assistant Teaching Professor and Director of Undergraduate Studies in the Department of American Studies at the University of Notre Dame. His scholarship is focused on American culture since 1960 and his publications include *Follow Your Conscience: The Catholic Church and the Spirit of the Sixties* and articles on topics including "A Military Surge for God" and "American Catholic Priests as Sixties Rebels."

David Cloutier, Ordinary Professor of Moral Theology/Ethics and Moral Theology/Ethics Area Director at the Catholic University of America. He is the author of four books and various articles. He is active in traditional and web-based media, having been published in *Commonweal*, *The Washington Post*, *U.S. Catholic*. His books include *The Vice of Luxury: Economic Excess in a Consumer Age*; *Love, Reason, and God's Story: An Introduction to Catholic Sexual Ethics*; and *Walking God's Earth: The Environment and Catholic Faith*.

John A. Coleman, SJ, moved into pastoral work after several decades of teaching and writing focused on Catholic Social Teaching. His institutional homes included Loyola Marymount University, the Jesuit School of Theology and the Graduate Theological Union in Berkeley, the University of Western Australia, Furen University in Taiwan, Catholic University of Leuven, and the Institute for Advanced Catholic Studies at the University of Southern California.

Very Rev. Thom Hennen, Vicar General of the Diocese of Davenport, IA.

Maryann Cusimano Love, Associate Professor of International Relations in the Politics Department of The Catholic University of America in Washington, DC while also serving as a consultant to the Holy See Mission at the United Nations and writing a bestselling series of children's books. Her scholarly publications include the book *Global Issues*

Beyond Sovereignty, and articles on topics including Just Peace, Holy See Diplomacy, Nuclear Weapons, Women, Religion and Peace, and Interreligious Peacebuilding.

William F. Murphy Jr., Theologian in Residence at St. Edmund's Retreat and Founder of the Initiative for Social Catholicism and a Better Kind of Politics, while also serving as Adjunct Professor of Theology at University of St. Mary of the Lake/Mundelein Seminary. He was previously a Professor of Moral Theology for over twenty years at various institutions and edited the *Josephinum Journal of Theology* for seventeen years. He has also previously edited four books through Catholic University of America Press and published numerous scholarly essays.

Roshnee Ossewaarde-Lowtoo, Assistant Professor at the Tilburg School of Catholic Theology in the Netherlands. Her present research concerns how to ensure that digitalization becomes a humanizing force and fosters the fulfilment of human needs of all. Recent publications address "wellness capitalism," economic justice and the EU's Green Deal.

Clemens Sedmak, Director of the Navonic Institute for European Studies and Professor of Social Ethics and concurrent Professor of Theology in the Department of Theology at the University of Notre Dame. His research centers on social ethics, the Catholic social tradition, and issues of poverty and justice. His recent books include *Enacting Integral Human Development*, *Enacting Catholic Social Tradition: The Deep Practice of Human Dignity* and *A Church of the Poor: Pope Francis and the Transformation of Orthodoxy*.

Matthew Shadle, independent scholar; author of *Interrupting Capitalism: Catholic Social Thought and the Economy* and *The Origins of War: A Catholic Perspective*, in addition to serving as associate editor of the *Journal of Moral Theology* and editor of the Window Light theology newsletter. He was previously Professor of Theology and Religious Studies at Marymount University in Arlington, VA.

Joseph Stiglitz, the 2001 recipient of the Nobel Prize in Economics, University Professor at Columbia University, Founder and Co-President of the Initiative for Policy Dialogue (IPD), Chief Economist for The Roosevelt Institute, Co-Chair of the High-Level Expert Group on the Measurement of Economic Performance and Social Progress for the

Organisation for Economic Co-operation and Development (OECD). He was formerly the Senior Vice President and Chief Economist of the World Bank and was the lead author of the 1995 (Second Assessment) Report of the Intergovernmental Panel on Climate Change, which shared the 2007 Nobel Peace Prize. His most recent books include *People, Power and Profits: Progressive Capitalism for an Age of Discontent* and the co-authored *Measuring What Counts: The Global Movement for Well-Being*.

Paul Vallely, internationally acclaimed writer, broadcaster, speaker, and consultant on philanthropy, ethics, religion, and international development. He is a Senior Research Fellow at the Global Development Institute, University of Manchester and author of acclaimed books including *Philanthropy: From Aristotle to Zuckerberg* and *Pope Francis: The Struggle for the Soul of Catholicism*. He is editor of *The New Politics: Catholic Social Teaching for the Twenty-First Century*.

Rev. Martin Zielinski (†) was Associate Professor of Church History at the University of St. Mary of the Lake, Mundelein Seminary. He published numerous scholarly articles in the *U.S. Catholic Historian*, the *Encyclopedia of American Catholic History* and *Chicago Studies*, while recently publishing annotations to the diary of Bishop William Quarter, who was the first bishop of Chicago.

Acknowledgments

CHAPTER 18 "AFTER NEOLIBERALISM," by Joseph Stiglitz of Columbia University was originally published by Project Syndicate. It is republished with permission.

Chapter 19 "Biophilic Economics," by Eric D. Beinhocker of the Institute for New Economic Thinking, Oxford was originally published in a thematic issue of *Dædalus: Journal of the American Academy of Arts & Sciences*. It is republished with permission.

Scripture quotations are from the New Revised Standard Version Bible, unless otherwise noted.

14

Introduction

New Hope for Ecclesial and Societal Renewal

William. F. Murphy Jr.,
Initiative for Social Catholicism

Abstract: This second of two volumes continues the effort begun in the first to foster not only synodal discussion but also action to live out a new era of Social Catholicism and "a better kind of politics," namely by appropriating more fully the Social Doctrine of the Church in response to the signs of our times. This chapter introduces this second volume by briefly reiterating some key points from the first before providing introductory remarks regarding the essays contained in this second volume. This second group of essays can be understood as illumining various steps on the path toward fending off the threat of dystopia and working in solidarity and social friendship to build a future worthy of the human family. These steps include the contemporary renewal of Christian humanism (chapter 15) and of human rights (chapter 16), learning to live as authentic Christians in a pluralistic society after the end of Christendom (chapter 17), working for a just and sustainable economic paradigm after the economic, sociopolitical and environmental failures of neoliberalism (chapters 18 through

21), becoming missionary disciples with a continual orientation toward the marginalized (chapter 22), overcoming the plague of racism buy building a multiracial democracy (chapter 23), fostering robust movements of social Catholicism apt for our age (chapter 24), realizing the Universal Call to Holiness through our earthly vocations in a spirit of solidarity (chapter 25), creatively employing social media to foster the social apostolate (chapter 26), cooperating beyond borders (chapter 27), fostering solidarity and mission through effective pastoral leadership (chapter 28), understanding the vastly different context for social Catholicism in the twenty-first century and how the social magisterium responds to this new context (chapter 29) and—in recognition of the signs of the times—understanding the grave threat posed by contemporary populism and the urgent need to overcome it through the better kind of politics of social Catholicism (chapter 30).

In the Context of Key Points from Volume 1

UNDER THE SUBHEADING OF "Historical Perspectives and Constitutional Democracy in Peril" and following a comprehensive introductory essay, the first volume proceeded to illustrate the nature of social Catholicism by introducing several examples of it from different countries including Cuba, Germany, France, and the United States. In their own times and places, these social Catholics reflected the essential aspects of the principles and methodology that would later be developed in the documentary heritage and masterfully synthesized in the *Compendium of the Social Doctrine* of the Church. Through their example, these earlier social Catholics can facilitate our prayerful consideration of how we might similarly demonstrate the Divine Love for the human family as our interdependence is increasingly evident in the face of a variety of challenges that threaten a dystopian future. As the *Compendium* illustrates in its second chapter on "Social Doctrine and Evangelization," to respond to such challenges with God's help and guided by the principles and methodology of social Catholicism is to recover a vital but underappreciated dimension of an authentically Catholic understanding of evangelization.

Given the contemporary prominence of radical antiliberalism and postliberal integralism, this first volume also sought to illumine how Catholic social doctrine and the social Catholicism that incarnates it should be understood in relation to different forms of liberalism and conservatism. In contrast to postliberal integralism, it highlighted the wisdom of the magisterial discernment—explicitly since St. John XXIII—to embrace key tenets of liberalism starting with equal human dignity, human rights and constitutional and democratic government. On this basis, it argued that Catholics should reject the illiberal excess of both the left and right while embracing key elements of "the political community" as we see described, for example, in treatment of that topic in the *Compendium*.

This first volume also went into considerable detail in discussing the various manifestations of the "hard right," understood as the now mainstream right that has forsaken democratic norms and institutions in a dangerous reach for raw political power. This hard right is not only openly authoritarian in its ambitions but has increasingly merited the label of neo-fascist based on embracing political violence and threatening to persecute political enemies who are increasingly dehumanized through the employment of the Hitleresque language of "vermin" and "enemies within." Given this frightening situation with clear parallels to interwar Europe, the concluding chapter 13 also proposed several theses regarding the primarily intellectual formation that will help contemporary Catholics to understand the signs of our times, starting with the urgent need to protect American democracy and renew it.

A Renewal of Humanism and Human Rights for a Social Catholicism after Christendom

Following this introduction, we get into the substance of the second volume with chapter 15, "Integral Human Development in the Information Age: Social Catholicism and Christian Humanism," by Roshnee Ossewaarde-Lowtoo, of the Tilburg School of Catholic Theology in the Netherlands. It revisits the topic of Christian humanism which—through the influence of Jacques Maritain—became central to Catholic social doctrine in the postwar decades and has remained so in the magisterial documents, although the fundamental stance of Christian humanism has faded in places like the United States where the Church has been pulled into more of a culture war model of social engagement. In this context, prominent conservative Catholics rail against the humanism of Pope Francis as if it were contrary to the Gospel, so the topic is of vital importance. The overlapping contemporary rise of the illiberal right, moreover, reflects a somewhat more explicit—or at least more strident—opposition to this humanistic vision, which has great relevance for the Church as the postliberal integralism embraced by many Catholics often looks more like the illiberal right than the social encyclicals, the *Compendium* or the Gospels, for that matter. For this reason, Ossewaarde-Lowtoo's updating of Maritain's Christian humanism by drawing upon the subsequent thought of Joseph Ratzinger, Charles Taylor and Paul Valadier makes a valuable contribution to this collection, especially as she also considers the need to foster a humanistic vision in an age dominated by digital technologies. As Catholics and the whole human family consider the disappointed hopes of the postwar liberal order and the threat of a dystopian future, this essay provides valuable orientation for especially those who have sufficient trust in God's providential care, hope in the divine power to save, and love for our neighbors to work in a Christian humanist mode of social friendship and solidarity for a future worthy of the human family.

In chapter 16, Peter Cajka of the University of Notre Dame introduces us to a promising renewal of historical scholarship on human rights, a topic that has fallen out of favor in recent decades for multiple reasons. These reasons begin with long-running conflicts over disputable assertions of rights primarily in areas of sexual and life ethics that depart from the traditional Christian norms that had permeated Christian cultures for centuries. This contributed to a widespread questioning of the very notion of human rights including criticism of the underlying rational justifications for them, especially given their presumed dependence upon the contested tradition of Enlightenment moral philosophy. The most influential of these critics included Alasdair MacIntyre and Leo Strauss, who exert a profound influence on the institutional infrastructure of the Catholic Church in the United States. Catjka's contribution introduces us to the contemporary renewal of historical scholarship on human rights among especially a new generation of scholars who were inspired by the groundbreaking work of Samuel Moyn, and who have deepened his work into what now meets the criteria of a distinct field of historical scholarship. This wave of recent research has resulted in a new appreciation for the role of Catholics in bringing human rights to the forefront in the postwar decades, who—it turns out—were reviving a tradition with deep but underappreciated roots. In so doing, this renewed scholarship has not only distanced human rights from the excesses of an Enlightenment tradition understood in opposition to Catholicism. It has also associated them more closely with the ongoing development of the Catholic social tradition as it joined in collaboration with those working to build a postwar world of peace, security and freedom. This recent scholarship on human rights initiated by Moyn, moreover, proposes ways to understand why the postwar hopes for a more peaceful and just world—with Catholics providing indispensable "salt and light" and the Church manifesting herself as and efficacious sign of unity—have been disappointed. For Moyn, these reasons center in the neglect of social and economic rights as globalization unfolded according to a market fundamentalist model in which rich and powerful countries and persons came to dominate the poor and devastate the natural environment. Although the magnitude of our problems discussed throughout this collection is sobering, progress toward understanding how they developed is an indispensable first step in addressing them, especially as it can alert us to the false solutions of populism, illiberalism, and postliberal integralism.

Chapter 17 is a reflection by Frederick C. Bauerschmidt of Loyola University Maryland on the role of the Church in society after the end of sixteen centuries of Christendom,[1] which can be understood as "the civilization inspired, ordered, guided by the Church." Bauerschmidt explores whether a "Marian-figural reading" of the story of the Church can suggest what a post-Christendom Social Catholicism might look like. This would see the Church as having more of a hidden life focused on the cultivation of the virtues apt for the household of God, which are also prerequisite for the public task of the Church. It would be "a story that includes both conflict and cooperation between the two cities." Sources of conflict would come from genuine disagreements about the common good since the culture no longer supports the Church's traditional positions on moral questions with considerable relevance to the social order including "the beginning and ending of life, the nature of marriage, and the proper understanding of sexuality and gender." This Marian-figural reading of the story would entail a politics of the Magnificat, where the Church embodies God's "care for the poor, the defenseless, and the

---

1. This end of Christendom is disappointing in one way for those who hoped the humanism of postwar Catholic Social Teaching would be a means of evangelization so that the Church might retain a prominent place in society. It is disappointing in another way for contemporary postliberals and integralists. They apparently want to reestablish the bonds between Church and an illiberal right-wing state so the former can use the coercive power of the latter to foster what they see as a kind of Christian society but which would actually be profoundly contrary to authentic Christianity and Catholicism.

outcast" by identifying with them, enabling "a love of preference for the poor" as a lowly servant. This is contrasted with the temptation—whether in alliance with the left or right—to "see self-assertion and domination as the primary means for establishing a just social order."

In relation to other essays in the collection, at least two key questions arise. The first is how this care for and identification with the marginalized relates to the role of the state. It would seem to accommodate, for example, the long recognition among social Catholics of the need for legislation and public institutions to serve the marginalized, but it would also seem to allow the "small government" approaches favored by conservatives informed by libertarian views reflecting deficient understandings of the common good. The second question is how this care for the marginalized would relate to those with obstacles to their full participation in the Church, such as the divorced and remarried or "sexual minorities," for lack of a better term. Again, it would seem that this approach could accommodate Pope Francis's emphasis on respecting their dignity and accompanying them, but it might also appeal to those more concerned with upholding the tradition of sexual and life ethics, such as by prioritizing a denunciation of the sins of the morally marginalized and aligning with a neofascist state to coerce them into repentance.

Symposium on New Economic Thinking After the Neoliberal Consensus

We next have a four-part symposium on Social Catholicism and New Economic Thinking After the Neoliberal Consensus. The first two short pieces come from prominent figures offering concise examples of the best thinking from outside the Catholic tradition whereas the second two come from accomplished thinkers in the Catholic tradition whose essays show how the Catholic social tradition—including the greatly underappreciated social thought of Pope Francis—aligns with the best secular thinking regarding not only the signs of the times, but also the way toward fending off dystopia and building a worthy future.

This symposium opens with our eighteenth contribution which is the republication of a short but influential piece by one of the most distinguished contemporary economists, the recipient of the 2001 Nobel prize Joseph Stiglitz of Columbia University. It is entitled "After Neoliberalism" and was originally published in 2019 to provide a concise introduction to the three main economic alternatives after what he describes as the spectacular failure of neoliberalism. He lists these as "far-right nationalism, center-left reformism, and the progressive left (with the center-right representing the neoliberal failure)." The first of these represents the Trumpian populism that threatens a mix of autocracy and kleptocracy. The second reflects the failed policies of Bill Clinton and Tony Blair that helped authoritarian China to become the world's dominant manufacturer, thereby alienating the American middle class and rending the social fabric. Stiglitz argues for the third alternative, which he calls the progressive left approach, which is defined in terms of four priorities, each of which I would argue are defensible and consistent with the Catholic social tradition. The first is to "restore the balance between markets, the state, and civil society." The second is to recognize that "the 'wealth of nations' is the result of scientific inquiry—learning about the world around us—and social organization that allows large groups of people to work together for the common good." This implies that markets be governed by "the rule of law and subject to democratic checks" as opposed to what Ronald Reagan frequently referred to as "the magic of the market," which—we were told by Reagan and a host of supporters—should be trusted to produce the best outcome. The third priority is to address "the growing problem of concentrated market power," especially that of corporations. The fourth is related, namely to "sever the link between economic power and political influence." In a nutshell, Stiglitz offers four reform proposals that would be supported by a wide range of leading economists, and would therefore align—in my opinion—with the Catholic social tradition, but are strongly opposed by the oligarchic interests that are able to obstruct reform of the American economy.

Chapter 19, entitled "Biophilic Economics," is another republication of a short work by a prominent author reflecting some of the best thinking from the perspectives of global management consulting and academia. It is offered by Eric D. Beinhocker, who is Professor of Public Policy and Executive Director of the Institute for New Economic Thinking at the University of Oxford, following a career in leadership at world's dominant management consulting firm, that is McKinsey & Company.[2]

---

2. The piece was originally published in a thematic issue of *Dædalus: Journal of the American Academy of Arts & Sciences* (2023). The whole thematic issue on "Creating a New Moral Political Economy" is recommended as an illustration of the level of dialogue in which contemporary social Catholics should be engaged if they are to make an informed contribution to collaboration toward the common good.

Recognizing the scientific consensus that our current economic practices are rapidly pushing the planet toward a mass extinction event, Beinhocker proposes a path toward "biophilic" markets, that is those compatible with life flourishing on earth. He argues that three conceptual shifts are required. The first is from a view that "sees nature as separate from human society" to one that recognizes their mutual interdependence, much like Pope Francis's insistence in *Laudato Si'* that "everything is connected."[3] The second conceptual shift is that "we must see markets not as mechanical equilibrium systems, but as dynamic, social evolutionary systems," that is "evolving social constructs" that we build to serve our needs.

The third conceptual shift is that the "market fitness function"—that is, those factors that determine whether an entity can flourish in a given market—must be understood as a social construct: something we create to serve our needs. It is not something like the law of gravity or "magic" as in the rhetoric of Ronald Reagan. We must, therefore, construct a market fitness function that fosters the flourishing of life on earth in contrast to the current one that unsustainably treats the planet as an infinite source from which to extract resources and a similarly infinite dump into which to deposit waste. Just like various states responded to the challenges of the industrial revolution by setting up regulatory frameworks that forced businesses to learn to operate without exploiting child labor, for example, Beinhocker argues that we need to set up frameworks establishing a "market fitness function" compatible with life on earth. In so doing, he builds the on the economic consensus of needed reforms represented by Stiglitz while also incorporating the living systems perspective demanded by contemporary science, while also indicating the kind of policies that can realistically reshape markets so they are conducive to ongoing life on earth.

Chapter 20 is by Anthony Annett who is affiliated with both Fordham University and the Sustainable Development Solutions Network, and who spent much of his career as an economist for the International Monetary Fund, with his last five years spent as speechwriter for two successive managing directors. His contribution is entitled "Toward a New Economics" which draws from his *Cathonomics: How Catholic Tradition Can Create a More Just Economy*. It illustrates how the Catholic social tradition aligns with the best contemporary economic thinking which

---

3. Francis, *Ladato Si'*, nos. 91, 117.

recognizes the need to work toward a new economic paradigm given the political and environmental unsustainability of the neoliberal one. Annett argues that neoliberalism's deficiencies can be traced to the principles of neoclassical economics, which are inferior to those of Catholic social teaching in the sense of being less attuned to human nature and therefore less likely to produce a healthy and sustainable economy. Annett argues that we are at an inflection point in history and we need to work intensely to build a new social democratic era, underpinned by the principles of Catholic social teaching and building on the success of the original social democratic movement in the postwar period. He does so through an insightful and compelling narrative about the rise and fall of the first social democratic era, including how the neoliberal one displaced it before failing through its inherent flaws, and why a new social democratic era is urgently needed.

Chapter 21 is by Matthew Shadle and is entitled "A New Vision for the Economy: Social Catholicism in the Twenty-First Century," drawing upon his book *Interrupting Capitalism: Catholic Social Thought and the Economy*. Shadle's essay aligns nicely with the previous three in seeking to address the problems we face after the breakdown of the neoliberal consensus. He does so while focusing on the prospects for and potential contours of a new era of social Catholicism in this evolving context. He astutely recognizes the changed social, economic, and ecclesial realities of our day and he is clear that a new social Catholicism would have to be appropriate for these contexts. He finds the social vision of Pope Francis invaluable for precisely this situation. In particular, Shadle highlights Pope Francis's understanding of "integral ecology," which adroitly employs the metaphor of the ecosystem for thinking about economic life thereby echoing the sensitivity to the biological sciences that we saw in Beinhocker.

Our next contribution is from Clemens Sedmak of the University of Notre Dame who writes on "Reimagining the World from the Peripheries: The Social Vision of Pope Francis." Sedmak takes Francis's famous call to "Go Out to the Peripheries" as capturing in a nutshell the Holy Father's social vision for a humane politics. He offers an exposition of this social vision in two major steps, drawing largely from the Holy Father's remarks on trips to various peripheries. The first step treats a much-overlooked topic, namely Francis's vision of Europe, which he sees as the beneficiary of a rich history nourished by the Gospel leading to the development of a humane politics of peace and hope that is a gift to be shared with all humanity. To the extent that Europe draws on the Christian wellsprings of its heritage, it will reach out beyond itself to the peripheries to share her gifts. The second part treats the idea of going out from self and to the "peripheries" which is the mark of a missionary discipleship that lives out the integral solidarity and friendship of social Catholicism.

Chapter 23 is offered by the recently deceased Rev. Martin Zielinski (†), who was a historian of Catholicism in the United States at the University of St. Mary on the Lake, Mundelein Seminary. His contribution is entitled "Social Catholicism and Race," and traces the history of Catholics between the postwar years and 1970, who came to work for racial justice against the legacy of slavery and Jim Crow segregation. This turns out to be a story of lights and shadows. On the positive side, exemplary Catholics wrote about and built institutions in support of racial justice. Leading up to the peak of the civil rights movement, there was an impressive array of interracial councils, education programs, a monthly journal, and broad collaboration to promote civil rights so that many Catholics were instrumental to the achievements of the Civil Rights movement. On the negative side, work and support for racial justice was perhaps more the exception than the rule among Catholics, with many clergy and laity passively or actively resisting initiatives for racial justice. Although excellent documents like the US Bishop's 2018 "Open Wide Our Hearts" have been produced in recent years, there does not seem to be anything comparable to the impressive infrastructure of the postwar decades, which suggests that there remains much more work to do on racial reconciliation and justice among American Catholics than is readily apparent.

Our next chapter is on "Mediating the Common Good: Social Movements in the Ecology of Social Catholicism." It is offered by Kevin Ahern of Manhattan College where he directs the Dorothy Day Center for Social Catholicism. As indicated by the title, Ahern's essay helps to round out the collection by providing an overview of the social movements that not only incarnate social Catholicism but often influence the magisterial social documents. It illumines the relationship between social movements and the church, and proposes a fourfold typology of social movements, also examining the way they mediate within a wider ecology of social Catholicism.

Chapter 25 on "The Worker's Paradise: Eternal Life, Economic Eschatology and Good Work as the Keys to Social Catholicism" is offered by David Cloutier of the Catholic University of America. In it, Cloutier articulates a framework for what he calls "good work" which moves beyond a reductionist understanding of labor in the context of a "consumerist eschatology" and toward a "sacramental" view consistent with the Universal Call to Holiness. It concludes with a consideration of some policy proposals regarding work that social Catholicism might pursue, helpfully illustrating the value of "critical realist sociology" to ensure due attention to the interaction of agency and structures. In so doing, he illustrates an approach that can be of use to contemporary social Catholics in addressing other areas of public policy.

Next, James Caccamo of St. Joseph's University in Philadelphia treats the topic of "Social Media, the Internet, and the Social Catholic Vision of a Better World." In it, he begins with an observation that while almost everyone today in the developed world is aware of social media, few contemporary American Catholics have any awareness of the tradition of social Catholicism, or how it might look in our century. Caccamo considers the contemporary reality of social media from the perspective of Catholic Social Teaching, beginning with a review of papal thought regarding internet and social media. Earlier generations of Catholic thought affirmed communications as a good, exemplified by God's act of revelation, and shared in by humans created in the divine image. This fundamentally positive understanding of communications opens the way to understand the use of social media as a sharing in God's work, thus—for example—it might be instrumental in building movements of social Catholicism. This goodness was affirmed in these earlier generations of Catholic thought on media whether technology was used in explicitly communicating the Gospel or in any mediation of truth, goodness and beauty.

The latest technologies provide even more power that can likewise be used for either good or evil. Regarding the greater contemporary concern about the increasing harm caused by the misuse of technology, Caccamo notes how Pope Francis breaks from a more neutral, instrumental affirmation of technology to recognize that they do not exist in a vacuum. In modern societies, they are influenced by a problematic technocratic paradigm which means their use is "conditioned by the vested interests of politics, economics, and corporate power." Indeed, "societies and technologies are in a mutually conditioning relationship in which cultural values and practices become embodied in our technologies and material productions." More recent Catholic thought, therefore, emphasizes "the negative impact of social media on expression of truth, particularly in the area of news," but also the propagation of disinformation, and the fostering of division and autocracy by appealing to our basest impulses of social prejudice, anger and hatred. Pope Francis is acutely aware of "the economic and manipulative aims that feed disinformation [and] are rooted in a thirst for power, a desire to possess and enjoy." As Caccamo explains in reference to *Fratelli Tutti*, Pope Francis is similarly aware of how social media has evolved to divide people into ideological camps of warring tribes. The Holy Father also recognizes, on the other hand, the potential for using social media for the good and strongly encourages that.

Caccamo also discusses recent social media trends on which social Catholicism can build, including sharing of accurate information and perhaps countering disinformation, serving as a means of connection during times of isolation such as the pandemic, and building solidarity to foster justice and secure a worthwhile future.

In chapter 27, Maryann Cusimano Love of Catholic University of America treats the topic of "Cooperating Beyond Borders: Catholic Social Teaching and the Global Human Family." In a time of increasing global crises that manifest the reality of human interdependence, this article begins with the contemporary lack of institutional structures in proportion to the problems. It then discusses how Catholic Social Teaching—including especially its contemporary developments as articulated by Pope Francis—reflects the global perspective and principles that not only facilitate our understanding of the challenges we face but also provides us with sound orientations toward addressing them. The Catholic social vision of an integral and solidary humanism did not come about by accident, moreover, but was forged in the experience of over two millennia of working in charity for justice and the common good.

Our next contribution is from Rev. Thom Hennen, the Vicar General of the Diocese of Davenport, IA who broadens our perspective to include that of pastoral leadership through an essay entitled "Bridging the Divide: Pastoral Leadership in a Time of Tribalism and Polarization." In it, Hennen reminds us that the challenge of fostering unity amidst the human vulnerability toward division is a perennial one, and was a major theme of New Testament writings, such as St. Paul's epistles. Henen helpfully illumines our contemporary situation with insights from the biological sciences, history and philosophy, and relates it to his own personal and pastoral experience which has helped him to grow in appreciation for the insights and priorities of Pope Francis.

Our penultimate essay draws upon the long experience of John Coleman, SJ to help us anticipate "The Future of Catholic Social Teaching." Coleman discusses the vastly different shape of global Catholicism in our century as compared to the preceding one. Contemporary social Catholicism will deal with an increasingly global Church, the ongoing legacy of the sexual abuse crisis, and the reduced mass attendance following the pandemic. It will also need to navigate the context of ongoing tensions between traditionalist or conservative Catholics and more progressive ones. Whereas the former—who include many clergy ordained in the last three decades—often dislike Pope Francis and post conciliar social teaching, the latter support CST and Pope Francis but are less likely to emphasize the priority of Catholic sexual and life ethics. Like our other contributors, Coleman sees the social teaching of Pope Francis as a major resource to address the challenges facing this evolving Church.

The epilogue is offered by Paul Vallely and is entitled "After Populism and Polarization: A Better Kind of Politics." I will highlight some key features of it, which is no substitute for a careful read of this rich essay that brings the collection to a fitting close. First, Vallely sketches a fourfold explanation of how we got to our contemporary crisis in which populism threatens to overthrow democracy rendering us helpless in the face of what the introduction to the first volume described as the polycrisis. Vallely's fourfold explanation includes not just the economic causes, but the related philosophical, social and cultural ones. Second, Vallely unpacks Pope Francis's distinction between "popular" leaders and "populists." Popular leaders, by Francis's account, appeal to and nurture the shared social and cultural bonds of "a people," where "a people"—in contrast to the ethno-nationalism often stoked by populists—has a future that is open to being broadened and enriched by others. "A people" in this sense is open to new insights into, for example, truth, goodness, beauty and solidarity as developed more fully in the "theology of the people" that he favors. "Populists," on the other hand, exploit a people's culture for power or advantage. Whereas popular leaders revere truth, populists are recognizable by their shameless trafficking in falsehood, which Vallely shows is a common feature of contemporary populists across the globe.

Third, and acknowledging that many will object that to even broach this topic is to engage in rhetorical hyperbole, Vallely picks up on some widely overlooked remarks by Pope Francis that he offered on precisely the day of Donald Trump's inauguration as President following the 2016 election. In this interview, Pope Francis expressed concerns about the parallels between today's populists and Adolf Hitler. Vallely explores these parallels through a review of the sixth chapter of *Mein Kampf*, Hitler's 1925 autobiographical manifesto. He shows that this infamous text "reveals a significant number of points of comparison" with contemporary figures like Donald Trump, who are unquestionably employing the most effective demagogic tactics from this playbook and building upon them.[4] Vallely discusses, for example, what former British Prime Minister Boris Johnson calls his "dead cat tactic," which gets its name from the image of throwing a dead cat on the dinner table when one is losing a debate. This tactic will quickly change the topic of discussion to something like "who killed the cat?" or "why did you throw that bloody cat on the table?" Similar tactics are employed by today's populists, who skillfully weaponize culture war issues as the path to political power without realistic policy proposals to address pressing needs, thereby fostering chaos. Although Pope Francis is widely dismissed by especially American critics, Vallely shows that he is not only astutely aware of these contemporary political dynamics and the threats they pose to the common good. He has also articulated organic developments of the Catholic Social Tradition to address them. His opponents, on the other hand, remain fixated on issues which—while grave in their own way—function as "dead cat" distractions from the existential threats to the common good, especially as this shared good exists in the public institutions of our constitutional democracies and in the natural environment.

Fourth, Vallely fleshes out how the better kind of politics encouraged by Pope Francis will grow out of a healthy "theology of the people" in our contemporary context. It will be grounded in solidarity, in "thinking and acting in terms of community," in cultivating virtues and forging interpersonal bonds, in addressing the structural causes of poverty and injustice, and in working to foster ways of living for everyone that are worthy of human dignity. It will be a politics not only for the people but with the people, giving them voice and fostering their agency so they don't look to populists for easy fixes, but are instead able to recognize the populists as another form of elites seeking power. Vallely suggests that, within this new politics, progressive and metropolitan liberals must build alliances with the "Left Behind" to help them become agents of their own destinies and to recover their sense of dignity. Such recovery of dignity is central to the "popularism" of Pope Francis, which can be

---

4. These include Hitler's discussion of how "Propaganda must appeal to the masses . . . [through] the feelings of the public rather than to their reasoning powers." It must "present only that aspect of the truth which is favorable to its own side." It must "be limited to a few simple themes and these must be represented again and again." Along with this, the mainstream media must be vilified.

understood as an "inclusive populism" that goes out to the peripheries of the marginalized. Through such an inclusive populism of social friendship in a better kind of politics, a new social Catholicism can—as Vallely concludes—"ride upon the same currents in global politics" that gave rise to populist polarization "to create something far more constructive—not an alternative to populism but a transcending of it," re-invigorating "our public life with this spirit of fraternity."

Bibliography

Francis. *Laudato Si': On Care for Our Common Home*. Vatican City State: Libreria Editrice Vaticana, 2015. https://www.vatican.va/content/francesco/en/encyclicals/documents/papa-francesco_20150524_enciclica-laudato-si.html.

Pontifical Council for Justice and Peace. *Compendium of the Social Doctrine of the Church*. Washington: USCCB, 2005. https://www.vatican.va/roman_curia/pontifical_councils/justpeace/documents/rc_pc_justpeace_doc_20060526_compendio-dott-soc_en.html.

15

Integral Human Development in the Digital Age

Social Catholicism and Christian Humanism

ROSHNEE OSSEWAARDE-LOWTOO, TILBURG UNIVERSITY

Abstract: Maritain's integral humanism was an important source of inspiration for the Catholic social doctrine, including Pope Paul VI's *Populorum Progressio*. The call for a "new humanism" has been repeated by later popes and, more recently, by Pope Francis. In this contribution the significance of Christian humanism in the present digital age is expounded by drawing on the more recent works of Joseph Ratzinger, Charles Taylor, and Paul Valadier. From a Christian humanist perspective, integral human development includes the reflective and critical use of (digital) technologies. Since these technologies are not self-governing, the development, implementation, and use of these technologies must be informed by rigorous thinking about the highest goods, values, ends, means, and priorities. Social Catholicism can safeguard the ideas, values, and practices that are conducive to integral human development but also criticize dehumanizing ideas and practices that undermine such development. It can accept the challenge of keeping the tradition of the care for wisdom, the soul, the stranger, and the world alive in the digital age.

Introduction: The New Context of Social Catholicism

SPEAKING IN TERMS OF an "age," "epoch," or "era" is a perilous thing to do, because it means either making claims or accepting the dominant discourse about the nature of a particular period in history. By interpreting our contemporary context as the "Digital Age," I am doing none of these. I am instead referring to a context in which human interactions and activities are largely mediated by digital technologies while at the same time generating an enormous amount of data that feed these same technologies. Behind the scenes are underpaid and invisible "ghost workers" who clean, code, and classify data. These data are put to a vast variety of uses, ranging from the "relevant" advertisements that appear on the internet pages that we visit, epileptic seizures apps, so-called "artificial intelligence"—AI—powered ghostwriters to deepfakes, profiling, and controversial criminal risk assessment algorithms. Our "Digital Age" is also characterized by the dominant political and corporate discourses that the "digital transformation" of economies and societies is necessary, desirable, and inevitable—and, correspondingly, by the international struggle for digital supremacy. Yet another race in the history of humankind. These old passions for prestige, power, and profit are an ironic reminder of the irrational premises that undergird all ideologies. Yet, the rational organization of societies, in which justice, civic friendship, and hence human flourishing prevail, has been the dream of all those humanists who believed that humans were capable of reason and hence of taming the violent forces in the depths of their human souls. The Catholic intellectual Jacques Maritain (1882–1973) was one of them.

Maritain's faith in reason was no (naïve) rationalism in the strict sense of the term. Instead, he conceived both reason and passions to depend on "goodness, love and charity" for their proper orientation to the good.[1] His integral humanism was an important source of inspiration for the Catholic social doctrine, including Pope Paul VI's *Populorum Progressio* (1967). The call for a "new humanism" has been repeated by later popes and, more recently, by Pope Francis in *Laudato Si'* (2015). This "new" or "full-bodied humanism" is one that strives after integral human development, which encompasses the whole human being, every human being, and all human beings. Given the spiritual nature of the human being, integral human development cannot be primarily and solely of an economic and technological nature. In Maritain's integral humanism

---

1. Maritain, *Christianity and Democracy*, 53.

and more recent versions of Christian humanism the paradoxical and non-static character of human "nature" is emphasized. Correspondingly, the transcendent vocation of humans in the "natural" world itself is re-articulated. The ontological interrelatedness between immanence and transcendence is thereby reasserted. Drawing on the works of the late Joseph Ratzinger (1927–2022), Charles Taylor (1931–), and Paul Valadier (1933–), I will develop what Maritain referred to as a "democratic philosophy of man and society," which is a humanist political philosophy that affirms the "absolute primacy of the relations of justice and law at the base of society, and an ideal not of war, prestige or power, but of the amelioration and emancipation of human life."[2]

According to this (Christian) humanist philosophy, the development of humanity and human societies is not a linear and necessary process but instead a "thwarted movement, purchased at the price of an heroic tension of spiritual and physical energies."[3] In the next section I explain "Christian humanism," introducing it both as a philosophy of the human and society and a counter-ideological resource in a world still dominated by variants of naturalistic materialism. I then move on to an important dimension of Christian humanism, namely, its understanding of human nature as the *imago Dei* (image of God). The three thinkers differ from mainstream conceptualizations of the *imago Dei* by their emphasis on the relational nature of the *imago Dei* and hence on *communion* as the highest human vocation. In the third section I elaborate on the implications of this understanding of the human vocation for integral human development in the context of digitalization. My argument is that the challenges that digital technologies give rise to are not only ethical but also existential: our engagement with (digital) technologies changes not only our practices but also our ways of thinking, feeling, and our aspirations. Christian humanism can take up the challenge of tirelessly recalling the highest goods, values, ends, means, and priorities that ought to guide the development, implementation, and use of these technologies. Moreover, digitalization does not override the persistent challenge of social, economic, and environmental (in)justice. In this regard, social

---

2. Maritain, *Christianity and Democracy*, 57. All translations of texts from Valadier's works are my own unless indicated otherwise. I have opted for a literal translation, which sometimes results in uncommon expressions in English. In order to maintain as much gender neutrality as possible, I have replaced the singular "man" (*l'homme*) with "humans" as often as possible.

3. Maritain, *Christianity and Democracy*, 121.

Catholicism, informed by Christian humanism, can recall the high standard of justice that is entailed by the ideal of communion. Social Catholicism, I conclude, has both a humanizing and critical function—for the sake of all human souls and hence a truly integral human development.

The Ontological Underpinnings of All Humanisms

The "new" humanism that Maritain advocated and deemed necessary was novel only relatively, that is, in comparison to the dominant anthropocentric forms of humanism.[4] He retrieved the core ideas of an integral humanism from the debris of Catholic intellectual traditions that had been either forgotten or corrupted. His *ressourcement*, however, would not have been possible without his faith in the power of truth and love and his own intense love for justice and his fellow beings. In other words, though the ideas for Christian humanism can be found in Christian thought itself, they need not be acknowledged. Such endorsement depends on particular ontological and anthropological assumptions and commitments, which we may not share. Two such crucial assumptions regard human "nature" and its ends and the conceived relation between transcendence and immanence. It is precisely at this level that Christian humanism diverges from an atheist humanism. Of course, it is not only about different beliefs and ideas but also, above all things, about our highest human possibilities and responsibilities here in this mortal life. These existential dimensions and implications of a religious humanism are very much overlooked by the author of *Humanism: A Very Short Introduction* (2011) when he asks, "do humanists miss out on something" when they give up religion?[5] For Stephen Law "Christian humanism" would be an oxymoron. But this might also be the case for Christians themselves. Yet, as I will explain in this section, an integral humanism lies at the very heart of Christianity and is thus not a modern phenomenon. It is certainly not a Christian version of the much more recent secular or "exclusive" humanism, to borrow Taylor's terminology.

"Humanism" and religion have often been opposed to each other ever since the Enlightenment and sometimes rightly so. Religions, however "revealed" they might be, are not immune to ideological distortions.

---

4. We may, however, wonder whether ideas and beliefs that have led to totalitarianism and to a priori limitations of intellectual and spiritual horizons can be called "humanist" at all.

5. Law, *Humanism*, 131.

Ironically enough, the consciousness of such possible corruption is itself religious since it presumes the notion of transcendence. One of the etymologies of ideologies is in fact "idols," the false gods—such as wealth and prestige—whose worship has been traditionally condemned by both religion and philosophy. However, when Law repeats the usual tirade against religion in general and Christianity in particular by claiming that religion prevents people from thinking and living life fully, he is not referring to a corrupted religion. He is asserting that religious "belief" is *essentially* a form of delusion. The humanist, according to him, has burst the magic "bubble of religious belief" and no longer believes in Santa Claus.[6] Of course, it is possible that Law has only had access to the shallow versions of religion and religious life. Nonetheless, it is hard to ignore the narrative of coming of age in his depiction of an (exclusive) humanism.[7] This understanding of humanism is terribly one-sided since it fails to recognize the faith that undergirds all humanisms. The post-humanist (or rather, anti-humanist) John Gray is not wrong to note that "the humanist belief in progress is only a secular version of this Christian faith."[8] The secularization of Christian faith consists in the eclipse of the original pre-scientific and even pre-rational grounds for the faith in humans, in the human capacity for self-transcendence, and in the re-conceptualization of progress as economic and science-driven technological progress.

Humanism rests on the belief that humanity must be and can be cultivated. This means that a certain degree of human freedom and reason is presumed. Though it is common to trace the roots of humanism to ancient Greece and Rome, homes to *paideia* and *humanitas*, respectively, it might be correct to go even further back to the "Axial Age," to understand the sources of the ideals of *paideia* and *humanitas*. "Axial Age" is a term coined by Karl Jaspers (1883–1969) to refer to the period roughly ranging from 800–200 BCE (or even earlier), when "new" religions and philosophies arose. Zarathustra, Confucius, Gautama, Socrates, and the Hebrew prophets are representative figures of this Axial Age. Characteristic for this axial (that is, revolutionary) age are the ideas of transcendence, individuality, and individual moral progress (self-transcendence). These are the key features of what Taylor calls the "Axial spirituality." In *A Secular Age* he shows how this axial spirituality has been active

6. Law, *Humanism*, 132.
7. Taylor, *Secular Age*, 589.
8. Gray, *Straw Dogs*, 4.

throughout Western history, from the late medieval period onwards. The idea of a transcendent realm and hence of transcendent norms of goodness and justice enables not only individual moral progress but also the criticism of social, political, and religious conventions. Prophets are precisely those who dare condemn iniquity and hence both unjust status quos and unjust "progresses." Of course, it is dubious that it is merely an *idea* that empowers people to transcend the instincts of self-preservation and self-interest. The *reality* that is implied by acts of self-transcendence and social/religious criticism is the possibility of the transcendent—or divine—empowerment of human selves. Another way of putting it is to say that transcendence permeates immanence and at the same time exceeds the observable—and even phenomenological—reality.

The idea of the intimate interrelation between immanence and transcendence has faded away in late medieval and modern times though it could be claimed that it was bound to have a tough time as soon as God was differentiated from the cosmos, and the human from extra-human nature. However, the actual constructed dichotomies between the natural and the so-called "supernatural" order, between the religious and the secular, and between faith and reason can be blamed on particular theological and philosophical ideas. In fact, the very language of the "supernatural" (and perhaps also of "immanence") reflects the confusion regarding the relation between nature and transcendence and hence (human) nature itself. As Taylor notes,

> In these practices of prayer and devotion, and in the reflections, say, of St. Francis de Sales, in his *Traité de l'Amour de Dieu*, God's presence in the world, however narrowed in the theories of theologians, is still very much felt. But devout humanism supposes that we can find within us that élan towards God on which we can build, the seed which we can nourish. . . . If our nature is really quite depraved, then the hope of finding this élan within us can be a snare and a delusion, a figment of our own pride. Recognizing our distance from God, we can only throw ourselves on his mercy, hoping that he will heal our ruined nature. We must obey his commandments from a distance in fear, rather than presume to approach him in love.[9]

---

9. Taylor, *Secular Age*, 227.

Such distance, even if philosophically and theologically conceivable, fails to take the full implications of Incarnation (and of creation) into account, as Ratzinger reminds his audience in his Regensburg lecture.[10]

There also seems to be much confusion regarding "transcendence," which appears to be some kind of (illusory) surplus that can be discarded at will without any detriment. The notion that transcendence is not an addition to an already full life but is constitutive of love, goodness, truth, and justice and is already present in human lives, including so-called nonreligious lives, might be hard to digest in historical contexts shaped by materialism. The restoration of the conceived intimate relation between immanence and transcendence, which is a precondition for Christian humanism, is an important dimension of the works of Ratzinger, Taylor, and Valadier. "Transcendence," in their cases, refers to divine transcendence, Spirit, and overabundant Life. Taylor distinguishes between two types of "acknowledgers of transcendence," namely, between those who hold that "secular humanism was just a mistake, which needs to be undone" and "others, in which I [Taylor] place myself, think that the practical primacy of life has been a great gain for humankind."[11] While supporting the affirmation of life, Taylor resists its *metaphysical* reduction to what he calls "ordinary human flourishing." In the latter case, what is being claimed is that there is necessarily nothing beyond ordinary human flourishing, either because we are too depraved to have any transcendent vocation or because there is no extra-human spiritual reality. Since these materialist, determinist, and naturalist approaches to humans and our worlds are oppressive and mutilating, Christian humanism has the important task of articulating the spiritual, moral, intellectual, social, and political preconditions for integral human development. In other words, it is not simply (or solely) a theoretical treatise on humans, but it is in and of itself a resource, a response to a world ruled by uncriticized ideologies.

The Christian humanist faith in humans is far from being blind. The conception of evil as permanent is part of Christian humanism, constituting a wisdom that has to be recalled time and again. But while this is one facet of human reality that tends to be overlooked, medicalized, or psychologized, it is not the only one. The greatness of human souls (persons), that is, our transcendent vocation also tends to be eschewed. As Henri de Lubac remarks, the description of the human as "a noble

---

10. Benedict XVI, *Faith, Reason, and the University*.
11. Taylor, *Secular Age*, 637.

creature in the capacity for majesty . . . seems in fact rather too noble for us. We may even come to find it too demanding."[12] *If* it is true that we are called to a life that can neither be created nor fulfilled by us and are by reason of this vocation also endowed with an irrevocable "dignity" here and now, then it means that anthropocentrism deprives us of ends proper to us and forces us to lower our aspirations. In this case, the question is not so much whether morality can be achieved within a closed immanent order—without extra-human power—but rather whether possible goods (realities) can be loved in this human life. Anthropocentrism, "secularism," and positivistic theories in general have no place for transcendent, extra-human sources. "Science" or "experience" is often used to legitimize the narrowing of our ontology. Yet, there is no such thing as a super-human entity called "science" but only scientists of blood and flesh, whose aspirations and works bear the marks of grandeur and depravity. As far as experience is concerned, it is dependent on cultures (implicit beliefs, ideas, values, and myths), temperaments, moods, and seasons. As Taylor rightly wonders, "who has decreed that the transformations we can hope and strive for in human life are restricted to those which can be carried out in a meaningless universe without a transcendent source?"[13]

A true humanism requires the negation of what Taylor calls the "limits of the regnant versions of immanent order" both in terms of theories and (political) practices.[14] In other words, it requires our dispelling the "secularist spin," which he especially sees in intellectual and academic circles.[15] "Spin" refers to the condition whereby human thinking is clouded by "a powerful picture which prevents one from seeing important aspects of reality."[16] This is also what the older Wittgenstein meant when he spoke of people being "captured by a picture." The secularist spin refers to the belief that the modern order is *necessarily* a naturalist order and that the highest human good is one that fits this order. Those in thrall to the secularist spin are neither gullible victims nor do they consciously acquiesce to the "scientific facts" that have revealed the naturalistic anthropology as being "true." Rationality, however defined, hardly plays a role in this enchantment. It is our background understanding that makes it difficult for us to imagine and experience a "natural" order

12. Lubac, *Mystery of the Supernatural*, 136.
13. Taylor, *Secular Age*, 589.
14. Taylor, *Secular Age*, 732.
15. Taylor, *Secular Age*, 549–50.
16. Taylor, *Secular Age*, 551.

that participates in a transcendent realm. Humans, Taylor explains, only respond to "facts" or "discoveries" against a certain "background," which makes sense of these "facts" (which are already the results of cultural interpretation and construction). We still have to make the information that we receive an "internal source."[17] Following Taylor's reasoning, we accept some claims and reject others in accordance with our implicit vision of human agency. Conversely, arguments and other technicalities do not play a decisive role in "convincing" us to keep or abandon our understanding of the self and of the world, however destructive and self-mutilating it happens to be. Of course, a destructive anthropology and ontology can be both religious and nonreligious. In the next section I outline a conception of human nature that avoids both an oppressive essentialism and a self-annihilating nihilism.

Human Nature as *imago Dei*

The anti-essentialist rejection of "human nature," contrary to the underlying intention and widespread belief, has not liberated humans but has allowed mechanistic and naturalistic conceptions of the human being to prevail. As a result, it is not uncommon to hear ourselves nonchalantly being described as great apes, brains in bodies, or a set of neurons.[18] The terminology "artificial intelligence" and the expectation or fear that machines will become super-humans reflect a strange confusion with regard to human nature and hence human intelligence. These claims would not have been so damaging if they did not determine our self-understanding, our relationships, and the ways in which we shape our worlds. The challenge that any philosophy of human nature faces is that of articulating that which makes us human while avoiding the many pitfalls that partly incited the anti-essentialist movement in the first place. The question regarding what makes us human is unavoidable if we wish to prevent dehumanizing practices. Our answers, however, can be dehumanizing, too, by being too narrow or too hubristic. In other words, any answer to the question of who the human is must capture what de Lubac referred to as the "human paradox," which is the situation of spiritual beings who reach fulfilment—our ends—by going beyond ourselves.[19] Ratzinger's,

---

17. Taylor, *Secular Age*, 568.
18. See also Midgley, *Are You an Illusion?*
19. Lubac, *Mystery of the Supernatural*, 102.

Taylor's, and Valadier's understanding of human nature as the *imago Dei* captures the spiritual and transcendent vocation or end of humans and hence avoids the biological or physical delimitation that is often conveyed by the terminology. Correspondingly, they retrieve the somewhat forgotten idea that all human beings are called to *theosis*, that is, to divinization. This conception of human exceptionality runs counter to (neo-)Aristotelian ideas of human nature, which are often implicitly assumed in discussions about human dignity.

The notion of the human being as the *imago Dei* raises a different and perhaps even more tortuous question since it concerns the "God" in whose image humans are thought to be made. The image of God, of course, determines the image of the human, God being the measure of the human. The psychotherapist Alfred Adler (1870–1937) thought it was a bad idea to teach children that they were made in the image of God. Children should not be taught the Bible, "at least not without a commentary, to the end that a child may learn to be content in this life, without assuming all manner of magical powers, and demanding that everyone be his slave, ostensibly because he was created in the image of God."[20] Alder's fear is not unreasonable. This is precisely why especially Ratzinger and Valadier go to great lengths to dispel pictures of a sovereign, self-loving narcissistic God. Ratzinger warns us that we should not distinguish too much between the God of faith and the God of the philosophers. In the end, reason is "God's great gift to man."[21] However, human reason (as well as imagination) has created a God whom Ratzinger calls "a relationless, self-orbiting Being."[22] This image of God has in turn fueled the human self-understanding as self-sufficient subjects, whom Taylor has dubbed "buffered selves." Of course, it could be argued that it is our self-understanding as independent and self-sufficient beings that was conducive to the picture of a sovereign, self-loving God. It is perilous to try to establish causal relations in these matters. In any case, it can be safely concluded that human self-understandings and conceptions of God are closely interrelated.

The consequences of the imitation of a god who is primarily associated with power and dominion have been pointed out by post- and antihumanists and (eco)feminists, among others. Ratzinger's Christocentric approach enables him to correct this image of God. The education of

20. Adler, *Understanding Human Nature*, 216.
21. Benedict XVI, *Caritas in Veritate*, 23.
22. Ratzinger, "In Search of Freedom," 4.

theosis is "the education of the cross," which is self-giving.[23] To imitate a God who is Love is therefore not an impossible or vague enterprise: to "be truly a human being means to be related in love, to be *of* and *for*."[24] It means being open to the gift of love. Against a Promethean understanding of God, Ratzinger stresses the "littleness" of God and the "little daily virtues"—which is a direct reference to Thérèse de Lisieux—which we can practice to become more like God. Valadier, similarly, distinguishes carefully between the egoist God and the God who is love. And like Ratzinger, he emphasizes the analogy between human beings and God:

> The divine model of the image, revealed by the Bible and hence through the economy of salvation, is that of a God Logos, Word, and reason, wisdom ordering everything and source of a Law that makes [us] live, merciful love, overabundant, and inexhaustible. It is this God whom humans resemble and not the imaginary Sovereign imagined by spontaneous religious sentiment. Created this way, humans are analogically endowed with the attributes of reason, wisdom, a regulating will, love, which are those of their Creator.... Hence, the more humans exercise their possibilities, the more they glorify God and conform to his image, make themselves what they must become.... Is this not a remarkable charter for a Christian humanism?[25]

Valadier, like Ratzinger, stresses the ontological relation between humans and God, reminding us why Augustine held that the true knowledge of oneself and the knowledge of God are intimately interconnected. Humans, similarly to God, are not self-enclosed individuals but fundamentally relational and hence self-giving.

Taylor sees the self-giving that stems from an overabundant love as the essence of the image of God. Consequently, for him "the highest good consists in communion, mutual giving and receiving, as in the paradigm of the eschatological banquet."[26] As he explains:

> Being made in the image of God, as a feature of each human being, is not something that can be characterized just by reference to this being alone. Our being in the image of God is also our standing among others in the stream of love which is that facet

---

23. Ratzinger, *Church, Ecumenism, and Politics*, 198.
24. Ratzinger, *'In the Beginning,'* 72.
25. Valadier, *Morale en désordre*, 204.
26. Taylor, *Secular Age*, 702.

of God's life we try to grasp, very inadequately, in speaking of the Trinity.[27]

Others have seen this ideal of communion as the dream of democracy or of civil society. Jean Bethke Elshtain, in her *Democracy on Trial*, has formulated this ideal as the following:

> It means both individual accomplishment as well as a sense of responsibility; it means sharing the possibility of a brotherhood and sisterhood that is perhaps fractious—as all brotherhoods and sisterhoods are—and yet united in a spirit that's a spirit more of good than ill will; it means that one is marked by history but not totally burdened with it and defined by it.[28]

We might be tempted to dismiss such language as hopelessly utopian. But Bethke Elshtain warns us that if we do so, we are also giving up the democratic ideal. The latter rests on the assumption that we are capable of civic friendship and justice, which are the essential constituents of a political community.

The primacy attributed to love by Ratzinger, Taylor, and Valadier has implications for their understanding of human dignity. The three men diverge from the dominant neo-stoic, Kantian conception of human dignity and instead opt for an approach that reflects the intrinsic relationality of human beings. What "captures the full force of the call we feel to succour human beings as human?", asks Taylor.[29] What does the Samaritan "see" in the one lying along the road and what moves him to risk his own life to save someone else's? Or in the case of newborns and growing children, what explains "this sense of awe, surprise, tenderness, which moves us so much when a new human being emerges"?[30] What relates us—*can* relate us—to each other in normal times and in extremis?[31] Valadier observes that the Kantian "high evaluation of the

---

27. Taylor, *Secular Age*, 701.
28. Bethke Elshtain, *Democracy on Trial*, 36.
29. Taylor, *Secular Age*, 678.
30. Taylor, *Secular Age*, 700.
31. I am emphasizing *"can,"* because our present phenomenology, following Taylor's reasoning, can be corrected by a more adequate ontology. At the same time, an ontology may also need to be corrected if it fails to "make sense of our ethical or moral lives, rightly understood" (Taylor, *Secular Age*, 608). The issue, therefore, is "how to align our best phenomenology with an adequate ontology, how to resolve a seeming lack of fit . . . either by enriching one's ontology, or by revising or challenging the phenomenology" (Taylor, *Secular Age*, 609).

human person based on reason, free will, communicational language, and the aptitude to dominate time" has backfired.[32] It is this dominant modern understanding of the person and of human dignity that is assumed by Peter Singer when he proposes to consider certain animals as persons and certain humans as non-persons. The "person," as he defines it, is not only sentient but "can [also] see that he or she actually has a life—that is, can see that he or she is the same being who exists now, who existed in the past, and who will exist in the future."[33] Infants and those who suffer from dementia and severe brain damage therefore do not fall under the category "person." Singer's post-enlightenment "antispeciesism" consists in "unsanctifying human life."[34] His solution to the anthropocentric conception of human exceptionality is to lower humans to their "proper" place, which is among other animals.

Valadier, on the other hand, holds that "moral autonomy" does not constitute human dignity. Instead, human dignity is to be found in "indignity" and not so much despite "indignity." While those who want to bring humans down to their proper level—that is, among other animals—find it hard to reconcile the horrors committed by humans with a dignity unique to humans, Valadier defends a lucid, non-Promethean humanism that is in itself humanizing.[35] According to him, Judaic and Christian traditions, Greek tragedy (especially Sophocles), and Montaigne (especially his skepticism) inspire such humanism.[36] These traditions share the common wisdom that "many things are worrying, but none is more worrying than humans."[37] Hence, Valadier notes that "if, according to the Bible, true wisdom begins with the fear of God, one can add with Greek tragic thought that it also goes through the fear of humans."[38] In other words, none of these traditions commits the mistake of believing in the "innocence" of humans, in the reign of innocence—now or ever—and in a future devoid of morbidity or violence.[39] At the

---

32. Valadier, *Un philosophe peut-il croire?*, 78.
33. See Singer, "Frequently Asked Questions."
34. Singer, *Unsanctifying Human Life*.
35. Valadier, "Exceptionnelle humanité," 783.
36. Valadier, "Exceptionnelle humanité," 784. I am aware of the fact that the term "Judeo-Christian" is contested among academics. However, since Valadier has recourse to it, I can hardly avoid it when referring to his thought.
37. Valadier, *Un philosophe peut-il croire?*, 82–83.
38. Valadier, "Mal politique moderne," 207.
39. Valadier, *Jésus-Christ ou Dionysos*, 86.

same time, they provide us with reasons for not despairing of ourselves. They affirm our capacity to transform ourselves and to cultivate our humanity. As Valadier remarks, "only those who know the worst of which humans are capable can *hope* in them, without illusion and in truth."[40] Valadier's integration of Greek tragic wisdom, Montaigne's skeptical wisdom, and religious wisdom constitutes a reply to Gray's (justified) criticism that "we have been reared on religions and philosophies that deny the experience of tragedy";[41] and that "for Christians, tragedies are only blessings in disguise: the world—as Dante put it—is a divine comedy."[42]

The coherence and viability of an integral or Christian humanism depends on whether it is able to address the criticisms levied at fundamental assumptions in traditional Christian thought. One such assumption is of course "God is love." In this context it is appropriate to recall a discussion between Ratzinger, Jürgen Moltmann, Eveline Goodman-Thau, and Johann Baptist Metz, during which the latter points out that the "love" of God, so often preached, fails to consider the "dark side of God." This dark side of God, according to him, is reflected in life itself, in the misery, and "abysmal suffering in creation, in God's creation."[43] Metz asks: "Is there . . . a God whom one can worship with back turned to such a catastrophe [Auschwitz]"?[44] Rather than trying to absolve God from blame, theology, according to him, should incessantly question God ("*rückfrage an Gott*").[45] For Ratzinger, too, words fail in the face of the horrors committed by humans and the indescribable suffering of so many.[46] Yet, he thinks that we cannot really blame God since we only see fragments and not the whole.[47] Without wishing to digress into theodicy, I must however note that this answer will not do for most of us. We cannot evade the objection that divine love is hard to find in a world that far too often resembles our wildest imagination of hell. This matter is closely related to Gray's criticism that Christianity has banned tragic consciousness.

40. Valadier, "Mal politique moderne," 207.
41. Gray, *Straw Dogs*, 194.
42. Gray, *Straw Dogs*, 99.
43. Peters, *End of Time*, 27.
44. Metz, "Suffering unto God," 611.
45. Metz, "Suffering unto God," 613.
46. Benedict XVI, *Visit to the Auschwitz Camp*, 1.
47. Benedict XVI, *Visit to the Auschwitz Camp*, 3.

Though the Christian idea of hope is not easily reconciled with the tragic vision of life, it must be emphasized that "hope" and "God's love" far too often become hollow and banal. The language of hope and God's love is bound to sound hypocritical when it is used by those who have not gone through hell on earth. Yet, "God is love" is not simply a "belief." Our self-understanding and our modes of living depend on this faith. Is it possible and legitimate to have "faith in the resources and the vocation of human nature" and in the "power of truth and the power of love," to borrow Maritain's eloquent words?[48] The analogy between humans and God—and hence the *imago Dei* idea—can help us here. It could be argued that it is out of love itself that we cannot accept a world that is torn by hate, cruelty, and suffering. It is out of love that we refuse to reconcile this reality with a God who is said to be Love. But if there is an analogy between human love and divine love, then we must conclude that it is divine love itself that prevents us from accepting things as they are and pushes us to keep on questioning and calling on God. Of course, I am here assuming that our discontent is truly driven by the love of the world and not by some pubescent rebellion against some imagined tyrannical father or mother. The above reasoning is supported by the phenomenology of love and compassion. Our compassion with the suffering of the world is not fully ours; it grows and moves us to action, on condition that we are willing to stand "among others in the stream of love."[49] This is when the mysterious intermingling of human and divine love takes place.

Christian Humanism and Integral Human Development in the Context of Digitalization

The language of (embodied) relationality and participation, which is prominent in the works of Ratzinger, Taylor, and Valadier, is perhaps the most important dimension of their Christian humanism that distinguishes the latter from other humanisms and non-humanist ontologies. The self-understanding that we are essentially open beings who are called to partake of divine love, reason, and wisdom clashes with our self-understanding as disengaged, buffered selves. Once again, it must be noted that we are not just dealing with different, conflicting *ideas* of the human and of the corresponding ideas or beliefs regarding the highest human

---

48. Maritain, *Christianity and Democracy*, 56.
49. Taylor, *Secular Age*, 701.

good, end, or vocation. These different self-understandings lead to different practices and hence different paths of development. At the same time, our lived realities also influence our ideas and beliefs regarding who we are, our aspirations, and our conception of the world. Digitalization entails both particular lived realities and ontological assumptions, which are further reinforced by digitalization practices. We must therefore understand both the phenomenology and ontology of digitalization in order to understand its implications for integral human development. In this section the main argument is that though digitalization enables communication where this was formerly lacking and provides individuals, private, and public organizations with useful information (data) that facilitates decision-making, care must be taken to prevent it from turning into an instrument of digital colonialism and cultural hegemony and hence from reifying a techno-scientific order. Christian humanism can function as a counter-hegemonic force by insisting on the human paradox, including the permanent reality of evil, and on the necessity of cultivating wisdom. In Ratzinger's words, it can recall "reason to the greatness of its task" and can thus assume "the Socratic function of worry."[50]

From a Christian humanist perspective, integral human development includes the reflective and critical use of (digital) technologies. Since the latter are not—and never will be—self-governing, the development, implementation, and use of these technologies must be informed by rigorous thinking about the highest goods, values, ends, means, and priorities.[51] In *Self-Improvement: Technologies of the Soul in the Age of Artificial Intelligence* (2022) Mark Coeckelbergh points out that the ambition to create "moral machines" to help moral decision-making "may promote the idea that being moral and doing the right thing is only or mainly about smart reasoning and following reason."[52] These moral machines will also inevitably promote a particular version of the good life since they, as Coeckelbergh reminds us, are thoroughly human and cultural. Hence, AI, however ethical it might become, "does not relieve us of the task and burden of examining ourselves and our society and finding out what the good life is"; we need "wisdom, not just clever reasoning or statistical and quantitative forms of knowledge."[53] Coeckelbergh's remarks make it clear that the challenge that digital technologies

50. Ratzinger and Flores d'Arcais, *Est-ce que Dieu Existe?*, 111.
51. See Midgley, *Utopias, Dolphins, and Computers*, 125.
52. Coeckelbergh, *Self-Improvement*, 76.
53. Coeckelbergh, *Self-Improvement*, 77.

pose are not only ethical but also existential. It is not simply a matter of "using" technologies in a right way or even developing fair and trustworthy AI. Our engagement with (digital) technologies changes not only our practices but also our ways of thinking and our aspirations. Moreover, technologies remain thoroughly *human* technologies despite the techno-scientific aspiration to transcend the human condition. Correspondingly, all digital technologies are cultural products. In this regard, Coeckelbergh convincingly shows that digital health and wellbeing, with all their apps that rely on AI, represent "wellness capitalism."[54]

The obsession with the self and "self-improvement" that is stimulated by digital technologies differs from the traditional care of the soul in a fundamental sense. The care of the soul or the self was embedded in physical communities (in the strong sense of term).[55] These physical communities are notoriously absent in our world today. While the traditional care of the soul had the twofold aim of cultivating wholesome selves who are able to accept and carry the responsibility for communal life, including political life, the contemporary obsession with the self reflects a narrow apolitical concern with individual emotional states. In a context of weak democracies digitalization reinforces what Taylor conceives to be a corrupted ethics of authenticity. A genuine and full-fledged account of self-fulfillment instead takes "the demands of our ties with others" and the "demands of any kind emanating from something more or other than human desires or aspiration" into account.[56] Valadier considers the "overflowing of the private into the public" through (digital) media as symptomatic of the increasing "depoliticization" of individuals.[57] In other words, digitalization both reflects and reinforces cultural and political trends and discourses. It also serves to mask the true nature of societal and global problems. The discourse that digitalization and, in particular, AI-driven digital technologies are the solution to all our global problems, including "scarcity," poverty, and the ecological crisis reflects the old positivist—and hence mechanistic—dream that technology will bring about salvation. From this techno-scientific perspective,

---

54. Coeckelbergh, *Self-Improvement*, 127.

55. The term "communities" is increasingly used in a very loose sense to refer to various collectivities, including "virtual groups." "Communities," in the strong sense of the term, are living and growing communities of persons who are bound to each other by fraternity (love) and justice.

56. Taylor, *Ethics of Authenticity*, 35.

57. Valadier, "Espace Public, Espace Privé," 3.

there is no doubt that conflicts, wars, hunger, illness, and even death can be solved by human technologies.

The motives behind digitalization certainly differ from context to context. Efficiency and better healthcare are apparent reasons for digitalization in the healthcare sector though we must bear in mind that "mainstream narratives around automation obliterate the amount of human labor that automation technologies still require."[58] Given the fact that digitalization reflects and reinforces dominant cultural values, prejudices, and particular ways of thinking and practices, it would be a miracle if it did not foster social atomism and a "culture of narcissism," a term to which Pope Francis has had recourse on several occasions. "Digital narcissism" is a widely used terminology in the media and, to a lesser extent, academic scholarship. However, (digital) narcissism is not simply self-centeredness. Christopher Lasch's understanding of the culture of narcissism is worth being recalled here.[59] Lasch and, more recently, Gilles Lipovetsky are referring to the inner emptiness and disintegration of selves.[60] In order to survive, these selves adopt the false unities or identities that are promoted everywhere thanks to social media. Of course, digital tools may also promote the idea of the genuine care of the soul in genuine communities. It may also remind individuals of their duties towards others and the world. Yet, digitalization is much more than digital channels of communication (which are moreover never simply neutral platforms). It is also—if not in the first place—the datafication of human activities, interactions, and of every possible aspect of human life. Datafication requires the *objectification* of these human phenomena. In a strong sense, digitalization therefore perpetuates the long tradition of objectification that we have inherited since early modernity. The ineffable dimensions of our human reality must therefore either be reduced to something that can be translated into data or simply negated.

Efficiency and comfort, though the apparent motives for digitalization, cannot explain the fascination with digital technologies, including AI-driven technologies such as (humanoid) robots. The urge to create purportedly conscious, sentient, and intelligent machines seems to reflect what Gabriel Marcel referred to as practical anthropomorphism.[61] In slightly different words, it can also be considered as a response to the

58. Carboni et al., "Eye for an AI," 5.
59. Lasch, *Culture of Narcissism*.
60. Lipovetsky, *L'ère du vide*, 76; Lasch, *Minimal Self*, 57.
61. Marcel, *Decline of Wisdom*, 41.

vocation to become like God and hence to be gods. The ancients were aware of this human desire to be gods, but they considered it as hubris. Though I think that certain responses to this vocation are indeed corrupted responses and hence hubristic, I would like to argue that the human desire to be a god should not be denied or chastised by reminding mortals that they ought not to cherish thoughts above their mortal condition. It is more fruitful, prudent, and less damaging to acknowledge the desire to be like gods or God as characteristic of humans. The question that then arises is whether we do indeed respond to our transcendent vocation when we try to create super-intelligent machines. Note that "intelligence" in this case is one kind of cognitive capacity, encompassing calculating, strategic, and procedural—that is, algorithmic—thinking. It is noteworthy that both "intelligence" and "creativity" are quite frequently considered as those features that make humans be like gods. Referring to transhumanist endeavors, Celia Deane-Drummond observes that the realization of the image of God "then becomes connected to the image of God by expressing a form of creative superintelligence. Humans share in this intelligence by becoming co-creators with God."[62] As I have argued above, Ratzinger, Taylor, and Valadier diverge from such dominant understandings of God/*imago Dei* by emphasizing that an overabundant love is the essence of God/*imago Dei* and, correspondingly, that communion is the highest human good.

As noted above, communion is both human communion and participation in God's love, involving the intermingling of transcendence and immanence. The ideal of communion has implications for both the content of and path to integral human development. The radical and hence uncomfortable implication of this ideal of communion for integral human development becomes clear in contexts where unjust conditions are in fact lawful. Consider, for example, socioeconomic contexts where unjust prices and wages, determined by the market, are legal. Slave wages at the beginning of supply chains are common in many sectors. Markets, contrary to some views, are far from being neutral exchange mechanisms or neutral spaces where equal players meet. The image of the market as a fair exchange place for peace-loving, trusting, and trustworthy actors is a fairytale told by the socioeconomically successful. More profound observers and the many struggling people in the real world confirm the Darwinian image of the market. Actual international markets today are

---

62. Deane-Drummond "Taking Leave of the Animal," 125.

not organically embedded in societies even if they are governed by certain rules and values. The latter are those of the most powerful players, who also set the rules of the game.[63] When weaker national economies participate in these international markets, they must comply with the rules set by others and accept the values of the powerful. Given these asymmetrical power relations, it is clear that markets are not the best and fairest way of allocating resources to fulfil the needs of everyone. Moreover, market prices do not reflect the genuine costs of production, which include real labor costs, the depletion of natural "resources," and the social, environmental, and health impacts of the production and consumption of certain products.

The ideal of communion resists what Maritain called the "anarchic conception of bourgeois materialism, according to which the entire duty of society consists in seeing that the freedom of each one be respected, thereby enabling the strong freely to oppress the weak."[64] It demands from us that we transcend the prevailing norms of justice. In the case of slave wages, we are urged to consider the needs of workers, who are above all things our fellow beings. So, it is not simply the case that we are being asked to consider those who are exploited as "ends" instead of "means." The ideal of communion calls on us to consider ourselves related to these strangers by an invisible bond of love and to give to them what is due to them in accordance with the demands of this relationship. The standard of justice that follows from the ideal of communion is thus much higher than the "traditional" conception of justice that involves giving to people what is due to them in accordance with their class, gender, status, merits, talents, or capacities. Needless to say, all these categories are conventions and far from being eternal criteria of distinction. Any "progress" that is achieved at the cost of the integral development of humans and of every human—yesterday, today, and tomorrow—cannot be considered as integral human development. The "progress of humanity" is nonsensical if "humanity" is an abstract idea that disregards individual lives who are purportedly the necessary sacrifices in the progress of humanity. Similarly, progress that is achieved at the cost of fundamental humanizing values, ideas, and practices—"truths"—is false progress.

---

63. See Bourdieu, *Social Structures of the Economy*, 195.
64. Maritain, *Christianity and Democracy*, 93.

Concluding Remarks: The Challenges for Social Catholicism

The challenges for integral human development in the digital age are both old and new. Digitalization reproduces and reinforces dominant habits of the heart and mind and practices. Yet, at the same time, it can replicate merely partial aspects of human realities since the latter cannot be fully objectified. This is not sufficiently considered in the development of AI-driven applications, such as self-tracking applications but also medical applications designed for diagnosis and suggestions of treatments. The underlying assumption is that selves can be quantified, are in a way transparent, and that we therefore know ourselves fully. We provide data, and we receive knowledge about ourselves generated by a machine. As Coeckelbergh notes, "our self becomes quantified. It is no longer the mysterious, dark, and complex self that is explored in novels and good old humanist psychology."[65] The damage would have been limited if our engagement with these false oracles did not affect our self-understanding and our understanding of embodiment. As Gavin J. D. Smith and Ben Vonthethoff point out, "the means of sensemaking is increasingly outsourced to and performed by auxiliary codifying mechanisms that are adjudged to encompass greater degrees of validity and reliability."[66] Extensive and intensive digitalization can therefore have a detrimental impact on integral human development by narrowing our self-understanding, competences—such as intuitive and sensorial knowing—and aspirations and, correspondingly, by legitimizing the conventional and ecologically harmful pathways to "progress." This is an old danger in a new form, namely, the proliferation of the mechanistic worldview inherent to naturalistic materialism and the corresponding practices. "A naturalistic materialism," Taylor remarks, "is not only on offer, but presents itself as the only view compatible with the most prestigious institution of the modern world, viz., science."[67]

Given the hegemony of naturalistic materialism, the probabilities that digitalization will be perpetuating materialist habits of the heart and mind are quite high, thereby blurring our transcendent vocation and integral human development. Social Catholicism can safeguard the ideas, values, and practices that are conducive to integral human development

---

65. Coeckelbergh, *Self-Improvement*, 62.
66. Smith and Vonthethoff, "Health by Numbers," 9.
67. Taylor, *Secular Age*, 28.

but also criticize dehumanizing ideas and practices that undermine such development. In our digital context the value, idea, and practice that runs the risk of being forgotten is wisdom, precisely the counterweight to hubris, according to Marcel.[68] Coeckelbergh seems to have realized this risk as well when he emphasizes our need to cultivate wisdom. Yet, wisdom is unlikely to be prioritized in an age that favors unambiguous knowledge geared to certainty, precision, utility, and mastery. Indeed, wisdom, as Abraham Heschel understood it, is the "intuition for the dignity of all things, a realization that things not only are what they are but also stand, however remotely, for something supreme."[69] Wisdom requires awe and reverence for the mystery of things. Since human life is well-lived only if it is lived in accordance with wisdom, social Catholicism can accept the challenge of keeping the tradition of the care for wisdom, the soul, the stranger, and the world alive. The Church, in particular, can embody this culture of love and care. According to Valadier, it/she can "give hope to humans by enkindling their desire to commit themselves to their full vocation."[70] He is well aware of the fact that the Church faces the burden of the past, which is in many cases a very recent past, and therefore emphasizes that the spokespersons of the Church must learn to be dialogue partners, acknowledge pluralism, and hence refuse to "dictate the only possible solution."[71] By affirming the "pluralist principle," the Church can perhaps play a crucial role in the realization of that "new organic and pluralist democracy" that was Maritain's dream.[72]

Bibliography

Adler, Alfred. *Understanding Human Nature*. New York: Greenberg, 1946.
Benedict XVI. *Faith, Reason, and the University: Memories and Reflections*. Rome: Libreria Editrice Vaticana, 2006.
———. *Caritas in Veritate*. Rome: Libreria Editrice Vaticana, 2009.
———. *Visit to the Auschwitz Camp*. Rome: Libreria Editrice Vaticana, 2006.
Bethke Elshtain, Jean. *Democracy on Trial*. New York: Basic, 1995.
Bourdieu, Pierre. *The Social Structures of the Economy*. Translated by Chris Turner. Malden, MA: Polity, 2008.

---

68. Marcel, *Decline of Wisdom*, 12.
69. Heschel, *Who Is Man?*, 88–89.
70. Valadier, *Inévitable morale*, 60.
71. Valadier, *L'Église en procès*, 140.
72. Maritain, *Christianity and Democracy*, 181.

Carboni, Chiara, et al. "Eye for an AI: More-Than-Seeing, Fauxtomation, and the Enactment of Uncertain Data in Digital Pathology." *Social Studies of Science* (2023) 1–26.

Coeckelbergh, Mark. *Self-Improvement: Technologies of the Soul in the Age of Artificial Intelligence*. New York: Columbia University Press, 2022.

Deane-Drummond, Celia. "Taking Leave of the Animal? The Theological and Ethical Implications of Transhuman Projects." In *Transhumanism and Transcendence: Christian Hope in an Age of Technological Enhancement*, edited by Ronald Cole-Turner, 115–30. Washington, DC: Georgetown University Press, 2011.

Gray, John. *Straw Dogs: Thoughts on Humans and Other Animals*. London: Granta, 2002.

Heschel, Abraham J. *Who Is Man?* Stanford: Stanford University Press, 1965.

Lasch, Christopher. *The Culture of Narcissism: American Life in an Age of Diminishing Expectations*. New York: Norton, 1978.

———. *The Minimal Self: Psychic Survival in Troubled Times*. London: Pan, 1984.

Law, Stephen. *Humanism: A Very Short Introduction*. Oxford: Oxford University Press, 2011.

Lipovetsky, Gilles. *L'ère du vide: essais sur l'individualisme contemporain*. Paris: Gallimard, 1983.

Lubac, Henri de. *The Mystery of the Supernatural*. Translated by Rosemary Sheed. New York: Herder & Herder, 1998.

Marcel, Gabriel. *The Decline of Wisdom*. New York: Philosophical Library, 1955.

Maritain, Jacques. *Christianity and Democracy; and, The Rights of Man and Natural Law*. Translated by Doris C. Anson. San Francisco: Ignatius, 1986.

Metz, Johann Baptist. "Suffering unto God." *Critical Inquiry* 20 (1994) 611–22.

Midgley, Mary. *Are You an Illusion?* Durham: Acumen, 2014.

———. *Utopias, Dolphins, and Computers: Problems in Philosophical Plumbing*. London: Routledge, 1996.

Peters, Tiemo Rainer, et al., eds. *The End of Time? The Provocation of Talking about God*. Proceedings of a Meeting of Joseph Cardinal Ratzinger, Johann Baptist Metz, Jürgen Moltmann, and Eveline Goodman-Thau in Ahaus. New York: Paulist, 2004.

Ratzinger, Joseph. *Church, Ecumenism, and Politics: New Endeavors in Ecclesiology*. San Francisco: Ignatius, 2008.

———. *'In the Beginning. . .': A Catholic Understanding of the Story of Creation and the Fall*. Grand Rapids: Eerdmans, 1995.

———. "In Search of Freedom: Against Reason Fallen Ill and Religion Abused." *Logos* 4 (2005) 1–5.

Ratzinger, Joseph, and Paolo Flores d'Arcais. *Est-ce que Dieu Existe? Dialogue sur la Vérité, la Foi et l'Athéisme*. Paris: éditions Payot & Rivages, 2006.

Singer, Peter. "Frequently Asked Questions." https://petersinger.info/faq.

———. *Unsanctifying Human Life: Essays on Ethics*. Edited by Helga Kuhse. Oxford: Blackwell, 2002.

Smith, Gavin J. D., and Ben Vonthethoff. "Health by Numbers? Exploring the Practice and Experience of Datafied Health." *Health Sociology Review* 26 (2017) 6–21.

Taylor, Charles. *The Ethics of Authenticity*. Cambridge: Belknap, 1991.

———. *A Secular Age*. Cambridge: Belknap, 2007.

Valadier, Paul. "Espace Public, Espace Privé." *Partie Prenante* 31 (1997/98) 1–17.

———. "Exceptionnelle humanité." *Études* 412 (2010) 773–84.
———. *Inévitable morale*. Paris: Éditions du Seuil, 1990.
———. *Jésus-Christ ou Dionysos: la foi chrétienne en confrontation avec Nietzsche*. Paris: Desclée, 1979.
———. *L'Église en procès: catholicisme et société moderne*. Paris: Calmann-Lévy, 1987.
———. "Le mal politique moderne." *Études* 394 (2001) 197–207.
———. *Morale en désordre*. Paris: Éditions du Seuil, 2002.
———. *Un philosophe peut-il croire?* Paris: Éditions Cécile Defaut, 2006.

16

After Moyn
Historians, the Catholic Church, and Human Rights

PETER CAJKA, UNIVERSITY OF NOTRE DAME

Abstract: Between 2015 and 2020 a new historiographical field came to life. Since the mid-2010s historians have published several books on the contribution of the Catholic Church to the creation and rise of human rights. Previously, historians considered human rights the secular product of the Enlightenment or the domain of secular activists like those in Amnesty International. After Samuel Moyn published his landmark work *Christian Human Rights* in 2015 historians have increasingly demonstrated how Catholics played an indispensable role in the theorization and diffusion of human rights discourses. Scholars have shown how Catholic intellectuals and activists drew upon natural law theory, the *nouvelle théologie*, and liberation theology to formulate distinct conceptions of human rights. Catholic human rights have been conservative and liberal, political and apolitical, fascist and democratic. This article is an intellectual history of this remarkable five-year transformation.

Introduction: A Renewed Era of Historical Scholarship on Catholics and Human Rights

TODAY IT IS IMPOSSIBLE to write the history of human rights without mentioning Catholicism. Just ten years ago, however, historians thought that the Catholic Church had little to do with human rights. The rights of man were the creations of Enlightenment savants or the exclusive intellectual property of Amnesty International activists; now, thanks to a collection of historians and their interlocutors, Catholics lay claim to the origins and contents of these modern ideas. They are now seen as responsible, in part, for the rise of human rights in the twentieth century. An unexpected historiographical transformation has taken place since 2015. What happened? The purpose of this essay is to show how historians came to associate human rights with Catholicism and to explain why this connection came about.

In the space of just five years, a new field has sprung up around the theme of Christian human rights. By 2020, a sophisticated body of works demonstrated the intellectual plurality of Christian human rights, and sought out the discourses in several global arenas, from Argentina to Poland to China. Christian human rights historiography was built through the normal channels and processes of scholarly research—a foundational text, a forum of essays, specialized monographs, and an edited volume. The alpha point of this field was Samuel Moyn's 2015 book *Christian Human Rights*, and from there, scholars built a field by debating and testing his claims. This essay follows the progress of the field from its provocative founding in 2015 to its maturation into a pluralized discourse by 2020.

The question as to why historians began studying Christian human rights is much more difficult to address, and I have let it for the essay's conclusion, where I also explore the implications of this historiographical turn for Catholic social teaching in the twenty-first century.

Moyn's Christian Human Rights as Catalyst

The origins are not difficult to uncover. A remarkable book published in 2015 by a significant historian gave life to a new subfield of historical inquiry. Scholars have been debating and testing the findings of Samuel Moyn's *Christian Human Rights* since the book's publication. Moyn can be somewhat hard to classify because he traverses fields such as legal theory, political theory, foreign affairs, global history, and the history of philosophy. But he is perhaps best described as an intellectual historian who takes a genealogical approach to the past. Genealogy, as pioneered by Friedrich Nietzsche and practiced by Michel Foucault, stresses the layered or sedimented aspects of human history. Humans add items gradually to an intellectual lineage, understood as a deep discourse, but they can also break sharply from a tradition under the right conditions. Genealogy starts with the present and digs into the past, almost like a drill, searching for the intellectual origins of the current moment. This method is helpful for detailing what Foucault famously called "the history of the present" while simultaneously stressing that the present could have turned out differently if historical actors had made different choices. Moyn tends to hone in on the sharp breaks form the past, and this is where we should start to unpack the claims he makes in *Christian Human Rights*.

Moyn interprets Pope Pius XII's 1942 appeal to the dignity of the human person as an epochal break with the past for both the Catholic Church and for liberalism. This argument for discontinuity was met with a chorus of objections that this essay addresses below. For now, however, the provocation can be seen in line with the evidence Moyn presents and explicates. Moyn contends that an exogenous shock administered by the Second World War prompted the Catholic Church's turn to human rights. That Catholics turned to human rights in 1942, before the conclusion of the war was clear, is pivotal in understanding the claims Moyn makes in his book. Catholics adopted the human person and human rights as a means to restrain the powerful fascist and communist states coming into existence in the 1930s and 1940s. Had the fascists conquered Europe, Catholics would have accepted the political order if it respected human rights. These rights made it possible for men and women to conform to God's order in an increasingly hostile and secularizing world. World War II taught Christians "that the cultivation of moral restraint depended on keeping the spiritual communities that offered their vision ethical life a home partly free from the state."[1]

The implications of Moyn's findings—and his tight framing of the sudden Catholic embrace of human rights—are profound. If Catholics

---

1. Moyn, *Christian Human Rights*, 12. Moyn previewed these arguments in an important article for an edited volume. See Moyn, "Personalism," 85–106; on the conservative origins of human rights, see also Duranti, *Conservative Human Rights*. For an excellent analysis of the modern papacy and human rights, see Chamedes, *Twentieth-Century Crusade*, 237–45.

of the 1940s are the originators of a human rights tradition then by extension that tradition has no direct correlation with liberal democracy. Human rights are conservative, and highly amendable to fascism. Thus, it is "more viable to regard human rights as a project of the Christian right, not the secular left."[2] Moyn emphasizes the Christian origins of human rights at times but he also wavers ever so slightly on occasion and acknowledges Catholics may have hijacked the French Revolutionary tradition and removed human rights from its previous secular moorings. Both findings, however, can be filed under the heading of "invention."

There is a third and final implication to be considered in addition to the conservative origins of human rights and its probable fascist affinities. To make his case for a sharp diversion in Christian intellectual history Moyn has to settle the question of tradition. He seems to agree with the classic formulation of the "invention of tradition" as laid out by Eric Hobsbawm and Terence Ranger in 1983.[3] Traditions are invented to suit present needs while creating imagined links to the past by way of discourse, contrived historical narratives, and ritual. Catholics who invoked human rights were "pretending they had always been there."[4] If you look back at history Catholics could hardly be considered champions of human rights given their suppression of religious liberty and denial of religious pluralism. Much had to change, then, for Catholics to truly embrace human rights. This narrative is so provocative and influential precisely because it is not celebratory for Catholics or for liberals. Catholics made human rights illiberal and contemporary seculars drawn uncritically on a highly exclusionary set of ideas.

The Significance of Moyn's Provocative Arguments: Universality, Economics

To grasp the gravitas of these arguments its helpful to step back to 2010, when Moyn published his blockbuster book, *The Last Utopia: Human Rights in History*. Though *Christian Human Rights* arrived like a lightning bolt in 2015, Moyn's turn to religious history does have antecedents. With his signature emphasis on contingency in a model of genealogical history, Moyn showed that human rights discourse exploded in the

---

2. Moyn, *Christian Human Rights*, 8.
3. Hobsbawm and Ranger, *Invention of Tradition*.
4. Moyn, *Christian Human Rights*, 5.

mid-1970s. A Google Ngram of "human rights" reveals a hockey stick, with the slope starting in the mid-1970s, with nearly an unabated rise, to circa 2005. Moyn claimed that previous historians who studied human rights overlooked the criterion that makes a right a human right: namely, that these concepts transcend the nation-state to achieve a supra-statism. To qualify as a human right that right has to exist outside of the framework of the nation state. The right gains recognition not through a constitution or bill of rights but with moral appeals that are universal in nature. Amnesty International's campaigns for human rights, in both communist and non-communist countries, is a case in point. In this sense, human rights vitiated the nation-state and the welfare state. The French Revolutionary tradition of rights linked rights to the state, making them more like civil or civic rights than actual human rights. In the end, human rights comprise a "Last Utopia" because the activists who flocked to these universal norms were fleeing the wreckage of socialism and communism.[5]

To further understand the importance of his 2015 book we must also move forward in time to 2019, when Moyn released the final installation of his trilogy on human rights, *Not Enough: Human Rights in an Unequal World*. Moyn is a genealogist but he also tends to write history from the perspective of a man of the Hegelian Left who sees the state and its institutions as crucial for fostering individual liberty and collective emancipation. The argument that Moyn made in 2019 is that human rights are well suited for an unequal, highly marketized society. Human rights are important ideological components of what we now call Neoliberalism, a political order built on the premise of market values and minimalist state interventions into the economy. How does *Christian Human Rights* fit into this intellectual history? For Moyn, Christianity helps to explain the negative quality of human rights as more concerned with the individual's moral preservation (and communal protection) than justice for a collective. Here we might note the limits of Moyn's notion of Catholic human rights as negative. Current Catholic teaching sees human rights as social in nature and at odds with neoliberalism. Catholic human rights are linked with universal distribution of goods, just wages, and sharing in ownership. These human rights, in other words, do call on state intervention to promote a common good. The social and economic development of the individual is captured in the phrase "integral

---

5. Moyn, *Last Utopia*.

human development." Catholics do make claims on the state to build a just world. Yet, for Moyn, human rights come at the expense of a modern social imaginary. Human rights suggest the attenuation of the powers of the modern state.[6]

Moyn on Maritain's Role as Synthesizer and Democratizer of Human Rights

The last aspect we need to address before moving onto the reception of *Christian Human Rights* is Moyn's treatment of Jacques Maritain. For everyone and anyone researching the history of Catholic human rights Maritain is a central, if not the central, figure to consider. Without a doubt, Maritain is the most important lay Catholic intellectual of the twentieth century, and one could make a claim that he is the most influential Catholic figure in the global Church in the years preceding the Second Vatican Council. It is simply impossible to write the history of Catholic human rights without addressing Maritain at length. Moyn treats Maritain according to the interpretations of conservativism and invention as discussed above. As Moyn notes, Pius XI and Pius XII made enduring contributions to the Catholic Church's human rights turn by attacking fascism and communism with encyclicals in the 1930s. But for Moyn, Maritain was both the synthesizer of an unwieldy discourse and its most adroit authenticator. Maritain "intercepted" an "episodic, unsystematic and selective" body of thought on human rights and rendered it solid, stable, foundational, and axiomatic.[7] Maritain did this by reconciling human rights with the Thomistic natural law tradition. Thomism now implied human rights and human rights now implied Thomism. How did this happen?

Moyn urges careful and critical analysis of this intellectual accomplishment. With the power of his pen, Maritain took a Catholic idea of human rights that countenanced fascism and linked it, forever it seems, to a Catholic notion of democracy. Historians and theologians still think of Maritain in terms of making Catholicism suitable for democracy. This historical revisionism "won the day" but Moyn warns us to see this move as inorganic. He calls this coupling of human rights to tradition, in a brilliant and unforgettable line, "a stroke of a master, or a sleight of hand,

---

6. Moyn, *Not Enough*.
7. Moyn, *Christian Human Rights*, 80.

or both."[8] Moyn leaves the reader some room to entertain the idea that Maritain bore rights out of the natural law tradition, finding the language there in a real empirical manner, but Moyn ultimately leans towards Maritain as a magician of political philosophy. He invented a tradition where one previously did not exist. Catholics ought to read Leo Strauss's *Natural Right and History* and recognize the gaping disjuncture between the Natural Law regime and the human rights dispensation. While Maritain goes unmentioned in *The Last Utopia*, the researcher who searches Moyn's impressive oeuvre for religion will discover a passage early on in the 2010 book outlining how the Natural Law tradition of Thomas Aquinas is completely opposed and antithetical to human rights.[9]

The Broader Study of Catholic Human Rights

While it is difficult to discern if *Christian Human Rights* dropped into a field already turning to Catholic human rights or if the book inspired this migration, it is clear that after 2015 several historians of modern Europe had become interested in exploring the relationship between the Church and human rights. To build an area of scholarly study Moyn's claims would have to be tested on other geographic areas of Europe (and beyond) as well as in regards to other schools of thought outside the natural law tradition. *Christian Human Rights* was a provocation, and not a comprehensive account meant to serve as a final word. It was a conversation-starter. Historians began seeking out and tracking Catholic human rights discourses in arenas *Christian Human Rights* did not consider. Piotr Kosicki, a prolific historian at the University of Maryland, took up the case of Poland in a 2017 article for *Modern Intellectual History*. Poland revealed the limits of what Kosicki called "the liberalizing trajectory" of

---

8. Moyn, *Christian Human Rights*, 83.

9. Moyn, *Last Utopia*, 21. Moyn notes that "if the idea of natural rights first emerged in the old language of natural law, it was so different in its intentions then and implications as to be a different concept. In modern times, most revivalists of natural law, usually Catholics, have regarded it as a disaster for their creed that it gave way to an apostate rights-based successor . . . the time and causes of the transition between natural law and natural rights have received massive attention in recent decades, in part because of the overestimation of how critical they were in the origins of today's human rights. The founding natural rights figures were, however, anything but humanitarians; on theoretical principle, they endorsed an austere doctrine that refused an expansive list of basic entitlements."

Catholic human rights.[10] This narrative suggests that Catholic human rights moved in an unbroken manner from Maritanian origins to the Second Vatican Council to John Paul II. While Moyn stressed the illiberal components of Catholic human rights, he still, according to Kosicki, contributed to the narrative of steady unfurling of Catholics rights discourses across the twentieth century by positing the 1930s and 1940s as an origin point that made possible later invocations of the idea. When one looks closely at the human rights language deployed by Wojciech Korfanty and the Polish Christian Democrats it reveals spikes and troughs of human rights talk. These dips and climbs are directly linked to the shifting political status quo. During the interwar period Korfanty spoke of the rights of human persons, understood as rights reserved only for Catholic persons, to challenge to the power of non-Catholics, specifically the Jews. When the Soviets occupied Poland in the aftermath of the Second World War, Kosicki shows that the Poles were made "Masters in their own home" and so they dropped the phrasings of human persons, dignity, and rights. From the mid-1940s to the 1960s, Polish Catholics seemed to have little use for human rights talk.

In addition to a temporal fluctuation that belied any narrative of steady progress, then, Kosicki shows human rights language was linked to national belonging. This is significant because it demonstrates how the Polish Christian Democrats were "hardly in lockstep with the Pius XI-driven rights talk" studied by Moyn.[11] Whereas Pius XI invoked human rights to challenge nationalism, the Polish invoked the language to "homogenize" the state.[12] Polish Catholics deployed rights languages with the goal of creating a communitarian ethno-state. With the homogenization accomplished after the arrival of the Soviets, the Poles had no immediate use for a moral discourse of dissent. Human rights disappeared in the 1940s and 1950s, but reappeared in the 1960s and 1970s as Polish Catholics contested Communist rule, having then turned back to dissent and with a new anti-authoritarianism. While Kosicki worked in the aftermath of Moyn's pathbreaking account, and perhaps drew upon *Christian Human Rights* as motivation to explore the Polish context in

---

10. Kosicki, "Masters," 100. Also by Kosicki, see *Catholics on the Barricades*. For another important study along these lines, see Hanebrink, *Christian Hungary*; Connelly, *Enemy to Brother*.

11. Kosicki, "Masters," 108.

12. Kosicki, "Masters," 108.

depth, he issued important correctives. Things were different behind the Iron Curtain.

In his 2018 book, *Catholic Modern: The Challenge of Totalitarianism and the Remaking of the Church*, historian James Chappel introduced important nuances into the history of Catholic human rights. His landmark work expanded understandings of the conservative elements of human rights (what he called "paternal") while adding a liberal wing (what he called "fraternal") to the historical understanding of the movement. It was quite inevitable that the more historians scoured the sources on Catholic human rights that more and more complexities would be introduced into the historiography. Chappel argued that the Catholic Church accepted modernity in the 1930s—defined by him as the spilt between a public sphere and a private religious sphere—in response to totalitarianism. Catholics abandoned the quest to run the state and dominate culture, and instead began looking to agitate for Catholic forms of life inside the modern framework that secularized the state and left religion to a private world. The paternal wing of this operation deployed human rights in an effort to force the fascist state to recognize a sacred space beyond its reach. Implied in this move is an acceptance of a new "strong state" as capable and willing to respect such rights.[13] One of the great values of Chappel's contribution is his recovery of a set of historical actors beyond the usual suspects of Catholic human rights historiography. He found in the work of German Jesuit Robert Lindhart and conservative French essayist Henri Massis—both defenders of fascism—a frequent mention of the dignity of the human person and human rights. Chappel tracked down pro-fascist human rights arguments in the writings of Dominican and Benedictine priests. He examined a political theory limned in popular books and religious journals. This paternal modernism accepted powerful fascist states that would "protect the welfare, property and rights of religious families."[14] A fascism that protected human rights proved an antidote against socialism and communism.

So much of the history of Catholic human rights, as mentioned above, hangs on the historian's interpretation of Maritain. We will meet more Maritains before the end of this essay. Chappel's Maritain is, to put it simply, much more liberal than Moyn's. Maritain, and his French contemporary Emmanuel Mounier, Chappel later wrote, were

---

13. Chappel, *Catholic Modern*, 84.
14. Chappel, *Catholic Modern*, 66.

not "inherently conservative."[15] Maritain embodies Chappel's notion of fraternal modernism. The French philosopher promotes human rights as an anti-statist and pluralist project. The fraternalists, like the paternalists, accepted a secular state and a world bifurcated into a modern state and a private, religious realm. But they preferred a smaller and weaker state complemented by a robust public sphere. For Maritain, human rights provided a baseline idea that Catholics could share with other modernist activists such as communists, atheists, liberals, and Protestants. It was a language all groups could speak so long as no one asked about the underlying metaphysical realties of the phrase. Importantly, Chappel shows that these human rights emerged "coeval with a newfound enthusiasm for global governance."[16] Maritain thought a form of global governance ought to preserve human rights. This too was anti-statist, and therefore modern, because it curbed the power of the nation-state in favor of a transcendent human rights politics. Chappel expanded the field of Catholic human rights considerably. Historians now proceeded with a duality of human rights: conservative in some contexts, yet liberal in others; paternalist in certain political arenas, yet fraternalist and globalist in others.

The year 2018 proved to be a watershed for Catholic human rights history. That year, just after Chappel dropped his book, a special forum on Christianity and human rights appeared in *The Journal of the History of Ideas*, edited by historians Udi Greenberg and Daniel Steinmetz-Jenkins. Christian human rights had truly arrived as a discrete unit of study. A growing group of historians recognized these religiously-inflected ideas as a vehicle to expanding their understanding of history since the French Revolution. We might return here to our essay's question: why did historians—often themselves ensconced in secular discourses—come to see religious ideas and religious actors as central to modern history? Why Christian human rights? Why the mid-2010s? Greenberg and Steinmetz-Jenkins allowed themselves to speculate in the forum's introductory essay. Their words are revealing in three ways. In the first place, the authors noted a type of exhaustion surrounding the secular side of the human rights story. While "the project of mapping human rights' origins and ascendancy may now be reaching its conclusion" the analysis of religion, and its relationship to rights, was just beginning.[17] Religion injected a jolt

---

15. Chappel, "Explaining the Catholic Turn," 77.
16. Chappel, *Catholic Modern*, 171.
17. Greenberg and Steinmetz-Jenkins, "Introduction," 408.

of life into modern history, offering a new way to address long-standing questions. Secondly, and relatedly, religion (a proposition much broader than Christian human rights) was itself making a comeback. Religious topics presented historians with the chance to study the "comprehensive visions" offered by Christians on well-trod domains like politics, economics, and sexuality.[18] Rights discourse in central to both the Christian vision for modernity and the direction of history since the French Revolution. Religious subjects shed light on concepts and trends European historians had been studying for many years. A final reason for the study Christian human rights is that they "often defied the category of the left and right."[19] Religion upended the usual grid of modern history and brought forth previously unseen dynamics. There were realities outside and beyond historians' normal taxonomies.

Reaching Farther Back

To really scrutinize the longer arc of this religious human rights story a historian would need to mine a moment in time well before totalitarian crises of the 1930s and 1940s. This is precisely what Stanford historian Daniel Edelstein did with "Christian Human Rights in the French Revolution," his contribution to the 2018 forum. In a sense, despite an expanding vision, historians still lived in the shadows of Moyn's provocation. Edelstein took a direct approach to defanging Moyn's claim that Christian human rights had been contrived in the 1930s and 1940s: he looked closely at the Catholic human rights discourse during French Revolution. Edelstein argued that Christian human rights had a much longer gestation than Moyn had suggested. While Moyn was correct that these rights "expanded" in modern times that did not mean that "the concept of human rights is new."[20] He presented evidence that Pope Pius VII, the Roman Catholic pontiff during the French Revolution (a man whom, we might recall, Napoleon placed in jail in 1809), was not opposed to human rights. He only "objected . . . to specific rights being recognized as human rights."[21] Edelstein made his case in the negative, arguing that an absence constituted a tacit endorsement. Pius VII did not favor total religious

---

18. Greenberg and Steinmetz-Jenkins, "Introduction," 408.
19. Greenberg and Steinmetz-Jenkins, "Introduction," 408.
20. Edelstein, "Rights in the French Revolution," 414.
21. Edelstein, "Rights in the French Revolution," 414.

liberty or complete freedom of expression. But, reaching deep into the tradition, Pius VII acknowledged a principle of self-preservation, or a duty to obey a law of nature. Catholics only rejected the French Revolution when it took extreme anti-clerical turns. Clergymen endorsed parts of the Revolutionary agenda before the National Assembly began seizing Church property or dissolving religious orders.

Edelstein drew upon the French Revolution moment and its distinction between acceptable and unacceptable rights to exfoliate the emerging scholarship on human rights, opening it up to a deeper past. Maritain did not create human rights with a "sleight of hand" or "invent a tradition."[22] From Aquinas (1225–74) to Francisco de Vitoria (1483–1546) to Francisco Suarez (1548–1617), Catholics incubated a genealogy of human rights; there would have been no need to make one *ex nihilo*. Edelstein concluded on a provocation of his own. Given this history, Catholics of the twentieth century "did not need to steer Catholic doctrine 180 degrees."[23] He encouraged historians to look much more closely at Pope Leo XIII's 1891 encyclical *Rerum Novarum*. The case made for social rights in that document echoed the arguments Aquinas made about self-preservation and a Catholic's duty to follow a natural law. "No significant break had to occur."[24]

A Detour on Origin of Human Rights: Historical Invention or Metaphysics

It is worth pausing for a brief moment to contextualize these claims. Let's step out of the 2018 forum for a quick detour. Claims about the perennial nature of Catholic human rights have followed *Christian Human Rights* from the start. Such rebuttals are easy enough to offer given the plethora of ideas and concepts found in the Church's two-thousand-year history. To explore this debate more deeply it is useful to offer a brief reception history of *Christian Human Rights* by analyzing some of its many reviews. Philosopher John Finnis, reviewing the book for *King's Law Journal*, claimed that natural law "entails" human rights, and that in using the word "duty" Aquinas was "talking about human rights even

---

22. Edelstein, "Rights in the French Revolution," 412.
23. Edelstein, "Rights in the French Revolution," 425.
24. Edelstein, "Rights in the French Revolution," 425.

though he did not use the phrase."[25] The theologian David Lantigua, in a review for *Studies in Christian Ethics*, wondered aloud why Moyn "did not adequately address the richer philosophical and theological beliefs informing dignity and human rights" such as the natural law, the common good, the Incarnation, and the Mystical Body of Christ.[26] Moyn read Leo Strauss but why did not he not take up the claims made by medievalist Brian Tierney in his classic 1997 book, *The Idea of Natural Rights*?[27] Why did he not consider Gallicanism, Jansenism, Conciliarism, or anti-Papalism?[28]

Moyn defended his approach in kind, citing World War II as the key moment in this history, and accusing Finnis of participating in the invention of tradition.[29] We might also highlight a brilliant line Moyn penned in his 2015 book: "universalistic languages have always had a historically specific and ideological meaning," he wrote, "which it is the mission of the historian to seek out."[30] While natural rights may have deeper valences across centuries, it was also a radically specific temporal discourse. We can be nominalists and historicists if we so choose. In a perceptive analysis of Finnis-Moyn exchange, historian Julian Bourg did not exactly call for a truce—the exchange itself had a longer history as insoluble—but he noted that both Moyn and Finnis are weary of an excessive individualism that came at the expense of communitarianism or collectivism. They parted ways over what brought rights into being, whether a "posteriori through historical effort" for Moyn or an "apriori in a metaphysically real cosmology" for Finnis.[31]

---

25. Finnis, Review of *Christian Human Rights*, 14–15.

26. Lantigua, Review of *Christian Human Rights*, 250.

27. Political theorist Carlo Invernizzi Accetti, suggesting another model, argued that the papacy took on the language of human rights in the 1960s but recast the ideas as "logical corollaries of the natural law" essentially hostile to liberalism. The papacy deployed human rights, then, but only as a means to affirm the authority of the natural law. Accetti, "Catholic Social Doctrine," 85.

28. For an excellent book that looks at these early modern ideas, see Breidenbach, *Our Dear-Bought Liberty*.

29. Moyn, "Tradition and Beyond," 27–34.

30. Moyn, *Christian Human Rights*, 67.

31. Bourg, "Alpine Climb," 45.

A More Important Debate: Can Catholics Be Modern?

It is beyond the scope of my essay to settle this dispute. In the end, it is less a matter of empirical spade work than the preference, politically and theologically, of the researcher. "Divergent basic commitments lead to different methodological positions, which in turn yield divergent substantive conclusions," Bourg reminds us.[32] It boils down, Bourg suggests, to the relationship between Catholicism and modernity. The debate over tradition and invention probably matters less than the question of whether or not Catholics can be modern. If Catholics deploy human rights language to impose norms on others (as Kosicki, Chappel's paternalistic wing, and Moyn note) then Catholic human rights is not modern. If Catholic human rights are a means to accept other modes of life (Chappel's fraternal wing), then perhaps turning to these rights can make Catholics modern. In being modern, Christianity keeps its traditions while "accepting that it is one voice among many."[33] Modern Christians would countenance several explanations for why an individual possessed rights.

Can we split the difference between tradition and invention? Certain moments can bring Christians to amplify previous existing ideas, but these revivals, we should note, changes the contents of those ideas. I argued in my own 2021 book, *Follow Your Conscience: The Catholic Church and the Spirit of the Sixties*, that a medieval notion of conscience informed an explosion of conscience discourse in the 1960s and 1970s United States. Modern tensions between the individual and obedience to law during the debates over artificial birth control and conscription into the military during the Vietnam War brought a long-standing notion in Catholic history of "forming and following conscience" back into a limelight.[34] Modern American Catholics believed they were acting on tradition by following conscience but were they inventing that tradition? While there are some grounds for compromise here, we cannot deny that by staking out a strong position on this question Moyn did a great deal to create this field of inquiry and expanding our knowledge of Catholic history. The debate will not be settled anytime soon but we can relish its productivity.

The 2018 forum proved crucial on another ground. On its pages, historian Sarah Shortall announced the implications that her research on

---

32. Bourg, "Alpine Climb," 44.
33. Bourg, "Alpine Climb," 57.
34. Cajka, *Follow Your Conscience*.

the *nouvelle théologie*, particularly the writings of French Jesuit Henri de Lubac, held for the history of Catholic human rights. Up to this point, the historiography had been concerned almost exclusively with the natural law school of thought. For Shortall, this overriding focus on Maritain and Mounier offered historians a false sense of unity shared by Christians who invoked human rights. Bringing de Lubac into view showed that "human rights were a far more divided project than the recent literature suggests."[35] The missing ingredient was a sustained examination of the theologies that underwrote Catholic human rights claims. De Lubac argued that human rights came from the reality that all human beings were members of the body of Christ who are ultimately oriented towards a spiritual end in Christ. All human beings have dignity and rights because they are called to be members of the body of Christ. De Lubac "rooted human rights and dignity in a theological anthropology that was difficult to square with secular human rights projects."[36] The foundations of these human rights are ecclesial.

Shortall considers Maritian's body of works from the perspective of this alternative theological prism. In her award-winning book published in 2021, *Soldiers of God in a Secular World: Catholic Theology and Twentieth Century French Politics*, Shortall shows how the nouvelle théologie was deeply concerned with the secularization of modern Europe. Scholars like de Lubac, along with Yves Congar and Gaston Fessard, restocked the foundation of the Church with medieval and early modern sources in an effort to help the Church participate in the modern world without succumbing to its corrosive secularity. In 1942, the same year, Shortall notes, that Maritain published *The Rights of Man and Natural Law*, Jesuits Pierre Chaillet, Fessard, and de Lubac issued a critique of fascism, in which they decried the system's violation of human rights. But "their theological justification for doing so could scarcely have been more different."[37] To put it bluntly: the French Jesuits thought Maritain was a secularizer. *Nouvelle théologie* held that Maritain's conception of human rights compromised the standing of the Church by legitimating the existence of secularity. Maritain drew a distinction between the natural and supernatural arenas of human life. This allowed him to pursue a politics of human rights that fostered engagement with non-believers. But for the *nouvelle théologie*, such a move produced entire spheres of existence

---

35. Shortall, "Theology," 449. See also by Shortall, *Soldiers of God*.
36. Shortall, "Theology," 448.
37. Shortall, "Theology," 452.

outside the Church, which was unacceptable. Maritain's division of temporal and spiritual milieus played into the hands of the secularization of Europe. Under this dispensation, grace would have to enter the world from an external source rather than exist in human nature. De Lubac held that "human life does not possess a natural end that is somehow distinct from its supernatural end."[38] The Church held authority over all persons—no separate secular sphere existed—and so human rights were based on the notion that all persons, including the Jews, could become Christians.

"There were not one but many forms of human rights in the 1940s," Shortall concludes.[39] The primary division that historians ought to attend to, she maintains, is "between those open to working with non-believers to enshrine human rights in constitution and international law" like Maritain, and those like de Lubac "who rejected secular human rights projects."[40] With this, Shortall opened up an entirely new dimension in the history of Catholic human rights and the history of twentieth-century Europe.

Shortall exposed much of the previous literature as having placed Catholic human rights into a preexisting political taxonomy, one often taken up uncritically by many historians. This distorted the ontologies of these rights and foreclosed the possibility of looking at the past in new ways. Moyn held that Christian human rights comprised a conservative political agenda, one open to fascism and then later foundational for the Christian Democracies that achieved ascendancy in post-World War II Europe. But the *nouvelle théologie* were equally critical of both totalitarianism and liberal democracy, and this should give historians pause. Shortall's interventions show that theological concepts can "migrate between the left and the right, or even inhabit both at the same time."[41] The way the *nouvelle théologie* framed human rights—as connected to the Mystical Body of Christ and an eschatology of future Christians—could not be "rendered into law."[42] These projects existed outside the right–left, fascist–democrat, political spectrum. Recall here that we have pointed out how human rights became rights not by way of politics or constitutions but through the realty that all humans were future members of

---

38. Shortall, "Theology," 455.
39. Shortall, "Theology," 448.
40. Shortall, "Theology," 448.
41. Shortall, "Theology," 458.
42. Shortall, "Theology," 457.

the Church. De Lubac and his ilk were suspicious of liberal democracy because, abetted by Maritain, these politics produced an autonomous and secular political grounding. They critiqued totalitarianism as related to liberal democracy in its aspirations to de-Christianize major swaths of existence. Shortall's subjects resisted—and called into question—the public/private grid deployed implicitly by Moyn and explicitly by James Chappel. In this sense, Shortall sets up de Lubac and Congar as forerunners to later critics of human rights liked Talal Asad, Wendy Brown, Saba Mahmood, and Michel Foucault. Human rights law depended on the identification and governance of a particular liberal human subject. In a sense, this subject belongs to the state, as the state brought such a subject into existence. Here the temporal sphere can become autonomous and an end-in-itself. This is precisely what de Lubac had warned his contemporaries about as early as the 1940s, albeit by offering his critique from the perspective of the supernatural.

Reaching Maturity as a Field: Plural and Critical

The field reached yet another milestone in 2020 with the publication of edited volume of essays, *Christianity and Human Rights Reconsidered*. The volume, edited by Steinmetz-Jenkins and Shortall, marked the entrance of religion and human rights into a phase of globalism and pluralism. Moyn's conservative origin story, foundational for the way it clarified the roots of Christian human rights, gave way to several competing explications of the contents of Christian Human rights and several explanations for the idea's twentieth century rise. Moyn, who wrote the preface to the volume, thought the field "passed a critical threshold." The two watchwords were "plural" and critical." The historiography of Christian human rights was, as of 2020, a scholarly "conversation in which no one gets the last word."[43] The speed at which the field grew—from a foundational text published in 2015 to a highly diverse set of essays in a volume published by Cambridge in 2020—is quite remarkable. The editors included essays on China, Africa, and Latin America, capturing the global turn in Catholic history as enshrined in John T. McGreevy's authoritative book, *Catholicism: A Global History from the French Revolution to Pope Francis*. Steinmetz-Jenkins' and Shortall's edited volume did indeed present evidence of a highly diversified field. Contributors wrote about Liberal

43. Moyn, "Preface," xi–xii.

Protestants, John Rawls, African Americans, and biopolitics. The editors, summarizing the findings of the volume, described Christian human rights as marked by "plasticity" and concluded that there existed "remarkable internal diversity within the Christian tradition."[44]

Broadening Human Rights Scholarship to Include Latin American Experiences

To become truly pluralist, the predominance of the North Atlantic needed to be displaced. The context and history of Latin America produced an alternative Catholic human rights discourse. In his essay for the edited volume, David Lantigua took aim at the European framing of Catholic human rights historians. Like Shortall's French theologians, Latin American theologians were suspicious of the collusion between markets and human rights. But they were critical on different grounds. Latin American theologians were "not personalist in orientation, but liberationalist."[45] Human rights spoke more to group liberation than they did to individual resistance to state power. Human rights politics, as practiced in the European and North American theaters, was beholden to a false notion that "society enjoys an equality that does not exist."[46] The narrow definition of human rights pursued by the Carter Administration in the late 1970s, for example, worked against the struggle for liberation from oppression by telescoping human rights onto the individual. "Distinct peoples rather than abstract individuals were the agents and recipients of justice," Lantingua wrote.[47] Human rights, as understood by liberation theologians, entailed a just wage, unionization, security, and even a right to basic survival. Lantingua not only makes a crucial contribution to pluralizing to human rights, but he offers a strong critique of Moyn's 2019 argument that human rights simply sooth over the defects of the neoliberal economy. The human rights of liberation theology were born in opposition to capitalism, not as a response to communism, and they offer a real political alternative to the "international imperialism of money."[48]

---

44. Shortall and Steinmetz-Jenkins, "Introduction," in *Christianity and Human Right Reconsidered*, 8, 13.

45. Lantigua, "Neoliberalism," 240.

46. Lantigua, "Neoliberalism," 249.

47. Lantigua, "Neoliberalism," 249.

48. Lantigua, "Neoliberalism," 249.

A crucial case study of human rights politics in Latin America came in the form of Theresa Keeley's 2020 book, *Reagan's Gun-Toting Nuns: The Catholic Conflict Over Cold War Human Rights Policy in Central America*. The Maryknoll nuns at the center of this book could not be described as personalists. They defined human rights "broadly" as "having the right to human dignity and self-determination, right to be free from hunger, sickness, and political and economic domination in their country and more broadly."[49] Keeley, a historian of American foreign affairs, traces the ways Maryknoll nuns fomented an intra-Catholic dispute over human rights that echoed in the policy-making circles of the Reagan administration. In the wake of the rapes and executions of two Maryknoll nuns in El Salvador in 1980, a type of political competition opened up in American politics to define human rights and the policies used to secure them. While the conservative Catholics in the Republican Party deployed human rights as a critique of the Soviets, these nuns were in El Salvador, Nicaragua, and Guatemala, spoke the language of human rights to push back against regimes that were crushing the poor. Keeley introduces another complexity to the historiography. The history of Catholic human rights, as Lantingua also suggested, must be broadened considerably when one factors in liberation theology in Latin America. While they proceeded with similar critiques of state power, Latin American liberation theology and the thinkers like Maritain worked in divergent intellectual worlds. These nuns, like the French Catholic resistance or even the right-wing personalists, denounced the use of concentration camps, paramilitary squads, extrajudicial executions, torture and rape. But their imaginary was far more capacious and social than the personalist human rights politics. Human rights were enmeshed in a collective liberation that realized a more equal and just society.

Conclusion

What explains the turn to Christian human rights? History is an enterprise of discovery—a mode of searching primary sources to answer questions that have become pressing. Moyn took a trip to the University of Notre Dame in 2007 to conduct research at the Jacques Maritain Center. The field began when he attempted to explain Maritain's turn to

---

49. Keeley, *Reagan's Gun-Toting Nuns*, 8. For excellent literature addressing Christianity and human rights in the American context, see Williams, *Defenders of the Unborn*; Zubovich, *Before the Religious Right*.

human rights in the 1940s. He could have followed up on any number of points uncovered in his research for *The Last Utopia*, but he chose religion. Why? Several excellent historians then continued to ask questions about Catholicism. It may be too soon to explain this scholarly turn, but two factors seem particularly salient. First, religion offered a new means to write political history. These scholars do make original interventions into religion and theology, of course, but they are primarily concerned with politics. Christian human rights are a means to tell the story of fascism, democracy, communism, and liberalism. Second, as mentioned by Greenberg and Steinmetz-Jenkins, Christian human rights offer a compelling means to continue to the tell the story of the rise of human rights. Human rights are still celebrated by many historians. Now, however, that some of the illiberal, conservative, and supernatural aspects of this story have been brought to the surface, will human rights still garner respect?

Human rights bring into focus the relationship between Catholic Social Teaching and the modern state. Every iteration of Catholic human rights—whether conservative Maritain, fraternal Maritain, secularizer Maritain, the *nouvelle théologie*, or liberation theology—triangulate the individual, the community, and the state. Catholic social teaching must recognize individual dignity while acknowledging the community and the consider this intricate balance of self and group as it interfaces with the Leviathan. The past can be of service in taking some new approaches. What historians have uncovered and debated has serious implications for Catholic social thought. It will remain the test of the Church's social theorists to move human rights beyond the illiberal and exclusionary approaches of the 1930s and 1940s. While acknowledging this sordid history, Catholic intellectuals should link human rights to an inclusive and more global agenda. Is this possible? Or should the intellectual baggage of human rights inspire a migration to new concepts? It remains a challenge for Catholics to uphold the common good while not reducing faith to a set of politics. Yet, Christian human rights ought to be a concept well-suited to promote a culture of democracy. The fraternal side of Maritain, the supernaturalism of the *nouvelle théologie*, and liberation theology will continue to be guides. Finally, the findings of these scholars show that a wide range of Catholic subjects—political theorists, theologians, laypeople, activists, missionaries, unions, revolutionary collectives—make Catholic human rights. Considered in conversation with the papacy, which connects human rights to an objective natural law, the continued invention of tradition or authentic development of tradition (depending on one's perspective) will produce creative tensions. It seems clear, however, that the correction to the narrow and individualist concepts of human rights offered by Pope Francis and liberation theologians is essential to any future Catholic human rights project. The future of Catholic human rights is as much in economics as it is in politics.

Bibliography

Accetti, Carlo Invernizzi. "Catholic Social Doctrine and Human Rights: From Rejection to Endorsement?" In *Christianity and Human Rights Reconsidered*, edited by Sarah Shortall and Daniel Steinmetz-Jenkins, 81–102. Cambridge: Cambridge University Press, 2020.

Breidenbach, Michael. *Our Dear-Bought Liberty: Catholics and Religious Toleration in Early America*. Cambridge: Harvard University Press, 2021.

Bourg, Julian. "The Alpine Climb between Paris and Rome." In *Christianity and Human Rights Reconsidered*, edited by Sarah Shortall and Daniel Steinmetz-Jenkins, 40–60. Cambridge: Cambridge University Press, 2020.

Cajka, Peter. *Follow Your Conscience: The Catholic Church and the Spirit of the Sixties*. Chicago: University of Chicago Press, 2021.

Chamedes, Giuliana. *A Twentieth-Century Crusade: The Vatican's Battle to Remake Christian Europe*. Cambridge: Harvard University Press, 2019.

Chappel, James. *Catholic Modern: The Challenge of Totalitarianism and the Remaking of the Church*. Cambridge: Harvard University Press, 2018.

———. "Explaining the Catholic Turn to Rights in the 1930s." In *Christianity and Human Rights Reconsidered*, edited by Sarah Shortall and Daniel Steinmetz-Jenkins, 63–80. Cambridge: Cambridge University Press, 2020.

Connelly, John. *From Enemy to Brother: The Revolution in Catholic Teaching on the Jews, 1933–1956*. Cambridge: Harvard University Press, 2012.

Duranti, Marco. *Conservative Human Rights Revolution: European Identity, Transnational Politics, and the Origins of European Convention*. Oxford: Oxford University Press, 2017.

Edelstein, Dan. "Christian Human Rights in the French Revolution." *Journal of the History of Ideas* 79 (2018) 411–26.

Finnis, John. Review of *Christian Human Rights*, by Samuel Moyn. *King's Law Journal* 28 (2017) 12–20.

Greenberg, Udi, and Daniel Steinmetz-Jenkins. "Introduction: Special Forum on Christianity and Human Rights." *Journal of the History of Ideas* 79 (2018) 407–9.

Hanebrink, Paul. *In Defense of Christian Hungary: Religion, Nationalism, and Antisemitism, 1890–1944*. Ithaca, NY: Cornell University Press, 2006.

Hobsbawm, Eric, and Terence Ranger. *The Invention of Tradition*. Cambridge: Cambridge University Press, 1983.

Keeley, Theresa. *Reagan's Gun-Toting Nuns: The Catholic Conflict Over Cold War Human Rights Policy in Central America*. Ithaca, NY: Cornell University Press, 2020.

Kosicki, Piotr. *Catholics on the Barricades: Poland, France, and "Revolution," 1939–1956*. New Haven: Yale University Press 2018.

———. "Masters in Their Own Home or Defenders of the Human Person? Wojciech Korfanty, Anti-Semitism, and Polish Christian Democracy's Illiberal Rights-Talk." *Modern Intellectual History* 14 (2017) 99–130.

Lantigua, David M. "Neoliberalism, Human Rights, and the Theology of Liberation in Latin America." In *Christianity and Human Rights Reconsidered*, edited by Sarah Shortall and Daniel Steinmetz-Jenkins, 238–60. Cambridge: Cambridge University Press, 2020.

———. Review of *Christian Human Rights*, by Samuel Moyn. *Studies in Christian Ethics* 30 (2017) 247–50.

McGreevy, John T. *Catholicism: A Global History from the French Revolution to Pope Francis*. New York: Norton, 2022.

Moyn, Samuel. *Christian Human Rights*. Philadelphia: University of Pennsylvania Press, 2015.

———. *The Last Utopia: Human Rights in History*. Cambridge: Harvard University Press, 2010.

———. *Not Enough: Human Rights in an Unequal World*. Cambridge: Harvard University Press, 2018.

———. "Personalism, Community, and the Origins of Human Rights." In *Human Rights in the Twentieth Century*, edited by Stefan-Ludwig Hoffman, 85–106. Cambridge: Cambridge University Press, 2011.

———. "Preface." In *Christianity and Human Rights Reconsidered*, edited by Sarah Shortall and Daniel Steinmetz-Jenkins, xi–xii. Cambridge: Cambridge University Press, 2020.

———. "Tradition and Beyond: *Christian Human Rights* in Debate." *King's Law Journal* 28 (2017) 27–34.

Shortall, Sarah. *Soldiers of God in a Secular World: Catholic Theology and Twentieth-Century French Politics*. Cambridge: Harvard University Press, 2021.

———. "Theology and the Politics of Christian Human Rights." *Journal of the History of Ideas* 79 (2018) 445–60.

Shortall, Sarah, and Daniel Steinmetz-Jenkins. *Christianity and Human Rights Reconsidered*. Cambridge: Cambridge University Press, 2020.

Williams, Daniel. *Defenders of the Unborn: The Pro-Life Movement before "Roe v. Wade."* New York: Oxford University Press, 2016.

Zubovich, Gene. *Before the Religious Right: Liberal Protestants, Human Rights, and the Polarization of the United States*. Philadelphia: University of Pennsylvania Press, 2022.

17

Christendom and the Marian Path of the Church

FREDERICK C. BAUERSCHMIDT, LOYOLA UNIVERSITY MARYLAND

Abstract: What does "Social Catholicism" mean after the end of Christendom, the sociopolitical formation that the philosopher Chantal Delsol describes as "the civilization inspired, ordered, guided by the Church"—a civilization that endured for sixteen centuries, beginning from the reign of Theodosius in the late fourth century, and that carried with it a host of presumptions about how Catholicism can and should be "social," but which lies now in its death throes? In this essay, I begin by briefly suggesting how Christendom narrowed our understanding of the social nature of the Church. I then turn to the analysis offered by Delsol of the rise and fall of Christendom. Last, I explore how locating the end of Christendom within a Marian-figural reading of the story of the Church can suggest what a post-Christendom Social Catholicism might look like.

The Church and/as Politics

THESE DAYS IT IS difficult, though not impossible, to find defenders of Christendom. For many Catholics, Christendom was the offspring of an unseemly power grab by the Church that brought about immense human suffering in the name of religion and compromised the Church's witness to the Gospel of Jesus Christ by seeking to make his kingdom into a worldly one. There are, however, some historically nuanced interpretations of Christendom that, while recognizing that Christendom cannot be reconstituted, also recognize that Church leaders in the fourth and fifth centuries were simply responding to the novel exigencies of the times, particularly the collapse of Roman Imperial structures, and that the sixteen hundred years of Christendom brought not simply human suffering and worldly compromise, but also a patrimony of arts, thought, and institutions.[1] One even finds some "integralists" who suggest that Christendom's day is not past and that it is, by virtue of its integration of the temporal and the spiritual and the subordination of the former to the latter, the only social order than can address modern ills.[2] But most Catholics accept that Christendom, if not entirely vanished, is today reduced to the fumes emanating from an empty bottle.

This does not mean, however, that Catholicism has become a purely private, apolitical affair, though some may wish it so. Of course, if one takes for granted that by politics we mean "statecraft"—elections and legislation and public policy decisions—it is difficult to think about the political nature of Catholicism outside of the construct of Christendom. But while the operation of states is certainly one of the activities that might fall under the category of the "political," the collapse of politics into statecraft is not the only way to think about the political. If we follow Aristotle in defining a political community as "a community established with a view to some good,"[3] then our understanding of the political widens considerably, allowing us to see the "political" character of various forms of human association that are involved with the cultivation of the good for human beings. Indeed, it raises the possibility that we might

1. See, for example, Wilken, *First Thousand Years*.
2. See the writings associated with the website *The Josias*, which sums up its "integralist" social vision as follows: "Catholic Integralism is a tradition of thought that, rejecting the liberal separation of politics from concern with the end of human life, holds that political rule must order man to his final goal. Since, however, man has both a temporal and an eternal end, integralism holds that there are two powers that rule him: a temporal power and a spiritual power. And since man's temporal end is subordinated to his eternal end, the temporal power must be subordinated to the spiritual power" (Waldstein, "Integralism in Three Sentences"). See also the sermon preached in 1985 at the traditionalist Catholic Pentecost Pilgrimage to Chartres by Dom Gérard, Abbot of Le Barroux, "An Exhortation to the Restoration of Christendom."
3. Aristotle, *Politics* 1.1 (1252a).

think of the Church herself as a "political" community, instituted by God for the sake of obtaining the good that is participation in the divine life. This could help us to make sense of the use of political terminology in the New Testament: not only the term *ekklesia* itself, which referred to the public deliberative assembly of the Greek *polis*, but also Paul's statement that our true *politeuma* is in heaven (Phil 3:20), or the description of the Church in 1 Peter as a holy *ethnos* (2:9), or indeed Jesus' own proclamation of God's *basileia*. It also can help us understand why early Christian writers, such as the author of the *Epistle to Diognetus*, speak of Christians as having their own distinctive *politeias*.[4]

Beginning with this broad understanding of the political as the shared pursuit of the common good, we can then proceed to make some important distinctions. Aristotle argues against those who would see the difference between various forms of human association as simply a matter of scale and not of kind.[5] Thus, for Aristotle, the household (*oikos*) is a different kind of association from the village (*kōmē*), and the village from the city (*polis*), and what distinguishes the *polis* from other forms of association is its end, for it aims at the highest good and thus subordinates to itself all those associations, such as households and villages, that only aim at partial goods. It is only the life of the *polis*—only political life—that is in a complete sense the good life for human beings.

And here we see why we cannot, according to the classical understanding of politics, restrict Christianity to the realm of the private, and why the social nature of Christianity must be thought of in specifically "political" terms. For Christianity from the outset arrives on the scene as a rival to the earthly *polis*, inasmuch as it claims to be the community that aims at what is truly the highest good, the good to which the goods pursued by all other forms of human association, including the *polis*, must be subordinated (in the sense of "ordered beneath"). It is only in the *ekklesia* of God that one lives fully the good life for human beings, for it is only within the Body of Christ that human beings can attain the supreme good of participation in the divine life. In light of this supreme good, the goods of all human political communities are revealed to be as fragmentary as the goods pursued by households and villages.

Unlike households and villages, however, earthly political communities are constantly tempted to claim for themselves ultimate human

---

4. *Epistle to Diognetus* 5.
5. Aristotle, *Politics* 1.1 (1252a).

loyalty and thus seek to heal their own fragmentariness with the *pharmakon* (remedy-poison) of prideful bluster. This is the thought to which Augustine gives exhaustive expression in *The City of God*. All the political communities of antiquity, in their inordinate self-exaltation, are for Augustine distorted shadows of the true City, which exists perfectly in the fellowship of the saints above, and which lives a life of pilgrimage within human history. Thus, for Christians to think politically is not simply to think about public policy or elections; primarily, it is to think about their common life in Christ's body and to think about how the Church, which claims to aim at the supreme good, ought, while in her *status viatoris*, to cultivate the civic virtues that befit citizens of the Heavenly City and to understand the relationship of these citizens to the earthly cities in which they dwell while on pilgrimage.

It is understandable why Christians of the fourth and fifth centuries would draw from this view of the Church as a human association whose end is the highest good the conclusion that this truth should express itself in a civilization inspired, ordered, and guided by the Church—that is, Christendom. At the same time, there is a sense in which the political nature of the Church was occluded by the advent of Christendom. Or, perhaps more accurately, the variety of ways in which the Church as *polis* might interact with the earthly *polis* became constricted in the Christian imagination, reduced to the Christendom model of the Church having her hands upon the levers of worldly power, either directly or indirectly. But as Christendom faded from our world, if not from our imaginations, Catholics began to ponder how the Church might think anew about her public, political nature, her role as witness to the nations concerning the true nature of humanity's highest good, and how worldly goods might be ordered beneath spiritual goods. It is from this situation that the "Social Catholicism" of Wilhelm von Ketteler and Leo XIII was born.

What are we to make of this fading of Christendom? To help with our evaluation, I now turn to a recent work by Chantal Delsol (b. 1947), whose analysis of the situation of the Church in France, where de-Christianization is well advanced (around half the population identifies as Catholic, but only about 5 percent attend Mass), offers us a sketch of what the increasingly post-Christian West might look like. More than that, Delsol offers a narrative that suggests ways in which we might understand the immense social upheavals brought about by both the genesis and the demise of Christendom and also suggests ways the Church might understand her public character at the end of Christendom.

The Birth and Death of Christendom

Chantal Delsol is a thinker well known for her political philosophy, and her work *La fin de la Chrétienté* (*The End of Christendom*) continues a line of inquiry that is well developed in other works. Her approach is marked by a philosophical anthropology that acknowledges the social and historical construction of human identity without totally abandoning all notion of human nature. In this sense, her project is not unlike that of Alasdair MacIntyre and leads her to pay close attention to the play of historical contingencies in such notions as human dignity. Rather than a static identity, for her human nature is a dynamic, evolving reality—indeed, if anything is "essential" to our nature it is our ceaseless desire to exceed that nature. As she writes memorably of the human person in her book *Qu'est-ce que l'homme?* (*What Is a Human Being?*): "Rooted, he wants to be emancipated from his roots. Put another way, he seeks an inaccessible dwelling place through a succession of temporary way stations."[6] The result is an Augustinian anthropology of the "restless heart" inflected by (post)modern historical consciousness. All of this informs her account of the fate of Christianity in the contemporary West.

Delsol begins by examining how a Church that so resolutely resisted modernity for two centuries in the name of Christian civilization came, since the 1960s, to embrace modern values such as religious freedom, values utterly at odds with Christendom. She also offers an analysis of early twentieth-century fascism and corporatism as integralist attempts to save Christendom that "proved to be worse than the disease."[7] Animated by a utopian nostalgia that proved to be merely the mirror image of modernity's utopian futurism, these sorts of movements fell prey to those, such as Charles Maurras, who wanted Christendom but really could care less about Christianity. In the end, these movements proved to be nothing but "the convulsions of a dying Christendom."[8]

Unlike thinkers like Jacques Maritain and, more recently, Jean-Luc Marion, Delsol is skeptical that old Christendom can be replaced by a "New Christendom" in which Christians co-operate with a benignly

---

6. Delsol, "Introduction to *Qu'est-ce que l'homme?*," in Hall and Seaton, *Lucid Mind, Intrepid Spirit*, 9.

7. Delsol, "Conclusion to *Qu'est-ce que l'homme?*," in Hall and Seaton, *Lucid Mind, Intrepid Spirit*, 16.

8. Delsol, *Fin*, 27. In France today, the embrace of Catholicism as a civilizational heritage, but not a living faith, is still a political force, sometimes referred to as "zombie Catholicism." See Gobry, "Zombie Catholics."

secular society in order to realize commonly held goods.[9] She is skeptical of this because she is generally skeptical that any society can, in fact, be benignly secular, or indeed secular at all. Secularity is a fantasy indulged in by intellectuals, but for ordinary people, "for whom common sense whispers that there are mysteries behind the door,"[10] religion of some sort is unavoidable. Our present moment is not one of secularization but of revolution, "in the strict sense of a cyclical return."[11] Ancient paganism is reborn, albeit in new forms marked by the sixteen centuries of Christendom. This revolution involves a kind of Nietzschean transvaluation both in morals ("the normative inversion") and in worldview ("the ontological inversion"). Though herself a committed Catholic, Delsol tries to retain a certain analytic detachment in describing these inversions of prior moral norms, seeking to cast herself as an observer of this moment of historical transition and not a partisan. What she does want to insist upon is the significance of this inversion, for the mores of a society form a kind of architecture of our existence, a structure more stable than codified laws, shaping not only our actions but our feelings and habits.

To shed light on our current situation, Delsol looks back to the birth of Christendom, the last great inversion of norms in the West. She insists upon what might seem at first contradictory claims: the advent of Christendom was both a radical break with the pagan past and was also unthinkable without that past as a basis upon which it was built. Christians constructed their civilization utilizing elements of pagan culture, in particular Stoic morality, though now "democratized" and framed within a new system of beliefs that transformed what was appropriated. In contrast to the profoundly unified religious world of the Romans, in which the gods and humanity were fellow citizens of the cosmos, Christianity

---

9. For Maritain, after the demise of the old Christendom, the Church's public role is to provide the state with the values it needs to sustain what he called "the democratic secular faith," a faith that was, if not Christian, at least "Christianly inspired" and forms a people that "at least recognized the value and sensibleness of the Christian conception of freedom, social progress, and the political establishment" (Maritain, *Man and the State*, 109). Marion does not use the term "New Christendom," but seems confident that "Christians furnish society with its best citizens from the point of view even of the interests of the city of men, because their disinterestedness toward earthly power makes them honest workers who are efficient and reliable in community life" (Marion, *Brief Apology*, 57–58). Delsol explicitly rejects Maritain's New Christendom approach, calling it one of "the last illusions" of the post-war era (Delsol, *Fin*, 155).

10. Delsol, *Fin*, 34.

11. Delsol, *Fin*, 36.

"introduced a dualism between the temporal and the spiritual, the here-and-now and the beyond, human beings and God."[12] The advent of Christendom brings a sharp reversal of societal attitudes regarding divorce, abortion and infanticide, suicide, and homosexuality. Delsol evinces a keen sympathy for those pagan Romans, conservators of traditional values, who felt that, with the advent of Christendom, they had entered "an intellectual and spiritual world torn apart," and she shows genuine admiration for those who continued to battle in the face of what was clearly inevitable defeat.[13]

So too, in our own day, the partisans of Christendom—whether in its old form, in integralism, or the new form proposed by Maritain and others—fight in service of what is, particularly since the 1960s, a manifestly lost cause. Delsol points to shifts in both laws and popular attitudes toward divorce, abortion, and assisted reproduction. Though there are pockets of resistance to these developments (particularly, she notes, in the United States), the path of this arc is clear: "humanitarianism, the morality of today, is a morality entirely oriented toward the well-being of the individual, without any vision of the human person [*vision anthropologique*]."[14] What we see is an "inversion of the inversion,"[15] an undoing of the revolution of the fourth century that made the ideals of Christianity socially enforced norms. This might be identified by enthusiasts for modernity as a result of our progressive realization of the inviolability of individual conscience with regard to ultimate questions, but Delsol resists any narrative of progress: "in each era, 'progress' consists simply in reconciling realities (laws, customs, mores) with diffuse and sometimes as-yet-unexpressed beliefs that evolve in silence."[16]

This suggests that human beings are not simply behavers but also believers. The moral norms of the ancient world changed because the beliefs of Christianity supplanted those of paganism, making long-accepted pagan practices appear odious. Delsol quotes Tacitus, whose remarks concerning Jewish monotheism applied no less to Christians: "They hold profane all that we hold as sacred and, on the other hand, permit all that we hold to be abominable."[17] In particular, Delsol ascribes to Judaism

12. Delsol, *Fin*, 51.
13. Delsol, *Fin*, 51.
14. Delsol, *Fin*, 64.
15. Delsol, *Fin*, 65.
16. Delsol, *Fin*, 76.
17. Delsol, *Fin*, 84, citing Tacitus, *Histories* 5.4.

and Christianity a key role in desacralizing the world. The dualism of Christianity, with its transcendent God standing over and against the world, replaced the "cosmotheism" of antiquity, which saw the cosmos itself as saturated with divinity. Or, more precisely, monotheism was layered on top of cosmotheism, as a "secondary religion" covering over (but just barely) the "primary religion" of humanity, which "arises, so to speak, on its own, proliferates without fertilizer, and instantly occupies and reoccupies a place as soon as it is free."[18] Christianity has been replaced not by atheism and secularity, as the Enlightenment *philosophes* foretold, but by a religion "more primitive and more rustic."[19]

Delsol notes numerous writers who have described modernity as parasitic on Christianity, but she prefers to speak of modernity as a "palimpsest" written over the Christian text, in the same way that Christianity was written over the text of antiquity. This is always the way that human societies work: "using all the possible materials" from the past, "but depriving them of their meaning in order to reinvent them for the benefit of a new epoch."[20] Just as Christendom replaced paganism, a religion founded in mythos, with one that claimed foundation in truth and persecuted those who denied that truth and clung to their myths, so now, in our postmodern moment, "truth" has once again been eclipsed by mythos. Yet this new mythos is ineradicably marked by the Christian appeal to "truth," for it does not breed tolerance, as the myths of antiquity did, but retains the moral force of the universalism and absolutism of the Christendom that it has overwritten. For Delsol, those whom the French refer to as *les Woke* "have taken over the concept of dogmatic truth, and excluded their adversaries from public life, just as the Church had excommunicated in times past."[21] The fate of the West is neither nihilism nor ancient pagan religion but humanitarianism: "the evangelical virtues . . . recycled to become a kind of common morality."[22] We are left with what Delsol calls, invoking Flannery O'Connor's *Wise Blood*, "the Church without Christ."

Blame for this outcome can be laid at the feet of Christendom itself: "in its pretention to establish itself as a civilization, Christianity ended up producing a monstrous avatar that is at the same time its alter-ego

---

18. Delsol, *Fin*, 87.
19. Delsol, *Fin*, 90.
20. Delsol, *Fin*, 115.
21. Delsol, *Fin*, 129.
22. Delsol, *Fin*, 133.

and its mortal enemy."[23] But, Delsol reminds us, Christendom is not Christianity but simply one sociopolitical manifestation of Christianity, and the demise of the former is not the demise of the latter. Nor does she see much point in lamenting the errors of Christendom. Even if we today rightly judge aspects of Christendom as distortions of the Gospel, Delsol's historicist sensibilities lead her to cast a jaundiced eye at excessive Christian breast-beating over the past, "which can resemble masochism,"[24] and she sees little point in condemning those in the past who did not have the benefit of our hindsight. Even Augustine, who expected very little from Christian emperors in terms of aiding people in their journey to the heavenly city, saw no reason for Christians not to try to make use of the peace of the earthly city. Today it seems obvious for us to ask, "who was making use of whom?" but this was not so obvious in the late fourth century. Delsol comes neither to praise nor condemn Christendom but to bury it.

She is, however, concerned that, in their fear of repeating the errors of Christendom, Christians will mute their distinctive voice: "To dialogue is not to dissolve oneself in the theses of the adversary, and one does not need to cease to exist in order to be tolerant—in fact, the opposite is the case."[25] But the call to Christian distinctiveness is not the integralist call for a return to Christendom. It is, as Delsol puts it, a call to "a spiritual revolution,"[26] which by worldly standards might issue in what looks like defeat. Christians must form their children "to carry themselves like Kierkegaard's knight of faith: resigned, but also able to walk toward the infinite."[27] Christians without Christendom must take up the role of witnesses rather than rulers and learn the virtues characteristic of a minority: "equanimity, patience, and perseverance."[28] Delsol does not see the social kingship of Christ as requiring his followers, in integralist fashion, to have their hands on the levers of temporal power. Yet, in rejecting integralism, she also seeks to avoid a progressivism that would dilute Christian witness into a vague spirituality. It is through robust witness, not through coercion, that the Church engages the world and seeks to change it.

23. Delsol, *Fin*, 161.
24. Delsol, *Fin*, 148.
25. Delsol, *Fin*, 152.
26. Delsol, *Fin*, 154.
27. Delsol, *Fin*, 155.
28. Delsol, *Fin*, 163.

The Marian Path of the Church

Delsol's narrative of Christendom—its rise and flourishing and demise—helps us understand where we are and what the next step forward might be. In a sense, she is doing what Augustine did in *The City of God*: narrating the rise and fall of earthly cities as well as the story of God's pilgrim people in order to discern the workings of God's providence in the world and to gain some idea of the virtues that are required in order to participate in the good life of the heavenly City while on pilgrimage. Delsol differs from Augustine inasmuch as the story of Christendom's rise and fall is added to those of the empires of the pagans. This, in effect, relativizes Christendom, making it, in at least one sense, simply another instantiation of the earthly city. But is that really all that can be said of Christendom? Is it really nothing but the earthly city, as it were, dressed up in vestments?

Delsol's narrative also raises some discomfiting questions for Social Catholicism, which often presumes a neutral public space in which the Church and other social actors cooperate. If the post-Christian world is not neutrally secular but is, in fact, a revived rustic cosmotheism inflected by the absolutist claim of the Christendom over which it has been written, then any account of social cooperation between the Church and the civilization of modernity will have to recognize an element of conflict in that relationship since the heavenly and earthly cities both seek to define the highest good for human beings. Indeed, this conflict seems manifest in the rejection, often in quite absolutist terms, by many today of the Church's position on such social questions as the beginning and ending of life, the nature of marriage, and the proper understanding of sexuality and gender. If Delsol is correct about the religious nature of modernity, does the conflict between competing accounts of the highest good get the last word?

To combine these two concerns, we might ask whether it is possible to narrate Christendom as a moment within the story of the heavenly city's earthly pilgrimage, a story that includes both conflict and cooperation between the two cities? Such a narration must move beyond the merely historical to a theological reading of history and the path of God's people. Pope St. John Paul II's 1987 encyclical *Redemptoris Mater* suggests that the life of the virgin Mary can be seen as charting the path of the Church's pilgrimage. He writes:

> Strengthened by the presence of Christ (cf. Mt 28:20), the Church journeys through time toward the consummation of the ages and goes to meet the Lord who comes. But on this journey—and I wish to make this point straightaway—she proceeds along the path already trodden by the Virgin Mary.[29]

He reiterates later, "[Mary's] exceptional pilgrimage of faith represents a constant point of reference for the Church, for individuals and for communities, for peoples and nations, and in a sense for all humanity."[30] John Paul seems to suggest that we ought to look to the life of Mary in order to understand the pilgrim path of Christ's body through history. In other words, we ought to read the history of the Church "typologically" or "figurally" in such a way that Mary is the antitype for which the Church is the type.[31] This typological identification of the Church and Mary is possibly as old as the book of Revelation and has represented a major trend in modern Marian theology at least since Matthias Scheeben in the nineteenth century.[32] What is relatively novel in John Paul's suggestion is that we are to see Mary not as a static image of the Church but rather as a figure in motion,[33] so that we see in the trajectory of Mary's life an image of the trajectory of the Church's path through history.

It is this suggestion—that the life and destiny of the Church is seen in the living icon-in-motion of Mary—that I wish to develop in what follows. I am not suggesting that we can find some sort of precise one-to-one correspondence between the events of Mary's life and the past and future events of the Church's history. Such a use of Scripture has rightly been viewed with suspicion in the tradition of the Church. However, I do wish to explore how John Paul II's claim that the Church's path through history is the one already trod by the Virgin might provide the broad outline of an interpretive framework for the Church's understanding of its distinctive path within the course of world history. If Mary is iconically figured in the Church, and if we can discern in Mary's life a trajectory,

---

29. John Paul II, *Redemptoris Mater*, no. 2, in *Mary*.
30. John Paul II, *Redemptoris Mater*, no. 6; cf. 37.
31. See John Paul II, *Redemptoris Mater*, no. 42.
32. Scheeben, *Mariology*, 1:211–18.
33. On Mary's distinctive relation to time, and the need for what we might call a "narrative Mariology," see René Laurentin, "Blessed Virgin Mary," in Henry, *Historical and Mystical Christ*, 266–69. Laurentin notes that the narrative of Mary's life given an "impression of a necessity," albeit not a logical necessity; rather, it is "the type of necessity that occurs in the order of art and of love" (267). It is only narrative that can do adequate justice to God's election of Mary in grace and her free response.

then from her life, we ought to be able to gain some insight into the historical trajectory of the Church and in particular how we might locate Christendom within that trajectory and how conflicts between the Church and the world might be negotiated.

While we can see in Mary's Immaculate Conception and early life a kind of parallel with the election of Israel and the "pre-history" of the Church under the Old Law, it is with the Annunciation that the figural relationship between Mary and the Church comes clearly into view. Just as, at the Annunciation, Mary conceived God the Son in her womb by the power of the Spirit, so too at Pentecost, the ecclesial Body of Christ is conceived by the power of that same Spirit. As *Redemptoris Mater* notes:

> In the redemptive economy brought about by the action of the Holy Spirit, there is a unique correspondence between the moment of the Incarnation of the Word and the moment of the birth of the Church. The person who links these two moments is Mary: *Mary at Nazareth* and *Mary in the Upper Room at Jerusalem.*[34]

John Paul points to Mary's presence to the Spirit on these two occasions as key in establishing her as the one whose life reveals the Church's journey through history. He writes, "In the Upper Room Mary's journey meets the Church's journey of faith."[35]

But as we move beyond the Annunciation-Pentecost typology into the post-apostolic period, such a figural reading of the historical path of the Church must be put forward with great tentativeness. This is especially the case with the question, particularly relevant to political theology, that I wish to pose now: how can this Marian-figural reading help us address the question of the seeming collapse of Christianity as a social and cultural force in the modern West? Delsol offers a historical and sociological analysis of that collapse, but how can it be understood theologically? What accounts for what John Paul II called, in relation to Europe, this "silent apostasy"?[36]

We might be tempted to answer, curtly, "sin." But as with every case of hardening human hearts, we ought to probe deeper to ask how God's providence is being manifested in this story of the Western world's seeming enthusiastic embrace of Christianity and then widespread rejection.

---

34. John Paul II, *Redemptoris Mater*, no. 24.
35. John Paul II, *Redemptoris Mater*, no. 26.
36. John Paul II, *Ecclesia in Europa*, no. 9.

How is it fulfilling God's will for the Church to endure this rejection, and how ought the Church to live her common life in the face of such rejection? What light can Mary's path shed on this experience of the Church?

Such a figural reading might proceed in something like the following manner. Just as Christ's natural body grew in secret in Mary's womb for nine months, so too the ecclesial Body of Christ grew in secret in the first three centuries. When "in the fullness of time, God sent his Son, born of a woman" (Gal 4:4), Christ was revealed not simply to Israel but was manifested to the nations, as embodied in the Magi. The Magi came to the Virgin Mother seeking the Son of God who was born from her womb; four centuries later the nations came to Mother Church seeking to be reborn with Christ in the womb of Baptism as sons and daughters of God. And just as the Magi came bearing gifts, so too the nations came to the Church bearing gifts: not gifts of gold, frankincense, and myrrh, but gifts of philosophy, art, music, literature, and law. The emergence of the Church as a public social and cultural force after the Peace of the Church was not, as some would have it, a simple betrayal of the Church's ethos as a "contrast society" and the emergence of a fundamentally unfaithful form of "Constantinian" Christianity.[37] The Church could no more have turned away the nations than Mary could have turned away the Magi; to do so would have been to fail in the mission of manifesting Christ as a light to the world.

Yet those who criticize Christianity's welcome of Imperial Rome do have a point, for the story of the Magi is inextricably intertwined with a story of betrayal. The bloody slaughter of the innocents and the Holy Family's flight into exile followed upon, indeed in a certain sense was occasioned by, the joyous visit of the Magi. And it is at this point that our Marian-figural reading of Church history becomes particularly delicate. Part and parcel of the story of the Magi is the story of their inadvertent betrayal of Christ to Herod. Of course, there is no hint of ill will on the part of the Magi, though perhaps there is an element of naiveté that belies the epithet "wise men." For in their quest for Christ they brought in their train a king who did not see in Jesus one to be worshiped but rather a rival claimant to royal power. In Herod we see the figure of the earthly city, all those forms of earthly power that establish themselves upon violence and are ruled by their own lust for domination.[38] Herod sees in Christ the

---

37. See, e.g., Lohfink, *Jesus and Community*, 181–85; Yoder, "Constantinian Sources of Western Social Ethics," in *Priestly Kingdom*, 135–47.

38. See Augustine, *De civitate Dei* 1.

antithesis and overcoming of precisely the kind of power that he himself wields, and thus he sees in Christ one who must be eliminated. Yet he masks his true intention, presenting himself as one who wishes to join in worship.

We see in the intertwined history of the Magi and Herod a figure of the ambiguous nature of the project of Christendom, the project of creating a Christian civilization, and the enduring interplay of cooperation and conflict between the Church and the world. In welcoming the nations, the Church also welcomed those who, as Augustine said, belonged to the Church by virtue of the outward bond of the sacraments but who interiorly remained citizens of the earthly city.[39] The gifts brought by the nations were genuine gifts, but for all that the dangers were no less genuine. To recognize this is not to reject wholesale the sixteen hundred years of Christendom that followed upon the Peace of the Church. But it is to see that this period was one of both promise and peril to the Church and her mission, just as the homage paid by the Magi was both promise and peril to the Virgin and her child. It is to see that only a discerning heart can distinguish the gift from the threat. It is also to see that one must be prepared to go into exile, to flee to Egypt, even if this requires abandoning certain of the less portable gifts.

But is it to the Holy Family fleeing into exile that we should look to understand the current situation of the Church in the West?[40] As much as Christians might feel misunderstood and marginalized by the modern developed world, I suspect it is a bit too dramatic to see the Church as actively threatened. Now that the Church, particularly in Europe, is seen by most people to be quaintly irrelevant, there seems no need to keep it in exile. Aggressive anti-clericalism and persecution of Christians seem, at least in the West, to decrease in direct proportion to the decrease in the

---

39. Augustine, *De civitate Dei* 1.35.

40. Here I would underscore that my reading of the Church's current location along the "Marian trajectory" is meant to apply primarily to the industrialized West. One thing that should be kept in mind in any attempt to follow Pope John Paul's suggestion that we see the Church as following a path through history that has already been trod by the Blessed Virgin is that all local churches do not always follow that path at the same rate. It seems, for example, that the Church in Africa has not (yet) experienced its own form of Christendom (as much as it may have suffered from certain aspects of the Christendom of the West), and consequently has not had the same sort of peril posed to it, has not yet had its own "Herods." If one accepts John Paul's suggestion, one might have some confidence that all local churches within the one Catholic Church will in some way follow the Marian trajectory, but how this following will play out in detail cannot be determined in advance.

perceived power and influence of the Church. Stripped of political and cultural power, Christianity and its cultural relics can occupy a minor, folkloric place in society.

At the same time, the remnants of Christendom cannot be ignored. As Delsol suggests with her image of the palimpsest, the post-Christian West is haunted by ghosts of the Gospel that hover just beneath the text of modernity. The gifts that the nations brought to Christianity under Christendom were given back to the nations to become part of the cultural patrimony of the West, even if the story of that origin is forgotten or repressed. Notions such as human dignity are rooted in Christianity, even if "dignity" is understood by the modern world in ways that diverge from the Church's understanding. Perhaps now seen only in the cloudy mirror of humanitarianism, the manifestation of the Gospel to the nations continues to mark the rustic neo-paganism of the putatively secular West and to find an echo there. Hardly exiled, the Church's faith has instead been pillaged and repurposed. Thus, something of a return from Egypt has occurred, and we might see the Church as living an ecclesial life that is figured in the "hidden life" of the Holy Family in Nazareth. This life is far from the glory and drama of the visit of the Magi but is rather a time in which the Church must seek to foster among the offspring of the ecclesial womb the same growth "in wisdom and in stature" (Luke 2:52) that Mary fostered in Jesus.

We ought not think that accepting a certain "hiddenness" to the Church's life means an accession to modernity's circumscription of Christianity to the realm of the private. Such circumscription must be resolutely resisted, for it presumes a delineation of public and private that Christianity from its outset has called into question.[41] As I noted above, Aristotle distinguished the household or *oikos* from the city-state or *polis*, not simply because of differences in scale but also because of differences in the kind of end that each form of association pursued. The *polis* is that form of association that deals with the highest, the most comprehensive, the most public good, while the *oikos* is the realm in which more restricted, private goods are pursued, goods that must be subordinated to the good of the *polis*. Indeed, in some ancient accounts, notably the one given by Plato in the *Republic* (or by Sophocles in *Antigone*), the goods pursued within the *oikos* are not simply subordinate but actually

---

41. The public-private distinction of antiquity—a division between *oikos* and *polis*—is not identical to the modern rendering of this same division, which is between the individual and the state.

inimical to those pursued in the *polis*, such that among those who are the guardians of the *polis* the *oikos* must be abolished.[42] Even in accounts more appreciative of the *oikos*, such as Aristotle's, the *polis* cannot be seen simply as the *oikos* writ large but as different in kind.

Yet from its inception, Christianity has blurred the difference between the *oikos* and the *polis*. Jesus' proclamation of the Kingdom of God is inseparable from Jesus' proclamation of God as Father and Christians as sons and daughters adopted in him, the unique Son of God, into God's household. Thus, the social body of the Church could be described alternately in *polis*-terms or in *oikos*-terms. In the Letter to the Ephesians, Christians are addressed both as "fellow citizens [*sympolitai*] with the saints" and as "members of the household [*oikeioi*] of God" (2:19).[43] Christian theology speaks not only of the heavenly City in which Christ the Lamb reigns but also of the economy of salvation and of Christ as the master of the house (*oikodespotes*) that is the Church.[44] What the Letter to Diognetus calls "the wonderful and confessedly strange character of the constitution of their own citizenship"[45] found concrete expression in the first centuries in the domestic setting in which the citizens of the pilgrim City gathered to celebrate the Eucharist as the *familia Dei*, an image that continues to this day in the Eucharistic liturgy.[46] Perhaps the most striking instance of the "household" character of the Church, however, is seen in the unprecedented roles that women have had in Christianity. Excluded from citizenship in the public realm of the ancient *polis* and restricted to the private sphere of the *oikos*, women found in the Church a kind of "public *oikos*" in which they were valued fellow-members without having to imitate the supposedly masculine virtues of self-sufficiency that were seen as necessary for political life.

Thus, in speaking of the Church entering into a "hidden life," I do not at all mean to say that the Church is relegated to the sphere of the

---

42. Plato, *Republic* 423e, 457a-b, 462.

43. On the significance of this passage from Ephesians, as well as illuminating comments on the *oikos–polis* distinction in antiquity and Christianity, see Hütter, *Suffering Divine Things*, 160–64.

44. See Ignatius of Antioch, *Ephesians* 6.1.

45. *Epistle to Diognetus* 5.

46. For example, the ancient Roman Canon (Eucharistic Prayer I) prays: *Hanc igitur oblationem servitutis notrae, sed et cunctae familiae tuae, quaesumus, Domine, ut placatus accipias* (*Ordo Missae*, §87.). Josef Jungmann notes, "God's people is here conceived of as a domestic group with God as its *pater familias*" (Jungmann, *Mass of the Roman Rite*, 2:184n22).

private. As I noted earlier, because the good that the Church pursues is the most common, the most comprehensive, of all goods—the good that is God, the Creator of all good gifts—the Church is always and everywhere the most public of human associations. Even in the upper room on the day of Pentecost, the Church was public and catholic in its pursuit of the highest good. Indeed, even in the home in Nazareth, the common life of the Holy Family was the supreme exemplar of the shared pursuit of the good. Thus, to identify the life of the Church today with the hidden life in Nazareth is not a sectarian call for retreat from public life but is rather to understand that the public task, the political task, of the Church is the "domestic" task of nurturing disciples through the cultivation of the virtues distinctive of the household of God. Those distinctive virtues are at the heart of the public witness of the Church before the watching world.

The Politics of the Magnificat

When we in turn ask just what are those virtues that are distinctive of the household of God, we see another aspect of the "hiddenness" of the Church's life, and Mary's Magnificat appears as a scriptural witness of particular relevance. As I noted, when Jesus proclaimed God's kingdom, that proclamation was inseparable from his proclamation of God as Father. This is, of course, first and foremost the proclamation (*pace* Harnack) that God is *his* Father. But it also says something about the nature of God's kingdom; it is the proclamation that God exercises his kingship in the form of fatherly care for the poor, the defenseless, and the outcast. In this Jesus brings to perfection the prophetic proclamation of God's care for the *anawim*, the "little ones." In the household of God, according to the letter of James, the pure and undefiled sacrifice (*threskeia*) is "to care for the widows and orphans in their distress" (Jas 1:27). But more than simply possessing the virtue of generosity toward those in need, the members of God's kingdom are to identify *themselves* with little children (Matt 19:14; Mark 10:15; cf. John 13:33); they are to understand *themselves* as the "little flock" that receives the kingdom as a gift (Luke 12:32); they must see *themselves* as the foolish, the weak, the lowly (1 Cor 1:26). Imitating the Lord who came not to be served but to serve (Mark 10:45), the politics of the household of God is based not on an economy of violence and coercion, the economy seen in a figure like Herod, but one of self-giving through self-identification with those in need, a self-identification that is embodied in ascetical practices of self-dispossession. These practices cultivate a capacity to make the concerns of the *anawim* one's own, to subordinate self-love to the love of those little ones who are especially beloved of God as the concrete means by which we subordinate love of self to love of God. This, to use Delsol's terminology, is the true "inversion"—both normative and ontological—brought about within the Christian economy of salvation.

This economy is given iconic form in Mary and her Magnificat. In the Magnificat, Mary sings of what *Redemptoris Mater* calls God's "love of preference for the poor,"[47] a love that, more than any act of violence, disrupts the economy of power, casting down the mighty from their thrones and lifting up the lowly. Amid the rise and fall of earthly cities, and even of Christendom, this is the true revolution, the only true basis for a human community in which the supreme good is sought. Beyond all calculation of advantage or even effectiveness, Mary's identification with the poor bursts forth from her realization of the generosity that God has shown to her. And in accepting this generosity, Mary must identify herself as a "lowly servant." It is this generosity and identification that the Church is called to make its own, not as the basis of a program for ameliorating social ills—though undoubtedly in a society in which a large number of people understood the cause of the poor to be their own cause the poor would be less exposed to savage exploitation—but as a way of bearing witness to the God who has done great things for his people. Like Mary, the Church loves and identifies with the poor because this shows forth most truly what it means to be the bearer of Christ, the bearer of good news incarnate.

This preferential love is a key aspect of the paradoxical public hiddenness to which the Church is called and is the characteristic civic virtue of God's household. The life of the Church is not hidden in private realms of individual or sectarian faith. Rather, the life of the Church is hidden because it is a life that, like Mary's, is identified with the little ones who are overlooked by the Herods of the world. It is a kind of "hiding in plain sight" that takes advantage of coercive power's tendency to overlook that which seems small and weak. The Church, like Mary, makes the cause of these little ones her own cause: the poor, the unborn, the homeless, the stranger, the condemned, the dying. The life of the Church is hidden in the lives of those who do not count in the economy of violence and

---

47. John Paul II, *Redemptoris Mater*, no. 37.

coercion, except as replaceable units of exploitation. As Chantal Delsol puts it, Christians must take as their model not the sixteenth-century Spanish philosopher and theologian Juan Ginés de Sepúlveda, who justified the conversion-by-conquest of the Americas, but the martyred Trappist monks of Tibhirine, who died because they would not abandon their Muslim neighbors.[48] If the Church faithfully lives out God's preferential love and identification with the poor, then the hiddenness of the Church is no failure but rather judgment upon the world.

We might have been tempted to think that the end of Christendom, the end of the period in which the world's rulers brought their gifts to lay at the feet of Mother Church, was the end of the Church's public role. But, in fact, it is simply the next step along the path that Mary has already trod. The "hidden life" of the Church in the West—her (at times unwilling) renunciation of worldly power—involves a deepening of the Church's Marian identity, as the Church, like Mary, learns to identify with the little ones of God rather than the mighty. Unlike Mary, the Church might have to repent for having at times been dazzled by displays of worldly power, for the type has not always conformed to the antitype. In the transition from epiphany to exile to hidden life, the Church has undoubtedly had to leave behind not only some gifts that were of genuine value but also some that were unfitting, in order, like Mary, to have its hands free to carry Christ.

In terms of the project of Social Catholicism, discerning the Marian path of the Church requires that we must reckon with the possibility of genuine conflict between competing accounts of the common good—in particular, those accounts that privilege the "little ones" versus those accounts, whether of the political "left" or the political "right," that see self-assertion and domination as the primary means for establishing a just social order. But we must also reckon with the possibility of genuine cooperation, the possibility that unexpected visitors from afar might arrive bearing gifts that will enrich our conception of the good. And to reckon with both of these possibilities requires an exercise of prudence that can distinguish the Herods of our day from the Magi.

Finally, we must bear in mind that if the trajectory of the Church's pilgrimage does in fact follow the trajectory of the Virgin's life, then the most significant events of that life are yet to unfold. The first miracle at Cana, the teaching of multitudes, the casting out of demons—the entire

---

48. Delsol, *Fin*, 169.

public ministry of Jesus—which the Church, like Mary, will be privileged to witness, lie ahead of us. And so, too, does the great conflict figured in Mary's vicarious sharing in Christ's passion and in the woman clothed with the sun. And so, too, does our being raised to eternal life in heavenly glory.

Bibliography

Delsol, Chantal. *La fin de la Chrétienté*. Paris: Cerf, 2021.
Gérard, Dom. "An Exhortation to the Restoration of Christendom." *Josias*, October 31, 2014. https://thejosias.com/2014/10/31/exhortation-to-the-restoration-of-christendom/.
Gobry, Pascal-Emmanuel. "Zombie Catholics vs. French Secularism." *America*, April 7, 2017. https://www.americamagazine.org/faith/2017/04/07/zombie-catholics-vs-french-secularism.
Hall, Lauren, and Paul Seaton, eds. *Lucid Mind, Intrepid Spirit: Essays on the Thought of Chantal Delsol*. Lanham, MD: Lexington, 2012.
Henry, A.-M., ed. *The Historical and Mystical Christ*. Translated by Angeline Bouchard. Chicago: Fides, 1958.
Hütter, Reinhard. *Suffering Divine Things: Theology as Church Practice*. Grand Rapids: Eerdmans, 2000.
John Paul II. *Ecclesia in Europa*. June 28, 2003. https://www.vatican.va/content/john-paul-ii/en/apost_exhortations/documents/hf_jp-ii_exh_20030628_ecclesia-in-europa.html.
———. *Mary: God's Yes to Man*. San Francisco: Ignatius, 1987.
Jungmann, Josef. *The Mass of the Roman Rite*. Translated by Francis Brunner. Notre Dame: Christian Classics, 2012.
Lohfink, Gerhard. *Jesus and Community: The Social Dimension of Christian Faith*. Philadelphia: Fortress, 1984.
Marion, Jean-Luc. *A Brief Apology for a Catholic Moment*. Translated by Stephen E. Lewis. Chicago: University of Chicago Press, 2021.
Maritain, Jacques. *Man and the State*. Chicago: University of Chicago Press, 1951.
Ordo Missae. Vatican City State: Libreria Editrice Vaticana, 2002. https://media.musicasacra.com/books/latin_missal2002.pdf.
Scheeben, Matthias. *Mariology*. Translated by T. L. M. J. Geukers. St. Louis: Herder, 1946.
Waldstein, Edmund. "Integralism in Three Sentences." *Josias*, October 17, 2016. http://thejosias.com/2016/10/17/integralism-in-three-sentences/.
Wilken, Robert Louis. *The First Thousand Years: A Global History of Christianity*. New Haven: Yale University Press, 2012.
Yoder, John Howard. *The Priestly Kingdom: Social Ethics as Gospel*. Notre Dame: University of Notre Dame Press, 1984.

18

After Neoliberalism[1]

Joseph E. Stiglitz, Columbia University

Editor's Abstract: This short piece by Nobel Prize winning economist Joseph E. Stiglitz is republished here with permission as a preface to our symposium on new economic thinking. It is included here as articulating a trustworthy overview of the leading options after the widely perceived failure of the "neoliberal" economic paradigm that had enjoyed a broad consensus for roughly the four previous decades. It was originally published with the following lead: "For the past forty years, the United States and other advanced economies have been pursuing a free-market agenda of low taxes, deregulation, and cuts to social programs. There can no longer be any doubt that this approach has failed spectacularly; the only question is what will—and should—come next."

WHAT KIND OF ECONOMIC system is most conducive to human wellbeing? That question has come to define the current era, because, after forty years of neoliberalism in the United States and other advanced economies, we know what *doesn't* work.

---

1. Copyright © Project Syndicate, 2019. Republished with permission.

The neoliberal experiment—lower taxes on the rich, deregulation of labor and product markets, financialization, and globalization—has been a spectacular failure. Growth is lower than it was in the quarter-century after World War II, and most of it has accrued to the very top of the income scale. After decades of stagnant or even falling incomes for those below them, neoliberalism must be pronounced dead and buried.

Vying to succeed it are at least three major political alternatives: far-right nationalism, center-left reformism, and the progressive left (with the center-right representing the neoliberal failure). And yet, with the exception of the progressive left, these alternatives remain beholden to some form of the ideology that has (or should have) expired.

The center-left, for example, represents neoliberalism with a human face. Its goal is to bring the policies of former US President Bill Clinton and former British Prime Minister Tony Blair into the twenty-first century, making only slight revisions to the prevailing modes of financialization and globalization. Meanwhile, the nationalist right disowns globalization, blaming migrants and foreigners for all of today's problems. Yet as Donald Trump's presidency has shown, it is no less committed—at least in its American variant—to tax cuts for the rich, deregulation, and shrinking or eliminating social programs.

By contrast, the third camp advocates what I call progressive capitalism, which prescribes a radically different economic agenda, based on four priorities. The first is to restore the balance between markets, the state, and civil society. Slow economic growth, rising inequality, financial instability, and environmental degradation are problems born of the market, and thus cannot and will not be overcome by the market on its own. Governments have a duty to limit and shape markets through environmental, health, occupational-safety, and other types of regulation. It is also the government's job to do what the market cannot or will not do, like actively investing in basic research, technology, education, and the health of its constituents.

The second priority is to recognize that the "wealth of nations" is the result of scientific inquiry—learning about the world around us—and social organization that allows large groups of people to work together for the common good. Markets still have a crucial role to play in facilitating social cooperation, but they serve this purpose only if they are governed by the rule of law and subject to democratic checks. Otherwise, individuals can get rich by exploiting others, extracting wealth through rent-seeking rather than creating wealth through genuine ingenuity.

Many of today's wealthy took the exploitation route to get where they are. They have been well served by Trump's policies, which have encouraged rent-seeking while destroying the underlying sources of wealth creation. Progressive capitalism seeks to do precisely the opposite.

This brings us to the third priority: addressing the growing problem of concentrated market power. By exploiting information advantages, buying up potential competitors, and creating entry barriers, dominant firms are able to engage in large-scale rent-seeking to the detriment of everyone else. The rise in corporate market power, combined with the decline in workers' bargaining power, goes a long way toward explaining why inequality is so high and growth so tepid. Unless government takes a more active role than neoliberalism prescribes, these problems will likely become much worse, owing to advances in robotization and artificial intelligence.

The fourth key item on the progressive agenda is to sever the link between economic power and political influence. Economic power and political influence are mutually reinforcing and self-perpetuating, especially where, as in the US, wealthy individuals and corporations may spend without limit in elections. As the US moves ever closer to a fundamentally undemocratic system of "one dollar, one vote," the system of checks and balances so necessary for democracy likely cannot hold: nothing will be able to constrain the power of the wealthy. This is not just a moral and political problem: economies with less inequality actually perform better. Progressive-capitalist reforms thus have to begin by curtailing the influence of money in politics and reducing wealth inequality.

There is no magic bullet that can reverse the damage done by decades of neoliberalism. But a comprehensive agenda along the lines sketched above absolutely can. Much will depend on whether reformers are as resolute in combating problems like excessive market power and inequality as the private sector is in creating them.

A comprehensive agenda must focus on education, research, and the other true sources of wealth. It must protect the environment and fight climate change with the same vigilance as the Green New Dealers in the US and Extinction Rebellion in the United Kingdom. And it must provide public programs to ensure that no citizen is denied the basic requisites of a decent life. These include economic security, access to work and a living wage, health care and adequate housing, a secure retirement, and a quality education for one's children.

This agenda is eminently affordable; in fact, we cannot afford *not* to enact it. The alternatives offered by nationalists and neoliberals would guarantee more stagnation, inequality, environmental degradation, and political acrimony, potentially leading to outcomes we do not even want to imagine.

Progressive capitalism is not an oxymoron. Rather, it is the most viable and vibrant alternative to an ideology that has clearly failed. As such, it represents the best chance we have of escaping our current economic and political malaise.

Bibliography

Stiglitz, Joseph E. "After Neoliberalism." *Project Syndicate*, May 30, 2019. https://www.project-syndicate.org/commentary/after-neoliberalism-progressive-capitalism-by-joseph-e-stiglitz-2019-15.

19

Biophilic Markets[1]

Eric D. Beinhocker, Oxford University

Abstract: Markets must be made biophilic: that is, compatible with life flourishing on Earth. To do so, we must abandon prevailing notions of market efficiency and reconceive markets as social evolutionary systems embedded in nature. Such a reconception enables us to see that constraining markets within biophysical boundaries would not result in zero-sum trade-offs with the economy, but instead would drive market evolution to new forms of prosperity.

NATASHA ISKANDER AND NICHOLA LOWE's concept of "biophilic institutions" forces analytical and moral clarity: Are our institutional arrangements compatible with life flourishing on Earth?[2] Do we want them to be? At present, the scientific and political evidence suggests the answer is "no." Human activity has caused the species extinction rate to jump to tens to hundreds of times the average of the past ten million years, causing many scientists to conclude that a mass extinction event is

---

1. This contribution was originally published in the Winter 2023 issue of *Dædalus* and is republished here with permission.
2. Iskander and Lowe, "Biophilic Institutions."

underway with little being done to stop it.[3] As Iskander and Low observe, our current theories frame debates as the economy versus life and we have chosen the economy. Iskander and Lowe's concept of biophilic institutions highlights the absurdity of both the framing and our choice. Earth's previous five mass extinction events saw losses of over 75 percent of species. It is unlikely that human civilization, let alone anything like a modern economy, would survive an anthropogenically induced sixth event. It is biophilic or bust.

In this essay, I extend Iskander and Lowe's concept and explore what it might mean for one specific set of economic institutions–markets–to become biophilic.

The standard economic answer to biophilia is to "price the unpriced externality," for example, by using taxes or tradeable permits to put a price on human activities that harm nature.[4] This has been done with some success for pricing power plant sulfur dioxide pollution and ozone-damaging chlorofluorocarbon emissions, but with much less success for carbon emissions. Despite decades of effort, only about 0.8 percent of global emissions are subject to a carbon price consistent with the Paris Agreement.[5] There are political reasons why this approach has failed—namely, powerful vested interests who fight back—but to see how markets could become truly biophilic, we need a different understanding of how markets operate and their relationship with nature.

There are three conceptual shifts that must be made. First, the dominant economic paradigm sees nature as separate from human society: an externality that provides an infinite source of resources and an infinite sink for waste. The standard economic "production function" has no concept of energy, entropy, planetary boundaries, or any other finite limits to growth. If one looks inside the theories, models, and ideologies that shape the decisions of finance ministries, central banks, regulators, the courts, investors, and businesses, one finds that nature rarely, if ever, appears. This simply does not reflect the reality that economic value creation is both wholly dependent on, and significantly impacts, nature—the two are mutually interdependent. When nature does appear,

---

3. Intergovernmental Science-Policy Platform, "Global Assessment Report"; Ceballos et al., "Accelerated Modern Human-Induced Species Losses"; Climate Action Tracker, "Glasgow's 2030 Credibility Gap."

4. Pigou, *Economics of Welfare*.

5. Calculation by the author using data from World Bank, "Open Knowledge Repository."

it is usually in the form of a trade-off with the economy. As Iskander and Lowe put it, "[our] most influential institutions operate as if nature and the economy existed in a zero-sum game."[6] This zero-sum mentality in turn frames climate as a cost-benefit problem in which the burden of proof is on the person showing that the "benefits" of preserving life on Earth are greater than the "costs" to the economy (again, think of the absurdity of this). This framing has provided an enormous political advantage to fossil fuel and other interests, who can portray themselves as champions of the economy versus environmentalists who want to kill jobs to save polar bears.

Second, we must see markets not as mechanical equilibrium systems, but as dynamic, social evolutionary systems.[7] Economics has traditionally viewed markets as gravitating toward a socially optimal allocation of resources. This equilibrium framework has impeded action on climate in multiple ways.[8] In particular, it has an inherent status quo bias, as it assumes that the current arrangements are optimal, and exogenous changes introduced by policy (for example, climate regulation) are typically assumed to reduce market efficiency and therefore social welfare (or again, in political speech, will "kill jobs and growth"). Furthermore, the equilibrium framing assumes that all change is marginal and expressed primarily through shifts in relative prices within the existing system. This perspective then encourages policymakers to focus on incremental rather than structural change, and to see carbon pricing as "the answer" instead of the broad array of policies, investments, and institutional changes required for system transformation.

Markets are evolving social constructs, arrangements of institutions that in turn facilitate the evolution of products, services, jobs, technologies, and business models.[9] Such an evolutionary economy is not static but dynamic, with history showing both periods of marginal change and periods of transformational, structural change (for example, the Industrial Revolution). Processes of change are endogenous, emerging from interactions of economic, technological, political, and environmental forces. As a dynamic, evolutionary system, there is no "optimal" end state, but one can say that, over history, differing economic arrangements have

---

6. Iskander and Lowe, "Biophilic Institutions," 82.
7. Beinhocker et al., "Inclusive Economics Is Complexity Economics."
8. Beinhocker and Farmer, "Make the Clean Stuff Cheap."
9. Beinhocker, *Origin of Wealth*.

varied greatly in delivering human well-being: there is certainly "better" and "worse."

What then drives economic evolution toward "better" or "worse"? All evolutionary systems are driven by a fitness function that selects what survives and grows in the system and what fails and disappears. In biological systems, genes that enhance an organism's fitness for its environment are more likely to survive and replicate, thus driving species evolution. In the case of the economy, the fitness function is socially constructed. One can think of the economy as a set of billions of experiments in products, services, jobs, technologies, and business models. Market competition sifts through these experiments, determining which survive, grow, and dominate, and which disappear. The market fitness function is determined by the interplay of consumer tastes, firm and investor behaviors, legal and regulatory rules, and normative beliefs about what are good outcomes. As those factors change over time, so too does the market fitness function: what is a "successful" business today is different from what it was in the past. Driven by economic theory, our current system is constructed on the belief that human welfare is best served when individuals maximize their consumption, firms maximize their profits, investors maximize their returns, and policy-makers maximize GDP growth.[10] These beliefs have played a powerful role in the market fitness function, evolving a system that is highly bio-destructive and whose impacts on human welfare are mixed at best.

This leads to our third conceptual shift: as a social construct, the market fitness function is a social choice. Orthodox economics treats the fitness function as if it were an exogenously determined law of nature, as if there is no alternative. Yet the variety of human arrangements in organizing economic systems over history and across cultures shows that it is indeed a social construction.[11] As such, we could choose a different market fitness function than the one we have today: we could choose one that is biophilic. Markets exist to serve society, and society therefore has a right to shape the market fitness function to its needs, including the need to avoid mass extinction. A society could choose to require that its markets operate within biophysical boundaries, and thus, firms could only be "successful" if they earned profits in ways that are biophilic. Such societal choices are most legitimately expressed through democratic institutions,

---

10. Henderson, *Reimagining Capitalism in a World on Fire*.
11. Graeber and Wengrow, *Dawn of Everything*.

which in turn put high demands on those institutions to shape the market fitness function in the right ways. There are legitimate questions as to whether our current institutions are up to the challenge, but in this case, there really is no alternative.[12]

I am not advocating central planning. I am not proposing, for example, that government bureaucrats should decide what quantity, price, and style of automobiles to produce. That work is the job of markets. Instead, I am arguing that society has a right to require that automobile manufacturers (and all other manufacturers) operate within biophilic boundaries. Forcing markets to operate within socially determined boundaries is nothing new. For example, in the early twentieth century, child labor was still common and when reformers began advocating to ban the practice, there was intense opposition from employers.[13] Paralleling today's debates over climate, industry interests argued that children were an economic resource to be exploited, and there was a zero-sum trade-off between child welfare and the economy: that is, ending child labor would "kill jobs and growth." But when the practice was finally banned in the United States in 1938, the mines didn't close, the farms didn't go bankrupt, and the factories didn't grind to a halt. Instead, markets did what evolutionary systems do; they adapted to the change in the economic fitness function, and firms figured out how to operate profitably without child labor (and those that didn't arguably deserved to go out of business). And not only was child welfare greatly enhanced, but longer-run economic performance was boosted as better educated children became more productive adults. Instead of zero-sum, the adaptive dynamics of markets turned the child labor ban into a positive-sum win.

Similar evolutionary dynamics would be at work if the market fitness function were changed to be biophilic. What would this look like in practice? At a minimum it would involve legally binding national economies to carbon budgets that led to net-zero emissions over a time period consistent with limiting warming to 1.5 degrees Celsius. The ultimate destination would be a global ban on net-positive emissions by 2050 (or "carbon abolition," as I call it).[14] Such legally binding emission limits would need to be backed by a full suite of regulatory tools and public investments, as well as carbon border adjustments to address trade

   12. Bednar, "Polarization, Diversity, and Democratic Robustness"; Drutman, "How Democracies Revive."
   13. Schuman, "History of Child Labor."
   14. Beinhocker, "I Am a Carbon Abolitionist."

with countries whose markets are not biophilic. Making markets truly biophilic would further require constraints on a broader set of environmental impacts (for example, waste, pollution, and habitat loss) to drive markets toward a "circular economy" that delivers human well-being with minimal waste and net resource use.[15]

The good news is that such a change in the economic fitness function would not result in inefficiencies and welfare loss—as predicted by traditional analyses—but would result in a massive wave of investment, innovation, and enormous welfare gains (perhaps even infinite welfare gains given the existential threat to future generations). As noted, when the fitness function changes, evolutionary systems adapt. The true genius of markets is not their static allocative efficiency but their dynamic adaptability. There is a long history of environmental policy sparking adaptation, innovation, and investment. Even the wholly inadequate policies of the past decades have triggered significant advances: solar power costs have dropped 82 percent, wind costs have fallen 39 percent, electric vehicle battery range has quadrupled, and the overall energy efficiency of the US economy has increased by 23 percent.[16] Instead of experiencing "de-growth," as some would advocate, markets with hard biophilic limits (as well as policies for a just transition) would find new ways to meet human needs within those constraints.[17] Instead of bio-destructive growth, we could have biophilic progress.

The economy and nature are not in zero-sum competition. They are mutually interdependent, co-evolving systems. Our current economic and political framework does not recognize this fact. Markets are among humankind's most powerful inventions. How we harness their innovative power, and to what ends, is a social choice. Choosing biophilia does not mean choosing to become poorer: it means choosing to become prosperous in a different way.

---

15. Vogel et al., "Satisfying Human Needs at Low Energy Use"; Ellen MacArthur Foundation, "Circular Economy Introduction."

16. National Renewable Energy Laboratory, "Decade of Cost Declines"; Statista, "Median Range of Electric Vehicles."

17. Hanauer and Beinhocker, "Capitalism Redefined"; O'Neill et al., "Good Life within Planetary Boundaries."

Bibliography

Bednar, Jenna. "Polarization, Diversity, and Democratic Robustness." *Proceedings of the National Academy of Sciences* 118 (2021). e2113843118 https://doi.org/10.1073/pnas.2113843118.

Beinhocker, Eric D. "Biophilic Markets" *Dædalus* 152 (2023) 94–99. https://doi.org/10.1162/daed_a_01965.

———. "I Am a Carbon Abolitionist" *Democracy*, June 24, 2019. https://democracyjournal.org/arguments/i-am-a-carbon-abolitionist.

———. *The Origin of Wealth: The Radical Remaking of Economics and What It Means for Business and Society.* Boston: Harvard Business School Press, 2006.

Beinhocker, Eric D., et al. "Inclusive Economics Is Complexity Economics." *Boston Review*, March 26, 2019. https://bostonreview.net/forum_ response/complexity-economists-economics-needs-embrace-transdisciplinary.

Beinhocker, Eric D., and J. Doyne Farmer. "A New Strategy for Climate: Make the Clean Stuff Cheap." *Democracy*, November 10, 2021. https://democracyjournal.org/arguments/a-new-strategy-for-climate-make-the-clean-stuff-cheap.

BloombergNEF. "2H 2017 Wind Turbine Price Index." May 9, 2018. https://about.bnef.com/blog/2h-2017-wind-turbine-price-index.

Ceballos, Gerardo, et al. "Accelerated Modern Human-Induced Species Losses: Entering the Sixth Mass Extinction." *Science Advances* 1 (2015). e1400253 http://doi.org/10.1126/sciadv.1400253.

Climate Action Tracker. "Glasgow's 2030 Credibility Gap: Net Zero's Lip Service to Climate Action." *New Climate Institute*, November 9, 2021. https://climateactiontracker.org/publications/glasgows-2030-credibility-gap-net-zeros-lip-service-to-climate-action.

Drutman, Lee. "How Democracies Revive." https://www.niskanencenter.org/how-democracies-revive.

Ellen MacArthur Foundation. "Circular Economy Introduction." https://ellenmacarthurfoundation.org/topics/circular-economy-introduction/ overview.

Graeber, David, and David Wengrow. *The Dawn of Everything: A New History of Humanity.* New York: Farrar, Straus, and Giroux, 2021.

Hanauer, Nick, and Eric Beinhocker. "Capitalism Redefined." *Democracy*, 2014. https://democracyjournal.org/magazine/31/capitalism-redefined.

Henderson, Rebecca. *Reimagining Capitalism in a World on Fire: How Business Can Save the World.* New York: Perseus, 2020.

Intergovernmental Science-Policy Platform on Biodiversity and Ecosystem Services. "Global Assessment Report on Biodiversity and Ecosystem Services." https://ipbes.net/global-assessment.

Iskander, Natasha, and Nichola Lowe. "Biophilic Institutions: Building New Solidarities between the Economy and Nature." *Dædalus* 152 (2023) 81–93.

National Renewable Energy Laboratory. "Documenting a Decade of Cost Declines for PV Systems." https://www.nrel.gov/news/program/2021/documenting-a-decade-of-cost-declines-for-pv-systems.html.

O'Neill, Daniel W., et al. "A Good Life for All within Planetary Boundaries." *Nature Sustainability* 1 (2018). https://doi.org/10.1038/ s41893-18-0021-24.

Pigou, Arthur C. *The Economics of Welfare.* 4th ed. London: Palgrave Macmillan, 2013.

Schuman, Michael. "History of Child Labor in the United States—Part 2: The Reform Movement." *Monthly Labor Review*, January, 2017. https://www.bls.gov/opub/mlr/2017/ article/history-of-child-labor-in-the-united-states-part-2-the-reform-movement.htm.

Statista. "Median Range of Electric Vehicles Offered on the U.S. Market between 2011 and 2021 (in Miles)." https://www.statista.com/statistics/1207912/us-evs-on-market-range.

Vogel, Jefim, et al. "Socio-Economic Conditions for Satisfying Human Needs at Low Energy Use: An International Analysis of Social Provisioning." *Global Environmental Change* 69 (2021) 102287. https://doi.org/10.1016/j.gloenvcha.2021.102287.

World Bank. "Open Knowledge Repository: State and Trends of Carbon Pricing 2021." https://openknowledge.worldbank.org/handle/10986/35620.

20

Toward a New Economics[1]

Anthony M. Annett, Fordham University and Sustainable Development Solutions Network

Abstract: This chapter makes the case for a new social democratic era, underpinned by the principles of Catholic social teaching. Following a highly successful original social democratic movement in the postwar period, there was a sharp turn in the neoliberal direction over the past four decades. This experiment largely failed, leaving behind vast amounts of inequality, exclusion, and environmental devastation. The chapter makes the case that neoliberalism can be traced to the principles of neoclassical economics, which are inferior to those of Catholic social teaching in the sense of being less in tune with human nature and less likely to generate healthy economies. It then discusses the roles of government, business, and labor, arguing that all economic activity—whether public or private—must be oriented toward the common good. Following this, it goes on to describe three core economic challenges that hinder human flourishing and undermine the common good—the crisis of employment, especially in the context of technological change; the crisis of inequality, as sharp divisions arise between rich and poor; and the crisis of environmental devastation, with particular attention paid to climate change. The final section argues

---

1. This chapter is based on Annett, *Cathonomics*.

for a new social democratic moment capable of addressing these challenges using the principles of Catholic social teaching.

Introduction: From Social Democratic to Neoliberal Moment

THE SOCIAL DEMOCRATIC ERA was remarkable. Taking shape in the immediate aftermath of the Second World War, it delivered three decades of record economic growth in tandem with full employment and low inequality. Regions like Europe, North America, and Japan saw rising prosperity—prosperity that was broadly shared. The "social democratic moment" did not eschew the role of markets, but rather recognized that well-being depended on mixed economies that harnessed the role of the state to complement the market. This era, then, was marked by robust welfare states, wide-ranging financial regulation, control of monopolies, strong unions and collective bargaining, and high marginal tax rates. It was a model that worked.

An important point is that the social democratic institutions encapsulated a spirit of solidarity and shared purpose. This in turn built trust and social cohesion, setting off a virtuous cycle. Debates were cast not only in terms of efficiency, but justice, fairness, and solidarity.

There are three explanations for this extended social democratic moment. First, the Great Depression and subsequent war utterly upended the faith in a self-correcting market. Free market economics had become intellectually bankrupt, and all accepted the need for the state to extend a guiding hand. Keynesian economics was ascendant. Second, the war itself generated an ethos of solidarity and self-sacrifice, which extended well into the postwar period and only really began to fade into the horizon when the generations shifted. Third, all politicians eyed communism nervously in the rearview mirror. In the aftermath of the war, communist parties made major gains among some large western European countries. Faced with an ideology promising an unrelenting progression toward a socialist future, those charged with managing capitalist economies needed to take the sting out of the communist tail.

I would argue that the social democratic moment was influenced by Catholic Social Teaching. The emergence of modern economic rights rooted in the idea of human dignity and codified in the Universal Declaration of Human Rights owed much to this body of thought. The same is true of Christian democracy, which supported the idea of a "social market economy" to protect families from the vagaries of capitalism. In a recent book called *Catholic Modern*, historian James Chappel describes the intellectual evolution of Catholic thought in this period. He describes a bifurcation of Catholic thought into what he calls "paternal" Catholicism—eying communism nervously and elevating the family as the basic unit of society—and "fraternal" Catholicism—which tended to be more left wing and more suspicious of fascism. The former gravitated toward Christian democracy and included the founding fathers of postwar Europe: Konrad Adenauer of Germany, Robert Schuman of France, and Alcide De Gasperi of Italy. The latter strand embraced progressive forms of social democracy, especially through institutional mechanisms of worker solidarity and a strong welfare state. But especially in the early years, and especially in the realm of economics, the differences between Christian and social democrats were narrow. All supported the state's role in regulating the economy in line with the common good, providing universal social services funded by taxes and social contributions, and empowering unions as a bulwark against excessive corporate power—the kind of power that greased the wheels of fascism and Naziism. In his magisterial history of postwar Europe, the historian Tony Judt makes this very point, noting that "Christian Democrats of the first post-war years saw free-market liberals rather than the collectivist Left as their main opponents and were keen to demonstrate that the modern state could be adapted to non-socialist forms of benevolent intervention."[2]

In the United States too, the New Deal era brought about by President Franklin Roosevelt was also influenced by the principles of Catholic social teaching. The New Deal codified the notion of economic rights in the United States. Its policies limited the excesses of the market, aimed at just and harmonious industrial relations, created dignified public employment for those in need, and protected people from various kinds of market risks. Its goals extended well into the postwar period and were widely accepted on both sides of the partisan divide.

But by the early 1980s, the zeitgeist was changing. The Great Depression was a distant memory, and the sense of shared solidarity cemented by war had faded away. And after the fall of communism in 1989, the free-market economy faced no ideological competition. And so was born the neoliberal era, where free markets once again proved ascendent and

2. Judt, *Postwar*, 81.

the postwar institutions were gradually weakened. Judt actually traces this back to the 1960s, an era in which the communitarian impulse of social democracy started to seem a little worn, to be replaced with an ethos of individualism.[3]

Following the oil shocks of the 1970s, which generated stagflation—a ruinous combination of high inflation and high unemployment—faith in capable technocrats to successfully manage the economy and generate full employment was fatally undermined. People were looking for new answers, and those new answers turned out to be old answers—the power of an uninhibited free market to generate, via the invisible hand, growth and prosperity. Instead of a solution, government was now seen as a problem.

The neoliberal creed was simple: faith in free markets to achieve general prosperity. So governments implemented policies such as deregulation of industry, relaxed constraints on the financial sector, wide-ranging privatization, lower taxes on capital and high-income earners, and curbed power of unions. All of these measures were supposed to promote efficiency, innovation, and competitiveness.

The problem is, this "neoliberal moment" failed, even on its own terms. To see this, we need to look at productivity, which is the leading driver of long-term economic growth. Here, economist Robert Gordon shows that for the US economy, the period before 1970 was vastly more productive.[4] Estimates of what economists call "total factor productivity"—a way to measure innovation and technological improvement—are three times higher in the period 1920–70 as what came afterwards. Neoliberal policies simply did not unleash the wave of supply-side growth as promised.

The neoliberal era was also one of rising inequality. During the social democratic era, gains were broadly shared among the various classes of society. During the neoliberal era, on the other hand, the rich began to run away with most of the gains. Growth trickled up, not down. According to the *World Inequality Report*, the world's top 1 percent bagged twice the gains from growth as the bottom 50 percent since 1980—a sharp departure from the social democratic moment. And the biggest winners turned out to be the global super-rich.

---

3. Judt, *Ill Fares the Land*.
4. Gordon, *Rise and Fall of American Growth*.

All in all, the neoliberal moment gave rise to enormous dysfunctions: a widening chasm between rich and poor; rising corporate control, concentration, and corruption; a decline of trust and social cohesion in the context of ever-more urgent social problems, including a mental health crisis; and an urgent environmental crisis. The destruction of virtues such as solidarity meant that neoliberalism simply lacked the tools to fix the problems it either created or inherited.

Neoclassical Economics vs. Catholic Social Teaching

The ideology of neoliberalism comes directly from the assumptions of neoclassical economics. As documented by Binyamin Appelbaum, neoclassical economics has extended its power and reach over the policy world, even extending into areas traditionally regarded as beyond the domain of economics over the past century or so.[5] I want to argue that these principles are fundamentally flawed, aligned neither with human nature nor with healthy economic and social functioning. Instead, I will argue that the principles of Catholic social teaching are more realistic and healthier.

I want to isolate the following ten principles of Catholic social teaching as the bedrock of a moral economy. All are predicated on human dignity, the notion that every human being—made in the image and likeness of God—has intrinsic worth. The ten principles are as follows:

- **The common good.** The common good is the good that arises from human relationships in and through which people achieve human flourishing in an Aristotelian sense.[6] In the political and economic sphere, it means that no one can be excluded, and all must be guaranteed the material bases of human flourishing.

- **Integral human development.** This is defined as the fullest development of the whole person and all peoples. It calls for the maximum unfolding of each person's potential, a vocation whereby people become active agents of their own development. Again, no one can be excluded from this vocation.

- **Integral ecology.** This is the idea that human and natural relationships are all interconnected, deeply intertwined, and part of a larger

---

5. Appelbaum, *Economists' Hour*.
6. See Hollenbach, *Common Good*.

whole, so that if we hurt nature, we end up hurting ourselves. This is an injunction to care for our common home.

- **Solidarity.** This is, in the words of Pope John Paul II, "a firm and persevering determination to commit oneself to the common good; that is to say to the good of all and of each individual, because we are all really responsible for all."[7] It is a moral response to human interdependence.

- **Subsidiarity.** This is the principle by which decisions are taken at the lowest level possible and the highest level necessary.[8] It insists that higher-level communities (including the state) should assist lower-level communities but not usurp their rightful autonomy. Sometimes the proper locus is local, sometimes national, sometimes global.

- **Reciprocity and gratuitousness.** This is a human-level principle embedding fraternity in economic relationships. It suggests that we give not out of compulsion or to get something in return but out of a logic of gift. Economic encounter is less about seeking one's own advantage than caring for the person on the other side of the exchange.

- **Universal destination of goods.** This is a new name for one of the oldest principles in the Judeo-Christian tradition—that the goods of the earth are destined for all without exception and without exclusion. It suggests that property rights, while valid, can never be regarded as absolute or unconditional.

- **Preferential option for the poor.** Drawing from the deepest roots of the Christian tradition, to a God who loves the poor, this principle says that all human action and all economic policy should be judged first by how it affects the poor, the least among us, the oppressed, and the discarded.

- **Catholic notions of rights and duties.** A right a moral claim that others are obliged to accept. In Catholic thought, rights are economic as well as political, always tied to the common good, and always linked to duties. People have a right to the bases of human flourishing.

---

7. John Paul II, *Sollicitudo Rei Socialis*, no. 38.
8. See Clark, "Subsidiarity Is a Two-Sided Coin."

- **Catholic notions of justice.** Justice is one of the cardinal virtues, concerned with giving people what is owed to them. Catholic social teaching recognizes different forms of justice. Commutative justice is the justice between two individuals. Distributive justice pertains to what the community owes the individual. And contributive justice in turn is what the individual owes the community.
- I now want to stack up these principles against those of neoclassical economics. See Table 1 for an elaboration of the different principles.

Table 1. Assumptions of Neoclassical Economics vs. Catholic Social Teaching		
	Neoclassical Economics	**Catholic Social Teaching**
Motivation of the person	Self-interest	Solidarity, reciprocity, gratuitousness
Good of the person	Satisfaction of subjective material preference satisfaction	Integral human development
Good of society	Aggregation of subjective material preferences	The common good
Market functioning	Competition	Competition, solidarity, reciprocity/gratuitousness
Standard of judgment	Pareto efficiency, economic growth	Universal destination of goods, preferential option for the poor
Understanding of rights	Property rights	Economic rights
Norms of justice	Commutative	Commutative, distributive, contributive
Role of government	Neutral referee, correct market failures	Solidarity, subsidiarity
Treatment of nature	Extractive (in service of GDP)	Integral ecology

First things first: what motivates the person? In neoclassical economics, it is self-interest. This goes back to Adam Smith's claim that without self-interest, the butcher, the baker, and the brewer would not supply the goods you want. In Catholic social teaching on the other hand, the motivating virtues, as we have seen, are solidarity, reciprocity, and gratuitousness. It is about caring for the person on the other side of the transaction.

In terms of the good of the human person, while Catholic social teaching points to integral human development, neoclassical economics is instead predicated on the maximization of subjective material preferences. Put simply, you try to consume the most you can, in line with your personal preferences, given the money you have. This has four separate implications. First, it bakes in Smithian self-interest as you are primarily interested in your own preference satisfaction. Second, preferences are subjective and hedonic. There is no role for perfection or ethical formation. You like what you like. Questions regarding the value or worth somebody's preferences are prohibited under the assumption that people's desires are sacrosanct. Third, what tends to matter is goods and services that can be purchased on the market. There is no role for the non-material aspects of wellbeing, including relational good, spiritual goods, or goods of nature. There is no role for the sense of meaning and purpose that tends to be constitutive of human flourishing, Fourth, since the aim is maximization, wants are unbounded. This leads in turn to the goal of endless economic growth. The Christian tradition instead insists that desires should indeed be bounded, needs should be limited, and lower goods should be subordinated to higher goods.

Just as individual good differs, so does the common good. As noted, neoclassical economics has no concept of the kind of fused interpersonal wellbeing that constitutes the common good. All it can do is add up a monetary value, which is often equated with Gross Domestic Product (GDP). This is compatible with vast amounts of exclusion, which is not true of the common good.

For Catholic social teaching, the standard of judgment is the universal destination of goods and the preferential option for the poor. For economists, on the other hand, the answer is Pareto efficiency. Pareto efficiency is the point that exhausts all voluntary trades that can satisfy preferences. In other words, it is no longer possible to make somebody better off without making somebody else worse off. Importantly, Pareto efficiency rules out distributional issues, which makes it incompatible with the universal destination of goods and preferential option for the poor.

Neoclassical economics emphasizes the importance of market competition in bringing about Pareto efficiency—it can show that, under highly rarefied assumptions, this is what happens. Catholic social teaching does not reject market competition outright; it just recognizes that cooperation is just as (if not more) important, especially as exercised through the virtues of solidarity and reciprocity. There is no support in the tradition for central planning or for completely throwing out all price signals from markets.

Speaking of government, neoclassical economics conceives of a limited role, relegated to the sidelines and making sure that property rights are respected. This is too simplistic, of course, as neoclassical economics does allow for government intervention in areas where markets clearly fail, such as with public goods. But its role is still limited. Catholic social teaching, on the other hand, sees a deeper role for government intervention through the twin principles of solidarity and subsidiarity (more on this below).

Neoclassical economics also only envisions one norm of justice—commutative justice. This is because, to achieve efficiency, property rights must be well defined, and all contracts well specified, complete, and respected. There is simply no role for distributive or contributive justice. Economists would argue that they simply do not belong to the domain of economics, but are more political in nature. The exact same argument comes with the recognition of economic rights. In neoclassical economists, the only "right" is to a fair market outcome, as otherwise somebody is not being allowed to satisfy their preferences or maximize their profits in the best way possible. This is why, even though neoclassical economics does not come out of the libertarian tradition, it is often aligned with it.

One final point: neoclassical economics really has nothing to say about the environment. It employs a default mode of extractivism in the service of unlimited economic growth. There is certainly no concept like integral ecology. Economists will argue that if a resource is scarce, the market will simply take care of the problem by bidding up the price.

The Roles of Government, Capital, and Labor

In Catholic social teaching, the role of the government is to support the common good, including in the economic domain. In this, it has no truck with either hands-off libertarianism or smothering collectivism. Libertarianism, in some sense going back to the political philosophy of John Locke, is predicated on self-ownership; you own yourself and your labor, therefore you are entitled to the fruits of your labor. Libertarianism elevates economic freedom and denies the existence of a common good—because "common" entails coercion and "good" robs freedom of its essence. On the other side of the spectrum, communism denies people their dignity, agency and initiative, reducing them to mere cogs in a socioeconomic machine. The criticism here is directed at the collective ownership of the means of production and the suppression of the right to private property, not the kind of mixed economies that took shape during the social democratic era.

In Catholic social teaching, the common good in the economic sphere is the proper domain of government. Government is not merely the outcome of a social contract between independent agents, but a natural entity ordered to the common good. Yet the role of the state is both activist and circumscribed: activist, because the common good is higher than the good achieved by the individual; circumscribed, because human dignity requires that the autonomy and agency of subsidiary associations be respected.

The government can best serve the common good by aligning itself with the twin principles of solidarity and subsidiarity. Solidarity calls on the government to ensure the provision of the basic goods necessary for integral human development, including income security, decent jobs, nutrition, healthcare, education, housing, and a sustainable environment. It is important to note that the market tends to under-supply many of these goods, which calls for a more activist role of the state. And owing to the principles of the universal destination of goods and the preferential option for the poor, the poorest must take special precedence in policymaking. This calls for a clear role for redistribution through the tax, spending, and transfer system.

In terms of the role of government, subsidiarity is also important. Subsidiarity, in this sense, calls for the state to regulate the market, so that it can best direct its initiative toward serving the common good. As Karl Polanyi argued, all market institutions are underpinned by a wide array of rules, policies, cultural norms, and shared values. The question to ask is: Do the basic rules of the game support or impede integral development and the common good? Subsidiarity calls for a proper balancing of the scales, with government support for what economist John Kenneth Galbraith called institutions of countervailing power—including unions, small businesses, consumer organizations, cooperatives, and regional and local banks. When setting the rules of the game, therefore, government should strive to respect, assist, and promote the interests of the wider inhabitants of the civil economy.

Just like government, business is also called upon to align its activities with the common good. This means its goal cannot simply be profit maximization, as assumed by neoclassical economics and endorsed by neoliberalism. Economist Colin Mayer notes that the corporation has existed, in one form or another, for thousands of years, and has always contained an element of public purpose.[9] Mayer notes that the origin of the word "company" is the Latin *cum panis*, or "breaking bread together," an etymology that relates to how Catholic social teaching views the corporation—as a "community of persons" oriented toward the common good.

In this vein, the Vatican produced a short document called *Vocation of the Business Leader* to tease out the implications of how business can practically serve the common good.[10] The document argues that business serves the common good in three separate dimensions: *good goods*, *good work*, and *good wealth*—a trifecta that provides an excellent lens through which to analyze the role of business.

In terms of *good goods*, business is called upon to meet human needs through the creation and development "goods that are truly good and services that truly serve." Thus, to be legitimate, business must produce goods with social value that contribute to human flourishing. It cannot be just about the maximization of subjective preferences, as assumed by neoclassical economics.

The second major way in which business contributes to the common good and human flourishing is through *good work*. One of the themes of Catholic social teaching is the priority of labor over capital. Work is also seen as a vocation for humanity, as human beings reach their full potential through dignified, meaningful work. Accordingly, society must prioritize access to decent work over profits.

The third dimension of how business supports the common good and human flourishing is through *good wealth*, creating sustainable wealth and distributing it justly. A key insight of Catholic social teaching is that companies should be able to make a profit and extend a social benefit at the same time. This certainly means that business must be responsible to a whole variety of stakeholders, including wider society and the environment. On this latter point, business is called upon to invest in sustainable development solutions.

---

9. Mayer, *Prosperity*.

10. Dicastery for Promoting Integral Human Development. *Vocation of the Business Leader*.

Just as with business, Catholic social teaching also sees labor as a vocation oriented toward human fulfillment and the common good. Indeed, it is legitimate to speak of a "joint vocation" of labor and capital, oriented toward the same end. This stands in stark contrast to neoclassical economics. The neoclassical paradigm sees labor as a factor of production, a cost to be minimized. It argues that, in labor market equilibrium, the worker is paid in terms of what they contribute to productivity. Again, neoclassical economics finds a natural ally in libertarianism as not only is this wage efficient, but it is also just, since the wage represents the outcome of free choices between worker and employer.

Given the importance of work to human flourishing, the promotion of secure and dignified employment emerges as a central goal of public policy. In terms of the dignity of work, the concept of the just wage is central—this goes all the way back to *Rerum Novarum*, the founding document of modern Catholic social teaching. Indeed, a just wage is regarded as one of the main ways to achieve the universal destination of goods in practice. Along with just wages, Catholic social teaching recognizes an array of rights due to the worker in line with justice and dignity. These include pensions; unemployment benefits; affordable or even free healthcare; family support; adequate rest, vacation time; and work environments that do not impede health, safety, and moral integrity. Catholic social teaching also respects the right to form unions and bargain collectively, once again in line with both solidarity and subsidiarity.

One further aspect of the vocation of labor from Catholic social teaching worth making is the idea that workers should be able to share in both the profits and the management of the firm. Such an arrangement would break down any conflictual relationship between capital and labor, uniting them in common purpose and joint vocation. Yet the practical application of these idea has been limited. A partial exception is the role played by codetermination in Germany and other continental European countries. The German model of industrial relations is based on worker representation on boards, work councils at the level of the enterprise that give employees a stake in decision making, and wage negotiation at the regional or sectoral level underpinned by strong unions. Neoliberalism, on the other hand, places a premium on what it calls flexible labor markets, based on the idea that these markets will adjust if free from institutional impediments. Yet as Keynes showed during the Great Depression, it is possible to have prolonged unemployment even with flexible labor markets.

Three Priorities: Inequality, Employment, Environment

Back in 1936, Keynes concluded his magnum opus, *The General Theory of Employment, Interest, and Money*, with the claim that "the outstanding faults of the economic society in which we live are its failure to provide for full employment and its arbitrary and inequitable distribution of wealth and incomes."[11] The same is true today, except for a third fault line that did not really exist in the time of Keynes—an existential environmental crisis.

Inequality

This rise in inequality is certainly a defining economic narrative of our era. Inequality within countries has widened sharply, so much so that in countries like the United States and the United Kingdom, the distribution of income is back to where it was during the Gilded Age. Globally, the world's top 1 percent bagged twice the gains from growth as the bottom 50 percent since 1980—a sharp departure from the social democratic moment. The really big winners over the past three decades were the global plutocrats, especially the cadre of billionaires whose wealth more than doubled as a share of global GDP over this period.[12]

What accounts for this rising inequality? The standard economic reason is a combination of technological change and globalization. The technology argument essentially says that the nature of technological progress over the past few decades has boosted the productivity of high-skilled workers over low-skilled workers. The globalization argument is also one based on fate. It says that countries that face more competition from places with lower wages lose out, especially lower-skilled workers in those countries. But these factors alone cannot explain the rise in inequality. All countries faced these factors, but not all faced similar trajectories of inequality. Inequality can also be explained by neoliberal policies including curbs on union rights and collective bargaining, the paring back of welfare states, lower taxes on the wealthy, increased corporate concentration and power, and enhanced financial deregulation. Inequality expert Branko Milanovic says it well: inequality with roots in economics tends to be reinforced by politics as the increasing power of

---

11. Keynes, *General Theory*.
12. Milanovic, *Global Inequality*.

elites allows them to bend policy toward their will, allowing it to become long lasting and self-perpetuating. Inequality boils down to political will.

From the vantage point of Catholic social teaching, inequality has the effect of shredding the sense of shared purpose needed to further the common good. The rich shrink into circles of social similarity, with greater distance from, and care for, their fellow citizens. Trust, cohesion, and social capital are depleted. In a landmark book called *The Spirit Level*, social epidemiologists Richard Wilkinson and Kate Pickett have demonstrated that inequality reduced empathy and trust across the board.[13] Their analysis linked a skewed income distribution to a litany of social ills, including high unemployment and economic insecurity; high personal indebtedness; poor nutrition; low life expectancy; high infant mortality; poor physical and mental health; more prevalent drug abuse; weak educational attainment; limited social mobility; more crime, violence, and imprisonment; and higher levels of obesity, more teenage pregnancies, and poor child well-being. In a follow-up book called *The Inner Level*, Wilkinson and Pickett drill down into the psychological dimension of the social dysfunctions wrought by inequality.[14] They trace these problems to status anxiety. People who lose out can be overcome by thoughts of inadequacy, self-doubt, low self-esteem, and depression. On the opposite end of the scale, people can gravitate toward narcissism and self-aggrandizement that serves as a mask for self-doubt. Wilkinson and Pickett show that mental disorders such as depression, anxiety, schizophrenia, and psychosis are more common diagnoses in more unequal societies.

Neoclassical economists will frequently argue that inequality is a cost to be paid for a dynamic economy. They argue that there is a trade-off between growth and equity, whereby the policies to achieve lower inequality lead to reduced incentives to work, save, and invest. But the evidence simply doesn't back this up. The IMF has shown that, contrary to traditional assumptions, inequality is associated with lower and less durable economic growth and that growth trickles up from the poor and middle classes, not down from the rich.[15] So high inequality even undermines the core tenets of neoliberalism.

---

13. Wilkinson and Pickett, *Spirit Level*.
14. Wilkinson and Pickett, *Inner Level*.
15. Ostry et al. "Redistribution, Inequality, and Growth"; Dabla-Norris et al. *Causes and Consequences of Income Inequality*.

Employment

Many of the same factors that make inequality worse also impinge on employment prospects, leading to a paucity of dignified employment, especially among those with lower levels of education. For these people in particular, work has become increasingly low paying and fragile, lacking protections, lacking dignity. In countries like the United States, the labor share of national income has been on the decline for decades, as capital captures a greater share of the pie. If the insights of Catholic social teaching are true—in the sense of work being a source of meaning, purpose, dignity, and identity—then the lack of decent work is bound to undercut human flourishing, create unhappiness, and reduce trust and social cohesion. The evidence seems to bear out these insights.

In terms of driving forces, globalization is a key factor, given competition from low-wage countries in a world of open borders. Corporations find it easy to outsource to locations with low pay, weak labor protections, and limited taxation. Globalization essentially boosts the power of capital over labor, and a globalization of financialization—with free movements of capital jetting across borders seeking the highest short-term return—makes matters worse.

The other major threat facing workers is the rise of robots and artificial intelligence, which has led to the replacement of more and more jobs—including in non-traded sectors shielded from globalization. Economist Carl Frey has explored how technological change has affected workers since the beginning of the industrial revolution.[16] He argues that some changes are labor replacing and some are labor enabling. Labor-replacing technologies make jobs and skills redundant, as machines can do the work. Labor-enabling technologies, on the other hand, make people more productive in their existing roles or create entirely new jobs. Frey argues that the technologies of the early industrial revolution were labor replacing, as craft workers lost out to factory machines. But he also argues that the technological waves of the twentieth century were more labor enabling—the development of technologies such as electricity and the internal combustion engine led to widespread prosperity, paving the way for the admixture of high growth and low inequality of the social democratic era. And these advances were bolstered by welfare institutions that protected workers from harsh swings of fortune.

---

16. Frey, *Technology Trap*.

But Frey's analysis is ultimately pessimistic; he argues that the era of artificial intelligence is another labor-replacing era. In his view, this technological revolution, despite the wonders it can produce, will look more like the early industrial revolution than like the twentieth century. It will boost inequality, both by rewarding the owners of capital and lowering the wages of low-skilled workers. These trends could easily provoke a backlash, just as in the early phases of the industrial revolution.

Environment

It is no exaggeration to say that we face an existential environmental crisis, which undermines the very conditions for human flourishing on the planet. It is no coincidence that Pope Francis devoted his important encyclical, *Laudato Si'*, to the precarious state of our common home.

A key point is that, owing to the scale of human activity, we are bumping up against some key planetary boundaries—boundaries which delineate a hospitable planet conducive to human flourishing. Scientific evidence identifies at least nine such boundaries, which should be regarded as gateways to a perilous world: climate change, ocean acidification, overuse of freshwater resources, land-use changes, interference with the nitrogen and phosphorous cycles (caused mainly by fertilizers), ozone depletion, chemical pollution, atmospheric aerosol loading (airborne pollution from burning fossil fuels), and a rapid loss of biodiversity in the context of ruptured ecosystems.

The most important of these boundaries is surely climate change, caused by the burning of fossil fuels that releases carbon dioxide and other greenhouse gases into the atmosphere. We stand on the threshold of a terrifying new reality. Right now, the concentration of carbon dioxide molecules in the atmosphere is higher than at any time in the past three million years, a time when the environment has been hotter and vastly more hostile. This existential crisis is the most serious of the twenty-first century. We face something of a paradox here. These fossil fuels powered the industrial revolution and so deserve a lot of credit for advances in human well-being. But there is a giant bug in the program. We now know that these fossil fuels are actively undermining the very potential they promise, by warming the planet on an unprecedented scale and speed. Human wellbeing will be increasingly undermined from ever more severe droughts, flooding, forest fires, heat waves, and storms. In the years to come, climate change will have enormous effects on agricultural output, human health, poverty, migration, political instability and conflict. In this sense, we are sowing the seeds of our own destruction. And the poor will be on the front lines of climate change, even though they shoulder the least blame for the cumulative carbon emissions that are warming the planet. We cannot blame neoliberal ideology for global warming. But with its utmost faith in markets, neoliberalism has proved wholly unable to grapple with and solve this problem.

Solving this problem amounts to one of the most complex challenges humanity has ever faced. The international consensus encapsulated by the Paris Agreement on Climate Change—signed by the nations of the world in 2015—calls for limiting warming to under 2 degrees, or ideally 1.5 degrees, above preindustrial levels. The world has already warmed by over one degree, so the margin of error is increasingly limited. And the trajectory right now is for this target to be missed. If countries do what they promise over the next decade, warming would still increase by 3 degrees Celsius by end of century. Even this assumes they will do what they promise, and there is not much evidence of this so far.

What is needed to solve climate change is to reach net zero carbon emissions by mid-century. This form of "deep decarbonization" has three key strands—improving energy efficiency, replacing electricity generated by fossil fuels (coal, oil, gas) with electricity generated by renewables (hydro, wind, solar, geothermal), and shifting from the direct use of fossil fuels for energy to electricity that is generated by clean sources. All of this represents an enormous challenge. But we have the technology and the financial resources to make it happen. What we lack is the political will, and indeed the "moral capital."

Conclusion: Toward a New Social Democratic Moment

I would argue that we are at an inflection point in history. Four decades of neoliberalism, influenced by the discipline of neoclassical economics, have brought us to the brink of disaster. The global economy has proven capable of generating vast amounts of wealth but little in the way of virtue. Billions of people are excluded from the basics of human flourishing. And as the elites retreat into ever-smaller circles of solidarity, the economic forces of technological change and financialization, plus a pattern of globalization that favors corporations and financial institutions lead to widening inequality and flattening opportunity. And hovering over these health and financial disasters is the environmental crisis, which threatens to bring everything crashing down in a catastrophic fashion.

History teaches us clear lessons in this regard. We know that economic frustration and anxiety can fuel demagogues and insular nationalists offering up scapegoats and easy answers. We are already seeing this, in many countries. Political polarization in the United States is at levels not experienced in generations. Even democracy itself seems under assault. I would even argue that we are at grave risk of a "1930s moment," in which faltering economic prospects and shriveling common good lead to dire political dysfunctions. This backlash can manifest in different ways—sometimes directed inward against plutocrats and domestic elites, sometimes directed outward against immigrants and global financiers. Either way, this kind of backlash poses a major risk to domestic institutions and even to democracy; such anxiety and insecurity provides fertile ground for authoritarian leaders and demagogues. And the backlash has the potential to undermine not only the domestic common good but also the global common good, as nations turn inwards and the institutions of postwar global governance weaken.

Against this backdrop, we surely need another "social democratic moment." Yet this movement must entail not a simple repetition of the past but rather a response tuned to current circumstances and contexts. In an insightful analysis, Thomas Piketty identifies three fault lines in the original social democratic model, fault lines that caused it to unravel. The first was the failure to develop a more just approach to property ownership, especially as encapsulated by German-style worker sharing in business decision-making. The second was the difficulty in extending progressive taxes on income and wealth to the era of enhanced globalization. The third was the inability to confront the challenge of inequality of education in an era of neoliberal "meritocracy."[17] I would argue that Catholic social teaching is perfectly poised to deal with these fault lines. Indeed, the only way out of the current conundrum is a new "virtue economics" that grounds the global economy in a new moral narrative, in a new social democratic consensus for the twenty-first century underpinned by what Pope Francis calls a new and universal solidarity.

---

17. Piketty, *Capital and Ideology*.

Bibliography

Annett, Anthony M. *Cathonomics: How Catholic Tradition Can Create a More Just Economy.* Washington, DC: Georgetown University Press, 2022.

Appelbaum, Binyamin. *The Economists' Hour: False Prophets, Free Markets, and the Fracture of Society.* New York: Hachette, 2019.

Chappel, James. *Catholic Modern: The Challenge of Totalitarianism and the Remaking of the Church.* Cambridge: Harvard University Press, 2018.

Clark, Meghan J. "Subsidiarity Is a Two-Sided Coin." *Catholic Moral Theology,* March 8, 2012. https://catholicmoraltheology.com/subsidiarity-is-a-two-sided-coin/.

Dabla-Norris, Era, et al. *Causes and Consequences of Income Inequality: A Global Perspective.* Washington, DC: IMF, 2015.

Dicastery for Promoting Integral Human Development. *Vocation of the Business Leader: A Reflection.* Vatican City: Dicastery for Promoting Integral Human Development, 2018.

Francis. *Laudato Si'.* Vatican City State: Libreria Editrice Vaticana, 2015. https://www.vatican.va/content/francesco/en/encyclicals/documents/papa-francesco_20150524_enciclica-laudato-si.html.

Frey, Carl Benedikt. *The Technology Trap: Capital, Labor, and Power in the Age of Automation.* Princeton: Princeton University Press, 2019.

Gordon, Robert J. *The Rise and Fall of American Growth: The U.S. Standard of Living since the Civil War.* Princeton: Princeton University Press, 2016.

Hollenbach, David. *The Common Good and Christian Social Ethics.* New York: Cambridge University Press, 2002.

John Paul II. *Sollicitudo Rei Socialis: On Social Concern.* Vatican City State: Libreria Editrice Vaticana, 1987. https://www.vatican.va/content/john-paul-ii/en/encyclicals/documents/hf_jp-ii_enc_30121987_sollicitudo-rei-socialis.html.

Judt, Tony. *Ill Fares the Land.* New York: Penguin, 2010.

———. *Postwar: A History of Europe since 1945.* New York: Penguin, 2005.

Keynes, John Maynard. *The General Theory of Employment, Interest, and Money.* London: Macmillan, 1936.

Mayer, Colin. *Prosperity: Better Business Makes the Greater Good.* Oxford: Oxford University Press, 2018.

Milanovic, Branko. *Global Inequality: A New Approach for the Age of Globalization.* Cambridge: Harvard University Press, 2016.

Ostry, Jonathan D., et al. "Redistribution, Inequality, and Growth." *IMF Staff Discussion Notes,* February 2014. https://www.imf.org/en/Publications/Staff-Discussion-Notes/Issues/2016/12/31/Redistribution-Inequality-and-Growth-41291.

Piketty, Thomas. *Capital and Ideology.* Cambridge: Belknap, 2020.

Wilkinson, Richard, and Kate Pickett. *The Inner Level: How More Equal Societies Reduce Stress, Restore Sanity, and Improve Everybody's Wellbeing.* London: Penguin, 2018.

———. *The Spirit Level: Why More Equal Societies Almost Always Do Better.* London: Lane, 2009.

21

A New Vision for the Economy
Social Catholicism in the Twenty-First Century

Matthew A. Shadle, Independent Scholar

Abstract: Faith in neoliberalism has been on the decline since the financial crisis of 2007–8. Catholic social teaching (CST) offers a compelling alternative view of the economy, yet "social Catholicism," the network of associations that historically has put CST into action, is in a decades-long state of dormancy. At its height in the middle of the twentieth century, social Catholicism went into decline starting in the 1950s as a result of secularization and the globalization of the economy. If social Catholicism is to have a future in the twenty-first century, it needs a new vision that responds to contemporary reality. Pope Francis offers such a vision with his teaching on "integral ecology," which turns to the ecosystem as a root metaphor for thinking about economic life. Building on this ecological vision, the economy can be conceived as an open, complex, and nonlinear system that can be gradually but radically transformed by the participation of individuals and organizations guided by CST. This ecological vision leads to a new way of thinking about business enterprises, social movements, and church-affiliated communities focused on linking faith and economic life that can give life to social Catholicism in the twenty-first century.

THE FINANCIAL CRISIS OF 2007 and 2008 had a devastating and long-lasting impact on the United States economy, not just in terms of traditional economic indicators like gross domestic product (GDP) and the unemployment rate, but also the harm to people's livelihoods: the loss of homes to foreclosure, the destruction of household wealth, and the waste of human potential through long-term unemployment. The crisis also damaged Americans' faith in the free-market economy and led people to seek alternative ways of organizing economic life. It was perceived as a serious failure of the ideology of neoliberalism. The term "neoliberalism" is used in a variety of ways, but here I am referring to perhaps the most common usage, the belief that barriers to trade and finance should be lowered, government spending should be cut, social services should be eliminated or privatized, and government intervention in the economy (through regulation, investments, etc.) should be minimized.[1]

One sign that neoliberalism is in decline is the fact that there has been a decided shift in American policy toward a greater role for the government in managing the economy. This was reflected in a flurry of bailouts, stimulus spending, and financial regulation in the aftermath of the crisis. Despite the rise of the small-government Tea Party movement in 2010, greater openness to government intervention has continued under the nationalistic populism of President Donald Trump and the more progressive populism of Joe Biden. The US government was also deeply involved in supporting the economy during the COVID-19 pandemic under those two presidents.

Despite this greater openness to government intervention in American economic policy, some of the problems associated with neoliberalism have lingered. The Occupy Wall Street movement, which emerged in 2011 in part because of the perception that the Obama administration had not gone far enough in reining in the excesses of the financial sector and addressing the underlying problems of the American economy, brought attention to the fact that the Wall Street executives who had caused the financial crisis were never held responsible for their actions. The Occupy movement likewise brought to increased public awareness

---

1. "Neoliberalism" is often described as the ideology behind a set of policies pushed on developing nations in the Global South by international economic institutions like the International Monetary Fund (IMF) and World Bank, especially throughout the 1980s and 1990s, but the term is also used to apply to similar policies applied in more developed countries, including the United States and the nations of the European Union. See Harvey, *Brief History*, for one influential and critical account of neoliberalism.

the issue of economic inequality, pointing out the vast distance between the wealthiest one percent of Americans and the overwhelming majority of people, an inequality that had grown rapidly since the beginnings of the neoliberal era in the 1980s. At a deeper level, there is an increasing sense of precariousness, a lack of solidarity, and an epidemic of loneliness[2] that fuels xenophobia, racial resentment, and populism on the one hand, and passivity and resignation on the other.

Catholic Social Teaching (CST)—the body of Church teachings on the economy, political life, and culture produced during the modern era—has long been critical of radical, free-market ideologies,[3] and so the apparent weakness of neoliberalism in the aftermath of the financial crisis has provided an opportunity for CST to have a renewed influence on economic life. Indeed, there has been a revival of interest in CST's economic teaching, particularly as an alternative to neoliberalism.[4] CST, for example, insists that the state has an important role in regulating economic life, greater than what is recognized by neoliberalism, although it insists that state activity must be guided by moral criteria; it must promote solidarity amidst our differences rather than exacerbating divisions, as is the case with nationalistic populism.[5]

It is in addressing the cultural and spiritual emptiness exacerbated by neoliberalism that CST has the most to offer, however. In recent years, the documents of CST have warned against thinking of social life solely in terms of the market and the state. As Pope John Paul II most clearly put it in his 1991 encyclical *Centesimus Annus*, "The individual today is often suffocated between two poles represented by the State and the marketplace."[6] Pope Benedict XVI similarly warned in his 2009 encyclical *Caritas in Veritate*, "The exclusively binary model of market-plus-State is corrosive of society."[7] For both popes, the problem with this "binary

---

2. In 2023, US Surgeon General Vivek Murthy identified an "epidemic of loneliness" as a public health emergency. US Department of Health and Human Services, "New Surgeon General Advisory."

3. For a thorough history of modern Catholic thinking on the economy, see my *Interrupting Capitalism*.

4. See Annett, *Cathonomics*, for a good example. Annett provides a more thorough description of neoliberal economics, or what he refers to as "neoclassical economics," and contrasts it with the economic vision found in CST.

5. Pope Francis's 2020 encyclical *Fratelli Tutti*, for example, is a powerful statement in favor of global solidarity in opposition to the rising tide of nationalism.

6. John Paul II, *Centesimus Annus*, no. 49.

7. Benedict XVI, *Caritas in Veritate*, no. 39.

model" is that it ignores the role of what they call society's "intermediate associations" or "civil society," that is, social groups like families, churches, labor unions, neighborhood associations, nonprofits, and so on that are motivated neither by profit nor power. These associations foster social goods that cannot be provided by the market or the government. They help overcome the loneliness fostered by modern living and create bonds of friendship and solidarity. Therefore, CST insists that we must nurture these associations and protect them from being dissolved by the market or overtaken by the state.

Intermediate associations also help generate the political power needed to counterbalance the concentration of power in the hands of the few and to promote necessary political and economic reforms. As the American theologian William T. Cavanaugh notes, expanding on the framing of Popes John Paul II and Benedict XVI, "The state and the market are not opposed forces but collaborate much more often than they contradict one another. . . . Free market ideology protects corporations from state curbs on corporate power while corporations simultaneously avail themselves of massive state subsidies and state protection from having to face the discipline of the market for reckless behavior."[8] The concentration of wealth generated by the free-market economy allows a small handful of people to have an outsized influence on the democratic system, in turn preventing meaningful reforms of both the economic and political systems. Intermediate associations and the alternative forms of economic organization encouraged by CST, particularly when they network with one another and with like-minded institutions, generate solidarity and provide people with a source of power with which to challenge the status quo.

Despite the riches of the Catholic social tradition, efforts to transform the US economy inspired by CST have been meager, especially when contrasted with the vibrant social movements of the early twentieth century, sometimes referred to collectively as "social Catholicism."[9] It is precisely the Catholic intermediate associations, social movements, and economic enterprises that were characteristic of earlier manifestations of social Catholicism that are sorely lacking (although by no means

---

8. Cavanaugh, *Field Hospital*, 124–25.

9. For an outstanding account of the history of social Catholicism, particularly in Europe, see Misner, *Social Catholicism*; Misner, *Catholic Labor Movements*. For social Catholicism in the United States, see Shadle, *Interrupting Capitalism*, 150–66, and the sources provided there.

completely absent) today in the United States. Developing ministries devoted to linking faith and economic life has not been a priority for the US Catholic Church over the past several decades. Although it would be both impossible and fruitless to try to recreate the organizations of the past, Catholics today need to adopt the spirit of these earlier movements and develop creative ways to organize new social movements and forms of engaging in economic activity while drawing on recent CST, particularly the ecological vision of Pope Francis. In the next section, I will examine some of the causes for the decline in social Catholicism before turning to proposals for how social Catholicism might have a future in the twenty-first century.

The Rise and Decline of Social Catholicism

The years after the Second World War were arguably the high point for social Catholicism, but the seeds of its decline had already been planted. In Western Europe, a dense network of associations, including those devoted to the spiritual and economic needs of workers and farmers, had been established, and powerful Christian Democratic parties promoted a platform reflecting the principles of CST. Latin America demonstrated similar tendencies, although on a smaller scale. In the United States, where Catholics were a minority, social Catholicism took a different form; US Catholics worked within secular organizations but nevertheless had an influence on their goals and policies. Even as social Catholicism was at its height, however, changes in the mission of these Catholic associations, secularization, and the rapidly-changing capitalist economy were conspiring to contribute to its relatively rapid decline in the decades that followed.

Social Catholicism at Its Height

In the decades before the war, Catholic Action emerged in Western Europe as an international organization of associations dedicated to forming lay people for engagement in the world, particularly in family life and the workplace. In some countries like Belgium, the Netherlands, France, and West Germany, Catholic Action associations were established geared toward specific social roles, or "milieus," like industrial workers, farmers, and students. The most well-known of these was the *Jeunesse Ouvrière*

Catholique (JOC), or Young Catholic Workers, founded in Belgium by Joseph Cardijn in 1924.[10] These movements provided spiritual guidance to their members appropriate to their social context, including training in the principles of CST.

Another important component of social Catholicism was the Catholic labor unions that had begun to be established in Europe in the nineteenth century and grew in number in the twentieth. By the Second World War, nationwide federations of Catholic unions had been formed in most countries of Western Europe, with some, such as in Germany, federating with Protestant and secular, non-socialist unions.[11] These unions offered a vision distinct from that of their much larger rivals, the socialist unions. Rather than advocating for class conflict, they promoted cooperation and mutual respect between workers and employers.

The postwar years also saw the emergence of the Christian Democratic political parties in Western Europe.[12] These parties became a major political force in European politics. Although strictly independent from the Church, these parties promoted a political ideology grounded in CST. The parties were also formally nonsectarian, and in countries like the Netherlands and West Germany, this meant the parties included both Catholics and Protestants. The Christian Democratic parties made two contributions to the shape of postwar social Catholicism. First, they provided national networks linking disparate social Catholic groups. For example, in some cases, associations of workers or farmers were constituent groups within the party, providing new members, mobilizing voters, and shaping party policy. The policies implemented by Christian Democratic parties likewise incorporated these social groups; for example, Catholic labor associations played a role in shaping labor policy and in administering social assistance programs.

The second contribution was that Christian Democratic parties provided a political platform embodying the ideals of social Catholicism, and CST more broadly. In the economic field, the parties advocated for what Kees van Kersbergen has called "social capitalism," an ideology that balances the dignity of the person, the social role of associations like the

---

10. Misner, *Catholic Labor Movements*, 121–42.

11. Misner, *Catholic Labor Movements*, 161–211, 231–54.

12. On the emergence and growth of Christian Democratic parties, see Kalyvas, *Rise of Christian Democracy*. For analysis of Christian Democracy in different national contexts, see the essays in Hanley, *Christian Democracy in Europe*; Kselman and Buttigieg, *European Christian Democracy*.

family and labor unions, and the responsibilities of the state.[13] Although there were different tendencies within the Christian Democracy movement, ranging politically from left to right, the parties provided a unifying set of principles, along with a national network of associations, that gave CST an influential voice in European politics in the years after the Second World War.

In Latin America, social Catholic organizations also emerged, although on a smaller scale than in Western Europe. Organizations focused on the needs of Catholic workers and the promotion of CST were established in those countries that saw the most rapid industrialization, and thus the growth in the middle class and working class, like Argentina, Chile, and Brazil.[14] Social Catholicism was mostly absent in those regions, like Central America, where the economy remained primarily agricultural. Latin America also saw the creation of Christian Democratic parties. The most well-known example is Chile, where Christian Democratic President Eduardo Frei governed from 1964 to 1970,[15] but Christian Democratic parties also had varying degrees of success in other countries, as well.[16]

In the United States, Catholics were a minority, although a relatively large one, in a Protestant-majority nation, and therefore social Catholicism there took a different form. Unlike in Western Europe, from its beginnings, Catholic labor activism in the United States was nonsectarian, beginning with the controversy over whether Catholic workers could join the Knights of Labor in the 1880s. Catholics were heavily involved in both the American Federation of Labor, the national federation of trade unions, and the Congress of Industrial Organizations, the federation of industrial labor unions, which merged into the AFL-CIO in 1955. Some of the policies advocated by the unions reflected CST, such as the "industrial council plan" put forward in the postwar years, which proposed a cooperative structure for managing labor relations, including representatives of the workers and employers, along lines similar to those implemented by Christian Democratic governments in Europe.[17] The

---

13. Kersbergen, *Social Capitalism*.

14. For example, see Mainwaring, *Catholic Church and Politics in Brazil*, 116–41, and the essays in Berríos et al., *Catolicism social chileno*.

15. Fleet, *Rise and Fall of Chilean Christian Democracy*.

16. Mainwaring and Scully, *Christian Democracy in Latin America*.

17. See Sinyai, *Schools of Democracy*, 116–22; Prentiss, *Debating God's Economy*, 199–235.

Young Catholic Workers also had a presence in the United States, providing spiritual formation for Catholic workers, but American Catholics also established the Association of Catholic Trade Unionists (ACTU), which not only formed Catholic labor leaders in the principles of CST, but also took on stances in major labor disputes.[18]

Similarly, although no Christian Democratic party was established in the United States, Catholics still played an important role in American politics. The minority status of Catholics in the United States, and the suspicion under which they were held regarding political matters,[19] made it impossible to establish a sectarian Catholic political party. Likewise, the fact that the nation remained overwhelmingly Christian, and that Protestant Christians participated in both the Republican and Democratic parties, prevented the emergence of a nonsectarian Christian Democratic party. Nevertheless, Catholic voters were an important part of the coalition that made the Democratic Party the dominant political force in the United States in the middle of the twentieth century. Catholics also influenced major policies of the era; for example, aspects of New Deal policy were influenced by the 1919 Bishops' Program for Social Reconstruction, a set of policy proposals produced by the US Catholic bishops, and the ideas of John A. Ryan, a Catholic priest and economist.[20] In the United States, the Catholic Church's political role took the form of advocacy and lobbying. The US bishops' Social Action Department (SAD), founded and first directed by Ryan, advocated for industrial policies guided by Pope Leo XIII's *Rerum Novarum* (1891) and Pope Pius XI's *Quadragesimo Anno* (1931).[21] Similarly, the National Catholic Rural Life Conference (NCRLC) advocated policies to protect family farms, encourage the development of rural cooperatives, and provide rural development (such as electrification and access to new technologies).[22]

---

18. See Prentiss, *Debating God's Economy*, 83–142; Seaton, *Catholics and Radicals*.

19. See McGreevy, *Catholicism and American Freedom*, for a history of the complex relationship between American Catholics and American political institutions.

20. McShane, "*Sufficiently Radical.*"

21. Prentiss, *Debating God's Economy*, 90–102.

22. Bovée, *Church & the Land*.

The Decline of Social Catholicism

Although it is important not to exaggerate the influence of social Catholicism, by the 1950s the organizations identified with that label were key social actors in Western Europe, were growing in Latin America, and helped give Catholics a public voice in the United States. By the 1970s, however, their influence had been greatly diminished. The factors that contributed to their decline were already present by the 1950s. First, many of the organizations themselves underwent a shift in mission, abandoning their explicit Catholic identity for more secular goals. Second, secularization, or declining religious belief and practice and the privatization of religion, particularly in Europe and the United States, significantly weakened social Catholicism. Finally, the rapid development of the postwar capitalist economy, fueled by globalization, undermined the associations at the heart of social Catholicism and contributed to increasing economic individualism.

As early as the end of the 1940s, some organizations associated with social Catholicism reevaluated their mission, eschewing their Catholic identity and shifting their emphasis from spiritual formation to a more exclusive focus on activism in economic and political affairs. A handful of movements in France focused on workers and families were the first to undertake this shift, but associations in other countries soon followed.[23] By the 1960s, the International Young Catholic Workers, representing JOCist groups worldwide, had shifted toward greater activism and less focus on the spiritual dimension. This shift within the JOCist movement had an important impact in Latin America, which saw a similar transition among social Catholic groups in the 1960s.[24]

This shift in mission was spurred by changing theological perspectives. Members of these organizations rejected the notion that their vocation was to promote a distinctively Catholic social order. Instead, the new theological approach drew on the doctrine of the Incarnation, the belief that Christ took on human nature to save it, arguing that their vocation was to be an "Incarnational presence" or "leaven" in the secular world, helping to bring to fruition the demand for justice already present in the world. This sense that the secular world was characterized by an intrinsic dynamic pushing toward social progress led some of these groups

---

23. See Duriez, "Left Wing Catholicism."

24. Ahern, *Structures of Grace*, 70–73. This transition was an important factor in the emergence of liberation theology in Latin America at the end of the 1960s.

to associate with communism, leading to conflicts with the Church hierarchy.[25] Perhaps the most well-known example is the worker priest movement. Established in France in the 1940s as an apostolate to the working class, these priests adopted the life of industrial workers, including laboring in factories and participating in labor activism.

Although these movements were right to sense that the notion of a fully Catholic social order was historically obsolete, their new self-identity was not sustainable. For one, these movements underestimated the extent to which the Church, as a social body, provided not just the spiritual formation but the sense of community needed to give these associations life. By eschewing their Catholic self-identity and disassociating from the Church, these organizations abandoned the broader cultural matrix that had been their source of human capital. Similarly, by making the secular world the touchstone for their mission, these organizations undermined their distinctiveness; existing secular organizations, often much larger and well-established, already filled similar functions. Indeed, by the 1960s, many of these organizations faced dwindling membership or merged with existing secular organizations.

Catholic associations and Christian Democratic political parties, even when they remained grounded in their distinctive Catholic identity, were significantly weakened by secularization, the widespread disaffiliation from religion or privatization of religious belief, particularly in Europe. Beginning in the late 1950s, there was a rapid decline in religious practice in Western Europe: in almost every country, church attendance rapidly dropped, there was a decrease in ministerial vocations across denominations, and fewer children were baptized and received religious education.[26] This decline in religious practice had a dramatic impact on Catholic associations and the Christian Democratic parties. Without a grounding in institutional religious practice, people's affiliation with Catholic social and political organizations rapidly declined.[27]

In the United States, religious practice did not decline in the same way as in Western Europe, at least not until more recent decades. The decline in Catholic subcultures in the United States, however, had a similar effect on social Catholicism in the US Catholicism. In the United

---

25. See my *Interrupting Capitalism*, 51–55, for more on this transition. Ahern also has a detailed discussion of shifting perspectives on the mission of Catholic organizations in *Structures of Grace*, 109–24.

26. McLeod, "Religious Crisis of the 1960s."

27. Kersbergen, *Social Capitalism*, 235–46.

States was primarily an immigrant phenomenon, and so Catholic culture thrived in social enclaves, whether immigrant neighborhoods in major cities like New York City, Boston, and Chicago, or in small towns populated by the descendants of immigrants. In these enclaves, distinctive Catholic subcultures emerged in which the transmission of the Catholic faith was inextricably intertwined with passing on the culture. These tight-knit subcultures had been foundational to the emergence of social Catholicism as it existed in the United States. After the Second World War, however, an increasing number of Catholics moved away from these enclaves, either moving to the suburbs or to different neighborhoods in cities. They became, in many ways, indistinguishable from their non-Catholic neighbors. In fact, for many Catholics, this blending in was perceived as the achievement of mainstream respectability and modernity.[28] In this context, in which the subcultures that had been central to the formation of US Catholics had largely dissolved and secular respectability was prized, the distinct organizations of social Catholicism went into decline, much as they had in Western Europe.

Lastly, rapid economic development in the postwar decades and the increasing globalization of the economy had a profound impact on social Catholicism. For one, economic growth in the United States and Western Europe led to increasing affluence and consumerism.[29] Although economic prosperity brought rising living standards, consumerism challenged spiritual and religious values. By the 1960s, warnings regarding the dangers of consumerism became a staple of CST. For example, in his 1967 encyclical *Populorum Progressio*, Pope Paul VI stated: "The exclusive pursuit of material possessions prevents man's growth as a human being and stands in opposition to his true grandeur."[30] Second, economic development and globalization have contributed to greater social volatility and mobility. Older industries become obsolete while new industries emerge; companies move factories and offices from one country to another; people move from one place to another in search of opportunity. Social Catholicism as it had developed in the twentieth century, however, was based in a sense of rootedness; a person's participation in community life was mediated through their *milieu* (or occupational grouping), their company, and their parish. In a world in which people are rootless, such associations cannot flourish.

28. See D'Antonio et al., *American Catholics*, 1–18.
29. Griffiths and Tachibanaki, "From Austerity to Affluence."
30. Paul VI, *Populorum Progressio*, no. 19.

What can we learn from the decline of social Catholicism in the twentieth century to help us develop a renewed social Catholicism for the twenty-first century and an alternative to neoliberalism? I think there are at least three lessons. The first is that social Catholicism should not be primarily focused on proposing an alternative economic "system," wholly formed, or offering a platform of economic policies. For one, secularization makes this impractical. In most of the world, Catholics simply do not have the popular democratic support needed to promote such a platform and do not have sufficient access to the levers of power to promote system-level change. Second, there are good reasons for abandoning such an approach. The economy is evolving rapidly, and so thinking in terms of a static platform of ideas and policies is not very effective. And theologically speaking, the purpose of CST is not to propose a distinctive, "Catholic" economic system or a set of specific policies, but to form individuals and communities that can transform the economic system in which they find themselves. Rather than focusing on a comprehensive platform, Catholics should focus on introducing new ways of living in the economy (new forms of business enterprise, labor organizations, social movements, etc.) and working with others to make gradual, piecemeal changes to the economic system to make it more just and sustainable.

The second lesson is that the "intermediate associations" that form the backbone of social Catholicism cannot be taken for granted but rather must constantly be created and recreated. Twentieth-century social Catholicism was built around the relatively stable communities of family, neighborhood, workplace, and social milieu, but in today's volatile global economy, these types of communities do not provide a secure foundation for social transformation. Catholics should be willing to build social movements and organizations centered around causes or social conflicts that can incorporate members with a variety of identities and affiliations. These organizations may be temporary, lasting only as long as needed to address an issue, or may shift from one issue to another depending on community needs. They should also be willing to form networks with other organizations that share their aims and approach.

The third lesson is related; Catholic organizations should emphasize their distinctive Catholic identity but do so in a way that is open to pluralism. Earlier social Catholics were right to gradually reject the idea of a distinctive Catholic social order, but this should not have meant abandoning Catholic identity entirely. The Church's social teaching offers something distinctive to society, including an integral vision of the human person that joins the spiritual and the material and a concrete way of life founded on Christ's gratuitous love. Catholic organizations and social movements should draw on that distinctiveness, but in a pluralistic society, this can take different forms, including organizations strongly affiliated with Catholic identity, interfaith organizations in which Catholics cooperate with people of other faiths, and Catholic participation in secular organizations.

In the rest of this chapter, I will show how recent documents of CST provide a theological and practical framework for this renewed social Catholicism. In particular, Pope Francis's social teaching, which takes the form of an ecological vision of social life, proposes a helpful way of thinking about the economy. Recent CST also offers guidance on what it might mean for Christian discipleship to lead to new forms of economic life with the potential to change the broader economy.

Pope Francis's Ecological Vision

Pope Francis's most well-known remarks on the market economy are probably those in his apostolic exhortation *Evangelii Gaudium*, which he wrote in 2013, the first year of his pontificate. Francis pointedly claims that the contemporary global economy is characterized by exclusion and inequality, and "such an economy kills."[31] He likewise challenges the ideology of the free market:

> Some people continue to defend trickle-down theories which assume that economic growth, encouraged by a free market, will inevitably succeed in bringing about greater justice and inclusiveness in the world. This opinion, which has never been confirmed by the facts, expresses a crude and naïve trust in the goodness of those wielding economic power and in the sacralized workings of the prevailing economic system.[32]

Although these remarks generated a great deal of attention and controversy, Francis does not develop his thinking on the economy in much detail in *Evangelii Gaudium*.

Pope Francis's most significant thinking on the economy can perhaps be found instead in his 2015 encyclical *Laudato Si'*. *Laudato Si'* is

31. Francis, *Evangelii Gaudium*, no. 53.
32. Francis, *Evangelii Gaudium*, no. 54.

often described as Francis's "environmental encyclical," and indeed it does identify the environmental challenges faced by humankind while calling on Christians to undergo an "ecological conversion" in which we grow to live out "our vocation to be protectors of God's handiwork."[33] The encyclical is much more than that, however; it lays out a grand panorama, exploring humankind's place in the cosmos and God's movement in the universe, bringing Creation into loving union with the divine. Francis also provides the blueprints for how Catholics can faithfully and fruitfully think about our life in society and our relationship with the natural world, of which we are a part. This blueprint includes ideas relevant for understanding economic life. One of the most important concepts Francis employs to present this vision is "integral ecology."

Integral Ecology

Through his use of the concept of "integral ecology," Pope Francis draws on the patterns of thinking characteristic of ecological science to explain our place in the world. In the first place, he uses ecological thinking in a quite literal way by pointing out that we human beings are a part of the ecosystem: "Nature cannot be regarded as something separate from ourselves or as a mere setting in which we live. We are part of nature, included in it and thus in constant interaction with it."[34] Although human beings are characterized by "signs of a uniqueness which transcends the spheres of physics and biology,"[35] we share a kinship with the rest of the natural world. Our social and economic life depends on the resources provided by nature, and our activity has a profound impact on the natural environment. For this reason, Francis insists that we cannot consider social problems like poverty and environmental challenges separately, but rather must address them in an integrated manner.[36]

Francis goes further, however, drawing on "integral ecology" as a root metaphor for explaining human society in its different aspects. A root metaphor is an image or analogy used to help make sense of a complex reality like human society.[37] For example, in earlier documents of

33. Francis, *Laudato Si'*, no. 217.
34. Francis, *Laudato Si'*, no. 139.
35. Francis, *Laudato Si'*, no. 81.
36. Francis, *Laudato Si'*, nos. 49, 139.
37. The concept of a "root metaphor" was first developed by the American philosopher Stephen Pepper in *World Hypotheses* and has been frequently used in

CST, Popes Leo XIII and Pius XI describe society in terms of the human body, emphasizing that the members of society play distinct roles but must work together toward the good of the whole.[38] Francis, on the other hand, turns to the metaphor of the ecosystem. As an "organic" metaphor like that of the body, the concept of integral ecology allows Francis to emphasize the unity and diversity of human society, but also allows for a greater emphasis on change ("evolution"), both amongst the different institutions of society and within society as a whole.

Ecosystems can be studied at different levels, ranging in scale from an individual organism and its interactions with the surrounding environment to the biosphere of the entire planet, and every system is comprised of multiple subsystems.[39] Using the concept of "ecosystem" as a metaphor, Francis describes the different systems making up human society. As already noted, he begins by describing "environmental ecology," which looks at humankind's interconnections with the natural environment.[40] He then turns to "economic ecology," which studies the systems of production, commerce, and consumption[41] and "social ecology," which studies the state, the law, civil society, and other social organizations.[42] Francis gives a great deal of attention to what he calls "cultural ecology," the systems of language, meaning, and symbol that make up the "historic, artistic and cultural patrimony" of the nations of the world.[43] Each of these human systems can be examined at different levels, ranging from the local to the global. Francis finally turns, however, to what he calls the "ecology of daily life,"[44] which he defines as "the setting in which people live their lives."[45] The ecology of everyday life involves both the built environment and the relationships that make up local communities. The ecology of everyday life is extremely local, and yet Francis is sensitive to the ways the other social systems—culture, the economy, the political

---

commentaries on Catholic social teaching, for example, Hollenbach, "Prophetic Church," 249; Verstraeten, "Re-thinking Catholic Social Thought," 67; Holland, *Modern Catholic Social Teaching*, 20–23.

38. See Leo XIII, *Rerum Novarum*, no. 19; Pius XI, *Quadragesimo Anno*, no. 69.
39. See, for example, Ehrman, "Ecology."
40. Francis, *Laudato Si'*, nos. 138–40.
41. Francis, *Laudato Si'*, no. 141.
42. Francis, *Laudato Si'*, no. 142.
43. Francis, *Laudato Si'*, nos. 143–46.
44. Francis, *Laudato Si'*, nos. 147–55.
45. Francis, *Laudato Si'*, nos. 147.

system—are mediated through this everyday environment. In the rest of this section, I will focus on how Francis's approach can enrich how we think about the economic system, or "economic ecology."

Systems Thinking

Francis's concept of "integral ecology" provides a blueprint for further reflection on the economy (and the other systems of human society) in terms of the systems thinking used in the field of ecology. In particular, the systems studied in ecology have three basic characteristics: they are open, complex, and nonlinear.[46] An ecosystem is *open* because it receives inputs from other systems, and this input shapes the functioning of the ecosystem. For example, the ecosystem comprising a pond and all the forms of life inhabiting it receives inputs in the form of rain, energy from the sun, and organic matter, like leaves, that falls into the water. An ecosystem is *complex* because it is made up of constituent parts (in this case animals, plants, other types of organisms, and non-organic elements) that all behave in different ways and interact with one another, all of which impacts the broader system. Lastly, an ecosystem is *nonlinear*. This means that, precisely because of its complexity and its varied interactions with other systems, an ecosystem may behave in unexpected ways and its development over time is relatively unpredictable. Ecosystems may generally follow a certain pattern over the course of their life cycle, but the precise course its development will take depends on a multitude of factors. The human systems identified by Pope Francis also possess these three characteristics.[47] Here I will focus on the economic system.

---

46. The ideas in this section are indebted to contemporary economists belonging to the school of institutional economics, particularly Geoffrey Hodgson and Tony Lawson. See, for example, Hodgson, *Evolution of Institutional Economics*; Hodgson, *Economics in the Shadow*; Hodgson, *Conceptualizing Capitalism*; Lawson, *Economics and Reality*; Lawson, *Reorienting Economics*.

47. Of course, because the concept of "ecosystem" is here being used as a metaphor, it is important to keep in mind the ways that human social systems are *different* from ecosystems, most importantly the role played by human agency. Although human agency is a causal power that is shaped by, and in turn shapes, the systems of which the person is a part in a way analogous to the causal activity of the constituent parts of a natural ecosystem, the human agent acts with contingent freedom while other organisms operate in a more-or-less deterministic fashion. See the essays in Finn, *Moral Agency*, for one account of how human agents and social systems, or structures, interact.

A New Vision for the Economy—SHADLE

The Economy as Open System

Every economy depends on inputs from outside itself to function. Business firms make use of natural resources like wood, water, and minerals to manufacture products, and machinery depends on energy produced from resources like oil and coal or from renewable sources like water and the sun. A shortage in any of these resources can lead to economic decline or to a search for alternative resources. Contrary to free-market ideology, the economic system also depends on the state; the state provides the system of law that governs contracts, provides for a right to private property, and provides the legal structure for firms and corporations.[48] Government taxation, regulations, and other interventions in the economy also impact how the economy functions. The economy also depends on "human capital," the knowledge, skills, and virtues needed to perform the jobs that make up the contemporary economy and to foster the initiative and creativity that keep the economy running. Much of this human capital is developed outside the economic system, however, particularly in families and educational institutions. The government also plays a role in developing human capital, not only through education, but also through social assistance programs that provide for basic human needs like healthcare and adequate living standards.

Until relatively recently, however, economists treated the economy as a *closed* system, downplaying the economy's dependence on these external inputs. Because things like natural resources and human capital are, in technical terms, "externalities," or inputs that originate outside the economic system, economists believed that their economic models did not need to give an account of where these inputs come from or how economic activity might impact their availability. In concrete terms, the treatment of natural resources as an externality led many economists to assume in their models that these resources are limitless, and to ignore how economic production could deplete the stock of those resources, undermining future production.[49] Similarly, economists have neglected the impact that marketing and the rapid development of new technologies

---

48. This claim is one of the main insights of institutional economics. See, for example, Hodgson, *Conceptualizing Capitalism*, 101–28, 204–34.

49. This argument has most forcefully been made by adherents to the school of ecological economics. See Costanza et al., *Introduction to Ecological Economics*.

can have on the cultural and educational institutions that provide for human capital.[50]

The notion that the economy is an open system is rooted in CST. As I already noted, Pope Francis explains how the economy is dependent on the natural environment for resources and insists that economic policy-making should always take into consideration environmental impact. In his 1991 encyclical *Centesimus Annus*, Pope John Paul II explores the interdependence of three distinct social systems: the economy, the state, and culture.[51] For example, he insists that the state must provide a "strong juridical framework" for the economic system,[52] and he likewise teaches that the state is responsible for regulating the economy to ensure rights are protected and providing for needs that cannot be met by market activity alone, including the protection of the environment.[53] He also explains that economic activity takes place within the context of culture and depends on culture for its health; economic problems such as excessive consumerism and disregard for the environment have their deepest roots at the cultural and spiritual level.[54] Pope Benedict XVI succinctly reinforces this point in *Caritas in Veritate*, where he notes that, although the market can be put at the service of human well-being (or "emancipation"):

> In order to do so effectively, it cannot rely only on itself, because it is not able to produce by itself something that lies outside its competence. It must draw its moral energies from other subjects that are capable of generating them.[55]

CST also treats the economy as an open system through its insistence that the economy, like all dimensions of social life, needs to be oriented by the Church's doctrine and transformed by divine grace. As Benedict states, "Economic, social and political development, if it is to be authentically human, needs to make room for the *principle of gratuitousness* as an

---

50. The sociologist Daniel Bell famously argued in *Cultural Contradictions* that capitalism has a tendency to generate a culture of consumeristic hedonism and instant gratification that undermines the virtues, like hard work and delayed gratification, needed for the continued functioning of the institutions of capitalism.

51. On Pope John Paul II's *Centesimus Annus*, see my "Twenty Years," and *Interrupting Capitalism*, 225–41.

52. John Paul II, *Centesimus Annus*, no. 42.

53. John Paul II, *Centesimus Annus*, nos. 34, 48.

54. John Paul II, *Centesimus Annus*, nos. 39, 51.

55. Benedict XVI, *Caritas in Veritate*, no. 35.

expression of fraternity";[56] in other words, commercial logic needs to be transformed by what he calls the "logic of gift,"[57] the logic embodied in Christian discipleship.

The Economy as Complex System

Just as the economy is interconnected with other systems, both natural and human, the economy is itself a complex system made up of interconnected organizations, institutions, and structures. Any modern economy is made up of a variety of different types of business firms and corporations of different sizes and structures, pursuing different interests and goals. Consumers likewise make purchasing decisions based on their needs and desires, and those of their families, but they are also influenced by the power of marketing and social pressure and are constrained by their household income and the availability of credit. These different economic actors not only operate within the structures of the economic system, but collectively shape those structures, leading to the slow evolution of the economy. The functioning of the economy is also shaped by large-scale institutions like the currency system, the banking system, and the tax system. These different economic actors and institutions interact with one another, generating the "emergent properties" of the economic system, that is, the causal powers we attribute to the market itself and call "market forces," "the laws of supply and demand," and so forth.[58]

One implication of this complexity is that different economies, even those that can be classified broadly as "capitalist," may look quite distinct from one another. This insight has inspired a growing study of the "varieties of capitalism."[59] Economies may favor different types of business firms (such as Germany's favoring of small and middle-sized enterprises, or SMEs, the so-called *Mittelstand*), develop different types of banking systems, and manage labor relations in a variety of ways (such as France's system of *paritirisme*, in which national labor associations and employers' groups work with government representatives to set labor policy). Nations also develop different types of social welfare programs to meet

---

56. Benedict XVI, *Caritas in Veritate*, no. 34.
57. Benedict XVI, *Caritas in Veritate*, no. 34.
58. On "emergent properties" see the discussion in Smith, *What Is a Person?*, 25–42.
59. The best-known text is Hall and Soskice, *Varieties of Capitalism*.

human needs not met through employment.[60] These various institutions reflect the different values and priorities of the societies that make them, and the interplay among these institutions leads to differing economic outcomes. Economic systems, even capitalist systems, cannot be treated as if they are identical.

There is some recognition of the economy as a complex system in CST. In his 1987 encyclical *Sollicitudo Rei Socialis*, Pope John Paul II, writing in the last years of the Cold War, argues that CST does not provide a "Third Way" between capitalism and communism, or any kind of alternative economic system or platform. It is an expression of theological truths about the person and transcends the level of ideology.[61] He suggests, however, that CST can inspire "changes and updatings" in both systems.[62] John Paul makes a similar point in *Centesimus Annus*, written in 1991 after the fall of communism. He explains that CST "has no models to present," but rather offers an "orientation" that can guide the market economy and individual business enterprises toward the common good.[63] These passages reinforce the notion, mentioned above, that the economy is an *open* system, dependent not just on physical inputs from outside the system like natural resources but on the spiritual "input" provided by the Church. But they also demonstrate that John Paul thinks that the capitalist economy does not operate as a mechanistic system, but rather can take different forms with different trajectories. The responsibility of CST is to offer a new way of participating in economic life and to transform the trajectory of the economic system.

The Economy as Nonlinear System

In the twentieth century, economic theories that insisted that the economy progresses along a linear, pre-determined path had a great deal of influence. Perhaps the most influential was Marxism. Karl Marx argued that society has evolved through a series of stages characterized by different economic systems, or "modes of production." The internal contradictions of the mode of production, which come to be expressed through

---

60. The classic work is Esping-Andersen, *Three Worlds*.

61. John Paul II, *Sollicitudo Rei Socialis*, no. 41.

62. Interestingly, in *Sollicitudo Rei Socialis*, Pope John Paul II leaves as an open question the extent to which the two systems are capable of accommodating these "changes and updatings." See para. 21, already cited.

63. John Paul II, *Sollicitudo Rei Socialis*, no. 43.

class conflict, are exacerbated by improvements in technology, leading to social revolution and the emergence of a new mode of production. Although the exact course of events may be unpredictable, social change follows a predetermined path based on material forces. Marxists believed that the internal contradictions of the capitalist system would sooner or later lead to a proletarian revolution and the emergence of communism, the final stage of social development.[64]

A second theory, modernization theory, was put forward in the capitalist West during the 1950s and 1960s to explain how the developing nations of the so-called "Third World" could advance economically and technologically to match the level of development in the "First World." According to the economist W. W. Rostow, for example, nations move through five stages of development, culminating in the stage of "high mass consumption." Each stage is characterized by different economic institutions and technologies, and a nation must progress through each stage as part of the development process. More developed nations can assist in this process by providing investment, aid, and technological assistance.[65]

In the years after the fall of communism in Eastern Europe in 1989, the belief emerged that there was a new consensus around democratic political institutions and neoliberal economic policies. Some even argued that humankind had reached the "end of history," a final stage of development in which people could live in peace and freedom, and all that was left to accomplish was to ensure the spread of liberty across the globe.[66] International economic institutions like the International Monetary Fund and World Bank confidently imposed a package of neoliberal policies that came to be known as the "Washington Consensus" on developing nations as a condition for development assistance.[67]

Contrary to these popular theories, however, the economic system does not follow a linear path, nor does it inevitably progress toward a predetermined endpoint. The economy is a nonlinear system. Its path is uncertain because it is dependent on inputs from outside the system (i.e., it is *open*), its constituent parts—consumers, business enterprises, institutions like currency, banking, and property law—interact in unpredictable ways (i.e., it is *complex*), and perhaps most importantly, the human

---

64. See, for example, Marx and Engels, *Communist Manifesto*, 219–33.

65. Rostow, *Stages of Economic Growth*. See also Peet and Hartwick, *Theories of Development*, 140–48.

66. The most famous expression of this view was Fukuyama, *End of History*.

67. Peet and Hartwick, *Theories of Development*, 90–107.

agents who make it up are free. This does not mean that economists cannot develop models that can predict economic outcomes in the short and medium term, but rather that we must exercise humility in predicting the future course of the economy, especially over the longer term, and should eschew grand theories of historical progress.

In the theological framework of CST, history *is* linear in the sense that all human activity will find its fulfillment in the *eschaton*, the return of the Lord and establishment of the Kingdom of God at the end of history. But CST has rejected linear, deterministic theories of economic or social development, primarily because the progress or decline of social institutions is dependent on human freedom. For example, just as CST rejected the deterministic historical materialism of Marxism, in *Centesimus Annus*, Pope John Paul II warns that we should not interpret the new social and political realities that emerged after the fall of communism as "mechanistic or fatalistic in character," but instead as "opportunities for human freedom to cooperate with the merciful plan of God who acts within history."[68] Even though global capitalism appears as the "victorious" economic system,[69] as we have seen, John Paul believes that humankind nevertheless faces choices over the shape the economy will take and therefore the direction of human development.

Indeed, Christian eschatology provides theological grounds for a nonlinear view of historical development *within* the linearity provided by history's trajectory toward the *eschaton*. Precisely because we live in the time before the *eschaton*, we live in a world that is characterized by both grace and sin. The Second Vatican Council's Pastoral Constitution on the Church in the Modern World, *Gaudium et Spes*, portrays this reality as a historical struggle: "All of human life, whether individual or collective, shows itself to be a dramatic struggle between good and evil, between light and darkness."[70] Similarly, it teaches that "A monumental struggle against the powers of darkness pervades the whole history of humankind."[71] Because of humankind's divided heart, the path of history is not set in stone; we can cooperate with God in fostering truly integral human development, or construct structures of sin that oppress people and hinder development.[72] In *Centesimus Annus*, John Paul warns

---

68. John Paul II, *Centesimus Annus*, no. 26.
69. John Paul II, *Centesimus Annus*, no. 42.
70. Paul VI, *Gaudium et Spes*, no. 13.
71. Paul VI, *Gaudium et Spes*, no. 37.
72. On the concept of "integral human development" in CST, see Benedict XVI,

that those who deny the reality of human sinfulness and who claim to know the course of history are tempted to resort to totalitarian methods in pursuit of perfection in this world; a just social order is one that recognizes our freedom and the limits imposed by human frailty.[73]

The ecological vision that emerges in recent CST, and especially in Pope Francis's teaching, provides us with not just an insightful way of thinking about the economy, but also a sense of the form a renewed social Catholicism ought to take. First, the economy is an open system, not just in the sense that it is dependent on natural and human resources that come from outside the system, but also in a theological sense: it depends on the "logic of the gift" embodied in Christian practice to be fully and authentically human. Catholic involvement in economic life, then, should take a distinctive form reflecting their religious commitments. Conversely, however, CST does not impose a fully-formed economic system of its own; that would simply be another form of "closed" system. Rather, and this is the second point, Christian economic practice acts as a catalyst of transformation in the economy. In ecological terms, it creates a "mutation," a change in the "organisms" that make up the system or in the environment they inhabit. These mutations can, in turn, lead to gradual changes in the overall system. Third, although global, structural factors certainly impact the economy, whether the economy ultimately serves authentic human development or becomes a system of oppression depends on human agency. And therefore, if CST is to have an impact, these agents need to be formed in a spiritual and ecclesial context.

Business Enterprises, Social Movements, and Church Organizations

If we think of the economy in ecological terms, then businesses, labor organizations, consumer advocacy groups, banks, and even social movements are the system's "organisms"—they inhabit the system, use up resources of various kinds, create their own "outputs," interact with each other, and in ways sometimes subtle, sometimes not, transform their habitat. Certain types of "organisms" gradually die off, while new forms take their place. The ecological vision of recent CST suggests that

---

Caritas in Veritate, 10–18. On "structures of sin," see John Paul II, *Sollicitudo Rei Socialis*, 36–37.

73. John Paul II, *Centesimus Annus*, no. 25.

Christian economic practices can be understood as new forms of life, or "mutations." Although most of these organisms are primarily focused on different forms of economic activity and only indirectly impact the economic habitat, social movements are formed specifically to change the habitat, to transform the institutions and structures in which economic activity takes place. To form Christians imbued with CST and equipped to form these new organizations and social movements, however, the Church will need to develop new types of associations and programs focused on this task.

Business Enterprises

Although still examining the economy in broad, even global terms, recent CST has increasingly focused on the individual business enterprise as one way that Catholics can transform economic life. For example, in *Centesimus Annus*, Pope John Paul II recognizes that profit is a legitimate goal for business enterprises. The problem is that business schools, at least traditionally, have taught that profit, or maximizing returns for shareholders, is the *only* real objective for a business. John Paul disagrees, arguing both that a business enterprise is a "community of persons" and is "at the service of the whole of society."[74] As a community of persons, a business enterprise has a responsibility to ensure that every employee is treated with dignity and respect and has an opportunity to participate in the governance of the enterprise. Business enterprises also have a responsibility to ensure that the goods or services they produce are not just meeting consumer demand, but truly contribute to authentic human development and the common good. Likewise, they should ensure that their work is conducted in an environmentally sustainable manner.

Pope Benedict XVI expands on these reflections on the business enterprise in *Caritas in Veritate*. He teaches that, "Today's international economic scene, marked by grave deviations and failures, requires a *profoundly new way of understanding business enterprise*." He then adds, "Old models are disappearing, but promising new ones are taking shape on the horizon."[75] Like John Paul, he affirms that a business enterprise is a community of persons and therefore the life of the enterprise should

---

74. John Paul II, *Centesimus Annus*, no. 35.
75. Benedict XVI, *Caritas in Veritate*, no. 40.

express the full range of human values rather than exclusively focusing on profits, a goal that can take different forms.[76]

The most direct way an enterprise can express this identity as a community of persons is as what Benedict calls "commercial entities based on mutualist principles,"[77] or cooperatives in which the workers have part or even full ownership of the company. Cooperatives have a long history in the Catholic social tradition, and as early as 1931, Pope Pius XI endorsed cooperatives, or what came to be called worker "co-determination," in which workers share in the ownership or management of the company, in his encyclical *Quadragesimo Anno*.[78] John Paul II likewise promoted similar structures in his 1981 encyclical *Laborem Exercens*, arguing that such participation best fulfills the workers' dignity as persons.[79]

Benedict considers other forms of enterprise, as well. For example, he describes business enterprises in which a certain percentage of profits are set aside to fund charitable foundations or to provide aid to developing nations. He cites the Economy of Communion movement, connected to the Focolare lay Catholic association, as an example of a network of such enterprises.[80] He also alludes to the notion of "corporate social responsibility," a term referring to a broad range of business practices focused on ethical governance and responsibility to the broader community, as another example of a new way of understanding business enterprise. Corporate social responsibility includes philanthropic activity, but also policies such as environmentally sustainable production, fair-trade practices, and ethical investing. Benedict suggests that these forms of business enterprise represent a "cross-fertilization" between the world of business and that of non-profits, or civil society.[81]

This focus on the business enterprise as a vehicle for living out Christian discipleship was reinforced during Pope Francis's pontificate by the release of the document *Vocation of the Business Leader: A Reflection* by the Pontifical Council for Justice and Peace (now the Dicastery for Integral Human Development) in 2014. The document insists that a Christian business leader lives out their faith not just in their private life,

---

76. Benedict XVI, *Caritas in Veritate*, no. 41.
77. Benedict XVI, *Caritas in Veritate*, no. 38.
78. Pius XI, *Quadragesimo Anno*, no. 65.
79. John Paul II, *Laborem Exercens*, nos. 14–15.
80. On the Economy of Communion movement, see Gold, *New Financial Horizons*.
81. Benedict XVI, *Caritas in Veritate*, no. 41.

but as someone who builds and shapes an organization.[82] In fact, one of the greatest dangers facing a Christian business leader is a "divided life," a split between one's faith and one's daily life, including one's work in business.[83] The document, therefore, sees business as a concrete way of putting faith into practice. It goes on to encourage business leaders to adopt many of the practices endorsed in the official documents of CST: treating employees and customers with dignity,[84] being mindful of how a business's goods and services contribute to the common good,[85] serving the needs of the poor,[86] and encouraging worker participation.[87] Interestingly, the document also examines some of the structural factors that make living out the Christian vocation of business challenging (and, as previously noted, that contributed to the decline of social Catholicism in earlier decades): the globalization of the economy,[88] new communications technologies,[89] and growing individualism and materialism.[90] Although these factors pose challenges, the documents insist that the principles of CST offer a practical response to them.[91]

The notion that social and economic change can be brought about through a variety of business strategies is also reflected in two initiatives of Pope Francis's pontificate. On the one hand, the Council for Inclusive Capitalism is a non-profit organization founded in partnership with the Vatican in 2020 that includes representatives from major corporations around the world—including Merck, DuPont, Bayer AG, Bank of America, BP, and Verizon—and from global non-profits. Members of the Council commit to implementing, and sharing with one another, corporate practices that reflect the Inclusive Capitalism Platform, which promotes global development, environmental sustainability, and ethical

---

82. Pontifical Council for Justice and Peace, *Vocation of the Business Leader*, nos. 7–8.
83. Pontifical Council for Justice and Peace, *Vocation of the Business Leader*, no. 10.
84. Pontifical Council for Justice and Peace, *Vocation of the Business Leader*, no. 30.
85. Pontifical Council for Justice and Peace, *Vocation of the Business Leader*, nos. 41–42.
86. Pontifical Council for Justice and Peace, *Vocation of the Business Leader*, no. 43.
87. Pontifical Council for Justice and Peace, *Vocation of the Business Leader*, no. 47.
88. Pontifical Council for Justice and Peace, *Vocation of the Business Leader*, nos. 8–19.
89. Pontifical Council for Justice and Peace, *Vocation of the Business Leader*, no. 20.
90. Pontifical Council for Justice and Peace, *Vocation of the Business Leader*, no. 24.
91. Pontifical Council for Justice and Peace, *Vocation of the Business Leader*, no. 26.

corporate governance.⁹² This initiative promotes positive change in the global economy through seeking to reform the dominant "organisms" in the economic ecosystem. On the other hand, in 2019, Pope Francis inaugurated the Economy of Francesco initiative, a movement that brings together young economists, entrepreneurs, and organizational leaders committed to living out CST in innovative ways through their businesses and non-profits. The movement holds annual meetings and provides online educational opportunities to participants.⁹³ The Economy of Francesco offers a more radical, and more explicitly Catholic, vision than could ever be implemented by BP or DuPont, but also lacks the Council's global influence.

Social Movements

One potential objection to this focus on new forms of business enterprise as a strategy for transforming the economy is that such small-scale activity will not be effective without changing the broader structures of the economy. In ecological terms, these new organisms, as wonderful as they may be in principle, are not adapted to the hostile environment of the global economy and will die out before they make a significant impact. There is no reason to assume, however, that worker cooperatives or companies that embody the spirit of the Economy of Francesco movement could not thrive in today's global economy, and there are many successful examples of such companies. Nevertheless, it is still important to bring about institutional and structural changes in the economy, both to create a more welcoming "habitat" for CST-inspired businesses and as a matter of economic justice. Advocating for these changes is the role of social movements.

Over the course of his pontificate, Pope Francis has given several addresses to the World Meeting of Popular Movements, a gathering of Catholic-affiliated social movements and non-profits from around the world that meets periodically in Rome and various other worldwide locations. In his 2015 address to these movements, given in Santa Cruz, Bolivia, Francis gave his most extensive remarks on the nature of social movements and their work.⁹⁴ First, he recognizes that social movements

92. See the Council for Inclusive Capitalism's website: https://www.inclusivecapitalism.com/.

93. See the Economy of Francesco website: https://francescoeconomy.org/.

94. Francis, "Address to the Second World Meeting."

emerge because people desire change: "We want change in our lives, in our neighborhoods, in our everyday reality."[95] Although the desire for change arises from the challenges of everyday life, people form social movements when they recognize that these challenges arise from institutions and structures that transcend the local: "We want a change which can affect the entire world, since global interdependence calls for global answers to local problems."[96] Social movements, therefore, give people broader reach in responding to economic and other social problems.

Francis is sensitive to the question of how people with little power, and who are often poor, can bring about such sweeping changes. He expresses hope, however, that it is such people, rather than the powerful, who will be the agents of justice: "The future of humanity does not lie solely in the hands of great leaders, the great powers and the elites. It is fundamentally in the hands of peoples and in their ability to organize."[97] He states that real social transformation is brought about through a gradual process rather than decisive action from a position of power; Francis compares the work of social movements to small seeds, planted by some, watered by others, and which others see sprout: "Each of us is just one part of a complex and differentiated whole, interacting in time."[98] He explains that the social movements can bring about change through their "ability to organize and carry out creative alternatives,"[99] creating new forms of economic and social life at the local level, but also through the "collaboration of governments, popular movements and other social forces."[100] In other words, he suggests that Catholic social movements should be willing to form networks with organizations that share similar goals, and even appropriate government agencies, to address structural problems. His image of social movements making up a "complex, differentiated whole" resonates with the ecological vision outlined earlier.

Within this complex, differentiated whole, social movements may take different forms regarding Catholic identity. Some social movements may adopt a distinctive Catholic identity, forming their members in the faith and explicitly working in accord with the principles of CST. In other cases, Catholic parishes or organizations may form interfaith networks

95. Francis, "Address to the Second World Meeting," 1.
96. Francis, "Address to the Second World Meeting," 1.
97. Francis, "Address to the Second World Meeting," 4.
98. Francis, "Address to the Second World Meeting," 2.
99. Francis, "Address to the Second World Meeting," 1.
100. Francis, "Address to the Second World Meeting," 3.

with other religious congregations or organizations, working toward common goals or promoting community organizing at the local level. In yet other cases, Catholics may participate in secular social movements. What unites these different forms of participation is being grounded in the life of the Church and sharing a commitment to live out the faith in the world.

Church Organizations

As many of the associations of social Catholicism unfortunately found out too late, that grounding is needed to sustain the life and identity of Catholic social movements. Today the Church must do more to encourage Catholics to link their faith with economic life and to engage in the forms of action outlined in the previous sections. The Church already has many of the tools needed for this endeavor but awaits creative leaders to help bring the faith into the economic sphere.

For example, the Church has an established tradition of forming communities and associations that provide spiritual formation to prepare Catholics for social action. As already noted, in the middle of the twentieth century, Catholic Action, particularly in its milieu-based form, organized Catholic workers in various industries to provide them faith formation and instruction in the principles of CST. In Latin America beginning in the 1960s, base ecclesial communities were formed among the poor, integrating the study of the Bible with discernment and practical action in response to the social, political, and economic challenges faced in daily life.[101] In more recent times, so-called "small faith communities" have become quite popular in the United States and elsewhere.[102] Although these communities are typically purely of a spiritual nature, they could be adapted to focus on integrating spirituality, CST, and practical reflection on the realities of economic life.

These communities could take a variety of forms. For example, drawing on elements of both Catholic Action and the base ecclesial communities, some could bring together workers from a particular sector, like retail and service, or include members devoted to a specific cause, such as promoting a living wage or improving sustainability practices for businesses. The communities could study the Scriptures or teachings of the Church and draw on them to reflect on their experiences or develop

---

101. See, for example, Dawson, "Origins and Character," 109–28.
102. Lee, *Catholic Experience*.

a practical course of action. Other organizations could, for example, bring together participants from the middle class and the working poor, hoping to build better understanding and solidarity while sharing their faith. These communities could be linked to a specific Catholic parish or sponsored by an interdenominational coalition of churches, depending on the context. These communities would serve their own, spiritual, purposes, but could also encourage the formation of other associations more actively involved in economic life. As with social movements, the Church needs a complex, differentiated network of communities like those envisioned here if social Catholicism is to have a future.

Conclusion

The age in which CST could be envisioned as proposing an alternative economic system to replace the neoliberal, capitalist system (or the communist system, for that matter) is over. If it is to thrive, social Catholicism in the twenty-first century will look quite different than it did in the twentieth. Pope Francis's ecological vision, building on earlier CST, provides a blueprint for how Catholics can think about the economic system and encourages Catholics to develop a variety of forms of business enterprise, social movements, and faith communities inspired by this vision, continuously evolving to respond to their environment, and networking with others across faiths to bring about institutional and structural change. In contrast to the arid individualist and profit-dominated vision of neoliberalism, contemporary CST offers a vibrant, organic, solidarity-based blueprint for economic life just waiting to be put into action.

Bibliography

Ahern, Kevin. *Structures of Grace: Catholic Organizations Serving the Common Good*. Maryknoll, NY: Orbis, 2015.

Annett, Anthony M. *Cathonomics: How Catholic Tradition Can Create a More Just Economy*. Washington, DC: Georgetown University Press, 2022.

Bell, Daniel. *The Cultural Contradictions of Capitalism*. New York: Basic, 1976.

Benedict XVI. *Caritas in Veritate: On Integral Development in Charity and Truth*. Vatican City State: Libreria Editrice Vaticana, 2009. https://www.vatican.va/content/benedict-xvi/en/encyclicals/documents/hf_ben-xvi_enc_20090629_caritas-in-veritate.html#_ednref112.

Berríos, Fernando, et al., eds. *Catolicismo social chileno: Desarrollo, crisis y actualidad*. Santiago: Centro Teológico Manuel Larraín, 2009.

Bovée, David S. *The Church & the Land: The National Catholic Rural Life Conference and American Society, 1923–2007*. Washington, DC: The Catholic University of America Press, 2010.

Cavanaugh, William T. *Field Hospital: The Church's Engagement with a Wounded World*. Grand Rapids: Eerdmans, 2016.

Costanza, Robert, et al. *An Introduction to Ecological Economics*. 2nd ed. Boca Raton, FL: CRC, 2015.

D'Antonio, William V., et al. *American Catholics: Gender, Generations, and Commitment*. Walnut Creek, CA: AltaMira, 2001.

Dawson, Andrew. "The Origins and Character of the Base Ecclesial Community: A Brazilian Perspective." In *The Cambridge Companion to Liberation Theology*, edited by Christopher Rowland, 109–28. New York: Cambridge University Press, 1999.

Duriez, Bruno. "Left Wing Catholicism in France: From Catholic Action to the Political Left: The *Mouvement Populaire des Familles*." In *Left Catholicism: Catholics and Society in Western Europe at the Point of Liberation, 1943–1955*, edited by Gerd-Rainer Horn and Emmanuel Gerard, 64–90. Leuven: Leuven University Press, 2001.

Ehrman, Terrence P. "Ecology: The Science of Interconnections." In *The Theological and Ecological Vision of Laudato Si'*, edited by Vincent J. Miller, 51–73. New York: Bloomsbury, 2017.

Esping-Andersen, Gøsta. *The Three Worlds of Welfare Capitalism*. Princeton: Princeton University Press, 1990.

Finn, Daniel K., ed. *Moral Agency within Social Structures and Culture: A Primer on Critical Realism for Christian Ethics*. Washington, DC: Georgetown University Press, 2020.

Fleet, Michael. *The Rise and Fall of Chilean Christian Democracy*. Princeton: Princeton University Press, 1985.

Francis. "Address to the Second World Meeting of Popular Movements." http://w2.vatican.va/content/francesco/en/speeches/2015/july/documents/papa-francesco_20150709_bolivia-movimenti-popolari.html.

———. *Fratelli Tutti: On Fraternity and Social Friendship*. Vatican City State: Libreria Editrice Vaticana, 2020. https://www.vatican.va/content/francesco/en/encyclicals/documents/papa-francesco_20201003_enciclica-fratelli-tutti.html.

———. *Laudato Si': On Care for Our Common Home*. Vatican City State: Libreria Editrice Vaticana, 2015. https://www.vatican.va/content/francesco/en/encyclicals/documents/papa-francesco_20150524_enciclica-laudato-si.html.

Fukuyama, Francis. *The End of History and the Last Man*. New York: Free, 1992.

Gold, Lorna. *New Financial Horizons: The Emergence of an Economy of Communion*. Hyde Park, NY: New City, 2010.

Griffiths, Richard T., and Toshiaki Tachibanaki. "From Austerity to Affluence: The Turning Point in Modern Societies." In *From Austerity to Affluence: The Transformation of the Socio-Economic Structure of Western Europe and Japan*, edited by Richard T. Griffiths and Toshiaki Tachibanaki, 1–24. New York: St. Martin's, 2000.

Hall, Peter A., and David Soskice, eds. *Varieties of Capitalism: The Institutional Foundations of Comparative Advantage*. New York: Oxford University Press, 2001.

Hanley, David, ed. *Christian Democracy in Europe: A Comparative Perspective.* London: Pinter, 1994.

Harvey, David. *A Brief History of Neoliberalism.* New York: Oxford University Press, 2007.

Hodgson, Geoffrey M. *Conceptualizing Capitalism: Institutions, Evolution, Future.* Chicago: University of Chicago Press, 2015.

———. *Economics in the Shadows of Darwin and Marx: Essays on Institutional and Evolutionary Themes.* Northampton, MA: Elgar, 2006.

———. *The Evolution of Institutional Economics: Agency, Structure, and Darwinism in American Institutionalism.* New York: Routledge, 2004.

Holland, Joe. *Modern Catholic Social Teaching: The Popes Confront the Modern Age, 1740–1958.* Mahwah, NJ: Paulist, 2003.

Hollenbach, David. "A Prophetic Church and the Catholic Sacramental Imagination." In *The Faith That Does Justice: Examining the Christian Sources for Social Change*, edited by John C. Haughey, 234–63. New York: Paulist, 1977.

John Paul II. *Centesimus Annus: On the Hundredth Anniversary of Rerum Novarum.* Vatican City State: Libreria Editrice Vaticana, 1991. https://www.vatican.va/content/john-paul-ii/en/encyclicals/documents/hf_jp-ii_enc_01051991_centesimus-annus.html.

———. *Laborem Exercens: On the Ninetieth Anniversary of Rerum Novarum.* Vatican City State: Libreria Editrice Vaticana, 1981. https://www.vatican.va/content/john-paul-ii/en/encyclicals/documents/hf_jp-ii_enc_14091981_laborem-exercens.html.

———. *Solicitudo Rei Socialis: On Social Concern.* Vatican City State: Libreria Editrice Vaticana, 1987. https://www.vatican.va/content/john-paul-ii/en/encyclicals/documents/hf_jp-ii_enc_30121987_sollicitudo-rei-socialis.html.

Kalyvas, Stathis N. *The Rise of Christian Democracy in Europe.* Ithaca, NY: Cornell University Press, 1996.

Kersbergen, Kees van. *Social Capitalism: A Study of Christian Democracy and the Welfare State.* New York: Routledge, 1995.

Kselman, Thomas, and Joseph A. Buttigieg, eds. *European Christian Democracy: Historical Legacies and Comparative Perspectives.* Notre Dame: University of Notre Dame Press, 2003.

Lawson, Tony. *Economics and Reality.* New York: Routledge, 1997.

———. *Reorienting Economics.* New York: Routledge, 2003.

Lee, Bernard J. *The Catholic Experience of Small Christian Communities.* Mahwah, NJ: Paulist, 2000.

Leo XIII. *Rerum Novarum: On Capital and Labor.* Vatican City: Libreria Editrice Vaticana, 1891. https://www.vatican.va/content/leo-xiii/en/encyclicals/documents/hf_l-xiii_enc_15051891_rerum-novarum.html.

McGreevy, John T. *Catholicism and American Freedom: A History.* New York: Norton, 2003.

McLeod, Hugh. "The Religious Crisis of the 1960s." *Journal of Modern European History* 3 (2005) 205–30.

McShane, Joseph M. *"Sufficiently Radical": Catholicism, Progressivism, and the Bishops' Program of 1919.* Washington, DC: Catholic University of America Press, 1986.

Mainwaring, Scott. *The Catholic Church and Politics in Brazil, 1916–1985.* Stanford: Stanford University Press, 1986.

Mainwaring, Scott, and Timothy R. Scully, eds. *Christian Democracy in Latin America: Electoral Competition and Regime Conflicts.* Stanford: Stanford University Press, 2003.

Marx, Karl, and Friedrich Engels. *The Communist Manifesto.* New York: Penguin, 2002.

Misner, Paul. *Catholic Labor Movements in Europe: Social Thought and Action, 1914–1965.* Washington, DC: The Catholic University of America Press, 2015.

———. *Social Catholicism in Europe: From the Onset of Industrialization to the First World War.* New York: Crossroad, 1991.

Paul VI. *Populorum Progressio.* Vatican City State: Libreria Editrice Vaticana, 1967. https://www.vatican.va/content/paul-vi/en/encyclicals/documents/hf_p-vi_enc_26031967_populorum.html.

Peet, Richard, and Elaine Hartwick. *Theories of Development: Contentions, Arguments, Alternatives.* New York: Guilford, 2009.

Pepper, Stephen. *World Hypotheses: A Study in Evidence.* Berkeley: University of California Press, 1942.

Pius XI. *Quadragesimo Anno.* Vatican City State: Libreria Editrice Vaticana, 1931. https://www.vatican.va/content/pius-xi/en/encyclicals/documents/hf_p-xi_enc_19310515_quadragesimo-anno.html.

Pontifical Council for Justice and Peace. *Vocation of the Business Leader: A Reflection.* Vatican City State: Libreria Editrice Vaticana, 2014. https://www.humandevelopment.va/content/dam/sviluppoumano/pubblicazioni-documenti/archivio/economia-e-finanza/vocation-of-business-leader/Vocation_ENGLISH_4th%20edition.pdf

Prentiss, Craig R. *Debating God's Economy: Social Justice in America on the Eve of Vatican II.* University Park, PA: Pennsylvania State University Press, 2008.

Rostow, W. W. *The Stages of Economic Growth: A Non-Communist Manifesto.* Cambridge: Cambridge University Press, 1960.

Seaton, Douglas P. *Catholics and Radicals: The Association of Catholic Trade Unionists and the American Labor Movement: From Depression to Cold War.* Lewisburg, PA: Bucknell University Press, 1981.

Shadle, Matthew A. *Interrupting Capitalism: Catholic Social Thought and the Economy.* New York: Oxford University Press, 2018.

Shadle, Matthew A. "Twenty Years of Interpreting *Centesimus Annus.*" *Journal of Catholic Social Thought* 9 (2012) 1–21.

Sinyai, Clayton. *Schools of Democracy: A Political History of the American Labor Movement.* Ithaca, NY: Cornell University Press, 2006.

Smith, Christian. *What Is a Person?* Chicago: University of Chicago Press, 2010.

US Department of Health and Human Services. "New Surgeon General Advisory Raises Alarm about the Devasting Impact of the Epidemic of Loneliness and Isolation in the United States." *HHS*, May 3, 2023. https://www.hhs.gov/about/news/2023/05/03/new-surgeon-general-advisory-raises-alarm-about-devastating-impact-epidemic-loneliness-isolation-united-states.html.

Verstraeten, Johan. "Re-thinking Catholic Social Thought as Tradition." In *Catholic Social Thought: Twilight or Renaissance?*, edited by Jonathan Boswell et al., 59–77. Louvain: Peeters, 2000.

22

Reimagining the World from the Peripheries

The Social Vision of Pope Francis

CLEMENS SEDMAK, UNIVERSITY OF NOTRE DAME

Abstract: This chapter offers a reflection on the social vision of Pope Francis, which it understands as the kind of community he wants to see. It proceeds in two steps. The first introduces Pope Francis' vision of Europe as an example of his political ethics. For Francis, Europe is both part of his personal heritage and a political entity with a rich history. This rich history leads to a humane politics offering a vision of peace and hope that can be a gift to all of humanity. In an age struggling with globalization, Europe is a test case to illustrate Francis' social vision. To the extent that Europe recovers its vital soul, which traces to the Gospel, it can advance the dignity of the human person, justice, freedom and solidarity. The second part discusses a central notion of Pope Francis' pontificate, the idea of going out from self and going to the "peripheries." This is what a Europe drawing upon its Christian soul will do, and what the Church will do anywhere she is in touch with her deepest sources of vitality. This section treats the fundamental commitment to the peripheries, the many kinds of them, and the way they shape the theological imagination.

Reimagining the World from the Peripheries—Sedmak

In his Pre-Conclave speech on March 9, 2013, then-Cardinal-Bergoglio expressed the invitation and the imperative to "go out to the peripheries:" "The Church is called to come out of herself and to go to the peripheries."[1] This idea of peripheries can be regarded as Pope Francis' social vision in a nutshell.

1 The Social Vision of Humane Politics: Pope Francis on Europe

During a meeting with representatives of civil society and the diplomatic corps as part of his apostolic journey to Portugal on August 2, 2023, Pope Francis remarked: "According to a debatable etymology, the name Europe derives from a word meaning the direction west. What is certain is that Lisbon is the most westerly capital of continental Europe and thus speaks to us of the need to open ever broader paths of encounter."[2]

The message here is twofold: (a) Pope Francis recognizes Lisbon as "peripheral" in a certain sense ("the most westerly capital of continental Europe) which gives it a special significance; (b) Pope Francis' social vision is based on openness and encounter, openness to encounters. This is a theme that runs through his pontificate.[3]

Pope Francis has probably paid less attention to matters European than his European predecessors John Paul II and Benedict XVI. But both his reflections on Europe and his travels to European countries send strong messages that help us understand key aspects of his political ethics. Pope Francis, whose father Mario Bergoglio had migrated to Argentina in the 1920s and whose mother Regina Maria Sivori had family roots in northern Italy, emphasized his family origins in a letter on Europe, addressed to the Secretary of State on the occasion of the fortieth anniversary of the Commission of the Bishops' Conferences of the European Community, the fiftieth anniversary of the establishment of diplomatic relations between the Holy See and the European Union, and the fiftieth anniversary of the presence of the Holy See as Permanent Observer at the Council of Europe. The letter is dated October 22, 2020, and contains the line that the European continent, "so dear to me, not only because of my family's origins but also because of the central role that it has had,

---

1. Akin, "Speech That Got Pope Francis Elected," no. 1.
2. Francis, "Address to Authorities," para. 5.
3. See Ejiowhor, "Pope Francis's Culture of Encounter," 185–208.

and, I believe, must continue to have, albeit with different accents, in the history of humanity."[4] In this way Pope Francis connects the personal and the political. Europe is significant on the micro-level of his personal roots, but also on the global macro-level because of its weight and responsibility. He has high expectations vis-à-vis Europe; he sees "the European vocation as one of committing, from her wealth of history, culture, civilization, solidarity, and interreligious dialogue, to provide a rich future vision for the whole of humanity. Pope Francis looks at Europe in the perspective of the global world."[5] This is a significant shift, "the transition from a German pope to an Argentinian pope, from a European to a Latin American, marked a paradigm shift. If the main horizon upon which the Ratzinger papacy operated was secularization and its many consequences, including the spread of relativistic thought, Francis's papacy is characterized above all by globalization, which he views above all from the viewpoint of the poorest. . . . What makes globalization so significant to the Pope's eyes is, first and foremost, as it is experienced by people who live outside Europe."[6] This view "from the outside" or "from the periphery" has shaped Pope Francis' moral and epistemological approach to Europe specifically, but also to social entities more generally. Europe is a good test case to illustrate the Pope's social vision.

Pope Francis has traveled to—what could be called—"the peripheries" of Europe, to countries like Albania (2014), Bosnia and Herzegovina (2015) Greece (2016, 2021), the Baltic states (2018), Bulgaria (2018), Romania (2018), Cyprus (2021), or Malta (2022). His first travel outside of Rome (July 8, 2013) led the Pope to Lampedusa, a place for migrants on their way from Africa to Europe. As an island at the geographical end and beginning of Europe Lampedusa stands for a peripheral place and first European refuge for peripheralized people. The visit says a lot about "Francis's attitude to Europe, where he firmly believes in welcoming refugees and migrants as a way of breathing new life into the Old Continent. Francis's first journey was a visit to a highly symbolic place."[7] In his

---

4. Francis, "Letter on Europe," para. 2.

5. Spadaro, "Gaze of Magellan," 332. Spadaro further suggests: "What is the vision for Europe of this non-European Pope? Bergoglio's gaze is a European gaze, because his roots are in Piedmont and his formation is radically European as well. He himself, in his discourse, recognises himself as a son 'who rediscovers in Mother Europe the roots of his life and faith.' But he is, at the same time, Argentinian and his experience of the Church is Latin American" (333).

6. Giovagnoli, "Francis," 458–59.

7. Giovagnoli, "Francis," 461.

homily in Lampedusa Pope Francis reflected on the question, "Where is your brother?" In a letter on the occasion of the tenth anniversary of his visit to Lampedusa Pope Francis (addressed to Archbishop Alessandro Damiano of Agrigento), Pope Francis repeats this question and underlines the commitment to the other members of the human family: "We must change our attitude; the brother who knocks at the door is worthy of love, hospitality and every care. He is a brother who, like me, has been placed on earth to enjoy what exists there and to share it in communion."[8]

By his travels he has highlighted places and people that are not normally counted among the most powerful. It is indicative that he spent his first Holy Thursday in a youth detention center washing the feet of young inmates.[9] During his Apostolic Journey to Romania he had a meeting with the Rom community on June 2, 2019 in Blaj and asked for forgiveness:

> My heart, however, is heavy. It is weighed down by the many experiences of discrimination, segregation and mistreatment experienced by your communities. History tells us that Christians too, including Catholics, are not strangers to such evil. I would like to ask your forgiveness for this. I ask forgiveness—in the name of the Church and of the Lord—and I ask forgiveness of you. For all those times in history when we have discriminated, mistreated or looked askance at you, with the look of Cain rather than that of Abel, and were unable to acknowledge you, to value you and to defend you in your uniqueness.[10]

The special concern with people in less fortunate circumstances is a characteristic of Pope Francis' pontificate and his social vision for Europe and the world. He has approached Europe from the peripheries.[11] At least four significant occasions stand out when reconstructing Pope Francis' vision of Europe. The first was his addresses to the Council of Europe and to the European Parliament on November 25, 2014. The second was his acceptance speech when receiving the Charlemagne Award on May 6, 2016. The third was his Address to the Heads of State and government of the European Union on the occasion of the celebration of the sixtieth anniversary of the Treaty of Rome on Friday, March 24, 2017.

---

8. Francis, "Letter on the Holy Father," para. 3.
9. See Pozza, "Una periferia difficile," 561–68.
10. Francis, "Meeting with the Rom Community," para. 2.
11. See Barbato, "Geopolitics of Papal Traveling," 1–18.

The fourth was his Address to the Commission of the Bishops' Conferences of the European Community on October 28, 2017. Additionally, and more recently, we could mention his address to the Participants in the Plenary Assembly of the Commission of the Bishops' Conferences of the European Union—on March 23, 2023—and his address during the meeting with authorities, civil society, and the diplomatic corps in Hungary on April 28, 2023.

I would like to draw the attention to two reference points Pope Francis uses to talk about Europe, and two key concepts.

1.1 Two Reference Points for "Europe"

In his address to the European Parliament in Strasbourg, France on November 25, 2014, Pope Francis used the much-quoted image of the grandmother, "no longer fertile and vibrant. As a result, the great ideas which once inspired Europe seem to have lost their attraction, only to be replaced by the bureaucratic technicalities of its institutions."[12] He is clearly concerned about the vitality of a social entity and the risk of sacrificing this vitality to social engineering and what he had called in *Laudato Si'* a technocratic paradigm.[13] He asked the same question in his Address to the Council of Europe on the same day of November 25, 2014: "To Europe we can put the question: 'Where is your vigour? Where is that idealism which inspired and ennobled your history? Where is your spirit of curiosity and enterprise? Where is your thirst for truth, a thirst which hitherto you have passionately shared with the world?'"[14]

In his acceptance speech in May 2016 when receiving the Charlemagne Award Pope Francis referred to the image of "Mother Europe:" "With mind and heart, with hope and without vain nostalgia, like a son who rediscovers in Mother Europe his roots of life and faith, I dream of a *new European humanism*."[15] Europe is challenged to renew itself. Interestingly enough, this point has been mentioned by Jacques LeGoff as a key characteristic of Europe—the ability to constantly renew itself.[16] The image of the grandmother indicates that Europe has lost this ability.

12. Francis, "Address to the Council of Europe."
13. Francis, *Laudato Si'*, nos. 101, 106–14.
14. Francis, "Address to the Council of Europe," para. 17.
15. Francis, "Address at Conferral of the Charlemagne Prize," para. 24.
16. LeGoff, *Birth of Europe*.

In the address in Lisbon in August 2023 mentioned at the very beginning of this article, Pope Francis recalled the treaty of Lisbon from 2007 and appealed to "a Europe capable of recovering its youthful heart," i.e., a vision of peace and hope. He even used the term "true Europe" ("the world needs Europe, the true Europe. It needs Europe's role as a bridge and peacemaker"). The true Europe has the ability of constant renewal—unlike a "grandmother." The image of the grandmother could remind us of the image of the 'deformed woman,' mentioned in Luke 13:10–17, who is unable to stand upright. Pope Francis evokes this image in his above-mentioned Pre-Conclave speech in connection with an inward-looking Church: "When the Church does not come out of herself to evangelize, she becomes self-referential and then gets sick."[17]

The parallel is obvious: an inward-looking Europe that is not open to the cry of the poor and the migrants, that develops into a fortress—is losing its vitality. In his address to the European Parliament in Strasbourg Pope Francis mentions the power of encounters:

> In Europe's present political situation, merely internal dialogue between the organizations (whether political, religious or cultural) to which one belongs, ends up being unproductive. Our times demand the ability to break out of the structures which "contain" our identity and to encounter others, for the sake of making that identity more solid and fruitful in the fraternal exchange of transversality. A Europe which can only dialogue with limited groups stops halfway; it needs that youthful spirit which can rise to the challenge of transversality.[18]

Transversality is a property that speaks to openness and disruption and the renewal that comes with that. In his pre-Conclave speech Cardinal Bergoglio characterized the pope as a man who "helps the Church to go out to the existential peripheries, that helps her to be the fruitful mother." The contrast between the image of the (fruitful) mother in the four minutes speech in March 2013 and the image of the (infertile) grandmother in the address in Strasbourg in 2014 is striking. It is, however, a bit surprising that the Pope suggests a negative message with the image of the grandmother, given his concern with the most disadvantaged, the elderly, the vulnerable. In 2021 he even instituted the World Day of Grandparents and Elderly (and entitled his message to the 2022

---

17. Akin, "Speech That Got Pope Francis Elected," no. 2.
18. Francis, "Address to the Council of Europe," para. 26.

World Day with the words from Psalm 92:15: "In old age they will still bear fruit").[19] Nonetheless, we see a clear message: the vision of a healthy social body is fertility and the ability to self-renewal.

The self-renewal depends largely on the roots. In the above-mentioned address to the European Parliament in Strasbourg the Pope draws on the Italian poet and priest Clemente Rebora (1885–1957) to invoke the image of the tree:

> In one of his poems . . . Rebora describes a poplar tree, its branches reaching up to the sky, buffeted by the wind, while its trunk remains firmly planted on deep roots sinking into the earth. In a certain sense, we can consider Europe in the light of this image. Throughout its history, Europe has always reached for the heights, aiming at new and ambitious goals, driven by an insatiable thirst for knowledge, development, progress, peace and unity. But the advance of thought, culture, and scientific discovery is entirely due to the solidity of the trunk and the depth of the roots which nourish it. Once those roots are lost, the trunk slowly withers from within and the branches—once flourishing and erect—bow to the earth and fall.[20]

The message from this image is related to the message from the grandmother-image in terms of the expectation of bearing fruit. But here the emphasis is more on the roots and the importance of memory as well as the stress on growth through a bold vision. In his address to the participants in the Plenary Assembly of the Commission of the Episcopates of the European Union (COMECE) on March 23, 2023, Pope Francis characterizes this bold vision by "the two great 'dreams' of Europe's founding fathers: the dream of unity and the dream of peace." He is particularly taken by the vision of Schuman, De Gasperi and Adenauer.[21]

The image of the tree points to organic growth as opposed to the above-mentioned temptation of social engineering as an expression of a "technocratic paradigm." The roots of Europe, according to Pope Francis, can be found in the complex history of Europe. This brings me to a second reference point Pope Francis provides for an understanding of

19. We can equally be surprised how the Pope treats the image of the "deformed woman" and we could ask the question whether the 'deformation' was constructed through social and cultural forces and whether the woman was a victim of circumstances beyond her control. Ironically, the woman referred to in Luke 13:10 is "on the peripheries" and clearly marginalized. See Gowler, *Limits of Radicalism*, 17–34.

20. Francis, "Address to the Council of Europe," para. 12.

21. Spadaro, "Gaze of Magellan," 335–36.

Europe. In his Charlemagne Award acceptance speech in May 2016 Pope Francis mentions Erich Przywara and his work *Idee Europa*—The Idea of Europe—which "challenges us to think of the city as a place where various instances and levels coexist. He was familiar with the reductionist tendency inherent in every attempt to rethink the social fabric."[22] Erich Przywara's text points to the complexity of Europe:

> For Przywara, the real idea of Europe is one that is open to the East. Europe has always been a crossroads, and its cultural development is unthinkable apart from what it has received—not only from ancient Greece (e.g., from Plato and Aristotle), but more importantly, as far as its Christian roots are concerned, from Asia Minor and Africa. And in this regard Przywara makes special mention of the North African theologies of Tertullian, Augustine, and Origen. An authentically European culture, therefore, will not be closed in on itself, but will actively go forth in dialogue.[23]

Przywara reconstructs the idea of a common good-oriented city that is bound together by a covenant rather than a sense of constant negotiating and re-negotiating.[24] The key idea is the unity based on something deeper than an endeavor to maximize one's advantages.

With a vision of Europe that is shaped by a sense of peripheries, "Przywara is critical of any form of 'Christian elite' who just 'escape into the region of some 'sacred separateness.'"[25] The call for the Church is a call "into the world," especially the margins. For Przywara, "following the example of Christ," the task of the Church is to go "outside the gate" (Heb. 13:12ff.) of one's own preserve and "wash the 'dirty feet' of a 'dirty world' on one's knees (Jn 13:1–14)." The similarity to Pope Francis is obvious.[26]

Here again we see the vision of a community that bears fruit through its openness and inclusivity, an openness based on encounters and service to the wider common good. In his address during the meeting with authorities, civil society, and the diplomatic corps in Hungary on April 28, 2023, Pope Francis described his vision of an open and inclusive community:

---

22. Francis, "Address at Conferral of Charlemagne Prize," para. 10.
23. Betz, "Francis, Przywara, and the Idea of Europe," para. 6.
24. Przywara, *Idee Europa*, 18–20.
25. Hikota, "Church as a Missionary Servant in the Godless World," 109.
26. Betz, "Francis, Przywara, and the Idea of Europe," para. 11.

> At this historical juncture, Europe is crucial, for thanks to its history, it represents the memory of humanity; in this sense, it is called to take up its proper role, which is to unite those far apart, to welcome other peoples and to refuse to consider anyone an eternal enemy. It is vital, then, to recover the European spirit: the excitement and vision of its founders, who were statesmen able to look beyond their own times, beyond national boundaries and immediate needs, and to generate forms of diplomacy capable of pursuing unity, not aggravating divisions.[27]

We can observe how a wide notion of a global common good is emerging that does not allow for a self-serving closeness that Pope Francis sees in attempts to build a European fortress. This becomes clear when we take a look at two key concepts Pope Francis uses when talking about Europe.

1.2 Two Key Concepts

The two key concepts I would like to mention are: multipolarity and "the soul of Europe."

"*Multipolarity*" is a term that points to the integration of peripheries. Pope Francis used the term to characterize the challenges of Europe in his address to the European Parliament in Strasbourg in 2014:

> To speak of European multipolarity is to speak of peoples which are born, grow and look to the future. The task of globalizing Europe's multipolarity cannot be conceived by appealing to the image of a sphere—in which all is equal and ordered, but proves reductive inasmuch as every point is equidistant from the centre—but rather, by the image of a polyhedron, in which the harmonic unity of the whole preserves the particularity of each of the parts. Today Europe is multipolar in its relationships and its intentions; it is impossible to imagine or to build Europe without fully taking into account this multipolar reality.[28]

The image of the polyhedron reflects Pope Francis's vision of overcoming the core/periphery divide.[29] A polyhedron overcomes the binary distinction between a center and margins, a core and a periphery—"in the

---

27. Francis, "Meeting in Hungary," no. 1.
28. Francis, "Address to the Council of Europe," para. 24.
29. Francis, *Evangelii Gaudium*, no. 236. See Cantalamessa and Williamson, "New Ecclesiology?," 442–54.

polyhedron there is coherence, there is unity, but there is also diversity, variety of positions, of culture, of identity."[30]

The vision of a discursive space and an experiential horizon beyond a center/periphery divide is Pope Francis's social vision:

> The image of a polyhedron can represent a society where differences coexist, complementing, enriching and reciprocally illuminating one another, even amid disagreements and reservations. Each of us can learn something from others. No one is useless and no one is expendable. This also means finding ways to include those on the peripheries of life. For they have another way of looking at things; they see aspects of reality that are invisible to the centres of power where weighty decisions are made.[31]

This is a vision of a decentered social and epistemological reality. There is a lot of theological work to do in order to reflect on the political, but also ecclesiological implications.

Before we inhabit a polyhedron we have to embrace many an exodus. Within the context of his Apostolic Journey to Lithuania, Latvia and Estonia Pope Francis addressed the "going out to the peripheries" in the Angelus of September 23, 2018 he used strong language, emphasizing we are called "to be the last of all and the servant of all; to go to the place where no one else wants to go, where no one travels, the furthest peripheries."[32]

Europe is not a space, but a process—in the spirit of Pope Francis' rule that time is greater than space.[33] Europe is a process which is characterized by three key skills—the skills to integrate, to dialogue, to generate.[34] Europe in its fertility is based on dialogue and the idea of "unity in diversity."[35] In his Address to the Commission of the Bishops' Conferences of the European Community of October 28, 2017, Pope Francis clarified the idea of an inclusive community based on dialogue:

> Today the whole of Europe, from the Atlantic to the Urals, from the North Pole to the Mediterranean, cannot miss the chance

30. Francis, "Address to Regional Journalistic Group," para. 3.
31. Francis, *Fratelli Tutti*, no. 215.
32. Francis, "Angelus Remarks," para. 3.
33. Francis, *Evangelii Gaudium*, nos. 222–25. See Pimentel, "Time Is Greater Than Space," 683–701.
34. Spadaro, "Gaze of Magellan," 336–38.
35. See Turkson, "Towards the Restored Europe," 11–18, 16.

to be first and foremost a place of candid and constructive dialogue, in which all participants share equal dignity. We are called to build a Europe in which we can meet and engage at every level, much as in the ancient *agorá*, the main square of the *polis*. The latter was not just a marketplace but also the nerve centre of political life, where laws were passed for the common good.[36]

We see the influence of the vision of Przywara and a deep understanding of unity, a kind of unity based on a holistic understanding of the person and reality. In the same address, Pope Francis made use of the notion of "integral human development." "A Europe that rediscovers itself as a community will surely be a *source of development* for herself and for the whole world. Development must be understood in the terms laid down by Blessed Paul VI." And then he quotes the famous characterization of "integral human development" from *Populorum Progressio*, no. 14.[37]

Integral human development includes integral social development and integral social development pays special attention to the margins and to the inner dimension.

This brings me to the notion of "*the soul of Europe.*" In his address to the European Parliament Pope Francis quoted an anonymous second-century author who wrote that "Christians are to the world what the soul is to the body,"[38] and he added the explanation: "The function of the soul is to support the body, to be its conscience and its historical memory. A two-thousand-year-old history links Europe and Christianity . . . This history, in large part, must still be written. It is our present and our future. It is our identity. Europe urgently needs to recover its true features in order to grow." The soul of Europe is clearly the Christian message in Pope Francis' view.[39] In his address to the Heads of State and government

---

36. Francis "Address to Bishops' Conferences of the European Community," para. 11.

37. Paul VI, Pope. *Populorum Progressio*, no. 14: "The development We speak of here cannot be restricted to economic growth alone. To be authentic, it must be well rounded; it must foster the development of each man and of the whole man."

38. Francis, "Address to the Commission of the Bishops' Conferences of the European Community," made the same point: "The author of the *Letter to Diognetus* states that 'what the soul is to the body, Christians are to the world' . . . In our day, Christians are called to revitalize Europe and to revive its conscience, not by occupying spaces—this would be proselytizing—but by generating processes . . . capable of awakening new energies in society" (para. 28).

39. And he sees the danger of denying these roots. Even though the language he chose was strong, it is not surprising that Pope Francis commented on the circulated idea to cancel Christmas in no unclear terms. Francis, "Press Conference on the Return Flight to Rome from Cyprus and Greece" observed: "It is an anachronism. This is what

of the European Union on the occasion of the celebration of the sixteith anniversary of the Treaty of Rome (Friday, March 24, 2017) Pope Francis claims that "at the origin of European civilization there is Christianity,"[40] (A. De Gasperi) without which the Western values of dignity, freedom and justice would prove largely incomprehensible.

One key term he reminds us of is the term "dignity." In his address to the European Parliament in Strasbourg Pope Francis emphasized the notion of a humanism centered on respect for human dignity:

> A Europe which is no longer open to the transcendent dimension of life is a Europe which risks slowly losing its own soul and that "humanistic spirit" which it still loves and defends. Taking as a starting point this opening to the transcendent, I would like to reaffirm the centrality of the human person, which otherwise is at the mercy of the whims and the powers of the moment. I consider to be fundamental not only the legacy that Christianity has offered in the past to the social and cultural formation of the continent, but above all the contribution which it desires to offer today, and in the future, to Europe's growth. This contribution does not represent a threat to the secularity of states or to the independence of the institutions of the European Union, but rather an enrichment. This is clear from the ideals which shaped Europe from the beginning, such as peace, subsidiarity and reciprocal solidarity, and a humanism centered on respect for the dignity of the human person.[41]

At the center of the vision of Europe is the idea of human dignity, as he underlined in his address to the Heads of State and government of the European Union on the occasion of the celebration of the sixtieth anniversary of the Treaty of Rome (Friday, March 24, 2017). Here, Pope Francis recalled the need for hope and enthusiasm which had shaped the days leading to the Treaty of Rome on March 25, 1957:

---

so many dictatorships have tried to do throughout history: think of Napoleon, think of the Nazi dictatorship and the Communist dictatorship. . . . It is a sort of watered-down 'laicity.' . . . It is something that historically has not worked. This makes me think of something that, speaking of the European Union, I believe is necessary. The European Union has to take in hand the ideals of the founding Fathers, which were ideals of unity, of greatness, and to be attentive not to open the door to forms of ideological colonization. This could end up dividing countries and lead to the failure of the European Union. The European Union must respect each country as it is internally structured, the variety of countries, and not seek to standardize."

40. Francis, "Address for the Celebration of the Treaty of Rome," para. 11.
41. Francis, "Address European Parliament," paras. 15–16.

"The founding fathers remind us that Europe is not a conglomeration of rules to obey, or a manual of protocols and procedures to follow. It is a way of life, a way of understanding man based on his transcendent and inalienable dignity, as something more than simply a sum of rights to defend or claims to advance."[42]

This commitment to human dignity leads to "the first element of European vitality,"[43] namely solidarity (that "gives rise to openness towards others."). Later he states that "affirming the centrality of man also means recovering the spirit of family, whereby each contributes freely to the common home in accordance with his or her own abilities and gifts." This attitude leads to concrete actions, "solidarity entails the awareness of being part of a single body, while at the same time involving a capacity on the part of each member to 'sympathize' with others and with the whole." In this sense, solidarity is connected to the common good—and an expression of "the soul of Europe" (as the value core, and the motivational center of the community).

Vitality is a sign that the soul of Europe is present and active. In his acceptance speech in May 2016 Pope Francis invoked the notion of "the soul of Europe: "Creativity, genius and a capacity for rebirth and renewal are part of the soul of Europe." He also observes that "resignation and weariness do not belong to the soul of Europe," and that "the soul of Europe is in fact greater than the present borders of the Union."

The notion of the soul of Europe is an invitation "to build a community fundamentally based on the Christian concept of the person. The essence of this idea was the recognition of 'transcendent dignity' in man as the foundation for the unity of Europeans and the functioning of their political and legal structures. As was the case with the initiators of the unification of Europe, Francis selected this aspect as the main thread in his reflection on the real potential of Europe and the need to return to what its spiritual unity is based upon. His reference to human dignity derived from God was also meant to emphasise the moral aspect of human nature."[44]

The most distinctive expression of the commitment to dignity and the common good is the commitment to peripheries. Pope Francis' social vision has to be approached through this lens as we have also seen in this approach to Europe.

42. Francis, "Address for the Celebration of the Treaty of Rome," para. 6.

43. All citations in this paragraph are from Francis, "Address for the Celebration of the Treaty of Rome."

44. Kozerska, "Pope Francis on Europe," 250.

2 The Vision of a Fundamental Commitment to Peripheries

In his Pre-Conclave Speech, Pope Francis used the idea of "peripheries" and the exhortation to "go out to the peripheries," as previously mentioned. The Pre-Conclave speech was most explicitly taken up in the Apostolic Exhortation *Evangelii Gaudium*, section 20, where he mentioned Abraham and the call to set out for a new land (Gen 12:1–3), the vocations of Moses and Jeremiah, and the invitation that "all of us are called to take part in this new missionary "going forth". Each Christian and every community must discern the path that the Lord points out, but all of us are asked to obey his call to go forth from our own comfort zone in order to reach all the "peripheries" in need of the light of the Gospel."[45]

Here, he connects the language of exodus and the language of peripheries; the peripheries can be associated with "a new land," even a "promised land" that makes the intentional move to the peripheries less of a sacrifice and more of the experience of gift and grace. The invitation to go forth from our comfort zones in order to reach the peripheries is a divine call, an imperative.[46] The appropriate response is obedience.

Pope Francis' social vision is the idea to go out to and to learn from and to grow in- the peripheries. We have seen the same dynamic in his dealings with Europe.

> His journeys as Pope on the European continent began from Lampedusa, 'Europe's gateway,' and therefore destination of a journey more European than Italian—and from Albania, a land in Europe that is not yet part of the European Union and has an Islamic majority. From these "peripheries," the Pope briefly rebounded, as it were, to the "centre," namely Strasbourg, to visit the European institutions; then he goes always towards the borders: Turkey, Bosnia-Herzegovina and Lesbos, other tragedy-laden "gates of Europe." . . . Mercy for Francis is expressed politically in freedom of movement. . . . He approaches Europe from her distant "periphery."[47]

---

45. Francis, *Evangelii Gaudium*, no. 20.

46. Interestingly enough, the "comfort zones" could also be doctrinal comfort zones; people can find themselves at the margins of established discourses: Scott, "Pope Francis and the Periphery," 1.

47. Spadaro, "Gaze of Magellan," 333.

The term 'peripheries' suggests a set power structure of a center and margins. It dates back to the 1950s when Raul Prebisch published a report for the United Nations Economic Commission for Latin America where he contrasted the (economically) developed center with the (economically) underdeveloped or even undeveloped periphery.[48] He consistently applied the model of a privileged center and an underprivileged periphery to his analysis of the Latin American economic context. He pointed to a connection between inequality and injustice in describing the dynamics of unequal exchange as the cause of a flow of surplus value from the periphery to the center. Urbanization and industrialization contribute to the widening gap (or, for that matter, the creation of) the core/periphery divide. This is probably Pope Francis' reference point when talking about peripheries, a message that is heard and perceived. His visit to Lesbos Island on April 16, 2016, for example, had a significant influence on European perceptions of migration.[49]

Pope Francis consistently works with the concepts of peripheries and margins—which calls for a new way of imaging a community: "Pope Francis' approach with regard to Europe currently involves pastoral support to the outskirts of the continent and a call for it to regroup in the centre.... Pope Francis is persistent in his pastoral and political decisions to favour small precarious countries on the periphery of Europe, where Catholics are a minority. By placing this emphasis on the Balkans, the man who urges his Church to come out and go towards those who are far away, also invites Europeans to become less Euro-centric."[50]

The focus on peripheries leads to a new way of seeing the world, but it has a price tag: the term comes with a normative implication, it is a power construct, a political construct that has the potential to exclude or create exclusionary practices of "othering" and "labeling."[51] That is

---

48. Prebisch, *Economic Development of Latin America*. Priebsch describes Latin America "as part of the periphery of the world economic system" (1) and laments the fact that not much has been written about economic growth and the peripheries (49); he outlines the reality of "the disequilibrium between incomes at the centres and the periphery" (6), mentions "the vulnerability of the periphery" (58) and the mission to increase the productivity at the peripheries (e.g., 10).

49. See Deiana et al., "Unexpected Influencer," 75–95.

50. Maillard, "Vatican's Outlook on Europe," 9.

51. See Lang et al., *Understanding Geographies of Polarization*. The point has also been suggested by Armondi, "Towards Geopolitical Reading of 'Periphery,'" 526, where she writes "Periphery as political construct . . . the role of state spatial-making in the process of constructing the narrative of peripherality of subnational territories, in national-territorial politics. It examines the concept of 'inner region' as it is employed

why the discourse on "peripheries" also comprises a discourse on the dynamics of peripheralization and the creation of peripheries. Within the discourse on peripheries certain problems have been identified with regard to peripheries research: the fuzzy language, an othering, simplified and negative discourse, the neglected heterogeneity and complexity of the (gendered, raced, classed) inequality within a peripheral context.[52] However, it seems that research into peripheries "is experiencing something of a renaissance or golden era at the current time."[53]

2.1 The Power of (Many Kinds of) Peripheries

There are many ways of defining "peripheries"—we can propose definitions based on income and income growth differentials, definitions based on economic structure, employment and population potentials, definitions based on welfare conditions, to name but a few. These are definitions that reflect the reality that economic activities tend to concentrate around some pivotal points. The level of development has a negative correlation with distance from a center. "The peripheries are associated with distance, difference, and dependence on external aid and the unfavorable phenomenon of marginalization and deprivation."[54]

We need to move from the center to the peripheries.[55] The Church "does not consider it a lost to go out to the peripheries or to change the usual perception when necessary."[56] This statement expresses the ("antiutilitarian") logic of the lost sheep, the logic of leaving everything behind to search for the lost one (cf. Matt 18:12). Peripheries ask us to make a choice. You can plan your life without being exposed to peripheries; this may be an expression of the "indifference" Pope Francis mentions on numerous occasions.[57] Many people can design their life in a way that it

---

in state spatial strategy focusing on territories that are 'locked' into a configuration outside the core, that is, territories that are peripheral and remote."

52. Pugh and Dubois, "Peripheries within Economic Geography," 267–75.

53. Pugh and Dubois, "Peripheries within Economic Geography," 267.

54. Klimczuk-Kochańska and Klimczuk, "Core-Periphery Model," 2.

55. Francis, "Address to Plenary Assembly of the Council of the Bishops' Conferences of Europe" referred to the central paragraph no. 20 of his *Evangelii Gaudium*: "As I wrote in the Apostolic Exhortation *Evangelii Gaudium*, we are called to be a Church which "goes forth," moving from the centre to the peripheries to go towards all, without fear and without diffidence, with apostolic courage."

56. Francis, "Message to Cardinal Sistach," para. 3.

57. See, for example, Francis, *Laudato Si'*, nos. 14, 25, 52, 92, 115, 232; Francis,

does not get in touch with peripheries. Losing touch with the peripheries means sacrificing learning opportunities. Pope Francis has repeatedly characterized the poor as those who can teach us important lessons that no one else can teach us.[58] People on the peripheries are agents, artisans of a new understanding of what matters.[59] He sees the peripheries as a place of learning and growth and spiritual enrichment. Peripheries ask us to make a choice—a choice very much in the spirit of a "preferential option for the poor."

In his homily for the Filipino community in the Vatican Basilica on December 15, 2019 the Pope identifies "the inhabitants of yesterday's and today's peripheries,"[60] as "vulnerable people . . . the oppressed, the hungry, the sojourners, the orphans and the widows" and refers to Psalm 146:7–9 where we read about the Lord "who executes justice for the oppressed; who gives food to the hungry. The Lord sets the prisoners free; the Lord opens the eyes of the blind. The Lord lifts up those who are bowed down; the Lord loves the righteous. The Lord watches over the strangers; he upholds the orphan and the widow." This reference does not only provide us with a clearer sense of what it means to be at the peripheries (to be powerless and dependent), it also alludes to the decentering of the center through God who establishes a new power structure and order. Those on the peripheries are those who are rejected by their communities and those who are at the center of the gospels.

Even though we have to choose to go out to the peripheries, the gospels themselves do not leave space for excuses. "According to the Gospel, an 'outgoing' Church is the only way. This is shown by the life of Jesus."[61] In his Address to Participants in the Fourth National Missionary Conference (November 22, 2014) Pope Francis makes this point again: "Jesus himself was a man from the periphery, from that Galilee far from the power centres of the Roman Empire and Jerusalem."

Fratelli Tutti, nos. 30, 57, 72, 73, 113, 199, 224.

58. Francis, *Evangelii Gaudium*, nos. 198–202. See also Sedmak, *Church of the Poor*; Eckholt, *Peripherie gehen*; see also Scott, "Francis and the Periphery," 3.

59. Dias, "Freire and Pope Francis on Dialogue," 91, explains that "a hallmark of Francis' papacy is a concern for the active place of the underprivileged, marginalized, and vulnerable in shaping policy, and action in their own history." Dias reconstructs parallels between Pope Francis and Paulo Freire's anticolonial approach to decenter the center.

60. Francis, "Holy Mass for the Filipino Community," para. 2.

61. Francis, "Message to the Participants in the Meeting for Friendship Among Peoples," said that "Nazareth was truly an insignificant village, a 'periphery'" (para. 4).

2.2 Peripheries and the Theological Imagination

Peripheries shape the imagination. Pope Francis believes that true transformation comes from the periphery. In an interview with Bernarda Llorente he quotes Amelia Podetti who said: "Europe saw the Universe when Magellan arrived at the South. That is, from the largest periphery, Europe understood herself. The periphery makes us understand the center. You may or may not agree, but if you want to know what the People feels, go to the periphery."[62]

When Pope Francis talks about peripheries he speaks about a space other than comfort zone and sphere of control. In an interview, quoted by Antonio Spadaro, the Pope paints a picture of the periphery as "the other place:" Normally we move in space that in one way or another we control.

> This is the center. In the measure in which we go out from the center and distance ourselves from it, we discover more things and, when we look at the center of these new things that we have discovered, new places, from these peripheries, we see that reality is different. One thing is to observe reality from the center and another to see it from the last place where you arrived. An example: Europe seen from Madrid in the 16th century was one thing; however, when Magellan arrives at the end of the American continent, he sees Europe from a new point reached and understands another thing.[63]

The focus on peripheries is an invitation to see the world in a new, fresh, invigorating way. The focus on peripheries is a moral commitment, and existential choice, and an epistemological option. In an interview with Antonio Spadaro Pope Francis expressed an epistemological conviction:

> I am convinced of one thing: the great changes in history were realized when reality was seen not from the center but rather from the periphery. It is a hermeneutical question: reality is understood only if it is looked at from the periphery, and not when our viewpoint is equidistant from everything. Truly to understand reality we need to move away from the central position of calmness and peacefulness and direct ourselves to peripheral areas. Being at the periphery helps to see and to understand

---

62. Llorente, "Interview [with] Pope Francis."
63. Spadaro, "Gaze of Magellan," 333.

better, to analyze reality more correctly, to shun centralism and ideological approaches.[64]

This resonates with another principle, Pope Francis had mentioned in *Evangelii Gaudium*: realities are more important than ideas.[65] The life realities of people on the margins say a lot about the center and the power structures, about inequality and injustice. The realities of the peripheries create a sense of urgency and fight the temptation of self-righteousness, be in society, in Europe, in the Church.

Pope Francis' vision of Europe is an illustration of his view of the Church as well—a body shaped by special attention to peripheries, by respect to multipolarity, and by dialogue and encounters. It is the vision of social processes, rather than social spaces. It is a reality-centered approach that cannot be implemented from offices and desks—through a "gray pragmatism" that is disillusioned with reality."[66] The "joy of the gospel" is very much where the gospels call us to move: at the peripheries.

Bibliography

Akin, Jimmy. "The 4-Minute Speech That Got Pope Francis Elected?" *Catholic Answers*, April 23, 2013. https://www.catholic.com/magazine/online-edition/the-4-minute-speech-that-got-pope-francis-elected.

Armondi, Simonetta. "Towards Geopolitical Reading of 'Periphery' in State Spatial Strategies: Concepts and Controversies." *Geopolitics* 27 (2020) 526–45.

Barbato, Mariano P. "Geopolitics of Papal Traveling: (Re)Constructing a Catholic Landscape in Europe." *Religions* 11 (2020) 1–18.

Betz, John. "Pope Francis, Erich Przywara, and the Idea of Europe." *First Things*, May 12, 2016. https://www.firstthings.com/web-exclusives/2016/05/pope-francis-erich-przywara-and-the-idea-of-europe.

Cantalamessa, Raniero, and M. Daigle Williamson. "The Ecumenism of the Polyhedron: A New Ecclesiology?" *Journal of Ecumenical Studies* 54 (2019) 442–54.

Dias, Darren. "Paulo Freire and Pope Francis on Dialogue: An Anticolonial Interpretation." *Espacio, Tiempo y Educación* 9 (2022) 83–98.

Deiana, Claudio, et al. "The Unexpected Influencer: Pope Francis and European Perceptions of the Recent Refugee Crisis." *Oxford Economic Papers* 75 (2023) 75–95.

Eckholt, Margit, ed. *An die Peripherie gehen: In den Spuren des armen Jesus—vom Zweiten Vatikanum zu Papst Franziskus*. Ostfildern: Grünewald, 2015.

---

64. Spadaro, "Wake up the World," 3–4.
65. Francis, *Evangelii Gaudium*, nos. 231–33.
66. See Francis, *Evangelii Gaudium*, no. 83.

Ejiowhor, M. "Pope Francis's Culture of Encounter as a Paradigm Shift in the Magisterium's Reception of Justice in the World: Implications for the Church's Social Mission?" *Journal of Catholic Social Thought* 18 (2021) 185–208.

Francis. "Address at the Conferral of the Charlemagne Prize." Vatican City State: Libreria Editrice Vaticana, 2016. https://www.vatican.va/content/francesco/en/speeches/2016/may/documents/papa-francesco_20160506_premio-carlo-magno.html.

———. "Address to Authorities, Civil Society and the Diplomatic Corps Lisbon Portugal." Vatican City State: Libreria Editrice Vaticana, 2023. https://www.vatican.va/content/francesco/en/speeches/2023/august/documents/20230802-portogallo-autorita.html.

———. "Address to the Commission of the Bishops' Conferences of the European Community." Vatican City State: Libreria Editrice Vaticana, 2017. https://www.vatican.va/content/francesco/en/speeches/2017/october/documents/papa-francesco_20171028_conferenza-comece.html.

———. "Address to the Council of Europe." Vatican City State: Libreria Editrice Vaticana, 2014. https://www.vatican.va/content/francesco/en/speeches/2014/november/documents/papa-francesco_20141125_strasburgo-consiglio-europa.html.

———. "Address to a Delegation of a Regional Journalistic Group of the RAI." Vatican City State: Libreria Editrice Vaticana, 2019. https://www.vatican.va/content/francesco/en/speeches/2019/september/documents/papa-francesco_20190916_giornalisti-rai.html.

———. "Address to the European Parliament." Vatican City State: Libreria Editrice Vaticana, 2014. https://www.vatican.va/content/francesco/en/speeches/2014/november/documents/papa-francesco_20141125_strasburgo-parlamento-europeo.html.

———. "Address to Heads of State and Government of European Union on 60th Anniversary of Treaty of Rome." Vatican City State: Libreria Editrice Vaticana, 2017. https://www.vatican.va/content/francesco/en/speeches/2017/march/documents/papa-francesco_20170324_capi-unione-europea.html.

———. "Address to Participants in the Plenary Assembly of the Council of the Bishops' Conferences of Europe." Vatican City State: Libreria Editrice Vaticana, 2017. https://www.vatican.va/content/francesco/en/speeches/2014/october/documents/papa-francesco_20141003_plenaria-conferenze-episcopali-europee.html.

———. "Angelus Remarks During Apostolic Journey to Lithuania, Latvia and Estonia." Vatican City State: Libreria Editrice Vaticana, 2018. https://www.vatican.va/content/francesco/en/angelus/2018/documents/papa-francesco_angelus-paesibaltici_20180923.html.

———. *Evangelii Gaudium: On the Proclamation of the Gospel in Today's World*. Vatican City State: Libreria Editrice Vaticana, 2013. https://www.vatican.va/content/francesco/en/apost_exhortations/documents/papa-francesco_esortazione-ap_20131124_evangelii-gaudium.html.

———. *Fratelli Tutti: On Fraternity and Social Friendship*. Vatican City State: Libreria Editrice Vaticana, 2020. https://www.vatican.va/content/francesco/en/encyclicals/documents/papa-francesco_20201003_enciclica-fratelli-tutti.html.

———. "Holy Mass for the Filipino Community: Omelia Del Santo Padre Francesco." Vatican City State: Libreria Editrice Vaticana, 2019. https://www.vatican.va/content/francesco/en/homilies/2019/documents/papa-francesco_20191215_omelia-comunitacattolica-filippina.html.

———. *Laudato Si': On Care for Our Common Home*. Vatican City State: Libreria Editrice Vaticana, 2015. https://www.vatican.va/content/francesco/en/encyclicals/documents/papa-francesco_20150524_enciclica-laudato-si.html.

———. "Letter of the Holy Father on the Occasion of the Tenth Anniversary of His Visit to Lampedusa." Vatican City State: Libreria Editrice Vaticana, 2023. https://www.vatican.va/content/francesco/en/letters/2023/documents/20230620-lettera-anniversario-visitalampedusa.html.

———. "Letter on Europe." Vatican City State: Libreria Editrice Vaticana, 2020. https://www.vatican.va/content/francesco/en/letters/2020/documents/papa-francesco_20201022_lettera-parolin-europa.html.

———. "Meeting with the Authorities, Civil Society and the Diplomatic Corps in Hungary." Vatican City State: Libreria Editrice Vaticana, 2023. https://www.vatican.va/content/francesco/en/speeches/2023/april/documents/20230428-ungheria-autorita.html.

———. "Meeting with the Rom Community." Vatican City State: Libreria Editrice Vaticana, 2019. https://www.vatican.va/content/francesco/en/speeches/2019/june/documents/papa-francesco_20190602_romania-comunita-rom.html."

———. "Message of Pope Francis to Cardinal Luís Martínez Sistach, Archbishop of Barcelona on the Occasion of the International Pastoral Congress on the World's Big Cities." Vatican City State: Libreria Editrice Vaticana, 2014. https://www.vatican.va/content/francesco/en/messages/pont-messages/2014/documents/papa-francesco_20141125_messaggio-pastorale-grandi-citta.html.

———. "Message of Pope Francis (signed by the Cardinal Secretary of State) to the Participants in the Meeting for Friendship among Peoples." Vatican City State: Libreria Editrice Vaticana, 2014. https://www.vatican.va/content/francesco/en/messages/pont-messages/2014/documents/papa-francesco_20140823_messaggio-meeting-amicizia-popoli.html.

———. "Press Conference of Pope Francis on the Return Flight to Rome from Cyprus and Greece." Vatican City State: Libreria Editrice Vaticana, 2021. https://www.vatican.va/content/francesco/en/speeches/2021/december/documents/20211206-grecia-volodiritorno.html.

Giovagnoli, Agostino. "Pope Francis: A New Way of Looking at the World." *Journal of Modern Italian Studies* 24 (2019) 456–67.

Gowler, David B. "The Limits of Radicalism: A Dialogical Response to 'Liberation' in Luke 13:10–17." In *Radical Christian Voices and Practice: Essays in Honour of Christopher Rowland*, edited by Zoe Bennett and David B. Gowler, 17–34. Oxford: Oxford University Press, 2012.

Hikota, Riyako Cecilia. "The Church as a Missionary Servant in the Godless World: Erich Przywara on the 'Holy Saturday' Form of the Church." *The Way* 59 (2020) 103–11.

Klimczuk-Kochańska, Magdalena, and Andrzej Klimczuk. "Core-Periphery Model." In *The Palgrave Encyclopedia of Global Security Studies*, edited by Scott N. Romaniuk et al., 1–8. Cham: Palgrave Macmillan 2019.

Kozerska, Ewa. "Pope Francis on Europe." In *The Right-Wing Critique of Europe*, edited by Joanna Sondel-Cedarmas and Francesco Berti, 245–60. New York: Routledge 2022.

Lang, Thilo, et al., eds. *Understanding Geographies of Polarization and Peripheralization: Perspectives from Central and Eastern Europe and Beyond*. London: Palgrave Macmillan 2015.

LeGoff, Jacques. *The Birth of Europe*. Translated by Janet Lloyd. Oxford: Blackwell 2005.

Llorente, Bernarda, "Interview [with] Pope Francis: We Do Not Come Out from a Crisis on Our Own—We Need to Take Risks and Take Each Other's Hand." https://www.telam.com.ar/pope-francis.

Maillard, Sébastien. "The Vatican's Outlook on Europe: From Firm Encouragement to Exacting Support." *Policy Paper* 135 (2015) 9. https://institutdelors.eu/wp-content/uploads/2020/08/vaticaneu-maillard-jdi-june15.pdf.

Paul VI. *Populorum Progressio*. Vatican City State: Libreria Editrice Vaticana, 1967. https://www.vatican.va/content/paul-vi/en/encyclicals/documents/hf_p-vi_enc_26031967_populorum.html.

Pimentel, Álvaro Mendonça. "Time Is Greater Than Space: The Principle of Social and Ecclesial Changes in Francis' Magisterium." *Perspectiva Teológica* 54 (2022) 683–701.

Pozza, Marco. "Una periferia difficile. La voce di Francesco dentro le carceri." *La Rivista del Clero Italiano* 7 (2014) 561–68.

Prebisch, Raul. *The Economic Development of Latin America and its Principal Problems*. Lake Succes, NY: United Nations Department of Economic Affairs, 1950.

Przywara, Erich. *Idee Europa*. Nuremberg: Glock und Lutz 1955.

Pugh, Rhiannon, and Alexandre Dubois. "Peripheries within Economic Geography: Four 'Problems' and the Road Ahead of Us." *Journal of Rural Studies* 87 (2021) 267–75.

Scott, Timothy. "Pope Francis and the Periphery." *CRC Bulletin* 11 (2014) 1–20.

Sedmak, Clemens. *Church of the Poor*. Maryknoll, NY: Orbis, 2016.

Spadaro, Antonio. "The Gaze of Magellan: Europe, Pope Francis, and the Charlemagne Prize." *Studies: An Irish Quarterly Review* 105 (2016) 331–41. https://www.cyberteologia.it/2016/05/the-gaze-of-magellan-pope-francis-european-dream/.

———. "Wake up the World: Conversation with Pope Francis about Religious Life." *La Civiltà Cattolica* 1 (2014) 3–17. https://onlineministries.creighton.edu/CollaborativeMinistry/PopeFrancis/Wake_up_the_world-2.pdf.

Turkson, Peter A. "Towards the Restored Europe. The Mission of the Church in Europe. The Vision of Europe from Pope John Paul II to Pope Francis." *Horyzonty Polityki* 10 (2019) 11–18.

23

Social Catholicism and Race

Rev. Martin Zielinski (†), University of St. Mary of the Lake / Mundelein Seminary

Abstract: This article provides a broad survey of Catholic teaching and action for racial justice in the United States, especially between the Second World War and 1970. It proceeds in seven sections beginning with the US Bishops' 2018 "Open Wide Our Hearts" in reflection upon the 2020 marches following the murder of George Floyd. The text sketches the development of Catholic Social Teaching in the United States on racism during these postwar decades, which reflected the ongoing influence of the first modern social encyclicals and their insistence on the dignity of every human person. On this basis, Catholics concerned with interracial justice worked to build a moral order reflecting not just social justice but also social charity. As social Catholicism entails the living out of our social doctrine, the essay naturally includes a discussion of some grass roots initiatives of social Catholics including dozens of interracial councils, education programs, a monthly journal, and broad collaboration to promote civil rights. It also discusses various diocesan efforts toward racial justice, which ranged from admirable to disappointing, due to both practical complexities and the persistence of racism in human hearts. At their best, Catholics were an important part of the civil rights movement, which helped to address some of the lingering effects of the Jim Crow era. At their worst, they were among the most strident segregationalists. In our contemporary situation marked by both old challenges regarding the ongoing legacy of slavery and new ones regarding today's outcast and vulnerable, Catholics will do well to understand their history so they can not only avoid the failings of the past but follow in the footsteps of those who confronted this evil and magnanimously labored for justice, human dignity and the solidarity of the human family.

I. Introduction

IN THEIR 2018 LETTER on racism, "Open Wide Our Hearts," the American bishops commented:

> With the positive changes that arose from the civil rights movement and related civil rights legislation, some may believe that racism is no longer a major affliction in our society—that it is only found in the hearts of individuals who can be dismissed as ignorant or unenlightened. But racism still profoundly affects our culture, and has no place in the Christian heart. This evil causes great harm to its victims, and it corrupts the souls of those who harbor racist or prejudicial thoughts. The persistence of the evils of racism is why we are writing this letter now. People are still being harmed so action is needed.[1]

The murder of George Floyd on May 25, 2020 provided further proof of the persistence of racism and the deadly harm it causes. More than one hundred years before "Open Wide Our Hearts" was published, W. E. B. Du Bois wrote in "The Forethought" to his book, *The Souls of Black Folks*, that "the problem of the Twentieth Century is the problem of the color line."[2] Subsequent events throughout the twentieth century have proved the accuracy of his statement. In our national efforts to address the issue of racism, many individuals and organizations have dedicated themselves to making the words of the Declaration of Independence a reality for all Americans. How has the Catholic Church in the United States contributed to these efforts? This article will examine some of the efforts of American Catholics to promote racial justice from the post-World War II era to 1970.

---

1. USCCB, "Open Wide Our Hearts," 6–7.
2. Du Bois, *Souls of Black Folks*.

II. Catholic Social Teaching on Racism[3]

The tradition of papal Catholic social teaching began with the 1891 encyclical *Rerum Novarum*. Pope Leo XIII lays out the rights and duties of employers and employees. One of the key duties of the employer is "not to look upon their work people as their bondsmen, but to respect in every man his dignity as a person ennobled by Christian character."[4] This concept of human dignity becomes the hallmark of Catholic social teaching. Regarding the issue of racism, one of the most thorough presentations on this topic prior to World War II was made by the prominent proponent for interracial justice Father John LaFarge, SJ.[5] His 1937 book, *Interracial Justice: A Study of the Doctrine of Race Relations*, became the Catholic primer on the topic Catholic teaching on race relations for more than twenty years. His essential thesis was "that interracial harmony is a positive construction in the moral order, not a mere adjustment of conflicting forces."[6] Using the 1931 encyclical of Pope Pius XI, *Quadragesimo Anno*, as a guide, LaFarge would argue that a true Christian social order is based on social justice and social charity.[7] The culmination of this argument appears in the conciliar document *Nostra Aetate*.[8]

Since few American Catholics at the time read LaFarge's book, the message for interracial justice needed other voices within the Catholic Church to propagate the idea. The united voices of the American hierarchy certainly could give gravitas to the message. Yet, between 1943 and 1958, only two statements were issued by the Administrative Board of the National Catholic Welfare Conference (NCWC)—predecessor to the subsequent National Conference of Catholic Bishops and current United

---

3. For an overview on American Catholics and Social Reform, see Piehl, "American Catholics and Social Reform," 332–39.

4. Leo XIII, *Rerum Novarum*, no. 20.

5. For a brief biography of LaFarge, see Hecht, "LaFarge." For a more extensive analysis of LaFarge's life and work, see LaFarge, *Manner Is Ordinary*; Hecht, *Unordinary Man*; Southern, *LaFarge and the Limits of Catholic Interracialism*. Hecht gives a sympathetic portrayal of LaFarge. The book by Southern is more critical of LaFarge.

6. LaFarge, *Interracial Justice*, vii.

7. LaFarge, *Interracial Justice*, viii.

8. In Paul VI, *Nostra Aetate*, no. 5 we read: "There is no basis therefore, either in theory on in practice for any discrimination between individual and individual, or between people and people arising either from human dignity or from the rights which flow from it. Therefore, the church reproves, as foreign to the mind of Christ, any discrimination against people or any harassment of them on the basis of their race, color, condition in life or religion" (cited in Flannery, *Sixteen Basic Documents*, 574).

States Conference of Catholic Bishops. In their 1943 letter, *Essentials of a Good Peace*, the Administrative Board of the NCWC was anticipating an Allied victory and the need to provide a vision for post-war social reconstruction. Near the end of the document, the members of the Administrative Board discussed the constitutional rights of the Black man.

> We owe to these fellow citizens, who have contributed so largely to the development of our country, and for whose welfare history imposes on us a special obligation of justice, to see that they have in fact the rights which are given them in our Constitution. This means not only political equality, but also fair economic and educational opportunities, a just share in public welfare projects, good housing without exploitation, and a full chance for the social advancement of their race. . . . In many of our great industrial centers acute racial tensions exist. It is the duty of every good citizen to do everything in his power to relieve them. To create a neighborhood spirit of justice and conciliation will be particularly helpful to this end.[9]

Given that Axis propagandists regularly pointed out the hypocrisy of the United States in claiming to fight for freedom and democracy while allowing segregation and racial inequality at home, the call for political and economic equality was promise that needed to be fulfilled. The reference to "acute racial tensions" in industrial centers was an implicit acknowledgement of how the recent migration of African Americans to Northern cities in search of jobs in the defense industries had created new challenges in the areas surrounding the defense industry plants. The American bishops provide no practical suggestions for how to accomplish these goals. They seemed to be relying on the goodwill of government and civic officials, as well as citizens to achieve these goals.

Fifteen years would pass before the American hierarchy wrote again about the matter of racial justice. In those intervening years, President Truman established the President's Committee on Civil Rights that recommended the desegregation of the United States military and federal employment. Two Presidential Executive Orders—9980 and 9981—made those recommendations legal. In 1954, the Supreme Court ruled in

---

9. Nolan, *Pastoral Letters*, 2:48. The members of the Administrative Board were Edward Mooney (Archbishop of Detroit), Samuel A. Stritch (Archbishop of Chicago), Francis J. Spellman (Archbishop of New York), John T. McNicholas (Archbishop of Cincinnati), Joseph F. Rummel (Archbishop of New Orleans), John J. Mitty (Archbishop of San Francisco), John F. Noll (Bishop of Fort Wayne), John Mark Glennon (Bishop of Erie), Karl J. Alter (Bishop of Toledo), and John A. Duffy (Bishop of Buffalo).

Brown v. Topeka that the doctrine of "separate but equal" no longer would apply in the field of education. The modern civil rights movement would begin when Rosa Parks refused to be seated in the "colored" section of a Montgomery bus. A year-long boycott of that public transportation system by African Americans brought integration to this means of public accommodation. The 1954 Supreme Court decision also unleashed an organized and violent reaction by many white groups to legal means to enforce integration.

In their 1958 statement, *Discrimination and Christian Conscience*, the American bishops noted "considerable progress was made in achieving these goals," namely those stated in the 1943 letter.[10] However, something had happened.

> Unfortunately, however, it appears that in recent years the issues have become confused and the march toward justice and equality has been slowed if not halted in some areas. The transcendent moral issues involved have become obscured, and possibly forgotten. . . . Our nation now stands divided by the problem of compulsory segregation of the races and the opposing demand for racial justice . . . But the time has come, in our considered and prayerful judgment, to cut through the maze of secondary or less essential issues and to come to the heart of the problem. . . . *The heart of the race question is a moral and religious one.*[11]

The bishops would go on to address the issue of personal differences among people. While recognizing some normal distinctions among people that may be subject to change, they stated: "it is unreasonable and injurious to the rights of others that a factor such as race, by and of itself, should be made a cause of discrimination and a basis for unequal treatment in our mutual relations."[12] They also said enforced segregation could not be reconciled with a Christian view since compulsory segregation "imposes a stigma of inferiority" and the historical records shows that segregation has led to "the denial of basic human rights."[13] As a guide to the future, the bishops offered the observation that "we may well deplore a gradualism that is merely a cloak for inaction. But we

---

10. Nolan, *Pastoral Letters*, 2:201.
11. Nolan, *Pastoral Letters*, 2:201–2; emphasis added.
12. Nolan, *Pastoral Letters*, 2:203.
13. Nolan, *Pastoral Letters*, 2:204.

equally deplore rash impetuosity that would sacrifice the achievements of decades in ill-timed and ill-considered ventures."[14]

The 1958 statement was more strongly worded than the 1943 one. It should have left no doubt in the minds of those Catholics who read the statement that one could not be considered a "Christian segregationist." These two episcopal statements represent the higher level of Church authority. However, much had been happening in these fifteen years at the grass roots of the American Catholic Church.

III. Grass Roots Initiatives in the Fight for Racial Justice

The most prominent Catholic group working to fight racial injustice in the post-World War II era was the Catholic Interracial Council of New York (CICNY). The organization was established in 1934.

> The object of the Council shall be to promote, in every practicable way, relations between races based on Christian principles, by creating a better understanding in the public as to the situation, needs and progress of the Negro group in America through the establishment of social justice and through practice of mutual cooperation.[15]

LaFarge and the other Catholic interracialist believed that one needed to recognize that interracial justice was a spiritual and moral issue and that this issue was connected to social justice. The group also connected the discussion of human rights with the American ideals of life, liberty, and the pursuit of happiness. The CICNY saw itself as part of the larger Catholic Action movement. The result was that the CICNY could promote itself as fully Catholic and fully American.[16]

In the years prior to the Second World War, the council concentrated on a program of education, especially at Catholic colleges in the

---

14. Nolan, *Pastoral Letters*, 2:205. The members of the Administrative Board of the NCWC were Francis Cardinal Spellman (Archbishop of New York), James Francis Cardinal McIntyre (Archbishop of Los Angeles), Francis P. Keogh (Archbishop of Baltimore), Karl J. Alter (Archbishop of Cincinnati), Joseph E. Ritter (Archbishop of St. Louis), William O. Brady (Archbishop of St. Paul), Albert G. Meyer (Archbishop of Chicago), Patrick A. O'Boyle (Archbishop of Washington), Leo Binz (Archbishop of Dubuque), Emmet M. Walsh (Bishop of Youngstown), Joseph M. Gilmore (Bishop of Helena), and Albert R. Zuroweste (Bishop of Belleville).

15. Quoted in Zielinski, "Working for Interracial Justice," 233–60.

16. Zielinski, "Working for Interracial Justice," 236–37.

New York and Philadelphia area. Through the publication of its monthly journal, *Interracial Review*, the council attempt to reach a wider audience to inform them about the principles of Catholic social teaching as related to interracial justice and to inform them about notable achievements of African Americans. Father LaFarge believed that most Americans did not hate African Americans but rather were ignorant about their history and concerns. This ignorance and apathy only could be overcome through various educational means.[17]

Although the council primarily concentrated its efforts to a Catholic audience, the group worked to establish connections with other interested organizations. The executive secretary of the CICNY, George Hunton, maintained regular contact with the National Urban League and the National Association for the Advancement of Colored People (NAACP). In 1955, he would be elected to the national board of the NAACP and become well informed on the plans and strategies of this organization at a critical time in civil rights history.[18]

With the outbreak of war in September 1939, the council shifted its efforts towards an important employment issue. Although the United States officially would not enter the conflict until December 8, 1941, the nation began to gear up its various defense industries. Too many defense plants in the New York area and around the country refused to hire qualified African Americans for work. The CICNY joined in the efforts with A. Philip Randolph, head of the Brotherhood of Sleeping Car Porters, and other civil rights leaders to end discrimination in the defense industries. Public pressure was directed on President Roosevelt to act. Only when a threatened March on Washington was organized did the President act. He established the Fair Employment Practices Commission to investigate the hiring practices in the defense industries. The issuing of Executive Order 8802 resulted in the postponement of the March on Washington.[19]

By the end of the Second World War, the CICNY had established a solid reputation among various civil rights organizations as a reliable

---

17. Zielinski, "Working for Interracial Justice," 236.

18. Zielinski, "George Hunton."

19. For the CICNY's involvement with the Fair Employment Practices movement, see Zielinski, "Working for Interracial Justice," 243–45. In 1943, A. Philip Randolph organized a National Council for a Permanent Fair Employment Practices Committee. George Hunton would serve on the executive committee of this organization.

For a more detailed account of the CICNY's efforts to promote a permanent committee, see Zielinski, "Doing the Truth," 338–84.

partner to promote the civil rights agenda. In the decade after the war, the CICNY would continue to support the establishment of a Permanent Fair Employment Practices Committee, participate in the Leadership Conference on Civil Rights, and support efforts for a civil rights bill which finally succeeded in 1957. In fact, George Hunton twice would testify before Senate subcommittees in favor of civil rights bills.[20]

As important as it was for the CICNY to network with other civil rights to demonstrate Catholic interest in the field, it was equally important for the council to work with other Catholic organizations. In the post-war era, this meant working with the Social Action Department of the National Catholic Welfare Conference (NCWC). On the initiative of the Social Action Department, George Hunton, as well as other members of Catholic interracial councils, were invited to participate in a two-day conference on social and economic problems of African Americans. One result was the recommendation that an advisory committee on black-white relations be established as part of the Social Action Department. Members of this committee met in Washington, DC, from July 2–5, 1946. Four committee reports dealing with economic life, civic rights, housing, and social work and health services were incorporated into a pamphlet published by the Social Action Department under the title of "Negro Problems in the Field of Social Action."[21]

Another Catholic group that the CICNY cooperated with was the Catholic Committee of the South which was formed in 1939.[22] The relationship between the two groups did not include any specific joint projects. Instead, it was more the matter of networking with Father LaFarge and George Hunton, attending some of the annual conventions of the Catholic Committee of the South, and publishing articles in the *Interracial Review* by key leaders of the committee. Unfortunately, the demise of the Catholic Committee of the South in 1956 limited the contributions of Catholic interracialists from the South in the aftermath of the *Brown v. Topeka* decision when massive white and Catholic resistance to integration might have been mitigated by leaders from the Catholic Committee of the South.

---

20. On the political involvement of the CICNY from 1952 to 1960, see Zielinski, "Doing the Truth," 385–427.

21. Zielinski, "Doing the Truth," 223–29.

22. For a history of this organization, see Martensen, "Catholic Committee of the South," 249–67.

One Catholic group that could have become an important ally in the promotion of interracial justice with the CICNY was the Knights of Columbus. Both Hunton and LaFarge were aware that some Knights councils in the New York area had begun to integrate in their local group. Still many African American candidates were discriminated against by the "blackball" voting process. By 1954, the Knights of Columbus had 594,000 members throughout all regions of the United States and in other nations.[23] The size, geographical diversity, and the parish-based connection made the Knights of Columbus a perfect group to help promote the principles of Catholic racial justice. In 1954, an application was made for the formation of an interracial Knights of Columbus council in Cleveland. After the application was rejected, an appeal was made to the Supreme Board of the Knights of Columbus. They rejected the appeal. The auxiliary bishop of Cleveland, Floyd Begin—a Fourth Degree Knight, was honored by the Knights at a local dinner. He used the occasion to denounce the decision of the Supreme Board for rejecting the application of an interracial council and criticized the practice of "blackballing" to reject members. The CICNY used editorials and articles in the *Interracial Review* to bring attention to this case. The group also corresponded with the Supreme Knight, Luke Hart, about having the Knights make a clear statement against discrimination. The problem here was that the Knights did not bar African Americans from the organization. There was nothing in their constitution that prohibited African Americans from joining. The difficulty was on the local level where notable cases of discrimination took place and made the news. What the CICNY and other supporters of interracial justice wanted was a clear statement from the Supreme Knight that the Knights of Columbus would not tolerate discrimination in its local councils. Between 1954 and 1964, the Supreme Knight, Luke Hart, faced a barrage of criticism from Catholic journalists, clerics, and bishops over the issue. In 1963, when a Chicago Knights of Columbus council rejected the application of Joseph Bertrand, a University of Notre Dame graduate and star athlete, the criticism reached new levels. Hart finally agreed that the matter would be discussed at the 1964 annual convention.[24]

The 1964 Knights of Columbus annual convention was held in New Orleans, but it would be a new Supreme Knight, John McDevitt, who

---

23. Kauffman, *Faith and Fraternalism*, 377.
24. Zielinski, "Doing the Truth," 234–36.

would oversee the discussion. This annual convention almost did not take place as the hotel where it was scheduled to be held informed the Knights that there was no African American would be allowed to stay at the hotel. Only when McDevitt threatened to move the whole convention and the Archbishop of New Orleans, John Cody, pressured the management was this restriction dropped. A resolution was adopted so that in order to reject an applicant one-third of the voting members of the council had to cast a negative vote rather than the previous practice of casting five blackballs.[25] This action was not the bold and unambiguous statement against discrimination that the CICNY would have hoped to have made. It was merely a satisfactory resolution to a decade-long controversy with one of the leading American Catholic organizations.

IV. Beyond Grass Roots Efforts

By 1960, there were thirty-five Catholic interracial councils in the United States. These councils needed the approval of their local ordinary for diocesan recognition. Although many of the councils looked to New York for some guidance and support, since that council was the premier one, would a national organization of interracial councils be able to accomplish more to promote interracial justice? In fact, this idea had been raised in the late 1940s and in the mid-1950s, but with no further action being taken. A more intentional effort to establish a national organization began in 1956 with discussion between leaders of the New York and Chicago councils. George Hunton from New York supported the idea of a national meeting as a means of providing a supportive environment for the local councils to discuss their experiences. On the other hand, Monsignor Dan Cantwell from Chicago believed that a national meeting should be a first step to establishing a national organization that would have a wider impact than the local councils.[26] After further discussions, planning, and fundraising, the decision was made to hold a national meeting of the Catholic Interracial Councils at Loyola University in Chicago beginning on August 28, 1958.

In his opening address, Father LaFarge called for the establishment of fifty new interracial councils around the country. Subsequent talks, panel discussion, and commission meetings discussed issues like

---

25. Kauffman, *Faith and Fraternalism*, 400–401.
26. Zielinski, "Doing the Truth," 141–42.

effective race relations, education, housing, employment, and parochial institutions. As with many meetings of this sort, resolutions were proposed and adopted by those attending. The opening paragraph of the first resolution said:

> As Catholics and as Americans, we acknowledge in a humble and contrite spirit our many individual and collective failures to fully implement the principles of Christian social justice and American democracy in regard to race relations.[27]

The final resolution called for the formation of an interim committee "to study the possibility of some form of closer association of the various Catholic Interracial Council."[28]

During 1959, two meetings of the interim committee were held in New York City and St. Louis. At the June 13–14 meeting in St. Louis, representatives approved the formation of the National Catholic Conference for Interracial Justice (NCCIJ). While emphasizing the autonomy of local councils, the new national organization would serve as a clearing house to assist the growth and development of the councils; articulate a philosophy for the Catholic interracial movement; represent the cause of interracial justice at national and international meetings; and hold a biennial meeting.[29] The NCCIJ became affiliated with the National Catholic Welfare Conference later that year as the Administrative Board of the NCWC passed a resolution on this.[30]

Two notable efforts of the NCCIJ were the planning, organization, and meeting of the 1963 National Conference on Religion and Race and organizing Catholic participation in the 1963 March on Washington. Regarding the first event, the idea for such a national conference had been proposed by Matthew Ahmann, executive directory of the NCCIJ, the previous year. The meeting opened on January 14, 1963, in Chicago. Some sixty-seven delegates representing various religious and civil rights groups were in attendance. The list of delegates represented a veritable "Who's Who" of the civil rights movement. Dr. Martin Luther King, Jr., Rev. Ralph Abernathy, and Rev. Fred Shuttlesworth of the Southern Christian Leadership conference were there. In addition to the host,

27. Quoted in Zielinski, "Doing the Truth," 157.
28. Zielinski, "Doing the Truth," 158.
29. Zielinski, "Doing the Truth," 165.
30. For more on the background of the relationship between the Chicago and New York councils and the formation of the NCCIJ, see Zielinski, "Doing the Truth," 139–68.

Albert Cardinal Meyer, prominent Catholic episcopal leaders included Archbishop Paul Hallinan (Atlanta) and Bishop Vincent Waters (Raleigh). Dr. Abraham Heschel (Jewish Theological Seminary) and Rabbi Seymour Cohen (Synagogue Council of America) added to the diversity of this ecumenical gathering. Members of the Southern Baptists, Hungarian Reformed Church, Lutheran Church, Quakers, Romanian Orthodox Church, Young Christian Mens' and Women's Association were present. This may have been one of the largest, most representative, and ecumenical gatherings on race in the history of the United States. In his opening address, Dr. King urged churches and synagogues to eliminate the roots of prejudice—fear—through education and to take the lead social reform. He thought this was a time for religious bodies to recapture a prophetic spirit.[31]

At the conclusion of the conference, the delegates unanimously adopted a declaration titled "An Appeal to the Conscience of the American People." In the first part of the appeal, racism was called "the most serious domestic evil." The Supreme Court decision against segregation was praised as were the non-violent protests of people against discriminatory practices. As the document noted "the fact that patterns of segregation remain entrenched everywhere" must be deplored.[32] The first part of the appeal ended with a note of repentance.

> We repent our failures and ask the forgiveness of God. We ask also the forgiveness of our brothers, whose rights we have ignored and whose dignity we have offended. We call for a renewed religious conscience on this basically moral evil.[33]

The second part of the document listed four challenges for the nation. Americans needed to seek a "reign of justice" in the areas of voting rights, open access to public accommodations, equal educational and employment opportunities, and open housing. The next challenge was to establish a "reign of love" and centered on the removal of racial obstacles so that past wounds do not become the cause of new ones. The third challenge was for people to seek a "reign of courage" whereby their faith would help them suffer for justice and love. The last challenge was

---

31. Zielinski, "Doing the Truth," 275–79.
32. Zielinski, "Doing the Truth," 281.
33. Zielinski, "Doing the Truth," 281.

a "reign of prayer" to the God who unites humanity as a family.[34] The "Appeal to the Conscience of the American People" concluded:

> We call upon all the American people to work, to pray and to act courageously in the cause of human equality and dignity while there is still time, to eliminate racism permanently and decisively, to seize the historic opportunity the Lord has given us for healing an ancient rupture in the human family, to do this for the glory of God.[35]

The second notable activity of the NCCIJ during 1963 was the March on Washington. At this event, Dr. King gave his famous "I Have a Dream Speech." 1963 was a very dramatic year in the history of the civil rights movement. A focus of attention during April and May 1963 was the city of Birmingham, Alabama. Dr. King had gone to that city to help lead public protests against segregation in the city. He was arrested on April 12, 1963 and spent his time in jail composing his famous "Letter from Birmingham Jail." Events escalated where hundreds of young students and children were arrested for marching. The city police decided to use fire hoses and police dogs to stop the marchers. The brutal scenes of police violence against the marchers shocked the nation. On May 12th, President Kennedy appeared on national television to promise federal aid to keep order and protect people. After Governor Wallace tried to prevent the enrollment of two African American students at the University of Alabama, President Kennedy again appeared on national television on June 11 to address the crisis. He noted that the issues of segregation and discrimination were not sectional, regional, or legislative issues but moral ones. This echoed the language in the American bishops 1958 statement on discrimination and conscience. Sadly, following this address a leader of the Mississippi NAACP, Medgar Evers, was murdered outside his home. When the President addressed Congress on June 19, he asked this legislative body to pass an omnibus civil rights bill that covered equal access to public accommodations, employment, and federal programs. Behind the scenes of these events, Matthew Ahmann of the NCCIJ was selected to be part of the organizing committee for the March on Washington that A. Philip Randolph and Bayard Ruskin announced earlier in the year.[36]

---

34. Zielinski, "Doing the Truth," 281–82.
35. Quoted in Zielinski, "Doing the Truth," 282.
36. Zielinski, "Doing the Truth," 244–48.

Prior to the actual event, Ahmann was active in getting visible Catholic support for the March on Washington. In July 1963, a letter of Cardinal Spellman was read in over four hundred New York parishes in support of interracial justice. That same month the executive board of the NCCIJ passed a statement calling for universal Catholic support of a civil rights bill as well as Catholic participation in the march. On the day of the March, Matthew Ahmann spoke to the estimated quarter million participants. He urged the audience to dedicate themselves to securing federal civil rights legislation. It is difficult to get an accurate number of Catholic who participated in this event, but photos show priests and nuns in attendance. Sitting on the dais in the front row was Father John LaFarge.[37] The Catholic interracial movement had come a long way since 1945 when it only was a diocesan based movement. It now had a national presence on the center stage of one of the most important civil rights events of the era.

V. Diocesan Efforts to Promote Racial Justice and Integration

The credibility of the American Catholic Church to promote racial justice needed specific action on the part of the bishops. If the concept of racial justice was more than theory, it needed to be practiced by Catholic institutions. Even prior to the 1954 *Brown v. Topeka* decision banning segregation, there were a few Catholic bishops that undertook the desegregation of Catholic schools in their dioceses.

In August 1947, Archbishop Joseph Ritter instructed his auxiliary, John Cody, to send a letter to the pastors of St. Louis stating that there would be no discrimination in parochial schools. Although organized resistance to the announcement came from Catholic laity, Archbishop Ritter threatened excommunication. When the dissidents sought to bring the matter to the Apostolic Delegate, Amleto Cicognani, he upheld Ritter's position.[38]

Another Southern bishop who took the lead in ending segregation in his diocese was Bishop Vincent Waters of Raleigh, North Carolina. In 1951, the bishop had issued a pastoral letter affirming the right of African

---

37. Zielinski, "Doing the Truth," 250–53.

38. For more on the history of the desegregation of Catholic schools in St. Louis, see Kemper, "Catholic Integration in St. Louis," 1–5. Prior to his appointment to St. Louis, Ritter had integrated the Catholic schools in Indianapolis.

American and white Catholics to worship together in any parish. Since Southern diocese accepted the "separate but equal" doctrine and had created separate parishes for African American Catholics, this new policy was ahead of even American judicial decisions. The implication of the pastoral letter took on greater importance in 1953 when Bishop Waters decided to merge the African American parish, St. Benedict, with the white parish, Holy Redeemer, in Newton Grove, North Carolina. Members of each parish were upset with the decision and met with Bishop Waters to present their views on the matter. On June 21, 1953, Bishop Waters had a letter read in all the parishes of the Diocese of Raleigh. It said:

> Therefore, so that in the future there can be no misunderstanding on the part of anyone, let me state here as emphatically as I can: There is no segregation of races to be tolerated in any Catholic Church in the Diocese of Raleigh. The pastors are charged with carrying out this teaching and shall tolerate nothing to the contrary.[39]

Bishop Waters would follow up his commitment to interracial justice by approving the formation of a Catholic Interracial Council in the Diocese of Raleigh. By 1959, there were four interracial councils in the diocese.[40]

One of the largest Catholic dioceses in the South was New Orleans. It also had one of the largest numbers of African American Catholics anywhere in the South. Under the leadership of Archbishop Joseph Rummel, the Archdiocese of New Orleans, had begun to address the issue of segregation in the early 1950s. He was opposed to segregated Catholic activities and the assigning of separate seats for African American Catholics in Catholic churches. When parishioners at the mission church in Jesuit Bend, Louisiana refused to allow an African American priest, Father Gerald Lewis, SVD, to say Mass, Rummel closed the mission church. In his 1956 pastoral letter on school desegregation, Archbishop Rummel clearly stated that racial segregation was morally wrong and sinful. His pastoral letter brought organized resistance from white Catholics who formed the Association of Catholic Laymen to oppose integration in Catholic schools.[41]

---

39. Quoted in Zielinski, "Doing the Truth," 209n78.

40. Zielinski, "Doing the Truth," 210–11.

41. For a history of desegregation efforts in New Orleans, see Rogers, "Humanity and Desire." For an account of the Jesuit Bend incident, see Ochs, "Deferred Mission," 519–28. For more on Catholic resistance, see Poche, "White Resistance in Post-War Louisiana," 47–68.

One form of resistance on the part of Catholics opposed to integration was the threat to withhold financial support for the Church. As a result, Archbishop Rummel decided to postpone the plans to integrate Catholic schools. He said that there was no change in his position, but he believed that further education on interracial justice was needed before moving forward. The delay would be for a year, and then when integration began it would be done one grade at a time. Unfortunately, even this postponement would last until 1962. The continuing opposition of the Association of Catholic Laymen resonated with some Catholics, especially as the group used newsletter to argue Rummel's plans for integration played into the hands of Communists.[42]

With the establishment of the Catholic Council on Human Relations in the Archdiocese of New Orleans in 1961 under Henry Cabirac, the plans for school desegregation moved forward.[43] When members of the Catholic Council on Human Relations met with the Archbishop in August 1961, they found him not as enthusiastic about desegregating the schools. Part of the reason may have been his declining health and age, but another reason Rummel was reluctant is that his superintendent of schools had not recommended any plans for desegregation. The superintendent, Monsignor Henry Bezou, expressed fears that if the Catholic schools undertook plans to desegregate then the state legislature might retaliate with legislation against Catholic institutions. After the meeting with the chancellor of the New Orleans Archdiocese, Monsignor Charles Plauche, who also served as the chaplain for the Catholic Council on Human Relations, Henry Cabirac, Monsignor Bezou, and a member of the Louisiana State Legislature, these concerns were alleviated. On March 27, 1962 Monsignor Henry Bezou announced that all Catholic schools in the Archdiocese of New Orleans would be open to any Catholic student. Anti-integrationist resistance continued and even three Catholic segregationists were excommunicated, the Catholics schools of New Orleans would be integrated.[44]

A final example of a Southern diocese dealing with the issue of integration and racial justice is Charleston. Between 1950 and 1974, the

---

42. Zielinski, "Doing the Truth," 200–203.

43. The Catholic Council on Human Relations was the Catholic Interracial Council of New Orleans by another name. The inclusion of the word "interracial" in its title would have too many negative connotations in this Southern city. The use of "human relations" was more acceptable.

44. Zielinski, "Doing the Truth," 204–6.

diocese undertook efforts to end segregation of Catholic organizations and institutions. In the early 1950s under Bishop John Russell, such Catholic organizations as Councils of Catholic Men, Women, and Youth and the Confraternity of Christian Doctrine had been integrated.[45] In September 1954, a Oratorian priest, Father Maurice Shean, desegregated St. Anne's parish school. It is difficult to tell from an article about this event how much Bishop Russell took the lead in this. The Oratorians had worked in African American parishes in the Diocese of Charleston for twenty years and were known for their pro-integration views.[46] The desegregation of St. Anne's was more by way of exception than the start of a diocesan wide effort to desegregate all the Catholic schools. Only under the leadership of a new bishop, Paul Hallinan, would the diocese make a more vigorous effort to desegregate Catholic schools and institutions. In the summer of 1959, Hallinan sent a letter to the priests of the diocese calling for a gradual plan of desegregation.[47]

One of the challenges for Bishop Hallinan was the fact that the religious order priests in the diocese staffed the African American parishes and the secular priests staffed the white parishes. Between the two groups of priests, there was little contact and communication. The result was that the diocesan priests showed little interest in the issue of integration. Hallinan tried to rectify this situation by sending them *An Elementary Catechism on the Morality of Segregation and Discrimination* in October 1960. It had been written by Bishop Albert Fletcher of Little Rock (Arkansas). The immorality of segregation was clearly stated in the pamphlet.[48] In the following year, Bishop Hallinan worked with Bishop Francis Hyland (Atlanta) and Bishop Thomas McDonough (Savannah) on a joint statement on racial issues. A decision was made to issue separate but identical letters. Hallinan's letter referred to the 1958 bishops' statement on discrimination. He also said that Catholic schools would admit African American students when it was safe to do so but not later than public schools. He also announced a program to explain Catholic teaching on racial justice through sermons, letters, and study groups.[49] Some opposition emerged when white Catholics formed the Organization of Catholic Parents with the goal of opening a Catholic

45. Newman, "Desegregation of the Diocese of Charleston," 29.
46. Newman, "Desegregation of the Diocese of Charleston," 29–30.
47. Newman, "Desegregation of the Diocese of Charleston," 32–33.
48. Newman, "Desegregation of the Diocese of Charleston," 34.
49. Newman, "Desegregation of the Diocese of Charleston," 36.

school for parents opposed to integration. In a written response, Bishop Hallinan informed members of that group that they would no longer be permitted to participate in Catholic activities beyond those of the sacramental life, and if they persisted in their opposition, they would be excommunicated.[50]

The process of integration in the Diocese of Charleston remained difficult under Hallinan's successor, Bishop Francis Reh. He found more support among the diocesan priests for his plans to integrate Catholic schools in 1964. However, a federal court decision ordered the city of Charleston to admit African American students. This federal decision actually forced a move up of the date of diocesan plans for integration to 1963.[51]

Yet, Catholic hospitals in the state of South Carolina continued to resist integration. Since these institutions were owned by religious orders, a bishop could only plead and cajole the hospitals to change their policies. Under Bishop Reh's successor, Bishop Ernest Unterkoefler greater progress would be made. Much of the pressure to integrate came because of complaints by the NAACP to the Department of Health, Welfare, and Education (HEW) that Saint Frances Xavier hospital violated clauses in the 1964 Civil Rights Act. Bishop Unterkoefler met with the administrators of the South Carolina Catholic hospitals who finally agreed to comply.[52]

In subsequent years, Bishop Unterkoefler had to oversee the compliance of the Diocese of Charleston with a 1966 HEW mandate that required Catholic schools to be in compliance with non-discrimination practices to be eligible for federal funds. This meant not only in the enrollment of students but also in the composition of the faculty. As he discovered in February 1967 survey, twenty-three of the forty Catholic schools had desegregated, but only three of the forty had more than token integration. He also found out that only nine of the Catholic schools had begun to integrate their faculty. When he reported to the US Commissioner of Education in April 1967, the bishop reaffirmed the desire of the diocese to receive federal funds. He pointed out that integration of white schools was progressing, but that only two of ten African American schools had desegregated. The reasons for this were the strong attachment of African American Catholics to their own African American parishes and schools and the reluctance of white parents to send their children to

50. Newman, "Desegregation of the Diocese of Charleston," 37.
51. Newman, "Desegregation of the Diocese of Charleston," 39.
52. Newman, "Desegregation of the Diocese of Charleston," 41.

predominantly African American schools. HEW accepted these reasons but wanted regular reports on the progress of desegregation.[53]

One practice that resulted from white resistance to school integration was that some parents sought to enroll their children in Catholic schools to avoid attendance in integrated public schools. Bishop Unterkoefler announced in 1970 that Catholics schools would not admit students whose parents were seeking to evade school desegregation.[54]

As historian, Mark Newman, concluded in his article on desegregation in the Diocese of Charleston:

> Despite more than a decade in trying to desegregate its schools and promote white Catholic acceptance, the diocese's efforts largely brought tokenism. Aware that white Catholics, like most other whites in South Carolina, preferred segregation, Catholic bishops had tied the pace of parochial school desegregation to public school desegregation, yet in both school systems, white resistance significantly limited change. The church's hierarchical polity, which in theory enabled a bishop to desegregate Catholic institutions, often proved ineffective, because many white Catholics adopted covert resistance by relocating to different neighborhoods, churches, and schools or by making blacks feel unwelcome in ostensibly desegregated institutions. . . . Federal pressure also was crucial in stimulating Bishop Unterkoefler's efforts to move school desegregation beyond tokenism but these foundered on the unwillingness of many white Catholics to accept significant desegregation. Even if Unterkoefler had acted earlier and more forcefully, it seems unlikely that the outcome would have been any different given the tide of white resistance he encountered in the Diocese of Charleston.[55]

Would the situation and reactions be any different in a Northern diocese? For reasons of space, only one Northern diocese will be considered, the Archdiocese of Chicago.[56] Unlike Southern dioceses where Jim Crow laws required the establishment of separate parishes for African American Catholics, most bishops in Northern dioceses followed a

---

53. Newman, "Desegregation of the Diocese of Charleston," 44.
54. Newman, "Desegregation of the Diocese of Charleston," 46.
55. Newman, "Desegregation of the Diocese of Charleston," 49.
56. The choice of Chicago is purely personal as the author is a priest of that Archdiocese and has served in African American parishes during his priesthood. For the most thorough treatment of integration in Northern diocese, see McGreevy, *Parish Boundaries*.

practice from the nineteenth century of establishing African American parishes on the model of national parishes for immigrant groups. Northern bishops also recruited religious orders such as the Josephites, Society of the Divine Word Fathers and others to minister to African American Catholics. What had been a good pastoral practice for European immigrants in the 19th century often led to de facto segregation of African American Catholics in Northern dioceses. White pastors who were reluctant or opposed to having African American Catholics attending their parishes simply would tell them that they had their own churches to attend.[57]

The end of World War II brought numerous social, political, and demographic changes to American society. In Chicago, the African American population grew by sixty-five percent between 1950 and 1960 to 813,000.[58] The traditional African American neighborhoods did not have a sufficient amount of adequate housing for this population. The post-war era also saw the growth of new suburbs around Chicago. African Americans desired to both reside in these areas as well as various neighborhoods in Chicago.

Archbishop Samuel Stritch had to face the issue of racial discrimination in archdiocesan parishes, schools, hospitals, and Catholic organization. His attitude on racial matters has been described as "laissez-faire" and reluctant "to attack racial discrimination in his archdiocese then only under the pressure of demographic, social, and political events."[59] Although not progressive on racial issue, Cardinal Stritch did allow a Catholic Interracial Council to be established in the archdiocese in 1945. Some shift in Stritch's attitude on racial issues seems to have occurred between 1943 and 1945 as the result complaints by a woman about the admission of an African American student to a Catholic school. Stritch believed that the refusal to admit the student would be a violation of Christian charity. By 1945, Cardinal Stritch allowed African American Catholic students to attend any Catholic school in the Archdiocese of Chicago. He did not make a public statement about this, but dealt with the issue on a case-by-case basis in correspondence with the pastor concerned.[60]

When it came to the matter of integration of Catholic hospitals, the Archbishop of Chicago took a more forceful stand. There were over

57. Avella, *This Confident Church*, 251–53.
58. Avella, *This Confident Church*, 251.
59. Avella, *This Confident Church*, 254–55.
60. Avella, *This Confident Church*, 259–61.

twenty Catholic hospitals in the Archdiocese of Chicago after World War II. Most were owned by religious orders that remained free to establish admission policies that excluded African Americans. Through the Archdiocesan Catholic Hospital Council, the Archbishop tried to affect a change in admission policy. He only succeeded with two hospitals—Mercy and Lewis. Most of the Catholic hospitals in Chicago continued to set their own admission policies. At a 1955 conference on the issue of race and Catholic hospitals, Cardinal Stritch did make a strong statement against discrimination. However, archdiocesan-wide change in admission policies only came after Chicago city ordinance in 1956 prohibited racial exclusion.[61]

Cardinal Stritch was less vocal when it came to integrated housing. Between 1946 and 1957, there were six outbreaks of violence to protest integrated public housing in the Chicago area. African American Catholics, moving into this housing, planned to attend local Catholic parishes. All these protests had Catholic participants opposing the project. In some instances, Catholic clergy also approved of the actions of lay Catholics.[62] Despite the efforts of members of the Chicago Catholic Interracial Council to help mitigate the violence by meeting with local pastors, only once did Cardinal Stritch take direct action. The suburb of Cicero was the site of racial violence in 1951 that made international headlines and required that assistance of the Illinois National Guard to restore order. Cardinal Stritch, stung by the bad press and upset by the violence, sent a letter to all the pastors in the area requiring them to preach on racial justice.[63]

Although Cardinal Stritch often was reluctant to speak out on matters of racial justice, he did have an auxiliary bishop, Bernard Sheil, who was less so. On a practical level, Bishop Sheil promoted interracial contact through his Catholic Youth Organization (CYO) which had been founded in 1930. The purpose of the CYO was to help reduce juvenile delinquency and provide positive and healthy activities for youth, especially during the Depression years. From the very start, African American youth from St. Elizabeth, St. Anselm, and Corpus Christi parishes participated in sports, summer camps, and educational events sponsored by the CYO. As an auxiliary bishop, Sheil would speak out against housing discrimination and racial injustice. Although Sheil's involvement with the CYO would terminate in 1954, the CYO gave thousands of Chicago

61. Avella, *This Confident Church*, 276–81.
62. Avella, *This Confident Church*, 264–72.
63. Avella, *This Confident Church*, 268.

Catholic youths the practical experience of interracial contact with one another for more than two decades.[64]

A new direction in racial justice took place with the departure of Cardinal Stritch to Rome and the arrival of Archbishop Albert Meyer, formerly of Milwaukee. In his first Lenten in 1959 pastoral letter, the new archbishop referred to the 1958 statement on discrimination and conscience. He said:

> I would like to emphasize the teaching of this statement, and to urge all of you to study it carefully and prayerfully, so that you may fully understand and realize in the practical conduct of your lives that "the heart of the race question is moral and religious. It concerns the rights of man and our attitude toward our fellow man.[65]

The archbishop would follow up the Lenten pastoral with a statement to the Presidential Commission on Civil Rights when the group held hearings in Chicago. With the help of a well-known Chicago activist priest, John Egan, a statement was drafted and edited by Meyer. Egan gave testimony before the commission and condemned, in Meyer's name, the residential segregation in Chicago. His opposition to residential segregation had a very practical example in 1959. In the norther suburb of Deerfield, a new integrated housing development was being built. Again, local residents opposed integrated housing. The local pastor refused to support the efforts of other religious leaders in the area to accept this integrated housing development. Although a clerical supporter of integration, Father Dan Cantwell, asked the archbishop to intervene with the pastor, Meyer relied on Cantwell to handle the matter. The North Shore chapter of the Catholic Interracial Council worked with other like-minded citizens to change the minds of Deerfield Catholics. This opposition, along with other delays, caused the builder to drop the project.[66]

If the actions of Archbishop Meyer were timid in the Deerfield integrated housing case, he was more forceful the following year in addressing integration of Catholic high schools. The recently created cardinal hosted a clergy conference on September 20–21, 1960, at Resurrection parish on Chicago's West Side. In his address to the Chicago priests, he said:

---

64. For a fuller treatment of the CYO's efforts in interracial relations, see Neary, "Crossing Parochial Boundaries," 23–37.

65. Quoted in Avella, *This Confident Church*, 299.

66. Avella, *This Confident Church*, 301–3.

> We must remove from the Church on the local scene any possible taint of racial discrimination or racial segregation from the whole community. . . . Every Catholic child of the Negro race . . . must have as free access to our schools as any other Catholic child on all levels of our academic training, elementary and secondary, as well as higher levels.[67]

No clearer statement had ever been made by any Archbishop of Chicago. In addition to all levels of schools, Cardinal Meyer wanted fraternal, parish organizations, and hospitals to be integrated.

It would be good to report that a new era of race relations developed after this 1960 clergy conference on race. However, in the next couple of years new racial tensions arose as the city of Skokie faced housing integration and the Lake Michigan beach, Rainbow Beach, on the South Side of Chicago became the site of conflicts between whites and African Americans wanting to integrate that beach. Most serious was the reactions of white Catholics to the 1966 march in Marquette Park by Dr. Martin Luther King Jr. and others to protest housing discrimination and segregation in the Southwest side of Chicago. During the march, one of the few African American Catholic priests of Chicago was dragged from his car and beaten. A religious sister had a brick thrown at her head. Dr. King later would comment that he had never seen such hate in Mississippi or Alabama.[68]

In a recent article, Matthew J. Cressler, details the reaction of self-described "good and sincere" Chicago Catholics to these integration efforts from 1965 to 1968. His primary source in the Archives of the Archdiocese of Chicago are over six hundred letters found in boxes labelled "Race Mail." All express the opposition of "good and sincere" Chicago Catholics to have integration forced on them. Some letters invoke the example of activist priests and nuns who erode obedience for law and order. Some of the writers claimed that forcing Catholics to accept integration was a form of totalitarianism like fascism or communism. Other writers argued that they were the "real" Catholics and those who supported integration were not genuine Catholics.[69] The overall impression is that support for racial justice seems to have made little headway in the Archdiocese of Chicago in the post-World War II era.

---

67. Quoted in Avella, *This Confident Church*, 307–8.

68. Avella, *This Confident Church*, 308–10. Also see Cressler, "White Catholicism," 273–306.

69. Cressler, "White Catholicism," 273–306.

VI. Catholic Media

In an earlier section of this article, the writings of Father John LaFarge were mentioned as a means to teaching racial justice. Along with his numerous publications, the journal of the Catholic Interracial Council of New York, *Interracial Review*, was another means to do so. Although the *Interracial Review* was found in numerous Catholic seminaries, colleges, and universities, it reached a limited audience. For most Catholics in the pews, another means to learn about interracial justice was through pamphlets found in the racks at the back of their church.

Between World War II and the early 1960s, Catholic publishers did produce a number of pamphlets addressing the issues of racial justice and racism. For example, the publisher, The Queen's Work, produced six pamphlets between 1941 and 1962 addressing such topics as "Fifty Ways to Improve Race Relations: Helping to Erase Race Heresy" in 1951 and "To a Christian Segregationist" in 1962.[70] Both Ave Maria Press and Liguori Press published some pamphlets in 1955 and 1957.[71] Generally, the writers would offer a critique of racism from theological, philosophical, social, economic, political, and historical perspectives. Included in the pamphlets would be practical suggestions to overcome discrimination and racism. The detrimental impact of segregation in the Catholic Church also was discussed.[72]

Some of the standard arguments against discrimination included the idea that discrimination was a violation of Church teaching in regard to the unity of the human family, the dignity of the person, and the oneness of Christians in the Mystical Body of Christ. The myth of racial superiority was attacked on scientific grounds of biology and physiology. Controversial topics such as interracial marriage and housing were discussed.[73]

Some opponents to these pamphlets—especially foes of Frank Riley's *Fifty Ways to Improve Race Relations*—believed his work promoted communist views. The major objection was that a list of recommended readings in the pamphlet included works of Communist sympathizers. Given the heightened anxiety of the McCarthy era, this charge could hurt

---

70. Anderson, "Pamphleteering against Race Prejudice," 3.
71. Anderson, "Pamphleteering against Race Prejudice," 4.
72. Anderson, "Pamphleteering against Race Prejudice," 4–6.
73. Anderson, "Pamphleteering against Race Prejudice," 9–13.

the credibility of the pamphlet.[74] Another controversial pamphlet was the 1962 work—"To a Christian Segregationist"—by the Jesuit Harold Cooper. It was published at the time when the Archdiocese of New Orleans was beginning to desegregate its schools. The format was a conversation between a Christian segregationist and Christian interracialist. The purpose was to show the contradiction between being a segregationist and claiming to be a Christian.[75]

One fact that is not clear from the article on Catholic pamphleteering is the number of pamphlets produced by Catholic publishers. These publishers clearly targeted the Catholics in the pews to educate them on racial discrimination and racial justice. How many Catholics in the pews actually took them is not clear. "Pamphleteering against prejudice informed the conscience. What was yet to be seen was whether or not it changed the heart."[76]

VII. Conclusions

This chapter has shown that American Catholic social teaching on race has historical roots that precede World War II. The issues of discrimination, segregation, and racial justice took on increased importance for American Catholics after the end of the war. Although the American bishops only issued two statements on these topics between 1943 and 1958, grass roots Catholic organizations such as the Catholic Interracial Councils and the Catholic Committee of the South worked to educate American Catholics on interracial justice and affect change within the Church and society. The Catholic Church in the South was impeded in its efforts to promote racial justice prior to 1954 by the Jim Crow laws. Even so, a few Southern bishops initiated efforts to integrate Catholic schools and organization. After the *Brown v. Topeka* decision by the Supreme Court, the pace of integration increased. So also did the strength of white Catholic resistance. The success in Northern Catholic dioceses was not dramatically better as the example from the Archdiocese of Chicago shows.

Catholics interested in interracial justice were not lacking. Bishops willing to make changes and clearly articulate Catholic teaching on

---

74. Anderson, "Pamphleteering against Race Prejudice," 15–18.
75. Anderson, "Pamphleteering against Race Prejudice," 21–25.
76. Anderson, "Pamphleteering against Race Prejudice," 26.

race discrimination were not absent. Support for racial justice from the Catholic media was available for Catholics in the pews. Are we left with the conclusion that the American Catholic Church failed to successfully educate her members on interracial justice? Massive white resistance to these efforts would seem to indicate that. That may be the easy answer.

Between 1945 and 1965, many "baby boomer" Catholics were educated in educational institutions that not only had desegregated but also included instruction on interracial justice. Many of these boomers then attended not only Catholic colleges and universities but secular and state schools with a more integrated student body. As they entered the work force and settled down in various neighborhoods and suburbs, they encountered other integrated environments. Unlike their parents or grandparents, these Catholics simply had more experience of an integrated American society.

The late 1960s and early 1970s did see a rise in urban riots as African Americans protested the economic and housing inequalities still evident in American society. The Black Power movement challenged the whole approach of Catholic interracialists. Yet, it is hard to imagine that any American Catholic in the 1970s was unaware of where the Catholic Church stood on racism, discrimination and segregation.

The insidious and destructive nature of racism in American society has been evident over the last six decades. Many believed that the passage of the 1964 Civil Rights Act and the 1965 Voting Rights Act had achieved all that was necessary for racial justice. These were a starting point to help build a just society. With the influx of Hispanic, Asian, and African immigrants in the last decade of the twentieth century and the first decade of the twenty-first century, American society has faced another challenge to promote racial justice.

American Catholics—bishops, clergy, religious, and lay—need to remain vigilant to how racism continues to manifest its evil in the Church and society. The multiple resources of the institutional Church certainly can help to address current forms of racism. The difficult task of conversion, not so much of mind, but of heart remains a challenge. We also have our spiritual resources to help. Despite evidence often to the contrary, Catholics believe that grace can change nature.

Bibliography

Anderson, R. Bentley. "Pamphleteering against Race Prejudice: The Catholic Press Attacks Jim Crow in Twentieth-Century America." *American Catholic Studies* 120 (2009) 3.

Avella, Steven M. *This Confident Church: Catholic Leadership and Life in Chicago, 1940–1965*. Notre Dame: University of Notre Dame Press, 1992.

Cressler, Matthew J. "'Real Good and Sincere Catholics': White Catholicism and Massive Resistance to Desegregation in Chicago: 1965–1968." *Religion and American Culture: A Journal of Interpretation* 30 (2020) 273–306.

Du Bois, W. E. B. *The Souls of Black Folk*. https://www.gutenberg.org/files/408/408-h/408-h.htm.

Flannery, Austin, ed. *Vatican II: The Sixteen Basic Documents*. Northport, NY: Costello, 1996.

Hecht, Robert A. "LaFarge, John." In *The Encyclopedia of American Catholic History*, edited by Michael Glazier and Thomas J. Shelley. Collegeville, MN: Liturgical, 1997.

———. *An Unordinary Man: A Life of Father John LaFarge, SJ*. Lanham, MD: Scarecrow, 1996.

Kauffman, Christopher J. *Faith and Fraternalism: The History of the Knights of Columbus, 1882–1982*. New York: Harper & Row, 1982.

Kemper, Donald J. "Catholic Integration in St. Louis, 1935–1947." *Missouri Historical Review* 73 (1978) 1–5.

LaFarge, John. *Interracial Justice: A Study of the Catholic Doctrine of Race Relations*. New York: American, 1937.

———. *The Manner is Ordinary*. New York: Harcourt, Brace, and Company, 1954.

Leo XIII. *Rerum Novarum: On Capital and Labor*. Vatican City: Libreria Editrice Vaticana, 1891. https://www.vatican.va/content/leo-xiii/en/encyclicals/documents/hf_l-xiii_enc_15051891_rerum-novarum.html.

Martensen, Katherine. "Region, Religion, and Social Action: The Catholic Committee of the South, 1939–1956." *Catholic Historical Review* 68 (1982) 249–67.

McGreevy, John T. *Parish Boundaries: The Catholic Encounter with Race in the Twentieth-Century Urban North*. Chicago: University of Chicago Press, 1996.

Neary, Timothy B. "Crossing Parochial Boundaries: Interracialism in Chicago's Catholic Youth Organization, 1930–1954." *American Catholic Studies* 114 (2003) 23–37.

Newman, Mark. "Desegregation of the Diocese of Charleston, 1950–1970." *The South Carolina Historical Magazine* 112 (2011) 29.

Nolan, Hugh, ed. *Pastoral Letters of the United States Catholic Bishops*. Vol. 2. Washington, DC: United States Catholic Conference, 1984.

Ochs, Stephen J. "Deferred Mission: The Josephites and the Struggle for Black Catholic Priests, 1871–1960." PhD diss., University of Maryland, 1985.

Paul VI. *Nostra Aetate: On the Relation of the Church to Non-Christian Religions*. Vatican City State: Libreria Editrice Vaticana, 1965. https://www.vatican.va/archive/hist_councils/ii_vatican_council/documents/vat-ii_decl_19651028_nostra-aetate_en.html.

Piehl, Mel. "American Catholics and Social Reform, 1789–1989." In *Perspectives on the American Catholic Church*, edited by Stephen J. Vicchio and Virginia Geiger, 332–39. Westminster, MD: Christian Classics, 1989.

Poche, Justin D. "The Catholic Citizens' Council: Religion and White Resistance in Post-War Louisiana." *US Catholic Historian* 24 (2006) 47–68.

Rogers, Kim Lacy. "Humanity and Desire: Civil Rights Leaders and the Desegregation of New Orleans, 1954–1966." PhD diss., University of Minnesota, 1982.

Southern, David W. *John LaFarge and the Limits of Catholic Interracialism, 1911–1963.* Baton Rouge: Louisiana State University Press, 1996.

United States Catholic Conference of Bishops. "Open Wide Our Hearts." https://www.usccb.org/issues-and-action/human-life-and-dignity/racism/upload/open-wide-our-hearts.pdf.

Zielinski, Martin A. "'Doing the Truth': The Catholic Interracial Council of New York, 1945–1965." PhD diss., The Catholic University of America, 1989.

———. "George Hunton." In *The Encyclopedia of American Catholic History*, edited by Michael Glazier and Thomas J. Shelley. Collegeville, MN: Liturgical, 1997.

———. "Working for Interracial Justice: The Catholic Interracial Council of New York, 1934–1964." *US Catholic Historian* 7 (1988) 233–60.

24

Mediating the Common Good
Social Movements in the Ecology of Social Catholicism

KEVIN AHERN, MANHATTAN COLLEGE

Abstract: For more than a century, social movements and social movement organizations have played a critical role in the development, articulation, and implementation of official Catholic social teaching. Time and again, they have proven to be essential components in making the principles of the church's social doctrine a reality. Nevertheless, their role and importance in the life of the church remains underappreciated and overlooked. Drawing from several examples, this paper situates the role of Catholic social movements and movement organizations in the wider ecology of social Catholicism. The paper begins with an examination of the relationship of social movements, broadly defined, with the church. The second part looks more specifically at the roles played by Catholic social movements and proposes a typology of four main forms. In the third and final part, this paper examines the mediating role of these collective agents within a wider ecology of social Catholicism. A more integral or ecological approach to ecclesiology, it argues, is needed to better understand and illuminate the work of these movements in the church and in society.

AT THE SECOND WORLD Meeting of Popular Movements in 2015, Pope Francis concluded his address with an impassioned call to action. "The future of humanity," he insisted, "does not lie solely in the hands of great leaders, the great powers and the elites. It is fundamentally in the hands of peoples and in their ability to organize." The pope here offers an important, yet often overlooked, insight for social Catholicism. Social movements, social movement organizations, and other collectives are critical elements in the just transformation of society. In other words, social movements are essential components in making the principles of Catholic social doctrine a reality.

Nevertheless, social movements, including Catholic social movements, are often overlooked in the study and promotion of Catholic social teaching.[1] Academic courses and media coverage of the church's social engagement tend to focus on the robust documentary heritage of papal encyclicals, the latest pronouncement by a pope, the work of inspiring individuals, the dynamics of robust institutional ministries, and the scholarly research of theologians. What is often missing is attention to the influence of what Gordon Zahn described as "Catholic social teaching from below," that is, the insights and experiences of Catholic social movements.[2]

Drawing from several examples, this paper situates the role of Catholic social movements and movement organizations in the wider ecology of social Catholicism. While imperfect, these collectives, operating with a range of forms and missions, serve as mediating forces in the development, articulation, implementation, and, sometimes, even the transgression of official Catholic social teaching. A more robust understanding of the role played by social movements can help scholars, church officials, and movement leaders better understand the challenge of enacting the vision of social Catholicism in the world today. But first, what are social movements and Catholic social movements in particular?

Social Movements and the Church

From the labor movement in the 1930s to the contemporary Black Lives Matter movement, social movements shape the contours of our public

---

1. Notable exceptions include Krier Mich, *Catholic Social Teaching and Movements*; Hinze, *Practices of Dialogue in the Roman Catholic Church*; Nepstad, *Catholic Social Activism*.

2. Zahn, "Social Movements and Catholic Social Thought," 43–54.

discourse. By their very nature, they are dynamic, fluid, and difficult to define. While people have long joined together in purposeful collectives, the term "movement" arose only in the seventeenth century, later evolving with the rise of the nation state, capitalism, communism, and the urban working class.[3] The role of social movements in the anti-establishment revolutions of the early modern period deeply shaped the way scholars first described the phenomena.[4] As such, scholarly attention is often on the role of movements working for or against change outside of established institutional channels.[5]

According to one definition dating from the 1960s, a social movement "is a purposive and collective attempt of a number of people to change individuals or societal institutions and structures."[6] Movements arise when people or preexisting groups come together for a common cause, usually with the goal of "seeking or halting change."[7] Not all social movements will agree on what change is or is not needed. They may even form in opposition to each other, as with the pro-life and pro-choice movements that have dominated American politics for decades.

Social movements may coalesce around charismatic individuals or arise organically. They can be focused on a specific issue, a specific class or people, or have a broad agenda. Movements, as David Hollenbach, SJ, writes, "empower people. They mediate between individuals and large social structures, giving the individuals who work together in the movement greater power to bring about social change than they could have alone."[8] Unlike robust established structures, movements allow for "degrees of participation," as members with varying levels of dedication and commitment to the cause surround a core group of militants.[9]

To achieve their ends, social movements often, but not always, create one or more *social movement organization* or SMO. These can include national networks with large budgets, international structures with

---

3. Buechler, *Social Movements in Advanced Capitalism*, 5. See also Melloni, "Movements" in the Church.

4. See Hannigan, "Social Movement Theory and the Sociology of Religion."

5. Snow et al, "Mapping the Terrain."

6. Zald and Ash, "Social Movement Organizations: Growth, Decay and Change," 329. See also Smith et al., "Social Movements and World Politics."

7. Snow et al., "Mapping the Terrain," 8.

8. Hollenbach, "Sustaining Catholic Social Engagement," 434. See also Berger and Neuhaus, *To Empower People*.

9. Schneiders, *New Wineskins*, 29.

formal consultative status with the United Nations (UN), and research institutes or centers. SMOs and their leadership play important animating roles in the wider movements. Consider the Southern Christian Leadership Conference and the National Farm Workers Association in US Civil Rights movements, 350.org and Greenpeace in the environmental movement, and the role of unions in the labor movement. While SMOs are important, the breadth and the depth of a movement cannot be reduced only to one or more organization associated with it.

SMOs, in turn, may create "umbrella organizations" to link groups with similar goals at a local, national, or global level in associations, federations, networks, or coalitions. An important example of a successful umbrella organization is the International Campaign to Abolish Nuclear Weapons (ICAN). This global coalition of organizations and groups was founded in 2007 with the goal of abolishing nuclear weapons. Modeled after the International Campaign to Ban Landmines, ICAN channeled the wider movement for nuclear disarmament, which includes many Catholic voices, to successfully push for the Treaty on the Prohibition of Nuclear Weapons. This historic treaty to ban the use and possession of nuclear weapons was signed in 2017 by a number of governments, including the Holy See. This historic achievement won ICAN the Nobel Peace Prize and a special audience with Pope Francis who voiced his support for their work. By January 2021, the efforts of ICAN and the wider movement for disarmament proved successful when the treaty reached the necessary number of state parties to enter into force. Like many other treaties and laws related to human rights, peace, and disarmament, this new treaty would not have developed without the influence of social movements and a number of SMOs advocating for change.[10]

While SMOs are important, the breath and the depth of a movement cannot be reduced only to one or more organization associated with it. A notable contemporary social movement is the Black Lives Matter movement, arguably one of the largest movements in US history.[11]

What began on social media in 2013 as "an affirmation for a community distraught over George Zimmerman's acquittal in the shooting death of seventeen-year-old Trayvon Martin" soon became a movement on the streets to mobilize responses to a number of high profile police killings of women and men of color, particularly with the killing of George Floyd

---

10. Beser, "People Who Made a Nuclear-Weapons-Prohibition."
11. Buchanan et al., "Black Lives Matter."

in 2020. While still a relatively recent social movement, the Black Lives Matter movement has changed conversations on race and law enforcements and had an impact in the 2020 elections. Much like the #MeToo movement, which highlighted the prevalence and pain caused by sexual assault, the movement to acknowledge the dignity of Black lives highlights the potential of social media to mobilize new forms of organizing. Like #MeToo, the #blacklivesmatter or #BLM hashtags spread worldwide across multiple social media platforms engaging a range of individuals with varying degrees of commitment.

Following the success and spread of the hashtag, the three original organizers, Alicia Garza, Patrisse Cullors, and Opal Tometi, created the Black Lives Matter Network, one of many SMOs associated with the movement. Over the next few years, the movement grew substantially in the United States and beyond and new SMOs and umbrella organizations were formed, including Movement for Black Lives a coalition of more than fifty groups with varying missions, memberships, and visions.

Even in the face of the COVID-19 pandemic, millions of people took to the streets to demonstrate for Black lives in this decentralized movement. According to some estimates, "about 15 million to 26 million people in the United States . . . participated in demonstrations" in May 2020 alone.[12] In 2021, Pope Francis likened the protests against the killing of George Floyd as an expression of a "Collective Samaritan who is no fool! This movement did not pass by on the other side of the road when it saw the injury to human dignity caused by an abuse of power."[13] In a recent book, Pope Francis makes a similar point:

> To know ourselves as a people is to be aware of something greater that unites us, something that cannot be reduced to a shared legal or physical identity. We saw this in the protests in reaction to the killing of George Floyd, when many people who otherwise did not know each other took to the streets to protest, united by a healthy indignation. Such movements reveal not just popular feeling but the feeling of a people, its "soul."[14]

This collective expression of the "soul" is also visible in a group of social movements known as *popular movements*. Broadly, the term popular movements points to grassroots efforts that join together those "whose

---

12. Buchanan et al., "Black Lives Matter," para. 2.
13. Francis, "Message of the Holy Father," para. 31.
14. Francis and Ivereigh, *Let Us Dream*, 101.

inalienable rights to decent work, decent housing, and fertile land and food are undermined, threatened or denied outright."[15] These include movements of landless farmers, indigenous peoples, workers without job security (and/or union membership), and those without adequate housing. Consequently, members of popular movements are more vulnerable and marginalized than other social collectives. In the US, this could include local community organizing efforts for affordable housing, indigenous peoples' groups, and movements of undocumented students.

In 2014, Pope Francis called representatives of popular movements to Rome for the first World Meeting of Popular Movements. Subsequent meetings took place in Bolivia (2015), Rome (2016), and online (2021). In 2017, a regional meeting in Modesto, California gathered Catholic faith leaders with leaders of popular movements and community organizers in the United States. This event was convened by the Vatican's department for Integral Human Development, the Catholic Campaign for Human Development, and the PICO National Network.[16] Participants represented some of the most active grassroots community organizing networks including the Gamaliel Foundation, PICO National Network, Service Employees International Union, US Federation of Worker Cooperatives, and the National Domestic Workers Alliance. Land, work, housing, migration, and racism were key themes in the discussions.[17]

In a 2020 letter to popular movements, Pope Francis uplifts their role in mobilizing those on the margins:

> If the struggle against COVID-19 is a war, then you are truly an invisible army, fighting in the most dangerous trenches; an army whose only weapons are solidarity, hope, and community spirit, all revitalizing at a time when no one can save themselves alone. As I told you in our meetings, to me you are social poets because, from the forgotten peripheries where you live, you create admirable solutions for the most pressing problems afflicting the marginalized. I know that you nearly never receive the recognition that you deserve, because you are truly invisible to the system.[18]

---

15. World Meeting of Popular Movements, "About."

16. PICO National Network, originally known as the Pacific Institute for Community Organizations, was founded in 1972 to mobilize and support community organizations. In 2018, it changed its name to Faith in Action.

17. Francis, "Message of the Holy Father."

18. Francis, "Letter of the Holy Father to the Popular Movements," para. 2.

In his 2021 video message to the Fourth World Meeting of Popular Movements, Pope Francis praised their work in the face of the pandemic and again challenged them to take action. Popular movements, he suggests, play an important role in carrying the voice of those on the margins. "We must listen to the peripheries, open the doors to them and allow them to participate. . . . How important it is that your voice be heard, represented in all the places where decisions are made."[19]

From a local popular movement of landless farmers to the global movement for nuclear disarmament, social movements transform people and politics in both visible and invisible ways. In some movements, Catholics play active roles in the struggle for social change; in others, Catholic leaders are not as active as they perhaps should be. But what about those collectives operating with a thick religious identity? What about Catholic social movements?

Catholic Social Movements

From one perspective, organized religion, and in particular the Roman Catholic Church with its robust centralized structure and history of established relationships to political regimes, embodies an opposing, top-down model to the dynamic bottom-up framework offered by the concept of social movements. This has contributed to what sociologist Patricia Wittberg, SC, describes as a resistance among social theorists who perceive "religion as a pillar of the status quo, a conservative institution that counsel[s] its adherents to accept their lot and await a heavenly reward."[20]

From another perspective, however, we can consider the church, defined as a people, to be a social movement or even a movement of movements that originated in a group of first-century Jews on the edges of the Roman Empire. Since its foundation, Christianity, and Catholicism in particular, has given rise to a range of dynamic movements that have bubbled up from the ground, often in response to social and political dynamics. As Wittberg points out in her study on movements of religious life, "individuals have participated in them for the same sorts of reasons that activists participate in other types of movements; they grow and decay subject to the same cyclic dynamics."[21] Some, like many movements

---

19. Francis, "Message of the Holy Father," para. 38.
20. Wittberg, *Rise and Fall of Catholic Religious Orders*, 5–6.
21. Wittberg, *Rise and Fall of Catholic Religious Orders*, 6.

of religious life, will encounter resistance and opposition from the church hierarchy before being formally granted official recognition. Others, like sixteenth-century reform movements or contemporary traditionalist groups who reject the Second Vatican Council, might be formally sanctioned or may break away completely from the Catholic church.

Catholic social movements, both those with official canonical recognition and those without any official mandate, exist in creative tension with the more centralized structures of church governance and authority. Like other social movements, Catholic social movements undergo life cycles of growth, bureaucratization, and decline. Decline, of course, does not always amount to dissolution or failure. Movements may succeed in their stated goals or they may experience moments of renewal that restart the cycle. The Benedictine movement, for instance, has been reformed and renewed multiple times over the centuries, giving birth to a range of groups including the Cistercians and Trappists.

As dynamic human collectives, Catholic social movements are often difficult to define and classify. Nevertheless, a look at the movements operating at an international level in the church today reveals a four types or clusters of movements.[22]

A. Religious Life

Arguably, communities of religious life are among the oldest movements within the church, and possibly some of the oldest social movements in the world. Originating among early communities of urban women and of desert monastics, new forms of religious life coalesced with Benedictine monasticism, the mendicant movements, societies of apostolic life, and the missionary and teaching congregations in the nineteenth century. Today, there are thousands of congregations ranging in size and scope from international groups like the Institute of the Brothers of the Christian Schools (Lasallian Brothers) to local diocesan congregations. These movements, in their many forms, often engage a range of individuals around a defining charism with core members living a regulated

---

22. Johan Verstraeten, offers a five-fold typology: (1) classical international Catholic movements, such as the Young Christian workers; (2) movements related to religious orders and congregations; (3) new ecclesial movements; (4) radical Christian groups linked with revolutionary movements; and (5) non-Christian movements where Christians play an important role. Verstraeten, "Catholic Social Thought and the Movements," 233–35.

(rule-based) life usually centered on the traditional vows of poverty, chastity and obedience.[23] Through this unique life-form, as Pope Francis points out, religious movements play a prophetic role in society:

> I am counting on you "to wake up the world," since the distinctive sign of consecrated life is prophecy. . . . Prophets receive from God the ability to scrutinize the times in which they live and to interpret events: they are like sentinels who keep watch in the night and sense the coming of the dawn (cf. *Is* 21:11–12). Prophets know God and they know the men and women who are their brothers and sisters. They are able to discern and denounce the evil of sin and injustice. Because they are free, they are beholden to no one but God, and they have no interest other than God. Prophets tend to be on the side of the poor and the powerless, for they know that God himself is on their side.[24]

Non-vowed members engage these movements to varying degrees. Some affiliate through formally established mechanisms for associates or "third orders." Others, including lay staff at SMOs sponsored by these congregations (e.g., schools, hospitals), may identify with the charism and mission of the movement in less formal ways. Increasingly, non-Catholic members are explicitly welcomed to associate with wider movements of religious. A recent text produced by the Brothers of the Christian Schools on the *Declaration on the Lasallian Educational Mission* exemplifies this growing sense of inclusiveness among some movements of religious life:

> Being Lasallian is, above all, a way of living, of being the bearer of values of one's religion, which are enriched when they are shared. Therefore, being Lasallian does depend on belonging to a particular culture or a religious creed. This conviction has made possible the existence and relevance of Lasallians who profess religions other than Catholicism or even those partners who do not subscribe to any religious faith or define themselves as indifferent.[25]

Over the past two decades, a range of charism-based networks or umbrella structures have formed to bring together members of these movement and their SMOs across geographic and institutional borders. For example, a non-Catholic professor at La Salle University in

23. See Schneiders, *Finding the Treasure*.
24. Francis, "Apostolic Letter to All Consecrated People."
25. Institute of the Brothers of the Christian Schools, *Declaration on the Lasallian Educational Mission*, 52.

Philadelphia can now connect directly with her peers at universities in multiple continents thought the International Association of Lasallian Universities without ever engaging a vowed brother.

Globally, the Franciscan movement is perhaps the largest movement of religious life. Since its foundation in the thirteenth century, this movement has grown to include orders of priests and brothers, cloistered nuns, active sisters, and a range of lay people who identify as Franciscan with or without any formal recognition. In their mission, Franciscans have created a great variety of SMOs from entire congregations and reform groups to hospitals and universities. Franciscan groups exist not only in the Roman Catholic Church, but also in Anglican, Lutheran and other protestant churches. In 1989, leaders of many of the Franciscan orders, under the Conference of the Franciscan Family, founded Franciscans International (FI) to be a voice for the Franciscan family worldwide, including groups of Anglican Franciscans. FI exercises this voice at the UN where they advocate "for the protection of human dignity and environmental justice."[26]

Likewise, among the Jesuit and wider Ignatian movement, a range of new networks have been created. In 2012, a group of Jesuits and lay partners began a project to map the various networks emerging within the Jesuit movement. Today, the project identifies eighty-four such networks.[27]

In the United States, one notable Jesuit network is the Ignatian Solidarity Network (ISN). Founded in 2004, ISN engages high schools, universities, and parishes with the aim of mobilizing advocacy and training "for social justice animated by the spirituality of St. Ignatius of Loyola and the witness of the Jesuit martyrs of El Salvador and their companions."[28] Among their activities, ISN organizes leadership programs for students, advocacy resources for Jesuit parishes, Solidarity on Tap programs for young adults, and the annual Ignatian Family Teach-In for Justice, the "largest annual Catholic social justice conference in the US."[29] In an average year, the annual teach-in brings together more than two thousand students and lay leaders to Washington, DC to learn, pray, and act on issues of social justice. While in DC, many conference participants often meet with members of Congress in order to advocate for issues of justice. This event grew out of earlier teach-ins that comprised part of the protest

---

26. Franciscans International, "Franciscans International."
27. Jesuit Networking, "Jesuit Networking."
28. Ignatian Solidarity Network, "About the Ignatian Solidarity Network."
29. Ignatian Solidarity Network, "Ignatian Family Teach-In for Justice 2021."

movement against the US Army's School of the Americas, a US military school which trained some of the military officers involved in the murder of six Jesuits and two companions in El Salvador in 1980.[30]

B. Specialized Catholic Action

In the wake of the second industrial revolution and First World War, a number of lay-led lay movements took root in Europe in the early days of modern social Catholicism. Pioneering initiatives in the late nineteenth century, such as the Oeuvre des Cercles Catholiques d'Ouvriers (Society of Catholic Worker Circles), Le Sillion, and the Fribourg Union, gave way to the formation of *movements of Catholic action and specialized Catholic action*.[31]

An important, yet often overlooked distinction must be made here between the general, often hierarchical model of Catholic action that emerged as an effort to defend the church's interests in secular societies and the approach of the specialized Catholic action. Specialized movements emphasize the autonomy and agency of the target milieu through an inductive or bottom-up approach.

The specialized vision here, as affirmed by the Second Vatican Council, is that the best evangelization happens when peers become apostles to their fellow peers, often in small cell groups.[32] The classic and pioneering movement here is the Young Catholic Worker (YCW) movement. Founded by a group of young women industrial workers in Belgium in 1912 with the help of Joseph Cardijn, the YCW (or JOC, in French) grew rapidly to over a hundred countries. At the core of the YCW is a spirituality centered on the Review of Life, sometimes referred to as the "see-judge-act" method, which was developed and popularized by specialized Catholic action. The YCW movement today is served by two global SMOs, the International Young Christian Workers (IYCW) founded in 1957 and the International Coordination of Young Christian Workers (CIJOC) founded in 1987.[33]

---

30. Gill, *School of the Americas*.

31. For overviews of the nineteenth-century efforts, see Bokenkotter, *Church and Revolution*; Cahill, "Catholic Social Movement; Vidler, *Century of Social Catholicism*.

32. Paul VI, *Apostolicam Actuositatem*, no. 12.

33. See Ahern, *Structures of Grace*, 63–84. As a separate structure, CIJOC grew out of concerns over perceived issues in the IYCW's adherence to Catholic values.

Following the creation of the YCW, young people of other milieus, including farmers, middle class, and students, created their own movements based on the same model. This was followed by adult counterparts. Today, there are over ten international Catholic movements in the specialized tradition. Many of these, like the International Movement of Catholic Students (IMCS-Pax Romana), were among the first Catholic movements to engage in advocacy in the UN system.

C. New Ecclesial Movements

New ecclesial movements represent a distinct grouping of Catholic social movements. These generally emerged in the mid to late twentieth century around a specific spirituality. They received considerable support under the pontificates of John Paul II and Benedict XVI as evidenced by the three World Congresses of Ecclesial Movements and New Communities organized by the Vatican (1998, 2006, 2014). Like many movements of religious life, the new ecclesial movements point to animating charisms in the lives of specific founders who were uplifted as "living saints" during their lifetimes.[34] Unlike specialized Catholic action, however, the new movements gather Catholics, and sometimes non-Catholics, of all milieus and ages, including lay people, priests, and religious who share their specific spirituality.

A notable example here is the Community of Sant'Egidio, which was founded in 1968 by Andrea Riccardi. Based in Rome, Italy, the movement gathers Christians from over seventy countries based in a common spirituality and the values of prayer, evangelization, friendship with the poor, ecumenism, and dialogue. Sant'Egidio is often best known for its direct service to the poor of Rome and for the role it played in the early 1990s in hosting the peace talks that ended the decades long Mozambican Civil War.[35] By playing an intermediary and conveying role in the peace talks, Sant'Egidio drew attention to the power of social movements and other non-state actors as agents of what is called multi-track diplomacy.[36]

Another new ecclesial movement of note is Focolare. Officially created as "Work of Mary" in 1943 by Chiara Lubich, Focolare is an

---

34. Leahy, *Ecclesial Movements and Communities*; Ahern, "Gemeenschappen van de Geest De Theologieën."

35. Riccardi et al., *Sant'Egidio*.

36. Diamond and McDonald, *Multi-Track Diplomacy*.

ecumenical Christian movement in over 180 countries with the stated "aim [of] contribut[ing] to building a more united world in which people value and respect diversity." At the core of the movement are "men and women who consecrate their lives to God with vows of poverty, chastity and obedience and live in separate households called 'focolares,' from the Italian word for 'hearth.'"[37] Among Focolare's more creative social initiatives has been a project on the economy of communion (EoC). Founded in 1991 in Brazil, the EoC seeks to achieve Focolare's goal of unity "through economic activity and enterprise."[38] The project today claims that the owners and founders of more than eight hundred businesses, including forty in North America, have committed to use their businesses to help serve the common good, including to "willingly share profits to help those in material need, provide opportunities for meaningful work, offer products and services that meet real human and social needs, and seek to manage their companies with moral integrity."[39] The EoC network, including the North American EoC Association, also facilitates mentoring and support for business owners as they seek to be agents of unity.

D. Issue Based Movements

In addition to those movements organized around a common charism (religious life and new ecclesial movements) or a common milieu (specialized Catholic action), there are numerous Catholic social movements organized around specific themes or topics. Issue based movements include groups working on issues like labor justice and sanctuary for migrants and refugees, networks fighting against human trafficking, and movements for church reform.

The theme of peace has long inspired Catholics. According to Ronald G. Musto, even in medieval times, tens of thousands of Catholics joined peace demonstrations, significantly outnumbering those who went on the Crusades.[40] In 1945, Catholics in Germany and France created Pax Christi as an international Catholic peace movement. Today, Pax Christi unites over one hundred member organizations worldwide

---

37. Focolare Movement, "About Us."
38. Economy of Communion, "What Is the EOC?"
39. Economy of Communion, "What Is the EOC?."
40. Musto, *Catholic Peace Tradition*, 87.

with the goal to "promote peace, respect of human rights, justice, and reconciliation."[41]

Throughout the twentieth century, nonviolence became an increasingly important theme for parts of the Catholic peace movement. Among Catholics, especially in the United States, the Catholic Worker Movement co-founded by Dorothy Day and Peter Maurin in 1933 and the United Farm Workers movement founded by César Chávez and Dolores Huerta in 1962 helped to draw attention to the value of nonviolence as both a Christian principle and an organizing tactic.

While the foundational goals of the Catholic Worker were first directed to address the reality and needs of the poor during the Great Depression, the movement, with its threefold vision of houses of hospitality, farming communes, and clarification of thought meetings, took on peace as a major theme in its efforts to radically embody Jesus's teachings in the Sermon on the Mount and about the works of mercy.[42] The Worker's controversial stance of pacifism and conscientious objection during the Second World War and later in during the Cold War and Vietnam War clashed with the official positions of the archbishops of New York over many decades.

The Catholic Worker's engagement in creative acts of nonviolence, such as their support for nonviolent labor actions (e.g., strikes, boycotts) and their public refusal to participate in Cold War air raid drills, inspired important acts of resistance during the Vietnam War. Members of the Catholic Worker, for example, were among the first to publicly burn their draft cards.[43]

By the late 1960s, Philip Berrigan, then a Josephite priest, his brother Daniel, a Jesuit priest, and other Catholic peace activists felt called to more confrontational acts of nonviolent resistance. This included the 1968 raid of a draft card office in Catonsville, Maryland. The images and news footage of the nine activists, including Philip and Daniel Berrigan and other Catholic religious, burning draft cards with homemade napalm drew increased attention to debates on the moral legitimacy of the war.

After a series of actions in the 1970s, this more radical wing of the Catholic peace movement focused attention on the Cold War arms race and the danger of nuclear weapons. In 1980, eight activists, including once again Philip and Daniel Berrigan, broke into the General Electric

---

41. Pax Christi International, "About Us."
42. Day, "Aims and Purposes."
43. Nepstad, *Religion and War Resistance in the Plowshares Movement*, 44–45.

Nuclear Missile Re-Entry Division in King of Prussia, Pennsylvania, where parts of the Mark 12A minuteman missile were manufactured. Inspired by the biblical call to turn weapons of war into plowshares, instruments of peace (Isa 2:4) the group used hammer and blood to deface the plant.[44]

Since 1980, there have been over seventy-five Plowshares actions following the model of the King of Prussia action, including one in 2018 at the Kings Bay Naval Submarine Base in Georgia, the home of several Ohio-class ballistic missile submarines.[45] Like the original activists, the seven members of the Kings Bay action felt called to take both real and symbolic action against the destructive nature of the nuclear weapons. The group included several members of the Catholic Worker movement; Martha Hennessy, the granddaughter of Dorothy Day; Elizabeth McAlister, the longtime Plowshares leader and widow of Philip Berrigan; and one Jesuit priest, Fr. Steve Kelly.[46] In 2019 a federal grand jury found them guilty of destruction of property, depredation of government property, trespass, and conspiracy.

Among the more dynamic issue-based movements to emerge in recent years has been the *Laudato Si'* movement, which was previously known as the Global Catholic Climate Movement, a coalition of over eight hundred Catholic groups including religious congregations and lay movements. Founded in 2015, the *Laudato Si'* movement seeks "to turn Pope Francis' *Laudato Si'* encyclical into action for climate justice, by undergoing our own ecological conversion, transforming our lifestyles and calling for bold public policies together with the wider climate movement." Among its actions, the movement asks individuals, families, parishes and organizations to sign a "*Laudato Si'* pledge" in which they agree to "Pray for and with creation, live more simply, and advocate to protect our common home."[47] Like other contemporary issue-based movements, this movement has strategically used social media and hashtags to mobilize young adults worldwide.

---

44. For a historical analysis of the Plowshares movement, see Laffin and Montgomery, *Swords into Plowshares*.

45. Laffin, *Plowshares Disarmament Chronology*.

46. For an analysis of the profile of the prisoners of conscience involved in the Plowshares movement, see Stanger, "Prisoners of Conscience," 535–49.

47. LiveLaudatoSi, "Sign the *Laudato Si'* Pledge."

The Ecology of Social Catholicism

Despite their dynamism, the role and potential of Catholic social movements remain underappreciated both inside the church and in wider studies of social movements. While scholars have given increased attention to social movements and other non-state actors, religious actors, and particularly Catholic social actors, remain overlooked as agents of change.

At the same time, when considering Catholic social teaching, scholarly and popular attention often focuses on the documentary heritage following the groundbreaking encyclical *Rerum Novarum* in 1891. Some approaches, however, consider these texts detached from the social movements that shaped them. This failure to appreciate the work of social movements is reinforced by persistent ecclesiological models that emphasize binary distinctions between the hierarchy and the laity.

A sharp division between the bishops, understood as the "teaching church" (or Ecclesia docens), and the laity, understood passively as "the learning church" (or Ecclesia discens), leaves little to no room to recognize social movements as playing a role in the development of Catholic social doctrine. As Amanda Osheim has written, such a division focuses attention "on the church's leadership and law, rather than [on] the abiding presence and continuing activity of the Holy Spirit throughout the church."[48]

One place where this distinction is clearly illustrated is in the footnotes used in papal encyclicals before Pope Francis. Other than a few references in *Populorum Progressio* and in *Sollicitudo Rei Socialis*, citations in papal encyclicals focus exclusively on biblical sources, the writings of saints (particularly St. Thomas Aquinas), and the insights of previous popes. Absent are direct references to the contributions of social movements, women, lay people, and non-Christians. Moreover, these documents tend not to cite sources perceived to possess less authority than the pope, excluding even statements of national bishops' conferences. Although Francis has significantly widened the conversation by referencing non-magisterial sources and the statements of episcopal conferences, there remains the impression that social encyclicals manifest very nearly out of thin air as if divinely inspired texts.[49]

What is needed is a more expansive approach to how social Catholicism is framed, one that takes seriously the dynamic interplay between official and unofficial sources of analysis. Social systems and network

---

48. Osheim, *Ministry of Discernment*, 23.
49. Ahern, "Follow the Footnotes."

theories support this broader perspective by pointing to the growing importance of the dynamic mediating role of networks and noninstitutional agents in the postmodern world.

Here, social Catholicism as reflected in the teachings of Pope Francis is informative. In his two social encyclicals, *Laudato Si'* and *Fratelli Tutti*, Francis has drawn attention to the interconnected reality of all creation and all people. *Laudato Si'*, in particular, commits itself to wider systems as it applies an ecological lens in the construction of an integral ecology. This approach affirms the multifaceted relationships of people with God, with others, with the world around us, and with one's deepest self.

Such an integral outlook that takes seriously networks, systems, and overlapping relationships can also be applied to social Catholicism in what might be described as an integral ecclesiology. Like an integral ecology, an integral ecclesiology offers a holistic and encompassing vision. It recognizes the varied connections and relationships that make up the church. An integral ecclesiology sees the church through an ecological lens, discovering not simply an institution centered around clerical power, but a community of the baptized with varied and complex social relationships internally and externally.

Such an ecclesiological lens illumines the role of Catholic social movements as mediators or conduits of information in at least four ways. First, social movements foster solidarity and share ideas across borders by mediating between people and groups who join together in a common movement. IMCS-Pax Romana, for example, was founded in 1921 as students from more than twenty countries sought to create a movement that would transcend political and ideological boundaries in the wake of the First World War.[50] This cross-border solidarity continues today, as students raise worldwide concern to the issues impacting members in different countries. For instance, following the recent coup in Myanmar, IMCS-Pax Romana and its partner organization for graduates organized online forums to give a voice for church leaders in the country to share their experiences with members in other countries and continents. Being a part of a movement with others from different social, political, and economic contexts can help to transform a "feeling of vague compassion" into a genuine sense of solidarity, or what Pope St. John Paul II defined as "a firm and persevering determination to commit oneself to the common

---

50. Weck, *Histoire de La Confédération Internationale*.

good; that is to say to the good of all and of each individual, because we are all really responsible for all."[51]

Second, Catholic social movements mediate between religion and the wider culture. By their very nature, Catholic social movements are instruments of public religion.[52] They stand at the intersection of faith and public life and consequently challenge models of secularization that seek to limit the voices of faith-based groups in the public sphere.

This mediating position often involves a type of translation. In one direction, Catholic social movements help to interpret public-political discourse into religious language. In the other direction, they help to translate issues and topics of religious concern using language accessible to wider audiences, including social media. Consider, for example, the work of the Global Catholic Climate Movement. In their website and resource materials, the GCCM interprets the scientific and public debates on climate change primarily for a readership of Catholic communities. At the same time, they take the Catholic concern for care of creation, as embodied by *Laudato Si'*, and translate those concerns into reader-friendly talking points, providing models of how to write letters to the editors of secular publications.[53]

In a very different way, the Plowshares movement communicates religious ideas in the public space through creative actions of disarmament. In their most recent action in 2018, activists left banners and graffiti with Biblical quotes on the Kings Bay naval base to communicate the peace concerns animating the Catholic social tradition. These religious ideas were also shared in sentencing statements made by the defendants during their trials. "I am attempting to help transform the fundamental values of public life," stated Martha Hennessy. She continued: "I am willing to suffer for the common good and for our sin of not loving our brothers and sisters, a condition that leads to war. War stems from our unwillingness to love one another as Christ has loved us."[54]

Third, Catholic social movements mediate between people and larger social-political structures. In one direction, movements can facilitate advocacy and flow of information from individuals and local groups to high levels of power (bottom-up). In another direction, movements

---

51. John Paul II, *Sollicitudo Rei Socialis*, no. 38.
52. Casanova, *Public Religions in the Modern World*.
53. Sisters of Mercy, "Writing Letters to the Editor on the Papal Encyclical."
54. Hennessy, "Sentencing Statement," para. 3.

also share and analyze information on what is happening in political structures with members on the ground (top-down).

Over one hundred Catholic organizations are involved some direct advocacy relationship with the UN system, a role recognized by *Gaudium et Spes*.[55] Consider, for example, the work of Franciscans International (FI). As an accredited NGO with the UN, FI gives voice to members of the Franciscan family in local communities where established political structures are unwilling or unable to respond to the needs of the community. This is especially impactful in the face of human rights abuses, such as their recent advocacy at the UN Human Rights Council on abuses taking place in West Papua. By bringing to Geneva local activists and victims of abuse, FI is able to draw international attention to abuses in ways that bypass national structures which are unable or unwilling to respond. Political scientists describe this type of work by NGOs as reflecting a "boomerang pattern of influence" whereby local "NGOs bypass their state and directly search out international allies to try to bring pressure on their states from the outside."[56] At the same time, FI helps to educate and form members on the nature and focus of the UN Human Rights bodies, including supporting trainings and formation on human rights. This information, in turn, empowers local members to mobilize for their rights.

Using different tactics, the GCCM also seeks to effect change in corporate and economic structures by mobilizing the collective power of investors. The GCCM has produced a series of resources, including a "Fossil Fuel Divestment Toolkit," to help organizations embody Catholic social teaching in their investment portfolios through divestment and shareholder advocacy.

Finally, Catholic social movements also mediate within the church between local believers and those in official ecclesial positions. Again, this dynamic flows in two directions. On the one hand, Catholic social movements raise awareness to new concerns, experiences, and ways of responding from the bottom up. On the other hand, these collectives, perhaps more than any other ecclesial space, are well suited to educate and form individual Catholics on the themes and teachings of the social tradition, a role explicitly recognized by the *Compendium of the Social Doctrine of the Church*.[57]

---

55. Paul VI, *Gaudium et Spes*, no. 90.

56. Keck and Sikkink, *Activists beyond Borders*, 12.

57. Pontificium Consilium de Iustitia et Pace, *Compendium of the Social Doctrine of the Church*, nos. 549–50.

Catholic social movements, in other words, play a fundamental role in the dynamic interplay between lived experiences of believers and the theories contained in official magisterial texts. Nearly every major development in official Catholic social teaching, from *Rerum Novarum* to *Fratelli Tutti*, reflects some prior initiatives by Catholic collectives. Consider the following two examples.

At the heart of the YCW and other movements of specialized Catholic action is the methodology of the Review of Life or see-judge-act. This inductive and action-oriented method was formulated and promoted for small group reflection by the YCW and its chaplain, Joseph Cardijn. In 1951, Pope St. John XXIII endorsed this method in *Mater et Magistra* as the approach for the church's social analysis. This official recognition had a significant impact on social Catholicism in the following decades. Nearly all subsequent social encyclicals are structured along these lines and several scholars have developed this approach into other methods of social analysis, including the pastoral circle.[58]

A more recent example can be seen in *Fratelli Tutti*. In chapter seven, Pope Francis engages important developments in the Catholic peace movement criticizing the just war tradition. In April 2016, the Catholic Nonviolence Initiative (CNI), a project of Pax Christi International, organized a conference of over eighty participants in Rome with the theme "Nonviolence and Just Peace."[59] This conference built on experiences of nonviolence in different places in the world, biblical reflection on Jesus's way of nonviolence, and decades of scholarship on new models for achieving and sustaining peace. In their final statement, participants called for changes in the official teaching of the church regarding war by moving away from the just war tradition and toward active nonviolence and a new framework of "just peace":

> We believe that there is no "just war." Too often the "just war theory" has been used to endorse rather than prevent or limit war. . . . We propose that the Catholic Church develop and consider shifting to a Just Peace approach based on Gospel nonviolence.[60]

This call renewed debates surrounding the possibility of any war ever being considered "just" and the legitimacy of absolute pacifism as a

---

58. Wijsen et al., *Pastoral Circle Revisited*.
59. Nepstad, *Catholic Social Activism*, 168–69.
60. Catholic Nonviolence Initiative, "Appeal to the Catholic Church," paras. 9, 11.

Catholic stance.⁶¹ Months later, Pope Francis took up several elements of the final statement, and in particular its framing of the value of nonviolence, in his 2017 World Day of Peace Message. While the message did not, as some may have hoped, condemn outright the just war tradition, it did uplift nonviolence more so than any other previous papal messages. In *Fratelli Tutti*, Francis offers a direct critique of the just war tradition as a valid stance in this particular moment. "It is very difficult nowadays," he writes, "to invoke the rational criteria elaborated in earlier centuries to speak of the possibility of a 'just war.' Never again war!"⁶² For the Catholic peace movement, *Fratelli Tutti* offered both an endorsement of years of activism as well as crucial support for their ongoing and future action. According to a statement by Pax Christi, it offers a "clear foundation for developing and integrating the theology and practice of nonviolence in the teaching of the Church."⁶³

Movements like the YCW and Pax Christi serve as laboratories and innovators in applying the Gospel to contemporary challenges. The sociologist and peace activist Gordon Zahn describes this dynamic as "Catholic social thought from below."⁶⁴ Initially, however, many of these "experiments" in discipleship may encounter resistance from church officials. While some of these on-the-ground responses may make mistakes, go "too far," or diverge from the Gospel mission, others will illuminate important issues and contribute to the development of doctrine. Nevertheless, the lack of official consultative processes for movements to share their lessons with the hierarchical structures and with each other may mean that some valuable insights are lost. Theologian Ellen Van Stichel raises precisely this concern: "The question is not so much what the official teachings add but rather what ideas and reflections they lose sight of and consequently delete from the Catholic social thought from below."⁶⁵

Here is where a more wholistic or integral approach to social Catholicism can be instructive. Rather than viewing social Catholicism in a hierarchical model with social encyclicals teaching the faithful where to go, an integral approach to the ecology of social Catholicism would take into account the dynamic interplay between different agents in the

---

61. For example, see Allman and Winright, "Protect Thy Neighbor."
62. Francis, *Fratelli Tutti*, no. 258.
63. Pax Christi International, "*Fratelli Tutti*," para. 2.
64. Zahn, "Social Movements and Catholic Social Thought," 52.
65. Van Stichel, "Movements Struggling for Justice within the Church," 291.

church and the presence of the Holy Spirit or sense of the faithful (*Sensus Fidelium*) in non-magisterial sources.

Such an approach complements the efforts of Pope Francis and many church reform movements to renew a sense of synodality and co-responsibility in the church. Speaking on the fiftieth anniversary of the Institution of the Synod of Bishops in 2015, Francis affirms the need to enhance the mutual flow of communication between the laity and the hierarchy. What is needed, he argues, is a renewed sense of synodality throughout the church. To this end, the church is called to become a "listening church," a community of believers "in which everyone has something to learn. The faithful people, the college of bishops, the Bishop of Rome: all listening to each other, and all listening to the Holy Spirit, 'the Spirit of truth' (*Jn* 14:17), in order to know what he 'says to the Churches' (*Rev.* 2:7)."[66] If this renewal of a more participatory model is to take place, as Francis envisions, then social movements have an important role to play in facilitating this process of mutual listening and learning in the unique ecosystem that is social Catholicism.

Conclusion

The year 2021 marked the fiftieth anniversary of *Octogesima Adveniens*, the 1971 apostolic letter by Pope St. Paul VI. Like Pope Francis, Paul VI clearly recognized the power and potential of Catholic social movements. Towards the end of this "call to action," *Octogesima Adveniens* calls on Christians to get involved in collective efforts for social transformation. "Christian organizations, under their different forms," he writes, "have a responsibility for collective action." Such action, he continues, stems from "the concrete demands of the Christian faith for a just, and consequently necessary, transformation of society."[67] Despite their important contributions and potential, Catholic social movements remain in many ways an underappreciated resource in the church. An ecological or integral approach to social Catholicism, as this paper proposes, helps to better illuminate the work of these movements and suggests at least four ways forward to strengthen and sustain their witness and work.

---

66. Francis, "Address Commemorating the 50th Anniversary of the Institution of the Synod of Bishops," para. 10.

67. Paul VI, *Octogesima Adveniens*, no. 51.

First, official Catholic social teaching, particularly papal encyclicals, would benefit from more explicit recognition of the non-magisterial sources that inspire them. This is not only a question of giving proper credit, but also offers a means to recognize those spaces in the church where the Holy Spirit is at work in bubbling up from the ground. While both *Laudato Si'* and *Fratelli Tutti* widen the frame of reference, more work is needed to recognize officially the ways the Holy Spirit is at work in these movements and the movements' effects on official sources.

Second, more work is needed by theologians, sociologists, and other scholars to more deeply understand the dynamics involved in Catholic social movements. Social theory, including the emerging work in systems and networks, can help inform analysis of how Catholic social teaching is formed and how it can be applied in the world. For theologians, in particular, this demands deepening engagements with communities and movements.

Third, increased attention to the mediating role played by these actors should also encourage greater financial and logistical support for their work. The Catholic Campaign for Human Development (CCHD), a program of the United States Conference of Catholic Bishops, already funds a number of important social movements and SMOs working at the local level in cities around the United States.[68] Internationally, there are several Catholic development agencies, including Catholic Relief Services. More support is needed, however, particularly to support and enhance the capacity of movements and SMOs in areas of the world with limited resources and those organized by and for underrepresented groups (e.g., youth, indigenous peoples). A global fund akin to CCHD might be one step forward in this regard.

Finally, a wider approach to the role of social movements in the landscape of social Catholicism helps to illuminate the need for greater coordination and communion both among different movements and between them and church hierarchy. Meetings like the three world congresses of Ecclesial Movements and the World Meeting of Popular Movements have the real potential to enhance communion, share information, and model best practices. Such spaces could be developed and expanded, both at the international level and at the diocesan and even parish levels; they should also be intentionally organized in such a way that no movements are excluded.

---

68. Korgen, *Beyond Empowerment*.

For more than a century, Catholic social movements have played a dynamic role in relation to the sources of Catholic social doctrine, functioning as mediators of ideas and experiences. While imperfect, these collectives often reflect a dynamic application of the Gospel to the contemporary world. As socially engaged embodiments of lived Catholicism, they possess an enormous potential to strengthen and promote the common good. Moving ahead into the twenty-first century, the future of social Catholicism, and possibly the common good, will depend on the dynamism of Catholic social movements.

Bibliography

Ahern, Kevin. "Follow the Footnotes." *America Magazine*, June 18, 2015. http://americamagazine.org/issue/follow-footnotes.

———. "Gemeenschappen van de Geest De Theologieën van de Nieuwe Katholieke Bewegingen." *Tijdschrift Voor Theologie* 57 (2017) 374–89.

———. *Structures of Grace: Catholic Organizations Serving the Global Common Good*. Maryknoll, NY: Orbis, 2015.

Allman, Mark J., and Tobias Winright. "Protect Thy Neighbor: Why Just-War Tradition Is Still Indispensable." *Commonweal*, June 2, 2016. www.commonwealmagazine.org.

Bartoli, Andrea. "Forgiveness and Reconciliation in the Mozambique Peace Process." In *Forgiveness and Reconciliation: Religion, Public Policy, and Conflict Transformation*, edited by Raymond G. Helmick and Rodney L. Petersen, 316–81. Philadelphia: Templeton, 2001.

Berger, Peter L., and Richard John Neuhaus. *To Empower People: The Role of Mediating Structures in Public Policy*. Studies in Political and Social Processes 139. Washington, DC: American Enterprise Institute for Public Policy Research, 1977.

Beser, Ari. "The People Who Made a Nuclear-Weapons-Prohibition Treaty Possible." *The Nation*, February 2, 2018. https://www.thenation.com/article/archive/the-people-who-made-a-nuclear-weapons-prohibition-treaty-possible/.

Bokenkotter, Thomas S. *Church and Revolution: Catholics in the Struggle for Democracy and Social Justice*. New York: Image, 1998.

Buchanan, Larry, et al. "Black Lives Matter May Be the Largest Movement in U.S. History." *New York Times*, July 3, 2020. https://www.nytimes.com/interactive/2020/07/03/us/george-floyd-protests-crowd-size.html.

Buechler, Steven M. *Social Movements in Advanced Capitalism: The Political Economy and Cultural Construction of Social Activism*. New York: Oxford University Press, 2000.

Cahill, Edward. "The Catholic Social Movement: Historical Aspects." In *Official Catholic Social Teaching*, edited by Charles E. Curran and Richard A. McCormick, 3–31. Readings in Moral Theology 5. New York: Paulist, 1986.

Casanova, José. *Public Religions in the Modern World*. Chicago: University of Chicago Press, 1994.

Catholic Nonviolence Initiative. "An Appeal to the Catholic Church to Re-Commit to the Centrality of Gospel Nonviolence." April 13, 2016. https://nonviolencejustpeace.net/2016/05/17/an-appeal-to-the-catholic-church-to-re-commit-to-the-centrality-of-gospel-nonviolence/.

Day, Dorothy. "Aims and Purposes." *Catholic Worker*, February 1, 1940. https://catholicworker.org/182-html/.

Diamond, Louise, and John McDonald. *Multi-Track Diplomacy: A Systems Approach to Peace*. 3rd ed. West Hartford, CT: Kumarian, 1996.

Economy of Communion. "What Is the EOC?" April 27, 2015. https://eocnoam.org/what-is-the-eoc/.

Focolare Movement. "About Us." https://www.focolare.org/en/chi-siamo/.

Francis. "Address Commemorating the 50th Anniversary of the Institution of the Synod of Bishops." October 17, 2015. http://w2.vatican.va/content/francesco/en/speeches/2015/october/documents/papa-francesco_20151017_50-anniversario-sinodo.html.

———. "Apostolic Letter to All Consecrated People on the Occasion of the Year of Consecrated Life." November 21, 2014. http://www.vatican.va/content/francesco/en/apost_letters/documents/papa-francesco_lettera-ap_20141121_lettera-consacrati.html.

———. *Fratelli Tutti, On Fraternity and Social Friendship*. Rome: Libreria Editrice Vaticana, 2020. https://www.vatican.va/content/francesco/en/encyclicals/documents/papa-francesco_20201003_enciclica-fratelli-tutti.html.

———. "Letter of the Holy Father to the Popular Movements." April 12, 2020. http://www.vatican.va/content/francesco/en/letters/2020/documents/papa-francesco_20200412_lettera-movimentipopolari.html.

———. "Message of the Holy Father." February 10, 2017. http://www.vatican.va/content/francesco/en/messages/pont-messages/2017/documents/papa-francesco_20170210_movimenti-popolari-modesto.html.

Francis, and Austen Ivereigh. *Let Us Dream: The Path to a Better Future*. New York: Simon and Schuster, 2020.

Franciscans International. "Franciscans International." https://franciscansinternational.org/.

Gill, Lesley. *The School of the Americas: Military Training and Political Violence in the Americas*. Durham, NC: Duke University Press, 2004.

Gold, Lorna. *New Financial Horizons: The Emergence of an Economy of Communion*. Hyde City, NY: New City, 2010.

Hannigan, John A. "Social Movement Theory and the Sociology of Religion: Toward a New Synthesis." *Sociological Analysis* 52 (1991) 311–31.

Hennessy, Martha. "Sentencing Statement." *Kings Bay Plowshares 7*, November 13, 2020. https://kingsbayplowshares7.org/2020/11/martha-hennessys-sentencing-statement-nov-13-2020/.

Hinze, Bradford E. *Practices of Dialogue in the Roman Catholic Church: Aims and Obstacles, Lessons and Laments*. New York: Continuum, 2006.

Hollenbach, David. "Sustaining Catholic Social Engagement: A Key Role for Movements in the Church Today." *Journal of Catholic Social Thought* 10 (2013) 431–47.

Ignatian Solidarity Network. "About the Ignatian Solidarity Network." https://ignatiansolidarity.net/about/.

———. "Ignatian Family Teach-In for Justice 2021." https://ignatiansolidarity.net/iftj/.

Institute of the Brothers of the Christian Schools. *Declaration on the Lasallian Educational Mission: Challenges, Convictions and Hopes*. Rome: Brothers of the Christian Schools Generalate, 2020. https://www.lasalle.org/wp-content/uploads/2020/07/La_Declaracio%CC%81n_ENG_web.pdf.
Jesuit Networking. "Jesuit Networking." https://jesuit.network/network/.
John Paul II. *Sollicitudo Rei Socialis: On Social Concern*. Rome: Libreria Editrice Vaticana, 1987. https://www.vatican.va/content/john-paul-ii/en/encyclicals/documents/hf_jp-ii_enc_30121987_sollicitudo-rei-socialis.html.
Keck, Margaret E., and Kathryn Sikkink. *Activists beyond Borders: Advocacy Networks in International Politics*. Ithaca, NY: Cornell University Press, 1998.
Korgen, Jeffry Odell. *Beyond Empowerment: A Pilgrimage with the Catholic Campaign for Human Development*. Maryknoll, NY: Orbis, 2015.
Krier Mich, Marvin L. *Catholic Social Teaching and Movements*. Mystic, CT: Twenty-Third, 1998.
Laffin, Arthur J. *The Plowshares Disarmament Chronology, 1980–2003*. Marion, SD: Rose Hill, 2003.
Laffin, Arthur J., and Anne Montgomery. *Swords into Plowshares: Nonviolent Direct Action for Disarmament*. San Francisco: Perennial Library, 1987.
Leahy, Brendan. *Ecclesial Movements and Communities: Origins, Significance, and Issues*. Hyde Park, NY: New City, 2011.
LiveLaudatoSi, "Sign the *Laudato Si'* Pledge." https://livelaudatosi.org/.
Melloni, Alberto, ed. *"Movements" in the Church*. London: SCM, 2003.
Musto, Ronald G. *The Catholic Peace Tradition*. Maryknoll, NY: Orbis, 1986.
Nepstad, Sharon Erickson. *Catholic Social Activism: Progressive Movements in the United States*. New York: New York University Press, 2019.
———. *Religion and War Resistance in the Plowshares Movement*. New York: Cambridge University, 2008.
Osheim, Amanda. *A Ministry of Discernment: The Bishop and the Sense of the Faithful*. Collegeville, MN: Liturgical, 2016.
Paul VI. *Apostolicam Actuositatem*. Rome: Libreria Editrice Vaticana, 1965. https://www.vatican.va/archive/hist_councils/ii_vatican_council/documents/vat-ii_decree_19651118_apostolicam-actuositatem_en.html.
———. *Gaudium et Spes: Pastoral Constitution on the Church in the Modern World*. Vatican City State: Libreria Editrice Vaticana, 1965. https://www.vatican.va/archive/hist_councils/ii_vatican_council/documents/vat-ii_const_19651207_gaudium-et-spes_en.html.
———. *Octogesima Adveniens: A Call to Action*. Rome: Libreria Editrice Vaticana, 1971. http://www.vatican.va/content/paul-vi/en/apost_letters/documents/hf_p-vi_apl_19710514_octogesima-adveniens.html.
Pax Christi International. "About Us." https://paxchristi.net/about-us/.
———. "*Fratelli Tutti*: A Foundation for Advancing Nonviolence in a Violent World." October 6, 2020. https://paxchristi.net/wp-content/uploads/2020/10/Fratelli-Tutti-statement-PCI.pdf.
Pontificium Consilium de Iustitia et Pace. *Compendium of the Social Doctrine of the Church*. Washington, DC: USCCB, 2004.
Riccardi, Andrea, et al. *Sant'Egidio: Rome and the World*. Maynooth: St. Paul's Press, 1999.

Schneiders, Sandra. *Finding the Treasure: Locating Catholic Religious Life in a New Ecclesial and Cultural Context.* New York: Paulist, 2000.

———. *New Wineskins: Re-Imagining Religious Life Today.* New York: Paulist, 1986.

Sisters of Mercy. "Writing Letters to the Editor on the Papal Encyclical." https://www.sistersofmercy.org/files/images/Justice/Earth/writing_ltes_tips.pdf.

Smith, Jackie, et al. "Social Movements and World Politics: A Theoretical Framework." In *Transnational Social Movements and Global Politics: Solidarity Beyond the State*, edited by Jackie Smith et al., 59–80. Syracuse: Syracuse University Press, 1997.

Snow, David A., et al. "Mapping the Terrain." In *The Blackwell Companion to Social Movements*, edited by David A. Snow et al., 3–16. Hoboken, NJ: Wiley Blackwell, 2004. https://doi.org/10.1002/9780470999103.ch1.

Stanger, Anya. "Prisoners of Conscience in the Plowshares and School of the Americas Watch Movements: The Politics of Privilege, Gender, and Religious Identity." *Social Movement Studies* 18 (2019) 535–49. https://doi.org/10.1080/14742837.2019.1597699.

Van Stichel, Ellen. "Movements Struggling for Justice within the Church: A Theological Response to John Coleman's Sociological Approach." *Journal of Catholic Social Thought* 10 (2013) 281–93.

Verstraeten, Johan. "Catholic Social Thought and the Movements: Towards Social Discernment and a Transformative Presence in the World." *Journal of Catholic Social Thought* 10 (2013) 231–39.

Vidler, Alexander Roper. *A Century of Social Catholicism: 1820–1920.* London: SPCK, 1964.

Weck, Guillaume de. *Histoire de La Confédération Internationale Des Étudiants Catholiques "Pax Romana" 1887-1921-1946.* Fribourg: Jendly, 1946.

Wijsen, Frans Jozef Servaas, et al., eds. *The Pastoral Circle Revisited: A Critical Quest for Truth and Transformation.* Maryknoll, NY: Orbis, 2005.

Wittberg, Patricia. *The Rise and Fall of Catholic Religious Orders: A Social Movement Perspective.* Albany: State University of New York Press, 1994.

World Meeting of Popular Movements. "About." http://popularmovements.org/about/.

Zahn, Gordon C. "Social Movements and Catholic Social Thought." In *One Hundred Years of Catholic Social Thought: Celebration and Challenge*, edited by John A. Coleman, 43–54. Maryknoll, NY: Orbis, 1991.

Zald, Mayer N., and Roberta Ash. "Social Movement Organizations: Growth, Decay and Change." *Social Forces* 44 (1966) 327–41.

25

The Worker's Paradise
Eternal Life, Economic Eschatology, and Good Work as the Keys to Social Catholicism[1]

DAVID CLOUTIER, THE CATHOLIC UNIVERSITY OF AMERICA

Abstract: The topic of work is underdeveloped in Catholic thought, despite its centrality to the modern encyclical tradition. In this paper, I develop a framework for "good work," that moves beyond the classic Catholic concerns with "good-enough work" in the direction of a "sacramental" view of work consistent with the Vatican II vision of the universal call to holiness. A chief challenge to practicing this view is the fact that modern economic thought treats work not as something good, but a "disvalue" that workers and firms both seek to minimize. Catholic thought must challenge this false "consumerist eschatology," especially by showing how the universal destination of goods is meant to be achieved through labor. I conclude the paper by looking at possible proposals for public policy that would aim at good work, rather than simply more and more consumption.

---

1. This essay is a slightly modified version of a plenary address at the 2021 Catholic Theological Society of America annual meeting and printed in the CTSA *Proceedings* 75 (2021) 1–18. Permission has been granted from the CTSA for this publication.

This past year, British anthropologist James Suzman published a book offering a "deep history" of work.[2] Suzman's book follows a line of inquiry that is not new—namely, that hunter-gatherers were "the original affluent society,"[3] living off the abundance of nature; the move to a more settled life—beginning with agriculture—was a kind of "fall" into economic scarcity. Accompanying this fall was a mythologizing of the goodness of work, aided further in recent centuries by a "scarcity economics," that provided a stick when the carrot of the myth of work's value wasn't enough. Suzman suggests that an analogy to the laid-back economic existence of the hunter-gatherers can now be recovered, thanks to ever-advancing robotics and AI historian James Livingston's recent book *No More Work: Why Full Employment is a Bad Idea* sums up this line more pithily, offering an "indictment" of the "moral universe" in which "meaningful work and the production of goods is somehow better for us than indolent leisure and the consumption of goods."[4]

Compare this anti-work line of thought with that represented by Swarthmore psychologist Barry Schwartz, whose published version of his TED talk, *Why We Work*, stresses the *importance* of meaningful and satisfying work for any sort of human flourishing. In addition to much empirical research, Schwartz draws on that noted American philosopher Bruce Springsteen, who argues that houses and TVs are the "booby prize" rather than the true American dream, and that he has to constantly discipline himself to realize that it's the work of making music that keeps him alive.[5] Springsteen, in turn, might be speaking for the various workers interviewed in Studs Terkel's 1970s classic, *Working*. Whether expressing frustration or gratitude for their various ordinary jobs, they invariably return to the presence or absence of *meaningful recognition of their tasks* as the key to working life. (e.g., the steel worker who laments his painful work but wishes the names of all the ordinary laborers who built it were somewhere inscribed on the Empire State building, so workers could point it out with pride to their children).[6] Facing up to the same

2. Suzman, *Work*.

3. The term is from anthropologist Sahlins, *Stone Age Economics*, an earlier exponent of this view. For an instructive early criticism of this line of thought, see Cook, "Structural Substantivism."

4. Livingston, *No More Work*, x. His "brutally simple" refrain is "fuck work."

5. Schwartz, *Why We Work*, 89.

6. Terkel, *Working*, xxxii. During the discussion period at the convention, a questioner helpfully reminded us also of the role of the "Mohawk skywalkers" in many such projects. See Evans, "How Mohawk Skywalkers Helped."

dynamics of automation, Schwartz ends with a rousing call for a society of "better doctors, lawyers, teachers, hairdressers, and janitors," whose work is *recognized* and contributes to "healthier patients, better-educated students, and more satisfied customers and clients."[7]

Should we seek less work or better work? It's easy enough to raise quickie objections to either one of these views, and each writer does try to take on these objections. I want us to focus instead on how wildly different the basic imagination of the good human society is in these two pictures. How should Catholics approach such radically different proposals?

We are not that well-equipped to do so. For a reality that is as central to human life as work is, Catholic theological ethics has an underdeveloped and fragmented perspective.[8] Despite the fact that the modern Catholic social encyclical tradition is founded on "the worker question," most of Catholic moral thought over the past century has centered its attention either on questions in sexual and life ethics or on various forms of individual and social provisioning for the poor. Catholic marriage prep? Check. Catholic charities? Check. The Catholic worker? Not so much. Where is work, the dominant reality of most lives? A sample of recent comprehensive works on Catholic Social Teaching (CST) illustrates this: at best, work is given a single chapter in a run-through of topics, sometimes less.[9] Jeremy Posadas recently demonstrated a similar neglect in the Society of Christian Ethics, noting only nine papers on the topic out of 761 sessions, dating back to 1975.[10]

Moreover, compared to that other central reality, marriage and family, the categories for the discussion of work are not well-defined. At least in our debates about sex and marriage, some core realities about faithful, loving relationship, mutuality, fruitfulness, and a concern for the good of vulnerable children are ubiquitous. That is to say, Margaret Farley and Janet

---

7. Schwartz, *Why We Work*, 90.

8. This paper focuses on the modern encyclical tradition. For an excellent, concise overview of resources from scripture and earlier in the tradition, see Kincaid, "Work and Vocation."

9. The textbooks by Brady (*Essential Catholic Social Thought*) and Benestad (*Church, State, and Society*) have a chapter, albeit later in both volumes, rather than in a foundational place. Dorr's classic study (*Option for the Poor and for the Earth*) devotes only three pages to the fundamentals of work, before turning to specific analyses of "indirect employer" and solidarity, both of which he aims at political structures. The recent collection of essays by Bradley and Bruegger (*Catholic Social Teaching*) includes chapters on many individual topics in the tradition, but omits work entirely.

10. Posadas, "Reproductive Justice."

Smith may not agree on how to understand and apply these terms. But we all recognize that these are the terms of the discussion. Moreover, these terms clearly structure the overarching magisterial documents, whether John Paul II's *Familiaris Consortio* or Francis's *Amoris Laetitia*. What is the comparable stable moral framework for conceptualizing work?

In this paper, I argue for and apply such a framework in three steps. First, I suggest that, like marriage, we need to approach work in terms of Vatican II's core idea of the universal call to holiness. Getting beyond a minimalism of decrying sins and only seeking what I will call "good-enough work," I argue for a vision of work rooted in the vocation to holiness that is shaped by not only natural ends, but also Christian eschatology. Second, such a vision rooted in Christian eschatology requires challenging the "eschatologies" implied in modern approaches to economics. Finally, I conclude by asking how social Catholicism can engage recent public policy proposals, some of which have been predicated on "the end of work" while others more promisingly have sought a reorientation of the economy in favor of work.

Work: Naming First Principles as Final Ends

In Catholic thought, the common starting point for ethical reflection on work would probably be dignity.[11] Yet starting with dignity throws off the inquiry from the start. If we have learned anything from the revival

---

11. A quick aside on the question of what counts as "work": Oliver O'Donovan's recent treatment of it provides a possible baseline. O'Donovan (*Entering Into Rest*, 102–34) suggests that work begins at the point others come to depend on our activity. He contrasts someone who chooses to prepare a dinner party for their friends this coming weekend with a chef running a restaurant. It's not so much the financial compensation that separates the cases, but that the chef's customers and employees depend on her showing up and undertaking the activity. This idea that people depend on you to "show up and do your job" is also what makes work meaningful. For example, the hospital custodians could see how the whole enterprise depended on them keeping up with their job; conversely, few things are as depressing as the sense that no one really cares whether I show up or not, because it doesn't matter. I do assume that, short of a radical reorganization of society, most adult persons of both sexes will spend a significant chunk of their lives on "work" that involves significant training, accumulated experiential expertise, and some degree of remuneration, as opposed to "dabbling" or a "hobby." I do think the rise of a gig economy and an extensive online market means more people will undertake work that does not conform to a certain framework. Finally, I do think that questions must be raised about various forms of household and community care work, historically women's work, that are evidently "work"—indeed, are certainly so by O'Donovan's definition of others being dependent on your showing up!—but are not recognized and remunerated as such.

of Thomistic virtue ethics, it's that moral first principles are matters of *final ends*—of "happiness," of teleology. Marriage and family arguments are teleological. Dignity can tell us something about the *basic conditions* that should hold for respecting persons, but in all persons and in all situations, not just work. Yet it doesn't tell us what work is *for*.

Immediately, we meet another challenge: the notion of heavenly *rest* tempts us to view work instrumentally—just as sexuality was long viewed largely in instrumental terms, since, after all, there is no marriage in heaven, either (Matt 22:30). So just as marriage was viewed primarily in terms of reproduction of the species, so too work aims merely at survival. Indeed, at worst and erroneously, some in the tradition viewed work as merely a punishment for sin, as some viewed marriage simply as a remedy for lust.

There is an undeniable element of truth in such eschatological asceticism—St. Paul remains unmarried (1 Cor 7:7, 26), or Jesus points to the lilies of the field (Matt 6:28). Yet, in light of the universal call to holiness, I take it that all sides of Catholic debate have wanted to repudiate such limited understandings of sexuality. So too must we repudiate a simply instrumentalized conception of work. Instead, we must start by *affirming* the goodness of work—and its goodness in eschatological terms, in terms that display how work is partially constitutive of what is ultimate. We must come to see work, as we have come to see marriage, in light of Vatican II's universal call to holiness, and especially in light of our vocation to self-gift.[12] I think Catholics should fundamentally opt for the side of Schwartz (better work) rather than Suzman (less work)—probably not a surprise, given I wrote a book against luxury![13]

12. See John Paul II, *Centesimus Annus*, no. 41 (hereafter cited as *CA*), where he re-describes alienation in capitalist societies in terms of "forms of social . . . production and consumption" that "make it more difficult to offer this gift of self and to establish this solidarity between people."

13. Cloutier, *Vice of Luxury*. Posadas, "Refusal of Work," outlines effectively what could be understood as the Christian anti-work position, one that explicitly defends the "refusal to work" and raises suspicions about the whole tradition. For a more extensive evaluation of Posadas' claims, see Cloutier, "Embracing Better Work: A Reply to Jeremy Posadas," in a forthcoming collection, *Theology of Work: New Perspectives*, edited by Gregorio Guitian. Here, I note briefly two things about his article. First, its advocacy for "less work" is predicated on the core idea that work is *not* an intrinsic element of our humanity. If Posadas is correct, then the basic claim (not just the details) of *Laborem Exercens* is simply false. Second, in his postulates at the end of the article, he (presumably intentionally) equates work with "the earning of wages" or the activity that supports those who earn wages. It is true that God does not "work for wages," but (in quite different ways), neither does the small-business owner and neither do

How should we describe work in light of the call to holiness? I will first make a distinction between "good-enough work" and "good work," and then distinguish between "good work" and what I will call "sacramental work," work that is understood as an effective sign of the fullness of God's kingdom.

Catholic ethics has spent most of its time talking about achieving good-enough work—work that is not fundamentally unjust or contrary to the dignity of the worker.[14] This is certainly a very important task; nothing I say here should be understood to diminish it. From Leo XIII onward, the modern encyclicals have stressed a basic set of themes: first and foremost, the just wage, but also safe working conditions, limitations on how much work can be extracted, and rights of association. Christine Hinze's recent benchmark book, *Radical Sufficiency*, outlines this tradition in the American context comprehensively. She starts from the work of John Ryan in overcoming "subnormal conditions,"[15] and then admirably expands his lenses to include issues like race and gender that were too often rendered invisible.

Achieving "good-enough" work is necessary . . . but limited. In a sense, it is no different from a sexual ethic that focuses on "thou shalt not sin." It is minimalist. It defines a basic level of adequacy for work, ruling out "inhuman" work, but it does not yet address the role of work in flourishing. As I said, left to itself, it tends to view work—as was the case with sexuality in pre-Vatican II theology—as little more than an instrumental reality of creaturely survival. As Pius XI said in *Quadragesimo Anno*, "Man is born to labor as the birds to fly."[16]

I. I certainly don't write articles "for wages." It seems that Posadas' claims aim at two specific targets: (a) his basic suggestion that the connection between work and daily necessities should be severed, and (b) the unjust conditions of a particular (not insignificant) group of workers. I (not Posadas) might define that group in terms of those whose wages offer little or no room for economic flexibility and whose labor is directly tied to hours worked. Those who work long hours in a tech company, a law firm, or a university are presumably choosing this, or at least they have other options for their lives. Posadas insists that we not treat work in the abstract, but should always make it particular. I agree—and the very wide range of particularities of work in an advanced economy suggest an analysis more complex than the one he offers!

14. Matz, *Introducing Protestant Social Ethics*, 126, also provides a nice example of Christians laying down benchmarks for good-enough in the 1908 "social creed" of the Methodists.

15. Hinze, *Radical Sufficiency*, 269.

16. Pius XI, *Quadragesimo Anno*, no. 61 (hereafter cited as *QA*).

By contrast, John Paul II notes at the outset of *Laborem Exercens* that properly speaking, "only man [sic] works," identifying work as "one of the characteristics that distinguishes man from the rest of creatures."[17] Even what the pope defines as the "objective dimension" of work involves the exercise of a dominion that goes beyond mere "daily bread." Human work is not simply toil, but involves the development of tools and knowledge that collaboratively generate a larger commons benefitting all (*LE* 5). John Paul also develops the (more morally determinative) subjective dimension of work: work is meant to make us more and more *human*, it is good for our humanity (*LE* 6).[18] In Hinze's book, this more expansive vision was present even in Ryan's work—Hinze calls it a "dream of livelihood" within "a broader, Catholic understanding of personal and common flourishing" that included developing a person's capacities, communities, and spiritual yearnings.[19] Lovely. Yet this idea of truly good work has not received sufficient development.

How to describe it—what are its ends? Schwartz talks about work that engages us so much that at least some of the time, it is "fun." It offers us sufficient autonomy to build skills and meet new challenges. It gives us opportunities for enlivening collaboration with others. And most important, Schwartz suggests, we find the work "meaningful" in the sense that what we do seems to make a difference in the world, whether small or large. There are no shortage of examples of this. Schwartz discusses an oft-cited intensive study of how hospital custodians understood the significance of their work, and how this understanding shaped the way they fulfilled their daily responsibilities.[20] Wendell Berry has led a generation of imaginations, including mine, back to a vision of a food system involving truly good work. No one needs to explain to a room of teachers this sort of good work. And finally, I was struck by the remarkable (if also disturbing) approach to good work that Michael Jordan reveals in the recent ESPN/Netflix documentary *The Last Dance*.

Note that the *opposite* of good work might still meet the criteria for good-enough work. We may feel like a cog in a machine (*LE* 15) or be governed by managerially-established, competitive carrot-stick incentive

17. John Paul II, *Laborem Exercens*, introductory paragraph (hereafter cited as *LE*).
18. This is the basic sense he describes with the aphorism "work is for man, not man for work."
19. Hinze, *Radical Sufficiency*, 4.
20. Schwartz, *Why We Work*, 12–20. For the details of the study, see Wrzesniewski and Dutton, "Crafting a Job."

systems.²¹ But this "not-good work" can still pay a just wage, offer secure benefits, give us vacation, and avoid breaking any laws where we might cheat or steal from a competitor.

Moreover, this distinction is invaluable in explaining two different sets of polling data from Gallup. On the one hand, Gallup has long done a complex operation of polling on what they call "workplace engagement," trying to help employers identify whether workers are, as they describe it, "involved in, enthusiastic about and committed to their work and workplace."²² Roughly speaking, this is "good work," especially in its subjective dimension—it suggests the actualizing of one's human capacities that is central to John Paul's description. Over time, the percentage of "engaged workers" has generally hovered around a third, sometimes rising (as it has over the last few years), sometimes dropping back. That data suggests that all too many workers are not really developing themselves as subjects in the way John Paul describes.

Yet, in a different poll, Gallup has for decades annually surveyed workers on a range of workplace issues, asking basic questions about satisfaction: are you satisfied with your pay, your benefits, your job security, your bosses, your safety, and the like.²³ Strikingly and consistently, workers say that in their current job, they are "completely" or "somewhat" satisfied with all these things at levels well over 70 percent, and often into the 80 percent range. For example, asked about their boss, year after year, around 10 percent of workers say they are somewhat or completely dissatisfied. And when asked the question about their overall job satisfaction, almost 40 to well over 50 percent respond they are "completely satisfied," and 83–92 percent are completely or somewhat satisfied.

What are we to make of this data? I admit when I first found it, I was quite taken aback. Certainly we shouldn't read it as if we've arrived at the worker's paradise. However, it should make us think twice about how exactly to name the problems we are facing. It is not 1891, nor 1931, at least in the United States and other developed economies. We have, in fact, achieved good-enough conditions for work for a large amount of the population. Should we, as Francis always reminds us, "go to the

---

21. Schwartz, *Why We Work*, 36–60.

22. Gallup, "What Is Workplace Engagement?" They also track "actively disengaged" workers, defined as "those who have miserable work experiences and spread their unhappiness to their colleagues." This number in 2020 was 13–14 percent. Harter, "US Employee Engagement Rises after Wild 2020."

23. Gallup, "Work and Workplace (Historical Trends)."

margins" of these numbers, seek out those who are still ground down, and especially those who are often very fragilely connected to the labor market? Absolutely.²⁴

But we should also recognize that the task we have now should be named differently from the task of a century ago. We must hold onto the "good enough" level, which faces real challenges (just ask the formerly good-enough taxi drivers or hotel workers about Uber and Airbnb), but also recognize that "good enough" is *not* good enough for a society with such abundance. It should not be a privilege of the few to enjoy one's work or find it meaningful. Truly good work is needed for all.

Yet we should not even stop there. Analogously to marriage, we can come to recognize that work can be "meaningful" in a supernatural sense, too; it can be graced. As one saint put it, "the sanctification of ordinary work" is "the hinge of true spirituality" for those "who have decided to become close to God while being at the same time fully involved in temporal affairs."²⁵

As Benedict XVI argued most clearly in *Caritas in Veritate*, the "astonishing experience of *gift*" must animate all of our work. He notes that all our economic activity should be marked by "quotas of gratuitousness,"²⁶ stressing that not only does every economic decision involve a moral judgment of justice, but also "works redolent of the spirit of gift,"²⁷ where we go the extra mile and give of ourselves beyond what is due to others. Can this language of self-gift be abused? Certainly—as it sometimes has been in sexuality. But that doesn't mean we disregard it. It is still true that work itself has sacramental potential, that rightly understood, it can share in the hope of CST to "shape the earthly city in unity and peace, rendering it to some degree an anticipation and a prefiguration of the undivided city of God."²⁸

---

24. For example, the interlocking challenges here (substance abuse, lack of mental health treatment, family breakdown, and the effects of mass incarceration, to name only a few) require a much more comprehensive approach. Dr. Gemma Tulud Cruz's plenary at the 2021 CTSA conference also outlined extensively the challenges faced especially in the global labor market, although even here, there is considerable data suggesting large populations have moved out of poverty in recent decades. In any case, as I mentioned, the thrust of my paper presumes the necessity of protecting and enforcing good-enough work.

25. Escriva, "Working for God," 61. I am indebted to my wife Melissa Moschella for this reference.

26. Benedict XVI, *Caritas in Veritate*, no. 39, (hereafter cited as *CV*).

27. Benedict XVI, *CV*, no. 37.

28. Benedict XVI, *CV*, no. 7.

What does this sacramentalized work look like? I'd highly recommend Michael Naughton's recent book *Getting Work Right*, which lives up to its title. Naughton's book follows in a line of reflection that focuses on Sabbath, observing, "If we don't get Sunday right, we won't get Monday right."[29] This is a paradoxical but central theological truth about the sacramental life as a whole: we best honor the thing itself by reminding ourselves that it *represents* something much larger. Just as sacramental marriage ultimately takes its meaning by a reference outside itself, so too sacramental work refers outside itself. Naughton prioritizes what he calls "primary institutions" of worship, family, and all forms of true friendship.[30] This is "leisure" in the correct sense, but it certainly differs from so much of what we think of as leisure—above all, the reference points of God and others are the critical ones. Perhaps we could be said to have this "leisure" best as a society if we had no such thing as a "leisure industry" (though that is an exaggeration).[31]

However, though sacramentalized work refers outside itself, to "Sunday," it possesses its own value, too. The goal, Naughton rightly notes, is to achieve a "wholeness" of life—not simply a work/life "balance" but a "genuine integration."[32] Here, the notion of gift is crucial; we give ourselves to the work and to the others with whom and for whom we work.[33] Theologian John Hughes' study, *The End of Work*, also emphasizes this extension of sacramentality in ordinary jobs. He criticizes any theology that involves "the removal of *divine intrinsic value* from the

---

29. Naughton, *Getting Work Right*, xi.

30. Naughton, *Getting Work Right*, 59.

31. Obviously a whole paper could be written on leisure, but see Kelly, *Fullness of Free Time*, for a recent insightful treatment, as well as Christine Hinze's excellent CTSA presidential address, "Remembering the Rest of Life". The complexity of leisure in the social discourse of the last 150 years is well-displayed in Snape, "Leisure Studies." See also Joseph Ratzinger, who argues that true liberation comes from work that is "integrated with culture" and that concerns itself with the "deepest questions" and "community in authentic humanity" (Ratzinger, "Freedom and Liberation," 246).

32. Naughton, *Getting Work Right*, 47.

33. One might contrast this approach with an example like the film *Babette's Feast*, which is often used as an exemplar of Catholic sacramentality. Insofar as the point is to combat an overly ascetical Protestantism, it is great. But it is kind of an easy win—who will not appreciate Babette's great generosity and the conviviality of a feast? Moreover, the entire circumstance of the movie makes the occasion a mega-Sabbath: Babette wins the lottery and blows it all on one, big feast. Presumably the next day, it's back to the basics! Babette "moments" are surely great, but the real challenge is how to infuse this into daily work.

material, empirical world," warning that such approaches simply abandon the workplace to "the world of total utility."[34]

The notion of work as involving self-gift is evidently more diffuse than its focused meanings in sacramental marriage. But the decisive guide for this task is found in Benedict's *Spe Salvi*, an encyclical whose contribution to CST is often overlooked. In it, Benedict offers a radically communal vision of Christian hope for eternal life, criticizing the tradition for shrinking its eschatological horizon to the individual, and thereby ceding the grounds of social salvation to others. The heart of this communal hope: the overcoming of sin understood as "the destruction of the unity of the human race" via redemption understood as "the reestablishment of community."[35] This can't just happen "after working hours"; in so many ways, we can come to understand our work as contributing to this great project of reestablishing unity, a process that necessarily will go *beyond* the practice of justice, given the history of sin in which we find ourselves. It is this *communal vision of eternal life*, in which the human race is finally unified, toward which our daily work can and should be directed.

Economics: The Dominance of Anti-Work Eschatologies

This threefold vision of the ethics of work—good-enough, good, and sacramental—within a Catholic eschatological vision is pretty easy to establish from the modern encyclicals, as I've indicated all too briefly. The real challenge comes when we try to bring this vision into dialogue with modern economics, in order to take the next step in the analysis: to ask what this vision requires to make it more and more a reality. Where does the root problem lie? The debate often quickly moves to a market-state binary: what should markets and/or states do? This is an *important* question, but it's not the *first* question we should raise. I'll assert here that such an argument is interminable insofar as one can easily point to evidence for how both markets and states can generate conditions that foster bad work, and both can also foster much good work, in all three ways.[36] The battle of anecdotes and even of structural examples does not produce a clear winner. So, both/and, not either/or.

---

34. Hughes, *End of Work*, 221–31.

35. Benedict XVI, *Spe Salvi*, no. 14.

36. You get Michael Novak on the market side, and the progressive tradition's portfolio of state policies on the other.

But there's a more serious *and prior* issue. Instead of questions of markets and states, we need to start the dialogue with modern economics in a different place, in order to generate better practical proposals: what eschatology is implied in modern economic thought, whether market-oriented or statist?[37] And how do the structures and culture generated by these theories affect how agents approach the world of work? It would take many monographs to handle these issues in sufficient detail, so for now, let me move quickly to the central knot that needs to be unraveled: modern capitalist economies produce a kind of schizophrenia about work.

On the one hand, many write in the tradition of Max Weber's classic thesis: capitalism requires a "work ethic," a commitment to hard work and saving that maximizes production and rewards those who are willing to work. The capitalist imperative to produce require more and more "work," eventually grinding down the most vulnerable workers in the process, and worse, making them believe it is noble to be ground down in this way.

On the other hand, standard economics assumes what might be called a "consumerist eschatology": the models presume that all work is "bad," a disvalue or cost to both firms and workers *that each seeks to minimize*. At the top of the income ladder are those who want to consume without working at all. But in the mainstream in which most people live, the models assume that firms seek to minimize labor (at least labor *cost*) by adopting more efficient production schemes and wage workers seek to minimize labor (at least labor *time*), attempting to sell the work at the highest possible price presumably with as much time off as possible. This set-up is obviously inherently conflictual—firms want low-cost, high-output labor and laborers want more compensation and more time off. But since both parties have some self-interests at stake—firms needs workers, workers need firms—they strike a bargain.[38]

Where does the bargain lead? There are of course market defenders—let the workers and firms strike their own bargains—and detractors—the state needs to protect vulnerable workers from the obvious power of large-scale capital. But the important thing is that *both* types of economists presume the same consumerist eschatology. On the one hand, defenders of neoclassical economics suggest the market works fairly well

---

37. I am using eschatology here loosely to indicate what is ultimate in some sort of last-things end state for the economy.

38. Borjas, *Labor Economics*, 4, describes these maximizing negotiations as the basic equilibrium defining the labor market.

in sorting out this bargain while the overall productivity of society expands.[39] In Harvard economist Greg Mankiw's textbook, he assumes that the question to be explained in this bargain is about the wage level, which is a matter of "why some people live in mansions, ride in limousines, and vacation on the French Riviera, while other people live in small apartments, ride a bus, and vacation in their own backyards."[40] Differentiated wages are *about leisure consumption*.[41] Harvard's George Borjas recites the same bargain: labor supply is defined in terms of workers *who seek well-being by consuming goods* "such as fancy cars, nice homes . . . and leisure." More tellingly, he notes that the slope of the labor supply curve is understood in terms of "how many additional dollars' worth of goods it would take to 'bribe' the person into giving up some leisure time."[42] It is interesting that Borjas supplies scare quotes around the word "bribe"!

Others are more skeptical about the bargain benefitting both parties: CST assumes that the state needs to provide what John Paul described as a "strong juridical framework"[43] for such bargains that (at least) maintains social peace and (at best) provides Keynesian demand management via government fiscal policy to save both firms and workers from excessive and destructive swings in the business cycle.[44] Through progressive taxation, the state also steps in to undertake some redistributive taxation

---

39. Economists do presume a set of worker protections and the like, such that all workers are theoretically protected from gross abuses. The question of what "worker protections" means is obviously contested, and the problem of extending such protections to those on the margins is significant, but few economists today argue for a pure-laissez-faire system.

40. Mankiw, *Principles of Economics*, 413.

41. To be fair, Mankiw notes plenty of problems with the basic model—the nature of some work may be more pleasant or enjoyable, and at certain levels the agent may prefer less work or at least less work time rather than enhanced consumption. Yet even *that* trade-off is described as hours spent working versus "hours you have to watch TV, enjoy dinner with friends, or pursue your favorite hobby" (Mankiw, *Principles of Economics*, 399). Even worse, it is then dismissed, since it would make the labor supply curve bend backwards, and therefore complicate the model too much. See Medaille, *Toward a Truly Free Market* for an accessible Catholic distributist critique of how economics models labor, including the key point about backward-bending curves.

42. Borjas, *Labor Economics*, 21, 30.

43. John Paul II, *Centesimus Annus*, no. 42. Even Pius XI notes that "capital . . . was long able to appropriate to itself excessive advantages" (*QA*, no. 54).

44. This is basically the picture assumed by the American postwar economy, with its "Treaty of Detroit" tamping down disruptive strife between workers and big companies and attentive countercyclical fiscal policy managing supply and demand in the overall economy. For an account of how unusual this period was, from the global dominance of America amidst the ruins of WWII to the homogeneity promoted by the rise of a mass media and decades of immigration restrictions, see Levin, *Fractured Republic*.

of rents. Those skeptical of the sufficiency of the Keynesian path can take the socialist step: instead of just regulating the firm-worker relationship, the state can take over the means of production and direct them for the benefit of the workers themselves.[45]

But to what end? Here the visions of Keynes and Marx ultimately agree with the Harvard economists: less work, more leisure. One author captured this eschatology by entitling his 2019 book "Fully Automated Luxury Communism."[46] When we center on market-versus-state arguments over "capitalism," we miss the built-in "consumerist eschatology"—the assumption by all parties that work is something to be minimized, and that at best it is an instrumental reality, enabling consumption. Work has only John Paul's objective dimension: it provides resources to spend outside the job, and it produces technologies and processes that further minimize the demands of work. These models describe how labor and wages work *in the dysfunctional context John Paul dubs "superdevelopment"*—a super-abundance of goods with no regard for "being" more.[47] And from the employer side, especially as the state does a better job supporting the worker, this means as many smart machines as possible. *Wall-E* world is not far away.[48]

Wall-E world—or more seriously, *Brave New World*—is in effect the economic eschaton. It is the place where socialist and neoclassical economic eschatologies converge, where work is minimized and where any remaining work is good-enough work. It doesn't generate good or sacramental work. Yet even before we get to an eschatological *Wall-E* world, we should recognize another problem with these consumerist models of the worker-firm bargain: how poorly they actually describe the mindset

---

45. To be fair, Marx was very reserved in his eschatological description. Heilbroner, *Worldly Philosophers*, 162, notes that "there is almost nothing that looks beyond the day of judgment to see what the future is like"; Speigel, *Growth of Economic Thought*, 476, notes that Marx wanted to resist the typical utopian descriptions of other socialists of the time (e.g., Owen). Still, Speigel includes his famous quote about fishing during the day and criticism after dinner.

46. The book is by Aaron Bastani and summarized by Lowrey, "Give Us Fully Automated Luxury Communism."

47. John Paul II, *Sollicitudo Rei Socialis*, no. 28.

48. *Wall-E* is a 2008 Pixar/Disney film about a time when the earth has been completely trashed, and humans now live in artificial space environments in which they passively consume resort-like pleasures and whir around from place to place in autonomous vehicular seats staring at constantly-on video screens. For reference, the iPhone had only been introduced to the world the year prior! Slides were shown during the convention presentation to illustrate these scenes.

of so many workers and even firms in today's world.[49] Neither maximizing income nor maximizing comfort and ease describes the approach to work seen in the diverse examples of farmers in Wendell Berry, Michael Jordan's dances, Barry Schwartz's hospital custodians, and many aspects of the jobs we do as academic theologians. In fact, the economic models miss almost everything important about those and hundreds of other examples of *good* work. Does good work require a certain amount of rest, fair compensation, moments where going to work is "easy"? Sure. But it would be all wrong to focus on agents *maximizing* these, just as it would be wrong to model firm behavior exclusively as profit maximization. Since the model distorts the agents involved in the labor bargain, it also offers us very little insight into what we really want to know, which is: what makes *these* custodians and *these* professors and *these* farmers and *these* basketball players possible? What are the conditions and structures that, while they can never guarantee good work (since by definition, good and sacramental work involves a certain sort of agency), can enable it and foster it?

The summary version of this discussion is that much market-versus-state economic debate is of little help to us because it doesn't actually aim us at a *worker's* paradise. It aims us at a *consumer's* paradise.[50] Now it's important to be fair here: setting strict Marxism to the side, mainstream economics, whether more market-oriented or more robustly Keynesian

---

49. Economic historians routinely note that the effects of capitalism on workers tend to imagine one particular form of worker, one calling it "stereotypes of the English capitalism of the 1850s" (Heilbroner, *Worldly Philosophers*, 169), and another noting the assumption that capitalism means the "increasing misery" and size of Marx's "proletariat" (Speigel, *Growth of Economic Thought*, 472). But work under capitalism turns out to be more complicated than that.

50. At an anthropological level, this conflictual frame also plays into a "good people-bad people" understanding of the world. This fundamental assumption of a divided world was rightly critiqued from the beginning by Leo XIII, who stated astutely in *Rerum Novarum*, no. 15 (hereafter cited as *RN*), that the "great mistake" in the doctrinaire socialism of his time was "the idea that class is naturally hostile to class; that rich and poor are intended by nature to live at war with one another." There are clearly structural critiques to be made of economics—the consumerist eschatology I've described is one such "structure of sin"—but the underlying anthropology of a world divided into heroes and villains should be rejected by a Christian anthropology that sees all people as sinners offered redemption in Christ. People are not Rousseauian innocents simply distorted by bad social structures. It is also the case, however, that we are not just self-interested, greedy knaves, an assumption that too often lies underneath apologetics for capitalism. These contrasting anthropologies could be seen as another way to contrast with the Christian vision of the person, good but fallen, in need of both the development of virtue over time and the gift of forgiveness and mercy on the way. Sacramental work would aim at both of these.

on government intervention, has historically focused on consumption because the problem to be solved was scarcity.[51] Such "scarcity economics" is often criticized by invoking Keynes's speculative essay, *Economic Possibilities for Our Grandchildren*. In that famous essay, written in 1930, Keynes suggests that within a century, productivity increases will in effect reduce returns to capital to zero. Productive capital will no longer be scarce, and so the "economic problem" will be solved.[52] I agree with those who have recognized that, at least in developed countries, we have (in the aggregate at least) overcome (this type of) scarcity, *and yet* we still have an economic system founded on it.[53] As if we don't have enough bread to go around!

Where I disagree with many anti-scarcity accounts is their idea that the problem that remains is simply intervening in the system in order to redistribute the artificially-scarce goods, thus achieving the universal destination of goods.

I disagree with this move to redistribution for two reasons. One, because (as I discuss at some length in my luxury book) one cannot overcome scarcity per se by redistribution *unless people self-limit their market desires to some level of basic necessities*.[54] Keynes himself *explicitly* distinguishes between "absolute" and "relative" needs. His post-scarcity economics is only about producing enough so that *absolute* "needs are satisfied."[55]

But, a second reason to object to mere redistribution is the neglect of good work: redistribution of the spoils of productive late capitalism

---

51. As Alfred Marshall, Keynes's predecessor and teacher put it, the purpose of economics is to identify "the cause and cure of poverty." Cited in Heilbroner, *Teachings from the Worldly Philosophy*, 210.

52. Keynes, "Economic Possibilities."

53. See, for example, Clark, "Wealth as Abundance and Scarcity."

54. Cloutier, *Vice of Luxury*, 160–69. Can we have enough food for all? Certainly. Can we have good schools for all? Not as long as some people want "better" schools and are willing to pay (in various ways) for them. Can we have (as Ben-Ami puts it) *Ferraris for all*? No, because people buy Ferraris in part for their symbolic value that obtains because of their scarcity, and if everyone has one, it won't be a Ferrari any more. Economists like Hirsch (*Social Limits to Growth*) and Frank (*Falling Behind*) are clear in explaining why.

55. Keynes, "Economic Possibilities," 365. He continues: "in the sense that we prefer to devote our further energies to *non-economic* purposes." Thus, highly productive economies cannot grow their way to Keynes's post-scarcity situation unless people (of all classes) curb their wants. Without curbing wants, scarcity competition just re-emerges no matter how much stuff there is.

still implies that fatal consumerist eschatology, that the universal destination of goods means *as little work as possible*.⁵⁶ What distinguishes Catholic social thought quite sharply here is the fundamental insight, articulated most clearly in *Laborem Exercens*, that capital should serve labor. John Paul insists that the priority of persons over things means that the accumulation of both natural resources and capital must be ordered to empowering the "subject" character of the person, to increase not simply their "output," but their humanity. "The only legitimate title" to the possession of the means of production, whether by market or state, "is *that they should serve labor*, and thus, by serving labor, they should make possible the achievement of the first principle of this order, namely, the universal destination of goods and the right to common use of them."⁵⁷ Thus, the true picture of just relations in a society is that *the universal destination of goods should come about through labor*.⁵⁸ In *Fratelli Tutti*, Francis explicitly reiterates this, noting that "helping the poor financially" is only a "provisional solution," and "the broader objective should always be to allow them a dignified life through work," adding "there is no poverty worse than that which takes away work and the dignity of work."⁵⁹ Once we have beyond-necessity productivity as a society, what we should seek, as agents *and* structurally, is not less work, but better work. Not more compensation, but better use of a firm's resources to make all workers not simply good-enough, but empowered for good work, and capable of sacramental quotas of gratuitousness. Not a consumer's paradise, but a worker's paradise, where the primary abundance is not more and more things, but more and more genuinely rewarding work for all.

---

56. In this regard, Keynes's own life is instructive. Despite clearly possessing the resources to work little or even not at all, he chose to work incessantly his whole life— and not simply on his scholarship, but on innumerable institutional tasks he could have easily left to others. Further, whatever the productivity imagined for capital in Keynes's scheme, his own way of life seems to rely heavily on the service work of others. Perhaps one could imagine a virtually costless life of zoom meetings, Jetsons-style automat meals, and Netflix streaming, but it strikes me that he—and we—would instead prefer train travel, convivial in-person campuses, manually-prepared meals, and live theatrical performances!

57. John Paul II, *LE*, no. 14.

58. This claim likely constitutes the basic contrast of my account here with the aforementioned anti-work account of Jeremy Posadas. Posadas contests in particular the tradition of connecting basic necessities to labor, while I have argued that labor is not merely instrumental to these needs, but rather that labor participation should be understood as intrinsic to how a post-scarcity society of abundance would function.

59. Francis, *Fratelli Tutti*, no. 162 (hereafter cited as *FT*).

Scenes from the Future: The End of Work or Working for the Proper Ends?

What does this mean in practical terms? The context of the present collection of essays is inspired by a vision of "social Catholicism" rooted in the original nineteenth century European Catholic movements that sought to address newly-emergent social realities. The tradition of Catholic social thought has insisted that at least one key way to address these realities is by participating in the political process to craft legislation that would reform social structures and processes. In the United States context, the contribution of John A. Ryan in advocating for a minimum wage is a classic example. But if our additional challenge is now to foster more "good" and "sacramental" work, what possibilities are there? It may be more challenging to do this in today's more complicated economy. As something of a counterexample to Ryan's effective advocacy for a policy that became entrenched, the US bishops' attempt at a high-profile intervention in debates about the economy received much criticism, and not just from nascent Catholic "theo-cons."[60] Social Catholicism must proceed with nuance and precision in the present context. Therefore, I want to start with some cautions about macro-policy solutions to the present challenges of work, before turning to some more promising pathways.

First caution: "good work" requires attention to both moral agents and micro-structures in the workplace—which is to say that it is greatly aided by the precision tools of critical realist sociology. As Daniel Finn, Daniel Daly, Matthew Shadle, myself and others have argued, critical realism allows careful attention to the *interaction of agency and structures*.[61] Good work is necessarily a matter of developing and exercising a certain sort of agency—and we need to give an account of that "virtue work ethic" in a way that is not simply "work hard." Yet this development of the virtuous worker is shaped by structural realities—these, however, are micro-realities, ones that vary from workplace to workplace, ones that look different in hospitals versus grocery stores versus universities. A similar attention to micro-structural realities might also address the real problem of moral luck, which is the subject of my respondent Kate Ward's excellent forthcoming book from Georgetown. One-size-fits-all macro-structural solutions simply do not fit to address these problems.

---

60. See, amidst the initial theocon critiques, for example, Greeley's intriguing objections to *Economic Justice for All* in "A 'Radical' Dissent."

61. Finn, *Moral Agency*.

Indeed, first of all, we should heed James Keenan's consistent calls for the university to focus on its own ethics, raising tough questions in our own institutions that we can do more than give papers about.[62]

Second caution: reliance on material incentives to self-interest—whether delivered via market or state—are fine to a point. Yet studies show that simply incentivizing self-interest has diminishing returns, some perverse outcomes, and, in the long run, erodes agent motivation toward shared and intrinsic goods.[63] So the categories of good and sacramental work are not chiefly going to be about getting self-interest right, but in fact shaping agents and organizations and citizens to get beyond the "what's in it for me" question.

A third caution is to recognize that conversations about "the future of work"—and especially the end of work—are complicated, speculative, and produce much disagreement among experts. In a longer space, I would engage in some detail three very different, yet all very expert, analyses.[64] For this plenary, we simply need to recognize that the future of work is not a certainty like gravity: rather, it involves questions about technology that, as Francis reminds us, "are not neutral" but "are in reality decisions about the kind of society we want to build."[65] To use a blunt yet complicated example, I am all for just wages, but a $15 *national* minimum wage is a good way to kill small retail for all but the highest-end

---

62. See Keenan, *University Ethics*. For example, isn't the reward system at universities skewed toward senior faculty? But isn't the problem really not faculty at all, but "administrative creep"? Or isn't the problem that well-off institutions simply add indefinitely to their advantage over others, in the ceaseless quest to the eschatological goal of becoming Harvard, while lecturing poorer institutions who can't charge high tuition and maintain endowments that provide enormous stock returns? These are really difficult questions for organizations to have frank, open discussions about, even though such things are known and said privately all the time. I am not suggesting magic-bullet solutions; indeed, the critical realist focus on specific agency/structure situations should excite us to look at the possibilities of improving work in our own backyards.

63. See the detailed and nuanced series of studies in Bowles, *Moral Economy*.

64. For a "this-time-is-no-different" analysis that suggests the pattern we have long seen of technological disruption simply leading to new jobs and roles in other areas of society, see Frey, *Technology Trap*. For a "no, this-time-is-different" account that suggests smart machines are much more disruptive than farm machinery and factory production, see Susskind, *World without Work*. For an analysis that suggests the disruption caused by current technologies simply can't be compared with the "one-time-only" leaps in labor-saving associated with electrification, water systems, combustion engines, and even basic home appliances like the refrigerator and the washing machine, see Gordon, *Rise and Fall of American Growth*.

65. Francis, *Laudato Si'*, no. 107.

luxury goods, particularly in lower cost of living parts of the country.[66] Amazon has zero problems paying $15/hour in part because it has a lot fewer workers, no matter where it operates. Plus, it clearly can automate to scale in ways others cannot. A $15 national minimum wage means advantage Amazon, which is a decision about the kind of society we want to build. As one economist puts it in explaining this future, reflecting the usual consumerist eschatology, "this is simply because people are more expensive than machines. The system will do everything in its power to get its work done with the minimum number of people. It is going to try to shed people whenever and wherever it can."[67] The context for his argument is the new low-wage field of video-game players, in which companies hire low-skill players to provide weak but still human competition for wealthier players, who will then vie to show off and show up these weaker players by buying various in-game enhancements![68] We shouldn't allow some broad hypothetical scenario to determine these choices. Nor is economics a science that is deterministic in this way, in any case. If we want to incentivize good work, instead of Amazon and video gaming vanity aids, we can do it.

How? I want to conclude by noting three bodies of work that offer promising steps *outside the consumerist eschatology of traditional economics* and instead develop policy packages that consider how to sustain abundance (i.e., the universal destination of goods) *through* labor, rather than around it. The three approaches are potentially complementary. Each moves at a level that one might call "pre-policy"—that is, they question assumptions that tend to keep us trapped in a certain set of policy options, especially the tendency to orient economic policy simply in terms of consumption-oriented growth.

The first is best represented by Oren Cass, a conservative policy wonk seeking to move Republican economic policy away from what he calls the misguided "economic piety" of globalist neo-liberalism, and toward a "productive pluralism." His key critique is that recent economic policy has made the "wrong trade-off," prioritizing the welfare of

---

66. I would stress that localities may well be able to pay and have good reason to set local minimum wages that are $15 or even higher.

67. Castronova, "Players for Hire," 202.

68. As economist Cowen, *Average Is Over*, 23, more cynically puts it, there is always room for workers to show up to make high earners with disposable income feel better, whether through yoga classes, video game players, or various consumer products and services that can help them with their virtue signaling!

consumers over the welfare of producers.[69] He offers a host of policy paths (some more debatable than others), but the most important is adjusting the tax and regulatory incentives that in their current form discourage both firms and workers from low and mid-skill work.

In one sense, Cass represents a set of claims about government action to support workers and existing industries, invest heavily in education, and supporting subsidiary communities that the political Left has supported for decades. Cass and the Left differ over key things—he is no fan of unions, nor of environmental regulation, both of which he thinks ultimately harm workers. But what is valuable about Cass is his attempt to make explicit a different kind of eschatology for the economy. One can see it most vividly in his critics from the political Right. For example, Glenn Hubbard has offered significant critiques of Cass. Hubbard says Cass supports "an intuitive but fatally damaging notion. He argues that from Adam Smith onward, economists have gotten the big picture wrong—the 'wealth of a nation' lies not in consumption or living standards but in jobs, good jobs, even particular jobs, using manufacturing jobs as the symbol of 'good jobs.'"[70] Hubbard goes on to express a reasonable concern that Cass's approach leads inevitably to government corruption in "picking" economic winners and losers—maybe, maybe not—but notice that his prior baseline critique is precisely that Cass has abandoned the consumerist eschatology! Cass is not maximizing the wealth of the nation. What Hubbard fails to see is that a critique of mercantilism in a world of scarcity may properly be aimed at increasing the human flourishing of all, but that in the situation of today's developed world, there can be a reasonable trade-off of some consumption in favor of sustaining better work. Cass's policy framework may not be perfect, but it helps us see what such a changed frame might look like.

The second promising body of work is represented by the Italian economic school advocating a "civil economy." The school's most prominent advocates have developed their approach in explicitly Catholic terms and have influenced papal teaching, especially *Caritas in Veritate*. More so than Cass, the civil economists are critical of the way in which capitalism's focus on efficiency via "the principle of contract" has the effect of crowding out "the principle of reciprocity," as a different kind of

---

69. Cass, *Once and Future Worker*, 2, 4.
70. Hubbard, "Enduring Logic."

genuinely two-way relationship.[71] Typical economic models make reciprocity instrumental to quantitatively-measurable contract. For example, if firms are generous to workers, the generosity is framed by traditional economists as the firm doing so *for the self-interested purpose* of maximizing productivity and profit. Eventually, the understanding of relations of reciprocity in society shrinks, as it is squeezed from the one side by a substitution of market goods for the more human goods of relationship (since the former are more easily acquired and systemically maximized), and from the other side by relationships of disinterested charity, brought in to compensate for the failures of efficiency.

This approach requires a way of attending to and encouraging existing forms of reciprocity—both measuring them at a macro level and seeing them at work structurally at a micro-level in particular workplaces. Whereas Cass's approach focuses on changing existing structural incentive systems, reciprocity's very character makes it resistant to incentivization! What instead is needed is a strong account of firms—perhaps not all firms, but many—as "necessary societies." The term "necessary societies" is borrowed from Russell Hittinger's work.[72] Hittinger's interpretation of CST has focused needed attention on the way the principle of subsidiarity is not so much a small/big question, as much as it is a question of the proper common goods of subsidiary communities, and the extent to which higher-order communities, especially the state, are meant to help them fulfill their proper functions, rather than replace the organization or subsume it entirely to the ends of the higher order.[73] To suggest that, at least in the modern world, firms are these sorts of communities is in effect to suggest that those engaged in banking, in medical care, in journalism, in universities, and in construction understand their firms as oriented to ends proper to the organization, such that workers are bound together by more than just money and personal ambition. How could we both measure and analyze the success of firms in developing this sort of common good ethos?

Finally, the third, most challenging possibility might be called "the road not taken"—represented by the (non-mythical) histories of British Luddites, American prairie populists, and Catholic distributists. Stripped of its sometimes questionable cultural nostalgias, such a path first and foremost recognizes the importance of what one might call

71. Bruni and Zamagni, *Civil Economy*, esp. 210–15.

72. Hittinger, "Three Necessary Societies."

73. See, above all, Hittinger, "Coherence of the Four Basic Principles of Catholic Social Doctrine."

"proprietorship," *the ability for skilled workers to maintain agency and control over the tools and processes by which they do their work.*[74] Such an approach is wrongly understood to be suspicious of technology per se—the suspicion is rather of what Francis rightly condemns as the technocratic paradigm, whereby technologies are implemented in ways that fundamentally serve those with the greatest power. Douglas Rushkoff's explicit advocacy for a "digital distributism" is an interesting example. One of the earliest and most insightful chroniclers of digital culture, his *Throwing Rocks at the Google Bus* explicitly recommends CST in its last chapter, in support of widespread, open-source digital platforms that are not operated for maximum profit.[75] The key elements of such a proposal demand something from both agents and structures. Structurally, this would require genuine dismantling of oligarchic and anti-competitive domination of the digital space. But it will also demand agents with a love of creative skill, and a formation of users in the admittedly more arduous (but ultimately more rewarding) work of learning how to take ownership in the tools of work and cooperate with others to foster that work. For Rushkoff, this would mean my trying to wean myself off of Microsoft's and Google's products as tools on which I am utterly reliant!

If you assembled Cass, Zamagni, and Rushkoff in a room and asked what legislation is needed to foster their visions, I'm not sure you would get agreement. But such disagreement illuminates the complexity of the actual situation with which we are faced. Cass's proposals clearly target the need to rebuild a more labor-intensive economy that produces goods through hands-on labor; the civil economists are envisioning an economy with stable workplaces of a human size; Rushkoff meanwhile accepts that the economic world will increasingly involve electronic transactions, and so the priority should be to avoid nineteenth-century-railroad-like monopolies on platforms and networks.[76] In one sense, they could be: a

---

74. The centrality of forms of worker ownership was prominent in earlier encyclicals (*QA*, nos. 61–63), and makes occasional appearances in more recent documents (*LE*, no. 14, envisioning each worker as a "part-owner of the great workbench," or *CV* 38, on various enterprises including cooperatives based on "mutualist principles"), albeit in less specified form. For a nice, accessible reminder of the centrality of cooperatives in CST, see Dodson, "Co-Op Pope." While specific forms of ownership are varied, the key point here is enabling certain sorts of worker agency.

75. Rushkoff, *Throwing Rocks*, 224–39.

76. As an aside, it is also noteworthy that these proposals—except crucially for Rushkoff, who understands the dynamics of digital firm evolution to depend on the venture capital system behind it—neglect the "financialized" background picture, where other parts of the economy become subordinated to finance, rather than served

small manufacturer of custom goods in the Midwest can market their products far more extensively digitally, but needs protection so that the platform managers do not suck away all the profits; if the firm becomes established in a solid market niche, it can stay where it's at and become a long-term, stable workplace infused with reciprocity. At the same time, they do not always cut in the same direction. It seems to me indisputable that firms are more likely to retain workers and develop them if they have a certain amount of market power that insulates them from competition. As previously noted, the Internet has certainly disrupted the taxi and hotel industries, and the list could go on. Moreover, Cass's argument in particular suggest the way in which both environmentalism and loose immigration policies serve the interests of elite knowledge consumers at the expense of those in a different class—a message that Rushkoff, for example, might find very hard to swallow.

That said, what unites these proposals is that none envision the response to technological productivity advances in terms of a consumerist eschatology—that is, in terms of an ever-increasing global marketplace in which we get better and better stuff *or* in terms of a state swooping in to redistribute the wealth generated by the technologies. Instead, they aim *to use the tools of productivity to create space for more good work*, to upgrade not the incomes from work as much as the experience of work. In so doing, they actually require more of all of us than do the typical market-state solutions.

This "more" is in part because we have fought the fight for "good-enough" work. We did not, however, build a worker's paradise; we built suburbia. Dilbert's office (the Gen X example) and David Graeber's "bullshit jobs" (the millennial example) present a different set of moral challenges than did the Homestead strikers. The "more" that is asked from us now is to rethink and elevate the ends for which we work. Instead of sending humans to Mars or inventing yet-more-miraculous devices, our aim should be to make "more" of the noble and enriching work we already know is possible. In so doing, "more" will be asked of us, too, because the standard playbooks for pathways to good-enough work aren't as easily available for creating good work. We will need more virtuous agents *and* we will need more cooperative and attentively curated workplace structures.

---

by it. The financialization becomes even more complicated with the rise of the "surveillance capitalism," built on big data and ultimately social control. See Zuboff, *Rise of Surveillance Capitalism*.

This is very much consistent with the "more" that lies at the heart of recent Catholic social tradition, the more the encyclicals call integral human development, which we might consider as another name for the universal call to holiness. Paul VI describes our movement toward this:

Less human conditions: the lack of material necessities for those who are without the minimum essential for life, the moral deficiencies of those who are mutilated by selfishness. Less human conditions: oppressive social structures, whether due to the abuses of ownership or to the abuses of power, to the exploitation of workers or to unjust transactions. Conditions that are more human: the passage from misery towards the possession of necessities, victory over social scourges, the growth of knowledge, the acquisition of culture. Additional conditions that are more human: increased esteem for the dignity of others, the turning toward the spirit of poverty, cooperation for the common good, the will and desire for peace. Conditions that are still more human: the acknowledgment by man of supreme values, and of God their source and their finality. Conditions that, finally and above all, are more human: faith, a gift of God accepted by the good will of man, and unity in the charity of Christ, Who calls us all to share as sons in the life of the living God, the Father of all men.[77]

Note how the passage becomes more challenging . . . when it moves beyond achieving good-enough conditions for all. Instead of upper-middle-class suburbia, the next step is a "spirit of poverty." Then comes working more and more in solidarity with others, in greater peace, with greater clarity about the values that unite us. Finally, we begin to make manifest our common journey toward a supernatural destiny, to radically communal eternal life.[78] It is a beautiful, challenging vision, full of the same hope for church and world that animated the work of Vatican II. This vision of integral human development leading on to the eternal hope of life in communion with God and all peoples of the earth—this is the only worker's paradise that can or will exist. Blessed are the ones who labor for this harvest.[79]

---

77. Paul VI, *Populorum Progressio*, no. 21.

78. It's this vision of Paul VI on which has been built John Paul II's defining of structures of solidarity in which "we are all really responsible for all," Benedict XVI's description of an economic world infused with gratuitousness and communion, and Francis's call for sobriety and a fundamental change of paradigm in the face of the crisis of the environment, poised to diminish so radically the most poor in the world.

79. I am deeply grateful to my colleagues Christina McRorie, Daniel Finn, and William Mattison, who read and commented on a draft, and also to those who posed questions at the CTSA convention.

Bibliography

Ben-Ami, Daniel. *Ferraris for All*. Bristol: Policy, 2012.
Benedict XVI. *Caritas in Veritate: On Integral Development in Charity and Truth*. Vatican City State: Libreria Editrice Vaticana, 2009. https://www.vatican.va/content/benedict-xvi/en/encyclicals/documents/hf_ben-xvi_enc_20090629_caritas-in-veritate.html#_ednref112.
———. *Spe Salvi*. Vatican City State: Libreria Editrice Vaticana, 2007. https://www.vatican.va/content/benedict-xvi/en/encyclicals/documents/hf_ben-xvi_enc_20071130_spe-salvi.html.
Benestad, Brian. *Church, State, and Society: An Introduction to Catholic Social Doctrine*. Washington, DC: The Catholic University of America Press, 2011.
Borjas, George. *Labor Economics*. 7th ed. New York: McGraw-Hill, 2016.
Bowles, Samuel. *The Moral Economy: Why Good Incentives Are No Substitute for Good Citizens*. New Haven: Yale University Press, 2016.
Bradley, Gerard, and Christian Bruegger. *Catholic Social Teaching: A Volume of Scholarly Essays*. New York: Cambridge University Press, 2019.
Brady, Bernard. *Essential Catholic Social Thought*. 3rd ed. Maryknoll, NY: Orbis, 2017.
Bruni, Luigino, and Stefano Zamagni. *Civil Economy: Efficiency, Equity, Public Happiness*. Bern: Lang, 2007.
Cass, Oren. *The Once and Future Worker: A Vision for the Renewal of Work in America*. New York: Encounter, 2018.
Castronova, Edward. "Players for Hire: Gamers and the Future of Low-Skill Work." In *The Digital Transformation of Labor: Automation, the Gig Economy and Welfare*, edited by Anthony Larsson and Robin Teigland, 200–212. New York: Routledge, 2020.
Clark, Charles M. A. "Wealth as Abundance and Scarcity: Perspectives from Catholic Social Thought and Economic Theory." In *Rediscovering Abundance*, edited by Helen Alford and Michael Naughton, 28–56. Notre Dame: University of Notre Dame Press, 2006.
Cloutier, David. "Embracing Better Work: A Reply to Jeremy Posadas." In *Theology of Work: New Perspectives*, edited by Gregorio Guitián. Forthcoming.
———. *The Vice of Luxury: Economic Excess in a Consumer Age*. Washington, DC: Georgetown University Press, 2015.
Cook, Scott. "'Structural Substantivism': A Critical Review of Marshall Sahlins' *Stone Age Economics*." *Comparative Studies in Society and History* 16 (1974) 355–79.
Cowen, Tyler. *Average Is Over*. New York: Penguin, 2013.
Dodson, Christopher. "The Co-Op Pope." *North Dakota Catholic Conference*, November 2015. https://ndcatholic.org/yourresources/editorials/column1115/.
Dorr, Donal. *Option for the Poor and for the Earth*. Maryknoll, NY: Orbis, 2012.
Escriva, Josemaria. "Working for God." In *Friends of God*, 55–72. London: Scepter, 1981.
Evans, Tony Tekaroniake. "How Mohawk Skywalkers Helped Build New York City's Tallest Buildings." *History Channel*, May 13, 2021. https://www.history.com/news/mohawk-skywalkers-ironworkers-new-york-skyscrapers.
Finn, Daniel, ed. *Moral Agency within Social Structures and Culture: A Primer on Critical Realism for Christian Ethics*. Washington, DC: Georgetown University Press, 2020.

Francis. *Fratelli Tutti*. Vatican City State: Libreria Editrice Vaticana, 2020. https://www.vatican.va/content/francesco/en/encyclicals/documents/papa-francesco_20201003_enciclica-fratelli-tutti.html.

———. *Laudato Si'*. Vatican City State: Libreria Editrice Vaticana, 2015. https://www.vatican.va/content/francesco/en/encyclicals/documents/papa-francesco_20150524_enciclica-laudato-si.html.

Frank, Robert. *Falling Behind*. Berkeley: University of California Press, 2007.

Frey, Carl Benedikt. *The Technology Trap*. Princeton: Princeton University Press, 2019.

Gallup. "What Is Workplace Engagement?" https://www.gallup.com/workplace/285674/improve-employee-engagement-workplace.aspx?g_source=link_WWWV9&g_medium=speedbump#ite-285701.

———. "Work and Workplace (Historical Trends)." https://news.gallup.com/poll/1720/work-work-place.aspx.

Gordon, Robert. *The Rise and Fall of American Growth*. Princeton: Princeton University Press, 2016.

Greeley, Andrew. "A 'Radical' Dissent." In *Challenge and Response*, edited by Robert Royal, 33–47. Washington, DC: EPPC, 1985.

Harter, Jim. "US Employee Engagement Rises after Wild 2020." *Gallup*, February 26, 2021. https://www.gallup.com/workplace/330017/employee-engagement-rises-following-wild-2020.aspx.

Heilbroner, Robert, ed. *Teachings from the Worldly Philosophy*. New York: Norton, 1996.

———. *The Worldly Philosophers*. 6th ed. New York: Simon & Schuster, 1986.

Hinze, Christine Firer. *Radical Sufficiency: Work, Livelihood, and a US Catholic Economic Ethic*. Washington, DC: Georgetown University Press, 2021.

———. "Remembering the Rest of Life: Toward a Rest-Inflected Theology of Work and Action." *Proceedings of the CTSA* 76 (2022), 67–85.

Hirsch, Fred. *The Social Limits to Growth*. Cambridge: Harvard University Press, 1976.

Hittinger, Russell. "The Coherence of the Four Basic Principles of Catholic Social Doctrine: An Interpretation." *Nova et Vetera* 7 (2009) 791–838.

———. "The Three Necessary Societies." *First Things*, June 2017. https://www.firstthings.com/article/2017/06/the-three-necessary-societies.

Hubbard, R. Glenn. "The Enduring Logic of the Wealth of Nations." *National Review*, March 1, 2022. https://www.aei.org/op-eds/the-enduring-logic-of-the-wealth-of-nations/.

Hughes, John. *The End of Work: Theological Critiques of Capitalism*. Malden, MA: Blackwell, 2007.

John Paul II. *Centesimus Annus*. Vatican City State: Libreria Editrice Vaticana, 1991. https://www.vatican.va/content/john-paul-ii/en/encyclicals/documents/hf_jp-ii_enc_01051991_centesimus-annus.html.

———. *Laborem Exercens*. Vatican City State: Libreria Editrice Vaticana, 1981. https://www.vatican.va/content/john-paul-ii/en/encyclicals/documents/hf_jp-ii_enc_14091981_laborem-exercens.html.

———. *Sollicitudo Rei Socialis*. Vatican City State: Libreria Editrice Vaticana, 1987. https://www.vatican.va/content/john-paul-ii/en/encyclicals/documents/hf_jp-ii_enc_30121987_sollicitudo-rei-socialis.html.

Keenan, James. *University Ethics*. Lanham, MD: Rowman & Littlefield, 2015.

Kelly, Conor. *The Fullness of Free Time*. Washington, DC: Georgetown University Press, 2020.

Keynes, John Maynard. "Economic Possibilities for Our Grandchildren." In *Essays in Persuasion*, 358–73. New York: Harcourt Brace, 1932.
Kincaid, Elizabeth Rain. "Work and Vocation." In *T. & T. Clark Handbook of Christian Ethics*, edited by Tobias Winright, 383–90. London: T. & T. Clark, 2021.
Leo XIII. *Rerum Novarum*. Vatican City State: Libreria Editrice Vaticana, 1891. https://www.vatican.va/content/leo-xiii/en/encyclicals/documents/hf_l-xiii_enc_15051891_rerum-novarum.html.
Levin, Yuval. *The Fractured Republic*. New York: Basic, 2016.
Livingston, James. *No More Work*. Chapel Hill, NC: University of North Carolina Press, 2016.
Lowrey, Annie. "Give Us Fully Automated Luxury Communism." *The Atlantic*, June 20, 2019. https://www.theatlantic.com/ideas/archive/2019/06/give-us-fully-automated-luxury-communism/592099/
Mankiw, N. Gregory. *Principles of Economics*. 5th ed. Marion, OH: Southwestern, 2009.
Matz, Brian. *Introducing Protestant Social Ethics*. Grand Rapids: Baker Academic, 2017.
Medaille, John. *Toward a Truly Free Market*. Wilmington, DE: ISI, 2010.
Naughton, Michael. *Getting Work Right: Labor and Leisure in a Fragmented World*. Steubenville, OH: Emmaus Road, 2019.
O'Donovan, Oliver. *Entering Into Rest*. Vol. 3, *Ethics as Theology*. Grand Rapids: Eerdmans, 2017.
Paul VI. *Populorum Progressio*. Vatican City State: Libreria Editrice Vaticana, 1967. https://www.vatican.va/content/paul-vi/en/encyclicals/documents/hf_p-vi_enc_26031967_populorum.html.
Pius XI. *Quadragesimo Anno*. Vatican City State: Libreria Editrice Vaticana, 1931. https://www.vatican.va/content/pius-xi/en/encyclicals/documents/hf_p-xi_enc_19310515_quadragesimo-anno.html.
Posadas, Jeremy. "The Refusal of Work in Christian Ethics and Theology." *Journal of Religious Ethics* 45 (2017) 330–61.
Posadas, Jeremy. "Reproductive Justice Re-Constructs Christian Ethics of Work." *Journal of the Society of Christian Ethics* 40 (2020) 109–26.
Ratzinger, Joseph. "Freedom and Liberation." In *Church, Ecumenism, and Politics*, translated by Stephen Wentworth Arndt and Michael J. Miller, 239–55. San Francisco: Ignatius, 2008.
Rushkoff, Douglas. *Throwing Rocks at the Google Bus: How Growth Became the Enemy of Prosperity*. New York: Penguin, 2016.
Sahlins, Marshall. *Stone Age Economics*. London: Routledge, 2017.
Schwartz, Barry. *Why We Work*. London: Simon & Schuster, 2015.
Snape, Robert. "Leisure Studies, Leisure History, and the Meanings of Leisure." https://leisurestudies.org/leisure-studies-leisure-history-and-the-meanings-of-leisure/.
Speigel, Henry. *The Growth of Economic Thought*. 3rd ed. Durham: Duke University Press, 1991.
Susskind, Daniel. *A World without Work*. New York: Metropolitan, 2020.
Suzman, James. *Work: A Deep History from the Stone Age to the Age of Robots*. New York: Penguin, 2020.
Terkel, Studs. *Working*. New York: Pantheon, 1974.
Wrzesniewski, Amy, and J. E. Dutton. "Crafting a Job: Revisioning Employees as Active Crafters of Their Work." *Academy of Management Review* 26 (2001) 179–201.
Zuboff, Shoshana. *The Rise of Surveillance Capitalism*. New York: Hachette, 2019.

26

#SocialCatholic

Social Media, the Internet, and the Social Catholic Vision of a Better World

JAMES F. CACCAMO, SAINT JOSEPH'S UNIVERSITY

Abstract: To talk about society in the twenty-first century necessarily means talking about the social, political, and economic juggernaut that is social media. Social media is something that the vast majority of Americans use, and often find to be a valuable addition to their lives. Yet, it also has significant issues that we experience in often very personal ways. This essay will consider social media from the perspective of Catholic Social Teaching. It will begin by laying out papal thinking about the internet and social media. It will then go on to explore how these theological and moral principles help us understand and speak to some of the complex social ethical issues of our time as they manifest themselves in recent trends in social media, and close by considering ways in which the Catholic approach to social media and its users could grow in order to be more effective and more fully embody the concerns that have animated Social Catholics since the nineteenth century.

Social Catholicism for the Twenty-first Century?—Volume 2

THE MOVEMENTS OF SOCIAL Catholicism in the nineteenth and twentieth centuries arguably stand as high points in the Roman Catholic moral tradition. Responding to the signs of their times—profound failures in basic human welfare resulting from changes in the economic structure of society brought on by the technological innovations of the industrial revolution—thinkers like Father Wilhelm von Ketteler drew upon the wisdom of the tradition to think anew about how society should function in order to best serve the good of all. Joining together with members of the laity and into study groups like the Fribourg Union, the Social Catholics were able to exert influence on industry as well as encourage the Vatican to consider its approach to workers and the economy. The movement would eventually spread to the United States, where clergy and Catholic communities adapted the European approach to the American context, shaping the labor movement in powerful ways that are still felt today. Along the way, Fr. John Ryan built upon the work of Fr. Ketteler and others, further articulating a Roman Catholic vision of an economic social ethic that would have a lasting impact. Social Catholicism was a true example of the genius of the Catholic tradition to pull together spiritual, social, and material realities into an intellectual and participatory movement that aimed to transform business, society, and government to create a world that more fully supported human flourishing.

Given this rich legacy, it is unfortunate that if you were to ask Catholics today about "Social Catholicism," few would likely recognize the term. Indeed, these days, the term "social" would be more likely to bring to mind a smartphone app than people of faith. That's because, since the advent of "Web 2.0" in the early 2000s, "social" has shifted to denote interacting and sharing information with others via online platforms. As of 2021, 72 percent of Americans use some sort of social media, up from just 5 percent in 2005.[1] Most of the first-to-market platforms in those early years of social media have since ceased operation, but they paved the way for the platforms that became household names like LinkedIn (2003) FaceBook (2004), YouTube (2005), Twitter (2006), Instagram (2010), Snapchat (2011), and TikTok (2016). As of late 2023, each of these platforms has between 550 million and 3 billion active users globally. In the US, their user bases range from 68 to 190 million. Not to be left out, the Vatican developed robust presences on Twitter, Instagram, Facebook, and YouTube. With so many people using social media, it is

---

1. Auxier and Anderson, *Social Media Use in 2021*.

no surprise that even for Catholics, "social" might not bring the Social Catholics to mind.

That said, while billions of people use social media, many pundits, priests, professors, politicians, and parents alike have raised questions about whether social media is actually helping create a better world. Like the Social Catholics of the nineteenth and twentieth centuries, we are witnessing the birth of a new economic, social, and political world that is emerging from a technological revolution. We have yet to see that this new world will more fully uphold the kind of dignity, community, and common good that the Social Catholics worked so hard to advance.

This essay will consider the role of social media in today's economic, social, and political context, grounded in the ethical perspectives of Catholic Social Teaching on Social Communication (CST on SC). It will begin with an overview of key ideas about social communication—the practice of reaching, communicating with, and influencing large groups of people—in the Catholic tradition as articulated in Vatican writing since 1936.[2] It will then examine the approach to social media and social uses of the internet that have developed over the past two decades.[3] With the approach laid out, the article will go on to explore how Catholic thinking on social media helps us understand some of the complex social ethical issues of our time, as well as places where the church might consider further development of the tradition both conceptually and in areas of practical implementation. Ultimately, this essay will show that CST has grown to offer an insightful and at times prescient approach to social communication through social media that could be further developed with an attention to real-world implementation at the core of the Social Catholic tradition.

---

2. Within CST, social communication has typically been defined along the lines of "those media which, such as the press, movies, radio, television and the like, can, of their very nature, reach and influence, not only individuals, but the very masses and the whole of human society, and thus can rightly be called the media of social communication." Paul VI, *Inter Mirifica*, no. 1.

3. For our purposes, "social media" refers to interactive, internet-based systems that individuals and organizations can use to share self-generated content (i.e., news, text, video, images, music, commentary) and interact with other users and posted content, ultimately for the purpose of self-expression, entertainment, social relations, and community. Vatican documents regularly speak (imprecisely) about social media activities or platforms using more general terms like "internet" or "computers." This essay will include such material in its analysis where they explore the kinds of creation and interaction that have become standard features of contemporary social media.

I: Key Concepts in Catholic Social Teaching on Social Communication

The work done by the Vatican to reflect on the theological implications and moral challenges of social media is part of a larger body of work within Catholic Social Teaching that focuses on the phenomenon of social communication. Explicit work on media in the modern era began in 1936 with the promulgation of an encyclical on film, *Vigilanti Cura*, by Pope Pius XI. Since then, the Vatican has examined new communication technologies as they emerged—including film, television, audio and video cassettes, cable television, computing, and the internet—through two encyclicals, two pastoral instructions, one Conciliar decree, two major sets of pastoral guidelines, fifty-seven annual World Communications Day (WCD) messages, and at least ten minor papal and Pontifical Council for Social Communications (PCSC) documents.[4] All told, more than two hundred thousand words have been published, creating a coherent and thoughtful set of ideas, approaches, and practical recommendations for media creators and audiences alike.

Notably, most of the development of the key concepts in CST on SC preceded the birth of social media and social uses of the internet. As a result, to understand the approach to social media, it is helpful to get a sense of these broader ideas. In particular, four stand out as foundational.

The Catholic approach to social communication begins with the idea that communication is a central divine activity.[5] As described in the Pastoral Instruction *Communio et Progressio*, communication forms the center point of the Christian understanding of the world: Jesus Christ. Despite human rejection of the offer of Divine love, God "made the first move to make contact with mankind at the start of salvation history. In the fullness of time, he communicated His very self to man, and the 'Word was made flesh.'"[6] Jesus was "the image of the invisible God . . . in

---

4. World Communications Day is an annual celebration dedicated to educating Catholics about issues in social communication instituted by Vatican II. The celebration includes a short message on a media from the pope. For a more detailed examination of the history of CST on SC up to 2005, see Caccamo, "Message on the Media."

5. It begins with this idea conceptually, but not chronologically, as it was not stated explicitly until thirty-five years after the first document on social communication, in Pontifical Council for Social Communications (PCSC), *Communio et Progressio*, nos. 8–11.

6. PCSC, *Communio*, no. 10.

and through [whom] God's own life is communicated to humanity."[7] But he was also "the Perfect Communicator" who proclaimed the message of divine love and salvation in both his words and "whole manner of life," "communicat[ing] to us His life-giving Spirit, who brings all men together in unity," and who "by His death and resurrection . . . shared with everyone the truth and life of God . . . more richly and lavishly than ever before."[8] Thus, by being both the one who communicates salvation as well as the content of God's communicative self-gift, Jesus was the "highest ideal and supreme example" of communication.[9] Indeed, "human history and all human relationships exist within the framework established by this self-communication of God in Christ."[10]

That said, God was not content to simply communicate and leave it at that. A second foundational concept in CST on SC is that social communication is central to being human. By being created in God's "own image," human beings "share . . . [in God's] creative power," a part of which is continuing the communication of love and goodness.[11] For Pope Pius XII, human beings are created to spread "the priceless treasures of God" like "good seed" within the human community.[12] The Pontifical Council would expand on this idea, saying that "it is part of the human vocation to contribute to [salvation history] by living out the ongoing, unlimited communication of God's reconciling love in creative new ways. We are to do this through words of hope and deeds of love, that is, through our very way of life. Thus, communication must lie at the heart of the Church community."[13] Rather than being optional, social communication is a necessary means by which individuals and the church contribute to the salvific work of God.

The documents suggest that there are two main ways in which media can support God's work. On one hand, social communication is about sharing truth with all who will hear. Spreading the Gospel is certainly a central part of this task. As noted in Vatican II's *Inter Mirifica*,

---

7. PCSC, *Aetatis Novae*, no. 6.
8. PCSC, *Communio*, nos. 11, 10.
9. PCSC, *Communio*, no. 10.
10. PCSC, *Aetatis Novae*, no. 6.
11. PCSC, *Communio*, no. 7. Later, see also Francis, *"Fear not,"* no. 1. Few World Communications Day messages have numbered paragraphs. Where they are absent, citations will indicate paragraphs by number according to their sequence.
12. Pius XII, *Miranda Prorsus*, part 1, introduction and section 1.
13. PCSC, *Aetatis Novae*, no. 6.

the Church has a duty "to announce the Good News of salvation also with the help of the media of social communication."[14] The Pontifical Council would expand on this idea, noting that "the Apostles used what means of social communication were available in their time.... Indeed it would be difficult to suggest that Christ's command was being obeyed unless all the opportunities offered by the modern media to extend to vast numbers of people the announcement of his Good News were being used."[15] In today's world, social communication is a primary location for spreading the truth that is the Gospel.

However, the mission of truth goes beyond evangelization to encouraging expression that embodies all truth. The initial understanding of social communication within modern CST was that it should function to "be a bearer of light and a positive guide to what is good" at the service of each person's development.[16] The artistic merits of social communication were not terribly relevant, so long as the communication acted as an "an influence for good morals, an educator."[17] While the Vatican was initially concerned about preventing people from seeing media that failed this test, it shifted to encouraging people to develop a "media conscience" so that they could discern on their own what is good and bad in media they encounter.[18] People are also called upon to create media that "contribute to the pursuit of truth and the speeding up of progress" through expressions grounded in "true interpretation of the dignity of man."[19] Over the years, the documents visit many ways media falls short, including inaccurate news, propaganda, and lack of access to information; falsehoods and manipulation in advertising; and pornography.[20] Yet, even though various media sometimes fall short, the Vatican consistently asserts that people have a right to both expression and information, as well as a duty

---

14. Paul VI, *Inter Mirifica*, no. 3.

15. PCSC, *Communio*, no. 126. See also John Paul II, *Rapid Development*, nos. 7–8.

16. Pius XI, *Vigilanti Cura*, part III, sec. 2.

17. Pius XI, *Vigilanti Cura*, part I, sec. 1.

18. Pius XII, *Miranda Prorsus*, part 4, sec. 2. On formation of conscience, creative abilities, and pastoral planning, see PCSC, *Communio*, nos. 109, 111, 120, 125, 133, 164–80; Congregation for Catholic Education, *Training of Future Priests*; PCSC, *100 Years of Cinema*, secs. IV and V.

19. PCSC, *Communio*, nos. 13, 14.

20. On news and information, see PCSC, *Communio*, nos. 33–47. On advertising, see PCSC, *Communio*, nos. 59–62; PCSC, *Ethics in Advertising*. On pornography, see PCSC, *Pornography and Violence*. Similar concern emerges in Synod of Bishops, *Final Document*, part I, para. 4.

to seek information that is truthful.[21] Guiding the media toward truth is a task for all Christians, but particularly the laity, who "especially must strive to instill a human and Christian spirit into these media, so that they may fully measure up to the great expectations of mankind and to God's design."[22]

On the other hand, social communication is not simply about delivering truthful messages. It is also about breaking down barriers between people, enabling them to draw closer into community. This aspect of community is the focus of the most significant document of CST on SC, *Communio et Progressio*. Written in response to a charge in Vatican II's *Inter Mirifica*, this document argues that the various means of social communication are necessary for society to function properly, and thus are required for establishing common good. When they operate well, the means of social communication help people come "into closer contact with one another" and learn about one another's hopes and fears, "deepen[ing our] social consciousness" and increasing the "unity and brotherhood of man."[23] This happens because communication is not merely the sharing of information. "At its most profound level it is the giving of the self in love."[24] Of course, not all communication goes that deep. But through authentic and honest communication that upholds the dignity of human persons, we can build bonds that support the good of all. Indeed, *Communio et Progressio* goes so far as to say that "the total output of the media in any given area should be judged by the contribution it makes to the common good."[25] This extends beyond the content of messages to an obligation to ensure that all nations have access to the tools of social communication, so as to avoid technological divides that impede economic and personal development for poorer nations.[26] Through sharing communication technologies, people will be more broadly empowered to spread truth and unity in support of continued work to advance God's creation.

This approach to the role of media probably makes sense in the context of a tradition that places great importance on sharing the story of Jesus Christ in order to create greater unity with God and others. Yet,

21. Paul VI, *Inter Mirifica*, nos. 5, 6, 12; PCSC, *Communio*, nos. 34, 36, 44–47.
22. Paul VI, *Inter Mirifica*, 3.
23. PCSC, *Communio*, nos. 6–8.
24. PCSC, *Communio*, no. 11.
25. PCSC, *Communio*, no. 18.
26. For instance, PCSC, *Ethics in Communications*, nos. 14–16, 20.

it also treats media a bit more optimistically than most people would these days. If so, the third foundational concept in CST on SC will likely be even more surprising, namely that the technologies that make up "the means of social communication"—film, radio, music, television, news, or internet—are "gifts of God."[27] Like human communication itself, these technologies have been "devised under God's Providence" to "unite men in brotherhood and so help them to cooperate with His plan for their salvation."[28] As such, they have an "allotted place in the history of Creation, in the Incarnation and in Redemption."[29] This idea was first raised in *Miranda Prorsus* in 1957, but was expanded steadily in documents like *Communio et Progressio* in 1971 and 1997's instruction *Ethics in Advertising*.[30] The tradition was certainly well aware that media can be used poorly, yet it remained essentially optimistic that with a bit of guidance, media would play its designated part in the salvation of the world.

The fourth foundational concept in CST on SC is that these means of social communication are, in and of themselves, morally neutral. While not stated explicitly at the outset, the germ of this idea can be seen in *Miranda Prorsis* alongside the notion that technologies are gifts of God. Pope Pius was optimistic about the "wonderful technical innovations" and their power to spread good, but acknowledged they did not always do so. Such failure was not attributed to "the techniques themselves," but rather to humans using free will poorly and abusing God's gifts.[31] *Communio et Progressio* expanded on this, noting that in addition to "good intentions and a clear conscience," communication must always speak truthfully.[32] But it was PCSC President Cardinal Foley who articulated this idea most directly in 1997, saying "there is nothing intrinsically good or intrinsically evil about advertising. It is a tool, and instrument: it can be used well, and it can be used badly."[33] Within the various philosophical approaches to technology, this would be referred to as "instrumentalism," or the idea that the moral significance of an action is not determined or conditioned by the technology used to carry

---

27. Pius XII, *Miranda Prorsus*, Introduction, sec. 1.
28. PCSC, *Communio*, nos. 12, 2.
29. PCSC, *Communio*, no. 15.
30. PCSC, *Ethics in Advertising*, nos. 1, 9.
31. Pius XII, *Miranda Prorsus*, part 1, sec. 3.
32. PCSC, *Communio*, no. 17.
33. PCSC, *Ethics in Advertising*, no. 9.

out the act.[34] (a.k.a.: "Guns don't kill people, people kill people.") When social communication is harmful, it is the result of moral failings of those who use the technologies poorly, often by misunderstanding the nature of freedom as license, and thus spreading falsehoods, manipulation, or division.[35] As a result, documents that touch on media generally include some enumeration of good and their bad uses. In *Caritas in Veritate*, for instance, Pope Benedict XVI notes that media always "need to focus on promoting the dignity of persons and peoples, . . . to be clearly inspired by charity and placed at the service of truth, of the good, and of natural and supernatural fraternity."[36] Guidance on the values and virtues that should inform media use is a central part of recent CST on SC, and helps users discern how to use the instruments of social communication in ways consistent with God's desires.

II. Catholic Social Teaching on Social Media

When the Vatican started to include social aspects of the internet in its reflections on communication, these four concepts were already firmly established, and so they provided the framework within which the new technologies were interpreted. As noted, work that focuses on the internet or social media within CST on SC is actually quite small, comprising fewer than twenty thousand words spread across World Communications Day messages, several minor PCSC documents, and brief passages in a few encyclicals. This should perhaps come as no surprise, given that use of the internet as a social tool is relatively recent and that social media really only emerged with the widespread deployment of participatory "web 2.0" technologies in the early- to mid-2000s. Indeed, the two longest Vatican documents on the internet—the Pontifical Council for Social Communications' *Ethics in Internet* and *The Church and Internet*—were written in 2002, before any of the platforms mentioned so far were created. So, much of what is said in the rich reflections on social uses of the internet are essentially extensions of previous CST on SC. However, several distinctive emphases have emerged already as popes have wrestled with the practical realities of social media use. And equally

---

34. For a more information on the idea of "instrumentalism," see Caccamo, "What's in a Tech?," 165–66.

35. See, for instance, PCSC, *Ethics in Communications*, nos. 4, 19, 28.

36. Benedict XVI, *Caritas in Veritate*, no. 73.

importantly, thinking about social media was shaped by the encyclical *Laudato Si'*, which took the bold step of reversing the foundational ideas that the technologies are gifts of God and are morally neutral.[37]

Connections with Previous CST on SC

Before introducing how thinking on social communication has developed and changed, it will be useful to identify two key ways of understanding social media that are firmly grounded in previous CST on SC. The first is that social media has great potential as a medium for evangelization. Given the centrality of this idea in the tradition, it is perhaps not a surprise that the internet was first seen as a "souped up" broadcast medium for the Gospel. In what was the first World Communications Day message focused on computing, Pope John Paul II noted in 1990 that "the Church must . . . avail herself of the new resources provided by human exploration in computer and satellite technology for her ever pressing task of evangelization."[38] He expanded on this in 2002, saying that the internet functions particularly well for evangelization because it can provide an unparalleled depth of information for ongoing catechesis and faith formation.[39] It is particularly important for reaching youth who "increasingly turn to the world of cyberspace as a window on the world." Pope Francis would later note (in a precursor to *Fratelli Tutti's* use of the Good Samaritan image) the usefulness of the web for ministering to those who are disconnected, "out on the streets," and in need of welcome into a Church that is "home for all."[40] While all can do this kind of ministry, young people (because they are already on social media) and priests (because of their key role in pastoral ministry) should make evangelization using social media a priority.[41]

Notably, as the social media era progressed, the initial tendency to view the internet as a one-way broadcast medium expanded to include aspects that we commonly associate with it today. Because it is built for

37. For a more expansive, pastorally-focused examination of Catholic Social Teaching on social communications and the internet up to 2014 (so, preceding Pope Francis' contributions), see Zsupan-Jerome, *Connected*.

38. John Paul II, *Computer Culture*, no. 8.

39. John Paul II, *Internet*, no. 3.

40. John Paul II, *Internet*, no. 3; Francis, *Culture of Encounter*, para. 8.

41. Benedict XVI, *New Technologies*, no. 9; Benedict XVI, *Priest and Pastoral Ministry*.

back-and-forth communication, social media is particularly useful for opening up the personal dialog central to evangelization.[42] Additionally, because it can enable users to share many different aspects of their day-to-day living, it can help people proclaim Christ through the fullness of their lives.[43] "It is not a matter of simply telling stories as such, or of advertising ourselves, but rather of remembering who and what we are in God's eyes, bearing witness to what the Spirit writes in our hearts and revealing to everyone that his or her story contains marvelous things."[44] Indeed, Pope Benedict goes so far as to say that "there exists a Christian way of being present in the digital world," which is "to witness consistently, in one's own digital profile and in the way one communicates choices, preferences and judgements that are fully consistent with the Gospel, even when it is not spoken of specifically."[45] In such pedestrian things as posting the small events of one's day-to-day existence, social media offers new ways to do the basic communicative act of evangelization.

A second way in which the approach to social media is consistent with previous approaches to media is that it breaks down barriers between people and enables them to draw closer into community. For those of us who spend even a little time on social media, this seems obvious. Social media satisfies our fundamental desire for communication and friendship because, "when people exchange information, they are already sharing themselves, their view of the world, their hopes, their ideals."[46] Social media enables an "entirely new world of potential friendships" by "open[ing] the way for *dialogue* between people from different countries, cultures and religions . . . [allowing] them to encounter and to know each other's traditions and values."[47] It also can help us cross barriers of social and economic marginalization, so that we "feel closer to one another, creating a sense of the unity of the human family which can in turn inspire solidarity and serious efforts to ensure a more dignified life for all."[48] Ultimately, whether we utilize digital tools or meet people

---

42. Francis, *Communication at the Service of Culture*, no. 9.
43. Benedict XVI, *Silence and Word*, nos. 7–8.
44. Francis, *Life Becomes History*, no. 5.
45. Benedict XVI, *Truth, Proclamation, and Authenticity*, no. 6.
46. Benedict XVI, *Truth, Proclamation, and Authenticity*, no. 6; Benedict XVI, *New Technologies*, nos. 3, 4.
47. Benedict XVI, *Truth, Proclamation, and Authenticity*, no. 5; Benedict XVI, *New Technologies*, no. 6.
48. Francis, *Culture of Encounter*, para. 2. Francis later quoted this in *Fratelli Tutti*, no. 136.

face to face, good communication "enrich[es] society" through creating understanding and communion.[49]

That said, while recognizing social media's power for sharing truth and building community, the Vatican is also quick to point out that social media cannot achieve either one on its own. Social media is inadequate to the task of sharing truth because the ways in which social media has been implemented do not lend themselves to the contemplation necessary to gain understanding and wisdom. Our "attention is fragmented" by the sheer volume of information that "exceeds our capacity for reflection and judgement,"[50] Focusing for brief periods of time on the texts and images that pass by our gaze in any given moment, we are no longer drawn to look deeper and reflect on our experience.[51] But "true wisdom . . . is not acquired by a mere accumulation of data which eventually leads to overload and confusion."[52] Instead, it is "the fruit of a contemplative eye upon the world" that is only found by setting aside "time and inner quiet to ponder and examine life and its mysteries."[53]

As with truth, human community cannot be created by social media alone. Despite providing new and valid opportunities for connection, in the end it is an "illusion that the *social web* can completely satisfy [people] on a relational level."[54] Because social media platforms have been designed to enable us to exert a very high level of control over our online presence and interactions, the friendships we create online can become "trivialize[d]" versions of the real thing.[55] There is a "tendency to communicate only some parts of one's interior world . . . constructing a false image of oneself, which can become a form of self-indulgence."[56] It is all too easy in digital spaces to avoid the difficult parts of friendship time, strategically avoiding "contact with the pain, the fears and the joys of others and the complexity of their personal experiences" by "choos[ing] or eliminat[ing] relationships at whim," and end up with unsatisfying

---

49. Francis, *Communication and Mercy*, no. 3.

50. Benedict XVI, *Truth, Proclamation, and Authenticity*, no. 5; Francis, *Culture of Encounter*, no. 3. See also Francis, *Fratelli Tutti*, no. 50.

51. John Paul II, *New Forum*, no. 4.

52. Francis, *Laudato Si'*, no. 4.

53. Francis, *Laudato Si'*, no. 4.

54. Francis, *Network to Community*, no. 8.

55. Benedict XVI, *New Technologies, New Relationships*, no. 7.

56. Benedict XVI, *Truth, Proclamation, and Authenticity*, no. 3; Francis, *Speaking with the Heart*.

relationships that are less about unity than narcissism.[57] The internet is an excellent "extension or expectation" of "direct human contact with people." But it is not a replacement for it.[58] "Ultimately *social network communities* are not automatically synonymous with community," but often "remain simply groups of individuals who recognize one another through common interests or concerns characterized by weak bonds" and individualism."[59] So, while clearly useful, social media brings with it a host of important limitations and failings that are difficult to avoid, even for someone with the best intentions.

Interlude on a Substantial Change

At this point, readers might be noticing some tensions between these more critical reflections on social media and some of the foundational concepts of CST on SC. And if so, that is entirely appropriate. As the social media era progressed, the realities of people's experience with the particularities of how social media platforms were implemented failed to line up with the essentially optimistic tradition. Social media had great potential to build on the strengths of the previous waves of media technology, but they didn't always deliver on that potential. In his 2008 WCD message, Pope Benedict XVI suggested that "humanity today is at a crossroads," saying that social communications "risk being transformed into systems aimed at subjecting humanity to agendas dictated by the dominant [ideological and commercial interests of the day."[60] Concern about the growing impact of external social forces on people's use of media corresponded with a broader concern about the role of technology and "progress" emerging in places like encyclicals, where technology is rarely discussed. The interplay between economics, politics, industry, and media and individual human choice was increasingly recognized as more than just a generalized influence, but rather a powerful coercive or even determinative force in the world.

This growing understanding led to what can only be described as a striking reversal of two of the foundational concepts at work in pre-social

57. Francis, *Fratelli Tutti*, 43; Francis, *Laudato Si'*, no. 47. Of course, this view is not exclusive to CST on SM. See, for instance, Turkle, *Alone Together*.

58. Francis, *Network to Community*, no. 17; Benedict XVI, *Truth, Proclamation, and Authenticity*, no. 5; PCSC, *Church and Internet*, no. 9.

59. Francis, *Network to Community*, no. 6.

60. Benedict XVI, *At the Crossroads*, nos. 3, 2.

media CST on SC. The changes came in the 2015 encyclical on the environment, *Laudato Si'*, where Pope Francis addressed the understanding of technology and the problematic "technocratic paradigm" that dominates western culture. First, in contrast to the notion that technologies are "gifts of God," Pope Francis says that "science and technology are wonderful products of a God-given human creativity."[61] This rephrasing shifts the giftedness away from the technological devices themselves and onto human persons, created as we are in the image and likeness of God. In making this change, Pope Francis takes a step away from the idea that all technologies necessarily have a place in salvation history, as was affirmed regularly in CST on SC. Instead, he makes central the approach taken previously to nuclear weapons, which stood outside of the "gift of God" paradigm, due to its prevailing lack of morally licit uses.[62] In doing so, he removes the halo from many technologies that have consistently been used poorly, to the detriment of both the ecological and media environments.

The second change in the foundational concepts at work in CST on SC relates to the traditional idea of moral neutrality. As noted previously, CST asserted that technologies are morally neutral: the moral character of any specific media was entirely the result of how the essentially good medium was used by a particular user for good or evil. But in *Laudato Si'*, Pope Francis could not have put the change any more starkly: "we have to accept that technological products are not neutral."[63] Pope Francis is making a significant claim here that independent of how they are used in a particular instance, technologies have moral species in and of themselves because they are embedded in social practices, values, and power relationships that bear their own moral weight. Technologies are never simply freestanding objects that exist in a moral vacuum. Rather, they "create a framework which ends up conditioning lifestyles and shaping social possibilities along the lines dictated by the interests of certain powerful groups. Decisions which may seem purely instrumental are in reality decisions about the kind of society we want to build," and are conditioned by the vested interests of politics, economics, and corporate power.[64]

61. Francis, *Laudato Si'*, no. 102. This language marks a shift for Pope Francis himself, having referred to the internet as "a gift from God" the year before in *Culture of Encounter*, no. 2.

62. John Paul II, *Address*, no. 3.

63. Francis, *Laudato Si'*, no. 107; Benedict XVI, *Caritas in Veritate*, no. 73, uses similar language to make the very different claim that technology can be morally evaluated.

64. Francis, *Laudato Si'*, no. 107. The break from previous teaching can also be seen indirectly in the fact that of the eleven notes in the thirteen paragraphs distinctly on

This new language marks an important conceptual change from instrumentalism to what is referred to as "cultural" or "technological materialism": the idea that societies and technologies are in a mutually conditioning relationship in which cultural values and practices become embodied in our technologies and material productions. Using these technologies then reinforces these ways of thinking or acting (e.g., the "technological paradigm"). This mutual conditioning can be at a rather abstract level, such as in the way in which the "specialization" and "fragmentation of knowledge" that facilitates scientific and technological progress in modern society has unconsciously led us to habits of understanding all of life in fragmentary rather than holistic ways.[65] At other times, it can be at a very practical level, for instance in the loss of cab driving jobs as the result of decentralized ride sharing apps. As Pope Francis would put it later in *Fratelli Tutti*, "'there are huge economic interests operating in the digital world, . . . creating mechanisms for the manipulation of consciences and of the democratic process'" that are made manifest in "the way many platforms work," and are not simply the result of isolated choices of individual social media users.[66] Like many of our choices in life, the way we use technology is a complicated and nuanced response to a variety of desires, circumstances, and perceived consequences.

Combined, these two changes marked a key point in the transition toward a more holistic and perhaps realistic appraisal of social media. While CST on SC still had many good things to say about social communication, the strong sense of optimism that often went along with viewing media as a "gift of God" throughout the twentieth century essentially disappeared.[67] While the most recent documents might be accused fairly of underplaying how rich and significant relationships can be even when lived out online, breaking away from the instrumentalist approach to understanding technology has enabled the tradition to look at social

---

technology, only two reference previous Vatican writing on technology. On the technocratic paradigm, see also *Laudate Deum*, nos. 20–28.

65. Francis, *Laudato Si'*, no. 110.

66. Francis, *Fratelli Tutti*, no. 45; quoting his post-synodal Apostolic Exhortation *Christus Vivit*, no. 89.

67. The phrase "gift of God" appears twice after *Laudato Si'*, but in both cases, the "gift" refers to something enabled by the technology—"broader horizons" and "possibilities for encounter and solidarity"—not the technologies themselves. See Francis, *Communication and Mercy*, no. 11; Francis, *Fratelli Tutti*, no. 205.

media in a more complex and nuanced way, recognizing a broader array of factors involved in technology use.

Distinctive Emphases in Light of Social Media

With this growing recognition of the ways in which social media may not be quite such a gift, but rather a complex set of technologies and use practices that are not entirely within the control of individual users, three distinctive emphases have emerged in CST on SC in light of the growth of social media. The first is a concern about the negative impact of social media on expression of truth, particularly in the area of news. Since *Inter Mirifica* and *Communio et Progressio*, CST on SC has strongly upheld the importance of journalism and news, asserting rights to information and expression, as well as a duty to seek accurate information, which are all necessary for the common good. However, the meeting of news and social media has not always led to the kind of accurate information that the tradition presumed when considering these rights. Perhaps more accurately, the internet "has proven to be one of the areas most exposed to disinformation and to the conscious and targeted distortion of facts and interpersonal relationships."[68] As Pope Francis observed in his WCD message on "fake news," people utilize social media's viral and algorithm-driven functionality to create "false but believable" information that grabs people's attention by appealing to our basest impulses of "stereotypes and common social prejudices, and exploiting instantaneous emotions like anxiety, contempt, anger and frustration."[69] "The sheer overwhelming quantity of information on the Internet, much of it unevaluated as to accuracy and relevance," certainly doesn't help people assess its veracity.[70] Nor is the economic model of journalism helpful, which "contributes to sensationalism and rumor-mongering, [and] to a merging of news, advertising, and entertainment."[71] Ultimately, "the economic and manipulative aims that feed disinformation are rooted in

---

68. Francis, *Fake News and Journalism*, no. 4; Francis, *Network to Community*, no. 2. By 2021, Pope Francis went so far as to say that "the risk of misinformation being spread on social media has become evident to everyone." Francis, *Communicating by Encountering*, no. 8.

69. Francis, *Fake News and Journalism for Peace*, no. 1.

70. PCSC, *Ethics in Internet*, no. 13.

71. PCSC, *Ethics in Internet*, no. 13.

a thirst for power, a desire to possess and enjoy," robbing people of the freedom that truthful information enables.[72]

A second distinctive emphasis that has emerged in CST on SC with the growth of social media is an awareness of the way in which social media has become a powerful tool for social fragmentation and isolation, grounded in the control afforded to users by content creation and filtering tools. As Pope Francis put it in the encyclical *Fratelli Tutti*, "a new lifestyle is emerging, where we create only what we want and exclude all that we cannot control or know instantly and superficially."[73] All too often, "people interact in homogeneous digital environments impervious to differing perspectives and opinions."[74] In part, this is connected to our filtered information intake: many people are more than happy to avoid "healthy confrontation with other sources of information that could effectively challenge prejudices and generate constructive dialogue," and would rather "barricade themselves behind sources of information which only confirm their own wishes and ideas, or political and economic interests."[75] But more fundamentally, "in the *social web* identity is too often based on opposition to the other, the person outside the group: we define ourselves starting with what divides us rather than with what unites us, giving rise to suspicion and to the venting of every kind of prejudice (ethnic, sexual, religious and other)."[76] The stories we find or create online are "often . . . destructive and provocative [ones] . . . that wear down and break the fragile threads binding us together as a society."[77] Instead of becoming tools for unity and self-gift, the particular ways in which social media has been implemented enhances our ability to separate ourselves from others.[78]

A third distinctive emphasis that has emerged in CST on SC along with the growth of social media is an increased attention to using social media for social good. As was the case with truth, concern that tools of social communication will benefit all nations has long been a

---

72. Francis, *Fake News and Journalism*, no. 1.
73. Francis, *Fratelli Tutti*, no. 49.
74. Francis, *Fake News and Journalism*, no. 1.
75. Francis, *Fake News and Journalism*, no. 1; Francis, *Culture of Encounter*, no. 3; PCSC, *Ethics in Internet*, no. 13.
76. Francis, *Social Network to Community*, no. 7.
77. Francis, *Life Becomes History*, no. 2.
78. Francis, *Fratelli Tutti*, no. 27; Francis, *Evangeli Gaudiem*, no. 87.

part of the CST on SC.[79] The approach to social media identifies that structural "digital divides" remain that impede economic and political development in many places. "We must, therefore, strive to ensure that the digital world, where such networks can be established, is a world that is truly open to all. It would be a tragedy . . . if the new instruments of communication . . . were not made accessible to those who are already economically and socially marginalized," separating them from access to resources that would contribute to their integral human development.[80] But as mobile technology has become nearly ubiquitous, the emphasis moved away from concerns about hardware. In its place arose an attention to the injustices caused by gaps in participation caused by bias and exclusion.[81] "Access to digital networks entails a responsibility for our neighbour whom we do not see but who is nonetheless real and has a dignity which must be respected. The internet can be used wisely to build a society which is healthy and open to sharing."[82] These injustices can be remedied by individual acts of creating a better online environment. This is critical because "people only express themselves fully [on social media] when they are not merely tolerated, but know that they are truly accepted."[83] Without that welcoming environment created by users, we may lose the opportunity to learn "the richness of human experience as manifested in different cultures and traditions."[84]

Together, these three areas of concern build upon the existing foundational concepts, as transformed in *Laudato Si'*, to offer a vision of social media that is alternately hopeful and stark. Yet, despite the concerns, the three most recent popes agree that believers should be involved in social media and the internet. As Pope John Paul II noted in 2002, "the Internet causes billions of images to appear on millions of computer monitors around the planet. From this galaxy of sight and sound will the face of Christ emerge and the voice of Christ be heard? . . . I dare to summon the whole Church bravely to cross this new threshold . . . so that now as in the past the great engagement of the Gospel and culture may show

---

79. For instance, PCSC, *Communio et Progressio*, nos. 65, 92; PCSC, *Intervention*, no. 5; Benedict XVI, *At the Crossroads*, no. 2.

80. Francis, *"We Are Members One of Another,"* no. 8.

81. See, for instance, PCSC, *Ethics in Internet*, no. 5; PCSC, *Ethics in Communications*, no. 21.

82. Francis, *Communication and Mercy*, no. 10.

83. Francis, *Culture of Encounter*, no. 4.

84. Francis, *Culture of Encounter*, no. 4.

to the world 'the glory of God on the face of Christ' (*2 Cor* 4:6)."[85] Pope Benedict XVI invited Christians to "join the network of relationships which the digital era has made possible" to share Christ in word and witness.[86] "This network is an integral part of human life" that Christians need understand to use effectively.[87] Even Pope Francis, who expressed more doubts than his predecessors about social media, sees it as a place that Christians should be. "While [the] drawbacks are real, they do not justify rejecting social media."[88] By approaching social media with a "certain sense of deliberateness and calm," listening, and accepting others, we will be able to appreciate them and their experiences more fully, creating a richer culture of encounter online in the process.[89] Pope Francis goes so far as to express the suspicion that "that great communicator who was Paul of Tarsus would certainly have made use of email and social messaging."[90] A decade before, Pope John Paul II made a similar connection St. Paul, suggesting as the "first Areopagus of the modern ages," Christians cannot legitimately be absent from the media.[91] Pope Francis extended this call, suggesting in no uncertain terms, "let us boldly become citizens of the digital world. The Church needs to be concerned for, and present in, the world of communication, in order to dialogue with people today and to help them encounter Christ."[92]

III. Helpful Insights: CST and Recent Social Media Trends

Over the course of the past eighty-five years, the Catholic tradition has probed each new technology of social communication, including the dominant new media of our age: social media. As was true for the Social Catholics who explored the new realities of labor and the economy in the nineteenth and twentieth centuries, the goal of this examination is to help us better understand the complex moral issues we face in our

85. John Paul II, *Internet: New Forum*, no. 6.
86. Benedict XVI, *Truth, Proclamation, and Authenticity*, no. 8.
87. Benedict XVI, *Truth, Proclamation, and Authenticity*, no. 8.
88. Francis, *Culture of Encounter*, no. 4.
89. Francis, *Culture of Encounter*, no. 4.
90. Francis, *Communicating by Encountering*, no. 9.
91. John Paul II, *Rapid Development*, no. 3.
92. Francis, *Culture of Encounter*, no. 10.

world. At its best, CST is more than just a way to reflect on what has already happened, but rather is a tool that both helps us apprehend the challenges ahead and consider ways to face them. Looking at some of the recent roles that social media has played in the United States reveals that the reflections on social media have done this.

One area where thinking on social media has proven insightful is in its role as a means for sharing information. As we have seen, CST has expressed concerns about the ability of social media to serve as a conduit for truth, particularly for information necessary for the welfare and governance of communities. Unfortunately, this concern seems well founded. According to Pew Research Center studies in 2020 and 2021, just under half of all adults in the United States (48 percent) report getting their news on social media platforms "often" or "sometimes."[93] But Pew also found that social media doesn't always increase understanding: for instance, 57 percent of those who get their political news via social media have "low political knowledge" and are "more likely to have heard . . . false or unproven claims."[94] This situation had significant effects during the 2016 elections, when coordinated Russian misinformation operations were propagated, particularly on Facebook and Twitter, dividing the country along ideological lines.[95] But the consequences of misinformation became even more dire during the COVID-19 pandemic. Disinformation about the disease and vaccines proliferated online, at times spread by individuals who use their credentials and reach to create what are essentially hubs of misinformation influencing hundreds of thousands of readers, and even clergy advancing claims that run counter to the guidance of the Pope and the USCCB.[96] All of this undermined the work of legitimate medical experts and public health officials to educate communities and create effective mitigation strategies, and exacerbated a social divide in which people shun information that contradicts their existing beliefs. It light of what happened, the words of the Pontifical Council from 2000 seem prescient: "the media also can be used to block community and injure the integral good of persons: by alienating people or marginalizing and isolating them; drawing them into perverse communities organized around false, destructive values; . . . [and] spreading

---

93. Walker and Matsa, "News Use across Platforms."
94. Mitchell et al., "Less Engaged, Less Knowledgeable."
95. Rebala, "Russia's Social Media War."
96. Frenkel, "Most Influential Spreader"; Siemaszko, "Wisconsin Catholic Pastor."

misinformation and disinformation."[97] The pandemic unfortunately demonstrated one of the more dire Vatican concerns about social media.

On the other hand, the pandemic also showed us places where social media plays a truly indispensable role in our everyday lives, serving as a point of connection during the isolation of lockdowns where people experienced the proverbial "giving of the self in love." During the pandemic, people took to social media in droves to express themselves through posting baking experiments, knitting projects, and songs; to offer their worries, sorrow, and grief; and even to pray and worship with one another. The pre-pandemic words of Pope Francis in 2019 seemed to capture what was to come when he said, "if the Net becomes an opportunity to share stories and experiences of beauty or suffering that are physically distant from us, in order to pray together and together seek out the good to rediscover what unites us, then it is a resource."[98] Notably, for many young people, the stark contradiction between the aspirational web and the complex realities of life in COVID led to a more critical take on the perfection presented on social media, spurring a shift toward valuing a more honest presence.[99] Of course, this does not mean that social media was able to overcome all of the disconnection spurred by the pandemic, particularly where lack of computer ownership and internet connectivity hampered ongoing employment and education for those who are economically disadvantaged.[100] This has been a factor for churches as well, where resource disparities have meant that many Christians around the country essentially went without access to their worship communities.[101] Those challenges notwithstanding, for many people, social media served as a lifeline through a very trying time.

A third area where Catholic thinking on social media has proven insightful is on the power of social media to create solidarity and liberation through sharing experiences. One hugely significant example of this is the #MeToo movement. Originally used by Tarana Burke in 2006, the phrase came into heavy use in 2017 following revelations of sexual abuse by Harvey Weinstein by women and men who took to social media to share their own stories. Following a tweet by actor Alyssa

97. PCSC, *Ethics in Communication*, no. 13.
98. Francis, *Social Network Communities*, no. 17.
99. Molla, "Pandemic Has Changed Social Media."
100. Tibken, "Broadband Gap's Dirty Secret"; Meckler and Natanson, "Lost Generation."
101. Pardes, "Giving American Churches Hell."

Milano encouraging people to share if they, too, had experienced abuse or harassment, the phrase "me too" flooded social media. "Facebook said that within 24 hours, 4.7 million people around the world engaged in the #metoo conversation, with over 12m posts, comments, and reactions."[102] The widespread sharing of stories helped bring to the forefront the extent to which marginalization and abuse of women exists in American society and has helped lift the taboo against speaking about such experiences in public. These changes have contributed to an increasing desire to hold perpetrators accountable and to seek greater equality for women more broadly. In the years following, America has seen the conviction and ouster of powerful men like Harvey Weinstein, Jeffrey Epstein, Larry Nassar; the resignation of New York Governor Andrew Cuomo; and a notable increase in discussion of equity for women, including the high-profile work for equal pay by the US Women's National Soccer Team and an effort to revive the ratification of the Equal Rights Amendment to the Constitution. Some have dismissed this movement as a "cancel culture" trying to silence those in power. But it seems more appropriate, in light of CST on social media, to say that social media has offered a new way for those who have long been silenced and shunned to lift their voices, join together, and work to bring forth a community of increased justice.

IV. Growing Edges: Insights from the Social Catholic Movement

As we can see, CST has offered an insightful perspective on social media. That said, there are also important ways in which it has not sufficiently accounted for the complexities social media's impact on individuals and communities. Indeed, if we draw upon the wisdom of the Social Catholic movement, three areas for development in the tradition become clear.

One area of Catholic thinking on social media that is ripe for development is moving beyond a focus on "content" to grapple with the ways in which companies wield the hidden power available to them through their technologies. One of the more well-known policy concerns of the Social Catholic movement was the just wage. There are a variety of components to this idea, but one key foundational aspect is human dignity, including the notion that "every person is an end in himself; none is a mere instrument to the convenience or welfare of any other human

---

102. Khomami, "#MeToo."

being."[103] Applying this concept to social media, it would be concerning if contemporary social media were built on systems that effectively transform social media users into means for the welfare of others, ultimately rendering them commodities rather than ends in themselves.

As it turns out, this is the case. It's generally known that platforms like Facebook surreptitiously harvest and sell user information to companies that use it to serve advertisements that, at times, are used designed to manipulate users.[104] What is less well known is the recent growth of third-party companies that surreptitiously aggregate social media data, particularly pictures and live streams, with location information obtained from service providers and apps, license plate and security camera data purchased from private vendors, and facial recognition technologies to provide nearly real-time data on people and activities. While it may seem like science fiction, companies like Banjo and Clearview, for instance, have provided such services to groups like the Justice Department, Interpol, and local law enforcement, and similar technologies have been used in China to carry out preemptive detention as well as surveillance of the Muslim Uyghur population.[105] The Catholic Church encountered this power of data in summer 2021 with the release of legally obtained, subsequently de-anonymized, social media information about the personal life of an USCCB general secretary, leading to his resignation.[106]

Whatever one's particular opinion is as to the merits of these particular cases, it is undeniable that social media platforms provide vast amounts of data to companies without the knowledge of the people from whom the data is gathered, rendering them instruments for the benefit of others. But it is also critical to note that there is no check on this free flow of information. As a result, data about the private lives of individuals becomes ubiquitous and available more and more broadly. While at times it might provide helpful information in a legitimate law enforcement effort, changing political winds could very easily lead to using this data outside of legitimate contexts for unjust acts like extra-judicial surveillance of journalists or legal migrants. CST's current focus on the content of social media, be

---

103. Ryan, *Economic Justice*, 113.

104. Bell, "Cambridge Analytica Controversy."

105. See, for instance, Hill, "May End Privacy"; Mac et al., "Clearview's Facial Recognition App"; Cobbler et al., "Surveillance Panopticon,"; Vanderklippe, "China Using Big Data"; Cockerell, "China's Surveillance Operation."

106. DeChant, "Catholic Priest Quits."

it sharing truth or building community, overlooks the way that platforms compromise human dignity to achieve their own particular ends.

A second area where Catholic thinking on social media could be developed is increasing appreciation of the limits that can be placed on the positive benefits of social media by powers offline. This connects to a second insight of the Social Catholic tradition, namely that the state has significant power at its disposal that can be used to compel actions by private entities to uphold dignity and rights, but always in a limited manner, lest they exert too much control.[107] As we have seen, CST lauds the power of social media to create community and build solidarity to pursue a better world. However, work for justice carried out via social media is a tenuous endeavor. For instance, 2021 marked the tenth anniversary of the Arab Spring, in which mass protests spread across the Arab world. Seeking democracy and economic change, protesters in many countries used social media effectively as a means of communication and organizing. While some change did occur in a small number of countries, what was once dubbed the "social media revolution" has had an arguably negligible, even negative, long-term impact across a host of measures including levels of democracy, internet freedom, and freedom of the press.[108] Indeed, the biggest lesson may have been learned by repressive governments, who now eliminate internet access at the first sign of unrest.[109] Of course, this is not to say that justice work using social media is fruitless. But it does mean recognizing that online efforts ultimately depend on governments allowing them to continue. It would thus be fruitful for CST on social communication be placed in dialogue with other parts of CST, such as those on politics and economics, to explore viable approaches to coordinate online and offline strategies for advancing the common good.

A third important area where Catholic thinking on social media could be developed is an increased understanding of the real challenges that social media poses for the church as an embodied community. One of the critical insights of the Social Catholic tradition is that people are relational beings. This can be seen, for instance, in the idea that dignified employment must allow for worker to gather with peers in unions or

---

107. Mich, *Catholic Social Teaching and Movements*, 11–14, 21.

108. Robinson, "Arab Spring at Ten Years." Even the "success story" that was Tunisia has recently fallen into political turmoil. See Ellali and O'Grady, "Tunisia's Fledgling Democracy."

109. For one example, see Smith-Spark, "Myanmar Junta Orders Internet Blackout."

"workingman's associations" for community and common cause.[110] This insight is certainly consistent with what we see in CST on SC's celebration of the power of social media to build bonds. At the same time, CST on social media consistently subordinates online relationality to those in physical spaces, particularly when engaging spirituality. As the PCSC put it, "virtual reality is no substitute for the Real Presence of Christ in the Eucharist, the sacramental reality of the other sacraments, and shared worship in a flesh-and-blood human community."[111]

For those steeped in sacramental theology, this claim probably seems self-apparent. But in the Summer of 2021, after a year of virtual Mass, the necessity of an embodied worship community may not be so obvious to others. On one hand, people have succeeded in developing new patterns and habits of spiritual community and sustenance while they were not able to join with others physically for prayer. While it took some adjusting, many people found ways to truly thrive spiritually, not just "get by," as they attended mass via livestream, did online retreats, and reflected on daily prayer and scripture posts. Social media has mediated true communion. On the other hand, physically gathered community has not necessarily become more attractive. Going into the pandemic, regular church attendance among Christians had already dropped to 47 percent, and church membership among people who identify as Catholic dropped eighteen percentage points to 58 percent over the last two decades.[112] The Church has also been involved in a number of high-profile disagreements coalescing around issues of political partisanship, access to sacraments, and what seems to some as failure to give due deference to a valid Pope. In this context, it seems eminently reasonable to choose to continue valuable spiritual practices that just happen to be online instead of a fractured community just because it happens to be in person. It is perhaps no surprise, then, that there is concern that "mere act of lifting the dispensation from the Sunday Mass obligation as the coronavirus pandemic eases won't be enough to get Catholics to come back to church."[113]

In the end, social media has provided a powerful, lived challenge to the Catholic claim that embodied community is necessary for a spiritually active life of Christian faith. This experience should not be ignored.

110. Mich, *Catholic Social Teaching and Movements*, 11–14, 21.
111. PCSC, *Church and Internet*, no. 9.
112. Jones, "Church Membership Falls."
113. Pattison, "Lifting Dispensation Is Not Enough."

While the insights of the Social Catholic tradition would support such community, it is incumbent upon the church to take this experience seriously and work to discern effective ways to engage it. Nearly twenty years ago, the PCSC essentially agreed, saying "pastoral planning should consider how to lead people from cyberspace to true community and how, through teaching and catechesis, the Internet might subsequently be used to sustain and enrich them in their Christian commitment."[114] This need remains to this day.

V. Conclusion

Modern Catholic Social Teaching is, in many ways, a dialog with an ever-evolving culture. This is certainly the case in its origins, when an upswelling of desire to respond to the needs of workers being crushed by the industrial revolution coalesced in the Social Catholic movement, which shined a light on new cultural realities that desperately needed attention. Given Social Catholicism's role in the development of the Church's social teaching, the fact that it was a "movement"—an organic emergence of shared concerns among a diverse group of people leading to common action across political, social, or religious lines—is particularly notable. The kind of fragmentation we see within society today, which is often supercharged by social media, makes that kind of "across-the aisle" action seem impossible.

Yet, the very social technologies so often used to divide offer us a great opportunity to support the development of a new Social Catholic movement. As we've seen, social media can be an effective way to share information, share experiences, and build relationships that can lead to understanding, compassion, and justice. As such, these tools offer the Social Catholicism powerful means for raising awareness about suffering and coordinating efforts to work against it that could span political and ideological divides, even within the Catholic Church. Of course, using social media to support such a movement would mean engaging in the difficult work of changing many of our social media practices to steer clear of what can only be described as the vices that many of us have unknowingly adopted. Thoughtlessness, falsehoods, reviling, ingratitude, boasting, quarreling, pride, anger, and fear (to use familiar categories from St. Thomas Aquinas) seem to characterize so

---

114. PCSC, *Church and Internet*, no. 9.

much of what happens online, the possibilities for prudence, justice, temperance, and fortitude seem little more than afterthoughts. Yet, as *Communio et Progressio* so poignantly put it, social communication is a way of "giving of the self in love" aimed at human communion. Social media can be used in ways characterized by *caritas*, that fundamental call for all Christians. Far-fetched as it might sound, we can imagine social media where people are patient and kind; not jealous, pompous or inflated; not rude, fixated on injuries, quick-tempered, or seeking their own interests; and where people ultimately rejoice not in wrongdoing, but in truth (1 Cor 13:4–6). Using social media in this way would help Social Catholicism create a faithful community and organize for change, and perhaps even serve as an example of power of the "Christian way of being present in the digital world."[115]

Bibliography

Auxier, Brooke, and Monica Anderson. *Social Media Use in 2021*. Pew Research Center, April 7, 2021. https://www.pewresearch.org/internet/wp-content/uploads/sites/9/2021/04/PI_2021.04.07_Social-Media-Use_FINAL.pdf.

Bell, Karissa. "Everything You Need to Know about the Cambridge Analytica Controversy." *Mashable*, March 18, 2018. https://mashable.com/article/what-is-cambridge-analytica.

Benedict XVI. *Caritas in Veritate*. June 29, 2009. https://www.vatican.va/content/benedict-xvi/en/encyclicals/documents/hf_ben-xvi_enc_20090629_caritas-in-veritate.html.

———. *The Media: At the Crossroads between Self-Promotion and Service: Searching for the Truth in Order to Share It with Others*. 42nd World Communications Day Message, January 24, 2008. https://www.vatican.va/content/benedict-xvi/en/messages/communications/documents/hf_ben-xvi_mes_20080124_42nd-world-communications-day.html.

———. *New Technologies, New Relationships: Promoting a Culture of Respect, Dialogue and Friendship*. 43rd World Communications Day Message, January 24, 2009. https://www.vatican.va/content/benedict-xvi/en/messages/communications/documents/hf_ben-xvi_mes_20090124_43rd-world-communications-day.html.

———. *The Priest and Pastoral Ministry in a Digital World: New Media at the Service of the Word*. 44th World Communications Day Message, January 24, 2010. https://www.vatican.va/content/benedict-xvi/en/messages/communications/documents/hf_ben-xvi_mes_20100124_44th-world-communications-day.html.

———. *Silence and Word: Path of Evangelization*. 46th World Communications Day Message, January 24, 2012. https://www.vatican.va/content/benedict-xvi/en/messages/communications/documents/hf_ben-xvi_mes_20120124_46th-world-communications-day.html.

---

115. Benedict XVI, *Truth, Proclamation, and Authenticity*, no. 6.

———. *Truth, Proclamation, and Authenticity of Life in the Digital Age.* 45th World Communications Day Message, January 24, 2011. https://www.vatican.va/content/benedict-xvi/en/messages/communications/documents/hf_ben-xvi_mes_20110124_45th-world-communications-day.html.

Caccamo, James F. "The Message on the Media: Seventy Years of Catholic Social Teaching on Social Communication." *Josephinum Journal of Theology* 15 (2008) 390–426.

———. "What's in a Tech? Factors in Evaluating the Morality of Our Information and Communication Practices." *Journal of Moral Theology* 4 (2015) 151–80.

Cockerell, Isobel. "Inside China's Massive Surveillance Operation." *Wired*, May 9, 2019. https://www.wired.com/story/inside-chinas-massive-surveillance-operation.

Cobbler, Jason, Emanuel Maiberg, and Joseph Cox, "This Small Company Is Turning Utah into a Surveillance Panopticon." *Vice*, March 4, 2020. https://www.vice.com/en/article/k7exem/banjo-ai-company-utah-surveillance-panopticon.

Congregation for Catholic Education. *Guide to the Training of Future Priests concerning the Instruments of Social Communication.* March 19, 1986. https://www.vatican.va/roman_curia/pontifical_councils/pccs/documents/rc_pc_pccs_doc_19031986_guide-for-future-priests_en.html.

DeChant, Tim. "Catholic Priest Quits after "Anonymized" Data Revealed Alleged Use of Grindr." *Ars Technica*, July 21, 2021. https://arstechnica.com/tech-policy/2021/07/catholic-priest-quits-after-anonymized-data-revealed-alleged-use-of-grindr.

Ellali, Ahmed, and Siobhán O'Grady. "Tunisia's Fledgling Democracy, Sole Survivor of the Arab Spring, in Crisis." *Washington Post*, July 27, 2021. https://www.washingtonpost.com/world/middle_east/tunisia-coup-saied-ennahda/2021/07/26/c1647c2c-ee05-11eb-81b2-9b7061a582d8_story.html.

Francis. *Christus Vivit.* March 25, 2019. https://www.vatican.va/content/francesco/it/apost_exhortations/documents/papa-francesco_esortazione-ap_20190325_christus-vivit.html.

———. *"Come and See" (Jn 1:46): Communicating by Encountering People Where and as They Are.* 55th World Communications Day Message, January 23, 2021. https://www.vatican.va/content/francesco/en/messages/communications/documents/papa-francesco_20210123_messaggio-comunicazioni-sociali.html.

———. *Communication and Mercy: A Fruitful Encounter.* 50th World Communications Day Message, January 24, 2016. https://www.vatican.va/content/francesco/en/messages/communications/documents/papa-francesco_20160124_messaggio-comunicazioni-sociali.html.

———. *Communication at the Service of an Authentic Culture of Encounter.* 48th World Communications Day Message, January 24, 2014. https://www.vatican.va/content/francesco/en/messages/communications/documents/papa-francesco_20140124_messaggio-comunicazioni-sociali.html.

———. *Evangeli Gaudiem.* November 24, 2013. https://www.vatican.va/content/francesco/en/apost_exhortations/documents/papa-francesco_esortazione-ap_20131124_evangelii-gaudium.html.

———. *"Fear not, for I am with you" (Is 43:5): Communicating Hope and Trust in our Time.* 51st World Communications Day Message, January 24, 2017. https://www.vatican.va/content/francesco/en/messages/communications/documents/papa-francesco_20170124_messaggio-comunicazioni-sociali.html.

———. *Fratelli Tutti*. October 3, 2020. https://www.vatican.va/content/francesco/en/encyclicals/documents/papa-francesco_20201003_enciclica-fratelli-tutti.html, 136.

———. *Laudate Deum*. October 5, 2023. https://www.vatican.va/content/francesco/en/apost_exhortations/documents/20231004-laudate-deum.html, 20–28.

———. *Laudato Si'*. May 24, 2015. https://www.vatican.va/content/francesco/en/encyclicals/documents/papa-francesco_20150524_enciclica-laudato-si.html.

———. *Speaking With the Heart "The Truth in Love" (Eph 4:15)*. 57th World Communications Day Message, January 24, 2023. https://www.vatican.va/content/francesco/en/messages/communications/documents/20230124-messaggio-comunicazioni-sociali.html.

———. *"That you may tell your children and grandchildren" (Ex 10:2): Life Becomes History*. 54th World Communications Day Message, January 24, 2020. https://www.vatican.va/content/francesco/en/messages/communications/documents/papa-francesco_20200124_messaggio-comunicazioni-sociali.html.

———. *"The Truth Will Set You Free" (Jn 8:32): Fake News and Journalism for Peace*. 52nd World Communications Day Message, January 24, 2018. https://www.vatican.va/content/francesco/en/messages/communications/documents/papa-francesco_20180124_messaggio-comunicazioni-sociali.html.

———. *"We Are Members One of Another" (Eph 4,25): From Social Network Communities to the Human Community*. 53rd World Communications Day Message, January 24, 2016. https://www.vatican.va/content/francesco/en/messages/communications/documents/papa-francesco_20190124_messaggio-comunicazioni-sociali.html.

Frenkel, Sheera. "The Most Influential Spreader of Coronavirus Misinformation Online." *New York Times*, July 24, 2021. https://www.nytimes.com/2021/07/24/technology/joseph-mercola-coronavirus-misinformation-online.html.

Hill, Kashmir. "The Secretive Company That Might End Privacy as We Know It." *New York Times*, January 8, 2020. https://www.nytimes.com/2020/01/18/technology/clearview-privacy-facial-recognition.html.

John Paul II. *Address of His Holiness John Paul II to Scientists and Representatives of the United Nations University*. February 25, 1981. https://www.vatican.va/content/john-paul-ii/en/speeches/1981/february/documents/hf_jp-ii_spe_19810225_giappone-hiroshima-scienziati-univ.html.

———. *The Christian Message in a Computer Culture*. XXIV World Communications Day Message, January 24, 1990. https://www.vatican.va/holy_father/john_paul_ii/messages/communications/documents/hf_jp-ii_mes_24011990_world-communications-day_en.html.

———. *Internet: A New Forum for Proclaiming the Gospel*. 36th World Communications Day Message, January 24, 2002. https://www.vatican.va/holy_father/john_paul_ii/messages/communications/documents/hf_jp-ii_mes_20020122_world-communications-day_en.html.

———. *The Rapid Development: Apostolic Letter to Those Responsible for Social Communications*. January 24, 2005. https://www.vatican.va/holy_father/john_paul_ii/apost_letters/documents/hf_jp-ii_apl_20050124_il-rapido-sviluppo_en.html.

———. *Redemptoris Missio*. December 7, 1990. https://www.vatican.va/holy_father/john_paul_ii/encyclicals/documents/hf_jp-ii_enc_07121990_redemptoris-missio_en.html.

Jones, Jefferey. "U.S. Church Membership Falls below Majority for First Time." *Gallup*, March 29, 2021. https://news.gallup.com/poll/341963/church-membership-falls-below-majority-first-time.aspx.

Khomami, Nadia. "#MeToo: How a Hashtag Became a Rallying Cry against Sexual Harassment." *Guardian*, October 20, 2017. https://www.theguardian.com/world/2017/oct/20/women-worldwide-use-hashtag-metoo-against-sexual-harassment.

Mac, Ryan, et al. "Clearview's Facial Recognition App Has Been Used by the Justice Department, ICE, Macy's, Walmart, and the NBA." *BuzzFeedNews*, February 27, 2020. https://www.buzzfeednews.com/article/ryanmac/clearview-ai-fbi-ice-global-law-enforcement.

Meckler, Laura, and Hannah Natanson. "'A Lost Generation': Surge of Research Reveals Students Sliding Backward, Most Vulnerable Worst Affected." *Washington Post*, December 6, 2020. https://www.washingtonpost.com/education/students-falling-behind/2020/12/06/88d7157a-3665-11eb-8d38-6aea1adb3839_story.html.

Mich, Marvin Krier. *Catholic Social Teaching and Movements*. Mystic, CT: Twenty-Third, 1998.

Mitchell, Amy, et al. "Americans Who Mainly Get Their News on Social Media Are Less Engaged, Less Knowledgeable." *Pew Research Center*, July 30, 2020. https://www.journalism.org/2020/07/30/americans-who-mainly-get-their-news-on-social-media-are-less-engaged-less-knowledgeable.

Molla, Rani. "Posting Less, Posting More, and Tired of It All: How the Pandemic Has Changed Social Media." *Vox*, March 1, 2021. https://www.vox.com/recode/22295131/social-media-use-pandemic-covid-19-instagram-tiktok.

Pardes, Arielle. "The Digital Divide Is Giving American Churches Hell." *Wired*, February 10, 2021. https://www.wired.com/story/covid-19-digital-divide-giving-american-churches-hell.

Pattison, Mark. "Lifting Dispensation Is Not Enough to Get Catholics Back to In-Person Mass." *Catholic News Service*, July 14, 2021. https://www.catholicnews.com/lifting-dispensation-is-not-enough-to-get-catholics-back-to-in-person-mass.

Paul VI. *Inter Mirifica*. December 4, 1963. https://www.vatican.va/archive/hist_councils/ii_vatican_council/documents/vat-ii_decree_19631204_inter-mirifica_en.html.

Pius XI. *Vigilanti Cura*. June 29, 1936. https://www.vatican.va/holy_father/pius_xi/encyclicals/documents/hf_p-xi_enc_29061936_vigilanti-cura_en.html.

Pius XII. *Miranda Prorsus*. September 8, 1957. https://www.vatican.va/holy_father/pius_xii/encyclicals/documents/hf_p-xii_enc_08091957_miranda-prorsus_en.html.

Pontifical Council for Social Communications. *100 Years of Cinema*. January 1, 1996. https://www.vatican.va/roman_curia/pontifical_councils/pccs/documents/rc_pc_pccs_doc_19960101_100-cinema_en.html.

———. *Aetatis Novae*. February 22 1992. https://www.vatican.va/roman_curia/pontifical_councils/pccs/documents/rc_pc_pccs_doc_22021992_aetatis_en.html.

———. *The Church and Internet*. February 28, 2002. https://www.vatican.va/roman_curia/pontifical_councils/pccs/documents/rc_pc_pccs_doc_20020228_church-internet_en.html.

———. *Communio et Progressio*. May 23, 1971. https://www.vatican.va/roman_curia/pontifical_councils/pccs/documents/rc_pc_pccs_doc_23051971_communio_en.html.

———. *Ethics in Advertising*. February 22, 1997. https://www.vatican.va/roman_curia/pontifical_councils/pccs/documents/rc_pc_pccs_doc_22021997_ethics-in-ad_en.html.

———. *Ethics in Communications*. June 2, 2000. https://www.vatican.va/roman_curia/pontifical_councils/pccs/documents/rc_pc_pccs_doc_20000530_ethics-communications_en.html.

———. *Ethics in Internet*. February 28, 2002. https://www.vatican.va/roman_curia/pontifical_councils/pccs/documents/rc_pc_pccs_doc_20020228_ethics-internet_en.html.

———. *Intervention by Archbishop John P. Foley for the World Summit on the Information Society*. November 18, 2005. https://www.vatican.va/roman_curia/pontifical_councils/pccs/documents/rc_pc_pccs_doc_20051118_un-ict_en.html.

———. *Pornography and Violence in the Communications Media: A Pastoral Response*. May 7, 1989. https://www.vatican.va/roman_curia/pontifical_councils/pccs/documents/rc_pc_pccs_doc_07051989_pornography_en.html.

Rebala, Pratheek. "Inside Russia's Social Media War on America." *Time*, May 18, 2017. https://time.com/4783932/inside-russia-social-media-war-america.

Robinson, Kali. "The Arab Spring at Ten Years: What's the Legacy of the Uprisings?" *Council on Foreign Relations*, December 3, 2020. https://www.cfr.org/article/arab-spring-ten-years-whats-legacy-uprisings.

Ryan, John A. *Economic Justice*. Library of Theological Ethics. Louisville: Westminster John Knox, 1996.

Siemaszko, Corky. "Wisconsin Catholic Pastor Who Preached against COVID-19 Vaccine Ordered to Step Down." *NBCNews*, May 24, 2021. https://www.nbcnews.com/news/us-news/wisconsin-catholic-pastor-who-preached-against-covid-19-vaccine-ordered-n1268352.

Smith-Spark, Laura, "Myanmar Junta Orders Internet Blackout as More Pro-Democracy Protesters Are Detained." *CNN*, April 3, 2021. https://www.cnn.com/2021/04/02/asia/myanmar-military-internet-blackout-detentions-intl/index.html.

Synod of Bishops. *Final Document from the Pre-Synodal Meeting*. http://www.synod.va/content/synod2018/en/news/final-document-from-the-pre-synodal-meeting.html.

Tibken, Shara. "The Broadband Gap's Dirty Secret: Redlining Still Exists in Digital Form." *CNET*, June 28, 2021. https://www.cnet.com/features/the-broadband-gaps-dirty-secret-redlining-still-exists-in-digital-form.

Turkle, Sherry. *Alone Together*. New York: Basic, 2012.

Vanderklippe, Nathan. "China Using Big Data to Detain People before Crime Is Committed." *The Globe and Mail*, February 27, 2018. https://www.theglobeandmail.com/news/world/china-using-big-data-to-detain-people-in-re-education-before-crime-committed-report/article38126551.

Walker, Mason, and Katerina Eva Matsa. "News Use across Social Media Platforms in 2021." *Pew Research Center*, September 20, 2021. https://www.pewresearch.org/journalism/2021/09/20/news-consumption-across-social-media-in-2021.

Zsupan-Jerome, Daniella. *Connected toward Communion*. Collegeville, MN: Liturgical, 2014.

27

Cooperating Beyond Borders
Catholic Social Teaching and the Global Human Family

MARYANN CUSIMANO LOVE, CATHOLIC
UNIVERSITY OF AMERICA

Abstract: We have more people, countries, and interdependent challenges than ever before. We must scale up and speed up our cooperative processes, to keep pace with the scale and speed of the global problems we face. Catholic ideas of a wider, global human family stand in stark contradiction to the rise of narrow, nationalist politics across the world. Forged in the fires of pressing global issues, a Catholic understanding of the global human family, the globalization of solidarity, and strong international institutions can help us address global issues that threaten life on earth, from climate change to nuclear weapons. The church is and has been a transnational institution since its inception. Today, CST expands with recent encyclicals *Laudato Si'* and *Fratelli Tutti*, further advancing themes synthesized in the *Compendium of the Social Doctrine of the Church*. These calls for integral solidarity come from the lived experiences of a large, diverse, and geographically dispersed community.

Cooperating Beyond Borders—Love

THREE VOICES ILLUSTRATE BOTH the urgent signs of our times, and how Catholic Social Teaching (CST) has evolved a global perspective to address these challenges to the human family. The first of these reflections is from Secretary General of the United Nations, António Guterres. The second is from St. John XXIII, and the third is from Pope Francis.

> Humanity is in the hotseat. The era of global warming has ended; the era of global boiling has arrived. The air is unbreathable. The heat is unbearable. And the level of fossil fuel profits and climate inaction is unacceptable. The consequences are clear and they are tragic: children swept away by monsoon rains; families running from the flames; workers collapsing in scorching heat. Leaders must lead. No more hesitancy. No more excuses. No more waiting for others to move first. There is simply no more time for that.[1]

> The attainment of the common good is the sole reason for the existence of civil authorities . . . the shape and structure of political life in the modern world, and the influence exercised by public authority in all the nations of the world are unequal to the task of promoting the common good of all peoples.[2]

> *Fratelli Tutti.* . . . Saint Francis of Assisi . . . calls for a love that transcends the barriers of geography and distance, and declares blessed all those who love the other "as much when he is far away from him as when he is with him." . . . fraternal openness allows us to acknowledge, appreciate and love each person, regardless of physical proximity, where he or she was born or lives.[3]

We must cooperate or die, literally. We have more people and more countries, in more close, interdependent connection, than ever before in human history. Yet our politics is out of sync with the global challenges we face. The world has a governance and cooperation problem; we need more of it, at a time when we have less of it. Pandemics, nuclear weapons, destructive changes in weather patterns, environmental pollution do not stop at the borders of countries, but our political responses to these challenges too often stop at the borders of sovereign states. Global problems move quickly across international borders, but our institutions move slowly and stop at country borders. We must build better means of cooperating than ever before. We need to scale up and speed up our

---

1. Guterres, "Remarks."
2. John XXIII, *Pacem in Terris*, nos. 54, 135.
3. Francis, *Fratelli Tutti*, no. 1.

cooperative processes, to keep pace with the scale and speed of the global problems we face. We urgently need new models, plural, of cooperation.[4] Catholic social teaching can help. Forged in the fires of pressing global issues, today Catholic social teaching in turn can help in resolving these global challenges.

Catholic ideas of a global human family stand in stark contradiction to the rise of increasingly nationalist politics across the world. This current trend cripples our abilities to cooperate effectively in the face of critical threats. Nationalist, so called "populist" politics of "me first/my group first" sow polarization, fear and distrust of others, and undermines the international cooperation and international institutions needed to solve global problems. At precisely the moment when we need greater capacity, strength, and trust in international institutions, rising nationalism undercuts all these. Pummeled by multiple global challenges simultaneously, the most vulnerable particularly are left to fend for themselves, at precisely the moment when they are least able to do so. A Catholic understanding of the global community can help us address global issues that threaten life on earth.

CST and Catholic institutions, provide much needed guidance for tackling global issues, and for promoting the view of a global human family. This is not a coincidence. From the beginning, Jesus ministered to people from all national backgrounds, and he sent the disciples to go out to all nations. The Catholic Church has been multinational since its inception. Today, that characteristic is even more pronounced. Urgent global issues forged CST, from addressing the threat of nuclear war (*Pacem in Terris*) to global environmental ecoside (*Laudato Si'*). In turn, through CST's affirmation of our interdependent human family (*Fratelli Tutti*), we are better able to resolve pressing global issues.

When reading the *Compendium of the Social Doctrine of the Church*, one can get the mistaken impression that CST emerged ethereal and "above the fray." That isn't true. CST emerged as the Church grappled with urgent global issues and continues to do so today. How to integrate diverse peoples isn't just a modern problem of nationalist supremacy and racism; it is a challenge the disciples grappled with since the Church's origins. Protecting human rights and stopping genocide isn't only a theological matter discussed in CST; the Church has been in the crucible of these issues from the Holocaust to the Rwandan genocide. Banning

---

4. Love, *Global Issues*, 418.

nuclear weapons isn't a problem the Holy See, a non-nuclear state, judges from the outside. The Catholic Church, incinerated in Nagasaki, was among the world's first victims of nuclear weapons. The Church in Asia was almost totally annihilated, and the Catholic Hibakusha (nuclear weapons survivors) were also among the world's first responders to the victims of nuclear weapons. When the Church advocates on behalf of humanitarian arms control, from banning landmines to banning nuclear weapons, it speaks from the Church's vast experiences as victims of these weapons and as providers of health care and humanitarian assistance to survivors. Today, CST expands with recent encyclicals *Laudato Si'* and *Fratelli Tutti* further advancing themes of the *Compendium*. These calls for integral solidarity come from the lived experiences of a large, diverse, and geographically dispersed community.

The Unity of the Global Human Family

The *Compendium of the Social Doctrine of the Church* makes clear that we are created to live in integral and rich relationships with peoples of all backgrounds, and with creation. This is not just theory. Catholic Social Teaching on human rights, just peace, integral ecology, and the need for cooperative capacity across ethnic, racial, national, and religious lines, have their roots in practice, within the Church as well as in external relations.

The Catholic Church is not a national church. The world's 8 billion people live in 193 countries and belong to over eight thousand national identity groups. The 1.3 billion followers of the world's largest single religion, Catholicism, live in every country in the world, and are members of diverse cultures, ethnicities, nations, races, and vocations. Catholics live even in the hermit kingdom of North Korea. Even in Saudi Arabia, where the Sunni faith is mandated by the state, there are over a million Catholics in the kingdom.

As I note in my book *Global Issues*, data show that demographically, the Catholic Church is distinct from most of the world's major religions, in ways that help it to address pressing global issues and advance the vision of a common human family. Geographically, most of the major religions never "left the cradle" where they were born. Most Hindus live in India; most Buddhists live in Asia. Islam originated in the Middle East, part of Asia, and most Muslims live in Asia and the Middle East. The world's fourteen million Jews live primarily in two countries, Israel and the US The exception is Christianity, and particularly the largest single sect in the world, Catholicism, who are most threatened in their "cradle" (the Middle East) but are more evenly dispersed across geographic regions.[5] A century ago two thirds of the world's Christians lived in the global north, in Europe and North America. Today that number is reversed; two thirds of Christians live in the global south. All global religions may choose to try to address global issues, helping the poor or protecting the environment, for example. However, these religious demographics mean that transnational networks of Catholic groups will be more available to address global issues, across geographic, class, and identity lines.

Catholicism has been multinational from its beginnings. Immediately, Jesus and his first followers spread the faith beyond Jews in his home region, to Romans, Samaritans, Greeks, Africans, and Asians. Catholicism predates the sovereign state by over 1,600 years. Because Catholicism is not a national church, not aligned with any sovereign state, nation, or tribe, Catholic believers and institutions have had to hone skills of intercultural encounter, dialogue, deep listening, and working with others, and to create institutions for cooperation across identity lines. From the origins of Christianity, when the apostles debated the *means* of inclusion of gentiles, Greeks, Romans, Samaritans, Africans, etc., into their Jewish origin religious movement, to today, the questions have turned on the *modalities* of inclusion, not on whether peoples from different identity groups could or should be included in the Church. The same debates are evident today. Catholics gathered from all over the world in the Synod on Synodality, where debates centered on the modalities and quality of inclusion, not on whether the Church should include people of very diverse identities.

In his travels to Iraq, Pope Francis showcased this lesson, noting the value that diverse identities bring to society in his travels to places of pain decimated by ISIS, where ISIS had conducted genocide against minority communities in the Nineveh plains. Pope Francis visited Iraq in 2021 in hopes of repairing and strengthening intercommunal relations after the destruction and division caused by ISIS. Where ISIS used sectarian and identity differences to divide and conquer, Pope Francis raised up these differences as strengths of a resilient society "As I look out at you, I can see the cultural and religious diversity of the people of

---

5. Love, *Global Issues*, 143.

Qaraqosh, and this shows something of the beauty that this entire region holds out to the future. Your presence here is a reminder that beauty is not monochrome but shines forth in variety and difference."[6] The Pope emphasized an insight of the Iraqi language, where locals do not use the word "minority" but instead discuss "component" groups, a recognition of how diverse groups are a strength and build up society.

The *Compendium* notes that the Catholic Church opposes racism in all its forms, and cannot condone nationalist/populist positions, the "culture wars," or the view that the "Clash of Civilizations" is inevitable. To support those positions violates *imago Dei* principles. In practice, such violations also promote internal fratricide within the Church, as well as external conflict in the world. Catholic social teaching developed as both pragmatic practices as well as religious principles for cooperative relations among the diverse national identity communities within the Church and on the planet.

A Pre-State Actor

The Catholic Church is not a non-state actor, but a pre-state actor.[7] This is an important distinction. Long before the sovereign state ever existed, millennia before the 1648 Treaty of Westphalia, the Catholic Church built robust transnational networks to address pressing problems, from reducing poverty to advancing health. The Church is the largest non-governmental provider of health care, education, social services, and humanitarian aid on the planet. The Catholic Church has also the oldest diplomatic corps on earth. This gives the Church robust networks to work with countries, governments, and international institutions, and to work directly with communities, civil society, and individuals. Thousands of years before the concept of sovereign countries was ever invented, religious organizations created institutions and performed (and still perform) functions which are today associated with sovereign states. Religious organizations had laws, courts, schools, universities, hospitals, media, humanitarian aid departments, diplomatic emissaries, etc., and registered births, marriages, and deaths, millennia before sovereign states ever created such institutions or engaged in these activities.

---

6. Francis, "Address to Qaraqosh," para. 1.
7. Love, *Global Issues*, 141.

Only a very small number of today's 193 sovereign states have been around since 1648. Most sovereign states are very new, only created after the end of European colonialism after the Second World War or after the end of the Soviet Empire in 1989. The sovereign state is a newcomer around the world today, often with limited response capabilities to global issues, while Catholic transnational networks are well-established, including in areas where the capacity and legitimacy of the sovereign state are limited. CST regarding subsidiarity and solidarity, the both/and importance of civil society as well as international law and institutions, is born from millennia of practice, before the invention of the modern sovereign state system.

Working Within and Beyond Sovereignty

The Catholic Church operates both beyond and within the sovereign state system, and it is not tied to it. Quite the opposite; church networks for solving pressing problems existed millennia before the sovereign state ever existed.

The Catholic Church today has a nuanced view of sovereignty. The Catholic Church preceded the sovereign-state system by sixteen centuries, then was a sovereign state, and now, while it no longer has armies, it operates both within and outside the sovereign state system.

The modern separation of Church and state was born from painful history. Catholic teaching today proclaims that while faith can be shared in a spirit of encounter and dialogue, it cannot be forced upon others, as noted by the School of Salamanca who articulated the Natural Law tradition and denounced brutality against indigenous peoples by European colonizers. The Catholic Natural Law tradition (which directly influenced the Universal Declaration of Human Rights) holds that all people have access to knowledge of right and wrong regardless of their religious or cultural traditions. God has written these truths in all hearts, including people of various cultural and religious traditions. Thus laws, policies, and programs pursuing the common good are possible among all, from all cultural traditions. War and repression of difference are not the means to grow the community.

Libraries have been written about Catholic approaches to peace, human rights, the Catholic natural law tradition, as well as the undermining of these gospel principles and practices as the Church moved from its early years to become "The Holy Roman Empire." Along with extensive lands, the Church became intertwined with medieval European power politics in ways which undermined and distorted Christianity's principles and practices of peaceful, open engagement with the other. Pope Benedict IX, and the Crusades, are a few exemplars of this problematic history so at odds with the discussion here of the *Compendium of the Social Doctrine of the Church*.

With the unification of Italy and the loss of the Papal states, the Catholic Church was liberated to return to its roots. A flourishing of Catholic transnational organizations, such as *Caritas Internationalis*, *Pax Christi*, and religious orders, brought organized practices of peacebuilding and cross-cultural engagement to all regions of the globe. After the ravages of World War II and the dawn of decolonialization, the number of countries exploded four-fold. Pope means bridge builder, and Saint Pope John XXIII convened Vatican II to build bridges across the new borders. But before the Council convened, Saint John Paul XXIII gave the directions for the church in the modern world in his encyclical *Pacem in Terris*. These principles were born of practice. Saint Pope John XXIII's appreciation of the importance of human rights and the global human family, and that state sovereignty is not absolute, was also forged from painful practice. He served as a diplomat in Eastern Europe during WWII, working to save European Jews from the Holocaust, including by producing baptismal certificates and Catholic identity papers to save lives and smuggle Jews out of the reach of the genocide. He is credited with saving thousands of Jews during the Holocaust and opening the door to constructive Judeo-Christian dialogue post-war.[8]

The Church operates in solidarity with those in need in other countries and welcomes the creation and strengthening of international institutions for better cooperation among sovereign states. Also, the Church operates in subsidiarity with community organizations, creating and strengthening cooperative civil society networks regardless of the capacity of states. This creates helpful principles and models for other international institutions, showing how they can be effective, whether or not sovereign states cooperate.

The Holy See is recognized as a micro-state, has a foreign service that exchanges diplomats with 183 sovereign states, and has a permanent observer seat at the United Nations. These characteristics of sovereignty

---

8. International Raoul Wallenberg Foundation, "John XXIII."

afford the Catholic Church a unique position among religious organizations and NGOs, with a foot in both camps, able to work readily with and negotiate with sovereign states while maintaining extensive operations and networks as a trans-state actor, operating across sovereign-state borders in all countries.

Yet sovereignty is not absolute. The Catholic Church believes the sovereign state exists to serve the human person and human communities, not the other way around. Thus, the church works with sovereign states where state institutions are able and interested in protecting the human person. Honoring subsidiarity, the Church also works at the community/sub-state level. And emphasizing solidarity, the Church also works at the levels of transnational networks and international institutions. Further, the work of the Church continues even where the state is predatory, antagonistic, or failing. For many of the world's most vulnerable, sovereign control is either absent or predatory. Nearly one-third of the world's population live in failed or failing states, absent the conditions of law and order, *tranquilitas ordinis*, that make human development possible. According to Freedom House, an overlapping two billion people live in forty-three countries where the state deprives them of basic human rights and freedoms. The worst of these states, like Rwanda in 1994, are predatory, killing their own people in genocides.[9]

The Catholic Church does not stand on the sidelines when sovereign states are unable or unwilling to protect human life and dignity and the common good. The Church works in a both/and manner, working to advance both the creation of effective international institutions of cooperation of sovereign states, and strong transnational institutions of collaboration among civil society groups. In NGO parlance, the Church is more like "Doctors Without Borders" than the International Red Cross, ready to act wherever people are in need, whether or not it has the prior permission of the sovereign state.

Yet a key difference with the international NGO comparison is that the church is not an external actor; it is already in-country around the world. Religious organizations and states operate differently regarding sovereignty. Religious organizations have a moral mandate to help "God's children," and do not stand on the sidelines and wait until state institutions are ready and able to provide services. Westphalia created a non-intervention norm for other states that does not apply to religious actors,

---

9. Love, "What Kind of Peace?"

who answer to a higher authority than state sovereignty. Some NGOs, like "Doctors Without Borders," also act wherever people are in need, whether or not it has the prior permission of the sovereign state. But a key difference with the NGO comparison is that Catholic organizations are both domestic and external actors; global religious organizations have believers and branches in countries around the world and are not only external actors. As stated in the Second Vatican Council's *Pastoral Constitution on the Church in the Modern World: Gaudium et Spes*, "The social order and its development must constantly yield to the good of the person, since the order of things must be subordinate to the order of persons and not the other way around, as the Lord suggested when he said that the Sabbath was made for man and not man for the Sabbath."[10] The protection of human life and dignity comes over deference to sovereignty; people come before states.

The UN and the US government have moved toward this position in adopting the Principle to Protect, "the idea that sovereign states have a responsibility to protect their own citizens from avoidable catastrophe, but that when they are unwilling or unable to do so, that responsibility must be borne by the broader community of *states*." But putting that principle into practice has been limited by state interests and concerns of state sovereignty.[11] States are failing to protect their citizens from the harms of climate change, and people are taking their claims to international institutions like the EU. Nuclear weapons states are not meeting their responsibilities to protect against the harms of nuclear weapons; the risk of nuclear war is the highest it has been since the 1962 Cuban Missile Crisis. In response, people have taken their concerns outside the vetoes of the Security Council, to the United Nations General Assembly to achieve a ban against nuclear weapons. Russia is committing genocide in Ukraine, and Ukrainians—through concerts and memes and persuasive speeches—are reminding others of their responsibilities to help protect against genocide and war crimes. While the international norm has advanced and the principle has developed, the actual protection is still underdeveloped.

---

10. Paul VI, *Gaudium et Spes*, no. 26.
11. UN Security Council, "Resolution 1674."

Principles in Practice: Stopping Nuclear War

As we mark the sixtieth anniversary of *Pacem in Terris*, the immediate precursor to Vatican II, we must note this as an important example of how CST was forged from practice. *Pacem in Terris* was written because Saint Pope John XXIII was asked to help stop nuclear Armageddon. In thirteen days in October of 1962, the United States and the Soviet Union almost blew the world to bits in a nuclear war.[12] The crisis began over the USSR's building nuclear missiles in Cuba, but soon escalated to a precarious confrontation over Cold War power balances, prestige, and the place of nuclear weapons in it all. At the height of the crisis, participants thought the chance of nuclear war between the US and USSR was about even, 50/50. Privately, Kennedy and Khrushchev both feared a nuclear exchange, but publicly, they struggled with how to walk away from the brink without losing face. In those dark hours, Kennedy did what many Americans feared he might when they elected the first Roman Catholic President; Kennedy turned to the Pope, suggesting the Pontiff might be able to open a back door dialogue with Khruschev. It was not the only back door JFK knocked on. ABC newsman John Scali, Columbia University President Andrew Cordier, the Brazilian government, even the President's brother Robert also carried messages. From those first words the Pope penned between Khruschev and Kennedy in the wee hours between October 23 and 24, 1962, emerged the encyclical, *Pacem in Terris*.

Before Vatican II opened the priest's position and the language of the mass to Catholics in the pews, *Pacem in Terris* opened the position and language of the Church to the world. For the first time, a papal encyclical was addressed not just to Catholics, but to the whole world, to all people of good will. And the language of the Pontiff's message was not only the specific language of Catholicism but was the common language of human rights. The encyclical echoes the Universal Declaration of Human Rights that "recognition of the inherent dignity and of the equal and inalienable rights of all members of the human family is the foundation of freedom, justice and peace in the world," but *Pacem in Terris* explains why. Human rights and dignity are God-given. All are created in God's image. Violations of this natural order fuel conflict. Institutions must serve the common good.

The global common good is an integral theme of *Pacem in Terris*. Working for "the common good is the sole reason for the existence of

---

12. Love, "Church and the Bomb"; Love, "Papal Vision."

civil authorities." The common good is so important that the term appears forty-six times in fifty-nine pages, as many times as "God" and nearly as many times as "Christ." *Pacem in Terris* laid out the Church's commitment to build peace and justice in the modern world. Vatican II created the organizational structures to intensify these efforts, particularly the Pontifical Council of Peace and Justice, and the corresponding Peace and Justice commissions throughout the world. Today the clergy sexual abuse scandals, followed by the pandemic, have depleted the resources of these Church Justice and Peace institutions, just as they are needed most to counter nuclear war and other global dangers.

These principles of Catholic Social Teaching, and the practices of encounter, dialogue, and common action skill sets further developed in *Laudato Si'* and *Fratelli Tutti*, are particularly necessary for the Church's very survival, amidst internal and external cultural pressures, as well as for the survival and health of the planet.

Continued Development of Intercultural Cooperation

CST continues to expand our views of the global common good to address today's challenges. Pope Francis' recent encyclicals, *Fratelli Tutti*, a companion piece to his previous encyclical *Laudato Si'*, extend CST in interaction with current problems, from the environment to intercultural peace. An encyclical is official, authoritative magisterium, a binding form of teaching in the Catholic Church. *Fratelli Tutti* and *Laudato Si'* are capstones,[13] drawing together centuries of Catholic teaching, informed by practices, of "*encuentro*," engagement, dialogue, and action for the common good, building community across religious, ethnic, and national identities. In *Laudato Si'* (LS), Pope Francis urges interreligious action for stewardship of our common home, inspired by Orthodox Patriarch Bartholomew. *Fratelli Tutti* (FT) was encouraged by Egypt's Grand Imam Ahmad Al-Tayyeb, and it is a deeper discussion of their interreligious action commitment, "Document on Human Fraternity for World Peace and Living Together." LS and FT urge moving seriously and systematically beyond mere "tolerance" of people from different national identity groups and religions, into deep, respectful relationships that better serve God, our common home, and the common good.

13. Love, "Interreligious Peacebuilding."

In these encyclicals Pope Francis continues the theological themes and processes of the Second Vatican Council, 1962–65, a period of Church renewal in the face of rapid social, economic, and technological change. The process of Vatican II included the participation of representatives from other religions, in respectful dialogue about the challenges and hopes in facing current challenges and discerning the "signs of the times." The resultant Church teachings were addressed to all people of good will (not addressed exclusively to Catholics). The theological themes of Vatican II included robust affirmations that God's love and gifts are present in all people of all faiths and cultures, therefore interreligious and intercultural engagement and action are necessary in order to serve God and to further the common good. FT and LS continue both the processes and the goals of intercultural and interreligious engagement for peace and the common good expressed in Vatican II. Fans of Vatican II are likewise fans of LS and FT. Critics of Vatican II remain unpersuaded by Pope Francis, LS, and FT.

A deeper examination of Vatican II is beyond the purview of this chapter. But for the average person, some of the most noticeable changes from Vatican II were from an internal focus to more open, outward engagement for the Catholic Church. Changes to worship services included use of diverse local languages, art, music, and culture, instead of Latin language and European music, art, and culture. The priest physically moved to face and engage the people, rather than turning his back on the congregation. Participation expanded, as lay people became more engaged in Church leadership and activities. Institutional structures promoting Justice and Peace committees were established from the Vatican to dioceses, parishes, and universities worldwide. And teaching on religious freedom and interreligious engagement was transformed. As Pope Francis noted on the Fiftieth Anniversary of *Nostra Aetate: Declaration on the Relation of the Church to Non-Christian Religions*, Vatican II's position on relations with other religions changed, "from indifference and opposition, we've turned to cooperation and goodwill. From enemies and strangers, we've become friends and brothers."[14] The title of an influential book puts it more sharply, contending that the Church's relations with other religions moved "From Confrontation to Dialogue."[15]

---

14. Francis, "Interreligious General Audience," para. 4.
15. Dupuis, *Christianity and the Religions*.

Vatican II solidly reinforced religious freedom, the human dignity of people of all faiths, and the value of interreligious engagement and action. Catholics are urged to positive relationships with non-Catholics, in *Nostra Aetate* (NA), to prudently and lovingly, through dialogue and collaboration with the followers of other religions, and in witness to the Christian life and faith, to acknowledge, preserve and promote the spiritual and moral good, as well as the sociocultural values found among them.[16]

These Vatican II teachings urge us to build robust relationships with others, not merely tolerate them. Vatican II had concrete application in the social justice work of the Catholic Church. For example, when Cardinal Hickey, Archbishop of Washington, DC, was appealing for support for refugees, a critic asked why the Church should use scarce resources to assist non-Catholics and non-US citizens. John Carr, longtime Director of the Office of Justice and Peace for the US Conference of Catholic Bishops, recalls Cardinal Hickey's eloquent response: "We shelter the homeless, educate those hungry for knowledge, and care for the sick, not because they are Catholic, but because we are Catholic. They are Jesus in disguise."[17]

Prior to Vatican II, interreligious work was often envisioned as "one way traffic." Missionary work in particular framed the work as converting "pagans." Today, the relationships among people of different faiths and cultures are multidirectional and mutually beneficial. While these changes were embraced by most Catholics, some traditionalists, then and now, argued that Vatican II and the *Compendium* moved the Church too far, too fast. Some lament the demise of medieval Christendom, and charge Vatican II with this demise (although the timing of their critique is several centuries off). The most extreme critics call Vatican II illegitimate along with all popes since 1962. Pope Francis has come under particular fire. Hailing from Latin America rather than Europe, engaging in outreach to other faiths, and critiquing the excesses and inequalities of global capitalism, have attracted particular ire. Urging the Church to be a poor Church for the poor and marginalized, and reaching out across identity groups, is consistent with the life and teaching of Jesus, but it has led some critics to label Pope Francis a communist, a socialist, while some even go so far as to call Pope Francis a heretic who is creating "a church run by Protestants, Islamists, and Jews."[18] And that's just coming from small but vocal groups in Catholic communities! As Pope

---

16. Paul VI, *Nostra Aetate*, no. 2.
17. Interview with the author.
18. Luxmoore, "Retired Archbishop in Poland," para. 6.

Francis noted, some who are opposed to change, neglect the history of the Church's development.

Without Borders

Rather than shrinking under the criticism, Pope Francis has doubled down on continuing the implementation of the spirit and processes of Vatican II, and amplifying CST. *Laudato Si'* and *Fratelli Tutti* are key in these regards. FT has been criticized as not breaking new ground, of being a sort of "Greatest Hits" which repeats and weaves together statements and themes made by Pope Francis in previous years, from his Abu Dhabi declaration to his addresses at the United Nations, his address to the US Congress, and his remarks at the Koudoukou mosque in CAR. This is entirely the point. FT weaves together Pope Francis teachings over the years. By elevating these into an encyclical, Catholic critics can neither avoid nor disavow them; they are now the official teaching of the Catholic Church. While Pope Francis' critics may not resonate with the messenger, FT ensures that they cannot easily disregard the message.

When Cardinal Bergoglio of Argentina was elected Pope, he chose the name Francis in order to model his papacy after St. Francis of Assisi, a man of poverty, peace, concern for the planet, and interreligious engagement and action, to show the resources the Church can bring to the urgent global issues of our day. Pope Francis' critics interpret the legacy of St. Francis differently; they see a man who engaged Muslims during the Crusades for the express purpose of converting their "heathen" souls. Pope Francis makes clear in the opening paragraphs of FT that he does not share that interpretation. His understanding of St. Francis of Assisi's approach and contributions eight centuries ago is worth citing fully. Intercultural and interreligious dialogue, encounter, and action are not nice pieties at the margins, but they are central to the faith, tangible demonstrations of fidelity to God's transcendent love beyond borders. And they are practical. Saint Francis of Assisi is a model because his love for others demonstrates the depth of his love of God, which flows unceasing and unperturbed by divides of human identities. A subsection of FT titled "Without Borders" illustrates how Pope Francis is inspired by Francis of Assisi's openness of heart to love everyone.

> There is an episode in the life of Saint Francis that shows his openness of heart, which knew no bounds and transcended

differences of origin, nationality, colour or religion. It was his visit to Sultan Malik-el-Kamil, in Egypt, which entailed considerable hardship, given Francis' poverty, his scarce resources, the great distances to be traveled and their differences of language, culture, and religion. That journey, undertaken at the time of the Crusades, further demonstrated the breadth and grandeur of his love, which sought to embrace everyone. Francis' fidelity to his Lord was commensurate with his love for his brothers and sisters. Unconcerned for the hardships and dangers involved, Francis went to meet the Sultan with the same attitude that he instilled in his disciples: if they found themselves "among the Saracens and other nonbelievers," without renouncing their own identity they were not to "engage in arguments or disputes, but to be subject to every human creature for God's sake." In the context of the times, this was an extraordinary recommendation. We are impressed that some eight hundred years ago Saint Francis urged that all forms of hostility or conflict be avoided and that a humble and fraternal "subjection" be shown to those who did not share his faith.

Pope Francis continually presents this saint as an important exemplar for contemporary Catholics.

He writes in the following section 4 of FT:

> Francis did not wage a war of words aimed at imposing doctrines; he simply spread the love of God. He understood that "God is love and those who abide in love abide in God" (1 Jn 4:16). In this way, he became a father to all and inspired the vision of a fraternal society. Indeed, "only the man who approaches others, not to draw them into his own life, but to help them become ever more fully themselves, can truly be called a father." In the world of that time, bristling with watchtowers and defensive walls, . . . Francis was able to welcome true peace into his heart and free himself of the desire to wield power over others. He became one of the poor and sought to live in harmony with all. Francis has inspired these pages.[19]

To honor this history, Pope Francis released *Fratelli Tutti* on the feast of St. Francis of Assisi. In case anyone should miss the point, he also traveled to the city of Assisi. He then signed the encyclical on the tomb of St. Francis of Assisi, after saying mass in the crypt church of the Basilica of St. Francis of Assisi. He surrounded himself with members of

---

19. Francis, *Fratelli Tutti*, nos. 3, 4.

the Franciscan orders who are followers of St. Francis of Assisi, while reminding the world that he took the name of Francis in order to follow the example of Saint Francis of Assisi, who served the poor, the planet, and the other/outsider, engaging in interreligious dialogue and action even during dangerous times of conflict.

Building on these themes of deep engagement across identity lines, peacebuilding, and healing, the heart of the encyclical is an extended exegesis on the parable of the Good Samaritan, the poster child for building peace across identity groups. As a Jesuit, Pope Francis uses the spiritual methods of St. Ignatius of Loyola's spiritual exercises. St. Ignatius Loyola was a Spanish nobleman and soldier. Wounded in battle, he had a spiritual conversion while convalescing in Loyola, northern Spain. He recorded his prayer methods, the spiritual exercises, which were adopted and spread by his followers, the Jesuit order. Originally, he sought to bring the gospel to Muslims and Jews in Jerusalem, but through this process of spiritual discernment, found God had another plan calling him, to educate and serve the poor in Rome and around the world.

In *Fratelli Tutti*, Pope Francis uses St. Ignatius' method of imaginative contemplative prayer, in which we are asked to imagine the gospel details concretely, as if imagining yourself as part of a movie scene. What do you see, smell, hear, feel, what do the characters and protagonists look like and say? Then imagine yourself present in the scene. What do you observe about the story from this "present at the scene" perspective? Using this Ignatian method, Pope Francis asks "Which of these persons do you identify with?", the injured person abandoned on the side of the road, the robber, the passerby, or the Good Samaritan? He invites us to an awareness of ourselves in all these roles at various moments in our lives, to a deeper understanding that all are our neighbors, not limited by identities or borders, and to a deeper commitment to build a better kind of politics, with a Good Samaritan heart, wide open to the world.

Pope Francis' theory of change is that creating a culture of encounter, of honest dialogue through differences, and common action toward the common good across identities, will create more sustainable social peace. This respectful intercultural engagement yields "reciprocal gifts," "a fruitful exchange," and "a better kind of politics," based on more inclusive love that integrates and unites. FT embraces a vision of integration and inclusion of differences, rather than assimilation, annihilation, and/or nationalist and populist exclusion. FT notes that just peace can only be built with expanded participation among people from different cultural identities, including those previously marginalized. He cites the intercultural and interreligious peacebuilding work of the Church around the world, noting lessons learned by the Bishops of South Korea, for example, that "true peace "can be achieved only when we strive for justice through dialogue, pursuing reconciliation and mutual development."[20] In other words, deep engagement with others to solve difficult global problems is not just "window dressing," it's what works to change hearts and to change policies.

Pope Francis emphasizes just peace,[21] and concludes the encyclical with an endorsement of the role of diverse actors in building peace. For those, including right wing Catholic politicians fomenting identity politics, looking for a scintilla of papal justification for new crusades, they will find none here. Pope Francis restates what the Church has lived and taught for decades: you can't kill your way to peace. Ignoring or stripping away differences brings conflict, not peace. Paths to peace require robust and respectful engagement of the other. Diverse cultural and religious actors must effectively work together to usher in more just, sustainable peace. *Fratelli Tutti* concludes with a return to the commitment, with the Grand Imam Ahmad Al-Tayyeb, to appeal for peace, justice, and fraternity. These are not just nice pieties about diversity. These are the practical means to build sustainable peace in the image of God. As the world now is at the greatest risk of nuclear war since the Cuban Missile Crisis,[22] since *Pacem in Terris*, CST again provides paths for de-escalation, and advancement of better relationships.

Institutions Are Relationships

The flags of all the world's countries fly outside the United Nations headquarters in New York City. It's a picture often used as the quintessential image of international institutions.

But in emerging CST, and church demographics, we see a different view. International institutions are not bricks and flags, but relationships. These commitments are not separate and stovepiped but interconnected. Laws and norms encode the promises we make to each other, our human

---

20. Francis, *Fratelli Tutti*, no. 214.

21. Love, "Just Peace and Nuclear Weapons"; Love, "Ethical Responsibilities of Nuclear Stewards."

22. Francis, "Treaty to Prohibit Nuclear Weapons"; OSV News, "U.S. Bishops Urge Critically Needed Progress."

rights and responsibilities. But the political institutions are outward signs of our connections as human family. The stronger our relationships, the stronger our institutions.

Thus, it was sobering to see empty seats for the 2023 United Nations high level meetings. Usually, the United Nations General Assembly chamber is full with leaders and people eager to see the heads of state who come to address the assembly. The United States was the only member of the P5 (five countries with permanent seats on the UN security council) to address the UN States have split in how to address the war in Ukraine, climate disasters, and other pressing global problems, and the UN, a state-based system, shows every crack. This snapshot of empty seats reveals lukewarm support for the institution and the challenges international institutions face, as well as the need for more robust institutions and church-based global networks to address global issues. It also reveals the need to strengthen our relationships.

By this view, the job of building institutions to serve the global common good is never done. Treaties are not signed and put on a shelf; neither is CST. Institutions, like relationships, must constantly be nourished and renewed. This long view of international institutions creates opportunities for grace and growth, building long term communities who build right relationships across identity lines, and accompany each other across time and borders. "Institutional reforms alone, however, cannot save us";[23] we need to reform the human heart. CST advances as our experiences advance of the challenges we face together. Moral learning advances with our practical learning. As we meet and work together regularly, over decades, we not only build knowledge and international policies together across identity groups, but we also build relationships, trust, and love, in *imago Dei*. The Catholic imagination raises our horizons in international affairs; our principles serve our practices, and our practices expand our principles. The institutions we create ought to reflect our relationships with our Creator.

Bibliography

Benedict XVI. *Caritas in Veritate: On Integral Development in Charity and Truth.* Vatican City State: Libreria Editrice Vaticana, 2009. https://www.vatican.va/content/benedict-xvi/en/encyclicals/documents/hf_ben-xvi_enc_20090629_caritas-in-veritate.html#_ednref112.

23. Caccia, "Emergency Special Session," para. 9.

Caccia, Gabriele. "Archbishop Caccia Addresses Emergency Special Session on Ukraine." Febrryar 22, 2023. https://holyseemission.org/contents//statements/63fe5755c8e6e.php.

Dupuis, Jacques. *Christianity and the Religions: From Confrontation to Dialogue.* Maryknoll, NY: Orbis. 2002.

Francis. "Address upon visit to Qaraqosh Community." March 7, 2021. https://www.vatican.va/content/francesco/en/speeches/2021/march/documents/papa-francesco_20210307_iraq-comunita-qaraqosh.html.

———. *Fratelli Tutti: On Fraternity and Social Friendship.* Vatican City State: Libreria Editrice Vaticana, 2020. https://www.vatican.va/content/francesco/en/encyclicals/documents/papa-francesco_20201003_enciclica-fratelli-tutti.html.

———. "Interreligious General Audience: On the Occasion of the 50th Anniversary of the Promulgation of the Conciliar Declaration *Nostra Aetate*." October 28, 2015. https://www.vatican.va/content/francesco/en/audiences/2015/documents/papa-francesco_20151028_udienza-generale.html.

———. *Laudato Si': On Care for Our Common Home.* Vatican City State: Libreria Editrice Vaticana, 2015. https://www.vatican.va/content/francesco/en/encyclicals/documents/papa-francesco_20150524_enciclica-laudato-si.html.

———. "Message of the Holy Father to the First Meeting of States Parties to the Treaty to Prohibit Nuclear Weapons." June 21, 2022. https://www.vatican.va/content/francesco/en/messages/pont-messages/2022/documents/20220621-messaggio-armi-nucleari.html.

Francis and Ahmad Al-Tayyeb. "Document on Human Fraternity for World Peace and Living Together." February 4, 2019. https://www.vatican.va/content/francesco/en/travels/2019/outside/documents/papa-francesco_20190204_documento-fratellanza-umana.html.

Guterres, António. "Secretary-General's Opening Remarks at Press Conference on Climate." July 27, 2023. https://www.un.org/sg/en/content/sg/speeches/2023-07-27/secretary-generals-opening-remarks-press-conference-climate.

The International Raoul Wallenberg Foundation. "John XXIII the 'Best Pope for Jewish People.'" April 28, 2014. https://www.raoulwallenberg.net/news/john-xxiii-the-best-pope-for-jewish-people/.

John XXIII. *Pacem in Terris: Peace on Earth.* Vatican City State: Libreria Editrice Vaticana, 1963. https://www.vatican.va/content/john-xxiii/en/encyclicals/documents/hf_j-xxiii_enc_11041963_pacem.html.

Love, Maryann Cusimano. "The Church and the Bomb: Holy See Diplomacy and Nuclear Weapons." In *The Vatican and Permanent Neutrality*, edited by Marshall J. Breger and Herbert R. Reginbogin, 203–24. Lanham, MD: Lexington, 2022.

———. "The Ethical Responsibilities of Nuclear Stewards." In *Forbidden: Receiving Pope Francis' Condemnation of Nuclear Weapons*, edited by Drew Christiansen and Carold Sargent, 287–97. Georgetown: Georgetown University Press, 2023.

———. *Global Issues beyond Sovereignty.* 5th ed. Lanham, MD: Rowman & Littlefield, 2019.

———. "Interreligious Peacebuilding and *Fratelli Tutti.*" In *Interreligious Peacebuilding: Routledge Handbook of Religious Literacy, Pluralism, and Global Engagement*, edited by Chris Seiple, and Dennis Hoover, 53–79. New York: Taylor and Francis, 2021.

———. "Just Peace and Nuclear Weapons." In *Forbidden: Receiving Pope Francis' Condemnation of Nuclear Weapons*, edited by Drew Christiansen and Carold Sargent, 172–80. Georgetown: Georgetown University Press, 2023.

———. "The Papal Vision: Beyond the Bomb." *Arms Control Today*, May 2020. https://www.armscontrol.org/act/2020-25/features/papal-vision-beyond-bomb#.

———. "What Kind of Peace Do We Seek?" In *Peacebuilding: Catholic Theology, Ethics, and Praxis*, edited by Robert R. Schreiter and R. Scott Appleby, 56–91. Maryknoll, NY: Orbis, 2011.

Luxmoore, Jonathan. "Retired Archbishop in Poland Says He Won't Keep Quiet about Pope as 'Heretic.'" *Crux, Catholic News Service*, February 28, 2020. https://cruxnow.com/church-in-europe/2020/02/retired-archbishop-in-poland-says-he-wont-keep-quiet-about-pope-as-heretic.

OSV News. "U.S. Bishops Urge Critically Needed Progress on Nuclear Arms Control." *NCR*, August 1, 2023. https://www.ncronline.org/news/bishop-urges-leaders-us-other-nations-make-critically-needed-progress-arms-control.

Paul VI. *Gaudium et Spes: Pastoral Constitution on the Church in the Modern World*. Vatican City State: Libreria Editrice Vaticana, 1965. https://www.vatican.va/archive/hist_councils/ii_vatican_council/documents/vat-ii_const_19651207_gaudium-et-spes_en.html.

———. *Nostra Aetate: Declaration on the Relation of the Church to Non-Christian Religions*. Vatican City State: Libreria Editrice Vaticana, 1965. https://www.vatican.va/archive/hist_councils/ii_vatican_council/documents/vat-ii_decl_19651028_nostra-aetate_en.html.

Pontifical Council for Justice and Peace. *Compendium of the Social Doctrine of the Church*. Vatican City State: Libreria Editrice Vaticana, 2004.

UN Security Council. "Resolution 1674 (2006)." https://digitallibrary.un.org/record/573969?ln=en&v=pdf.

28

Bridging the Divide
Pastoral Leadership in a Time of Tribalism and Polarization

Thomas J. Hennen, Diocese of Davenport, IA

Abstract: Drawing from both the treasury of the Catholic Church's social tradition and the best of modern social science, this contribution seeks to frame the pastoral challenges of our time, marked by deepening divisions within society and the church. After setting up the main issues, the author offers a personal reflection based on his own ministerial experience and then proposes the beginning of a path forward.

Introduction

> I urge, brothers, in the name of our Lord Jesus Christ, that all of you agree in what you say, and that there be no divisions among you, but that you be united in the same mind and in the same purpose. For it has been reported to me about you, my brothers, by Chloe's people, that there are rivalries among you. I mean that each of you is saying, "I belong to Paul," or "I belong to Apollos," or "I belong to Cephas," or "I belong to

Christ." Is Christ divided? Was Paul crucified for you? Or were you baptized in the name of Paul? (1 Cor 1:10–13)[1]

IT IS TEMPTING TO believe that we live in the most divided time in the history of the world, our country, and the church. We do not. It is clear from this short passage from St. Paul's first letter to the Corinthians that even the early Christian community faced great divisions within itself. Division is nothing new. What is new is the speed and extent to which division can spread in an age when information (or disinformation, as the case may be) is at our fingertips. For all their potential to inform and unite people, the internet and social media also act as powerful accelerants in the wildfire of "alternative facts," outright propaganda, divisive rhetoric, identity politics and the like. We no longer take the time to ponder, question, converse with others, and consider other viewpoints before forming opinions of our own. By the time we begin to understand something better, the world is on to the next thing.

As in any age, the Catholic Church is not immune to the various challenges and the dominant ethos of the present time. We might wish the church to be a bastion of calm reason in what seems like a world gone mad, but we are very much in the midst of that world and, therefore, subject to its influence. The question then becomes how do we as the church learn to be in the world but not *of* the world? How do we maintain a sense of eternal perspective, balance, and objectivity? How do we act as an agent of real unity in an increasingly fractured society? These are questions that the pastoral leadership of the church will have to address in the coming years. In this paper I hope to better lay out the nature of the problem, offer some personal reflection based on my own ministry as a priest, and begin to chart a possible path forward based on the best of our Catholic social tradition.

Setting Up the Problem

As I have already mentioned, division among human beings is nothing new. Our understanding of the origins of that division, however, is something we have come to understand better over time, and especially in recent years with the advance of the biological, psychological, and social sciences. Setting aside, for the moment, the theological roots of this

---

1. All biblical citations in this chapter are from the NAB.

division, there are three layers to this division we can isolate: biological, historical/political, and philosophical.

The bad news is that even at a basic biological level human beings are primed for division. Biological anthropologist and neuroscience expert Robert M. Sapolsky notes, "Our brains distinguish between in-group members and outsiders in a fraction of a second, and they encourage us to be kind to the former but hostile to the latter. These biases are automatic and unconscious and emerge at astonishingly young ages."[2] According to Jonathan Rauch in his 2021 book *The Constitution of Knowledge*, the evolutionary value of this is simple: survival. He writes, "People are biased for a reason: for early humans, not much changed from one day to the next, and survival often depended on reacting fast."[3] Biases develop from primitive pattern recognition and cognitive shortcuts, assessing threats and enlisting allies. Not all of this is wrong, as Rauch notes: "Even today, there is usually nothing wrong with using heuristics: that is, applying decision-making shortcuts based on intuitions and snap judgments and rules of thumb, some learned, some evolved,"[4] but the reality is that we instinctively divide ourselves.

The good news is that how we act on these instinctive snap judgments, whether through conflict, persuasion, or intentional cooperation is much more "up for grabs," at least if we believe in free will. Additionally, there is some good news in the fact that these in-group/out-group categories described by Sapolsky are not fixed. Even so, it is something of an uphill climb for us as human beings to begin to break down these categories and foster genuine, more universal cooperation among ourselves.

Add to this biological aspect of human discord a whole lot of ugly human history and our task does not get any easier. One recent example of scholarship on this from the specifically American context is Heather Cox Richardson's *How the South Won the Civil War*. Richardson addresses head on the "American paradox" that the same men who said, "All men are created equal," as stated in the Declaration of Independence, believed this only in a qualified sense, "men" being understood as white, land-owning, males.[5] She notes, "The conflict between a hierarchical society and one based on equality is rooted deeply in European-American society, and it

2. Sapolsky, "This Is Your Brain," para. 4.
3. Rauch, *Constitution of Knowledge*, 27.
4. Rauch, *Constitution of Knowledge*, 27.
5. Cox Richardson, *How the South Won*, xv.

is a battle America has fought from its founding."[6] Ultimately, Cox Richardson argues that while there has undoubtedly been progress, many of the underlying conflicts within American culture and our political system remain. In this sense, the South "won" the Civil War. It follows, for our purposes, that the Catholic Church in the United States cannot ignore these lingering issues or assume that we are somehow untainted by them, as aspects of our own history in this country demonstrate.

Finally, there is a philosophical layer to this as well, added to the biological and historical. Summarizing the thesis of seventeenth century English philosopher Thomas Hobbes' *Leviathan*, Rauch writes: "Left to themselves . . . people live not in orderly hierarchies but in a state of constant competition and rivalry, riven by personal and tribal struggles for power. The state of nature, Hobbes argued, is a state of war against itself."[7]

Grafted onto this social and political understanding of human beings as being fundamentally in conflict with each other is also a new kind of epistemology, which is Rauch's ultimate concern. This revolution comes from the eighteenth century Scottish philosopher David Hume. Rauch, again, summarizes this well when he notes that earlier philosophers "assumed that humans naturally incline toward truth and that reason, God's unique gift to our species, would guide us,"[8] but Hume "believed that reason is like the navigator in the passenger seat, able to suggest directions but not to steer the car, and that our emotions and moral intuitions are in the driver's seat."[9]

Both Rauch and social psychologist Jonathan Haidt, in his book *The Righteous Mind* grab onto this to explain, in part, how we arrived at this point of sociopolitical and epistemological turmoil. Haidt states, "I had found evidence for Hume's claim. I had found that moral reasoning was often a servant of moral emotions, and this was a challenge to the rationalist approach that dominated moral psychology."[10] Haidt's preferred analogy is that of a "rider" (reasoning, specifically language-based reasoning, or "controlled processes") astride a great "elephant" (intuitions or "automatic processes," more nuanced than simply "emotions").[11] Whatever control the rider may think he or she has is illusory. Building

---

6. Cox Richardson, *How the South Won*, 204.
7. Rauch, *Constitution of Knowledge*, 21.
8. Rauch, *Constitution of Knowledge*, 22.
9. Rauch, *Constitution of Knowledge*, 22.
10. Haidt, *Righteous Mind*, 29.
11. Haidt, *Righteous Mind*, 53.

on Hume's assertion that reason (the rider) serves the passions (the elephant) and not the other way around, Haidt concludes that "If you want to change people's minds, you've got to talk to their elephants."[12] Similarly, Rauch contends that "when forming political loyalties, we rationalize backward from our emotions and intuitions—yet we will swear that we are reasoning forward from our policy views."[13] Like it or not, Haidt and Rauch, are on to something here.

From a Christian pastoral perspective, we must honestly acknowledge a certain reality in what Hobbes and Hume (as re-presented by Rauch and Haidt) are saying. At the same time, though, we need not buy completely into this dark anthropology or resign ourselves to perpetual strife. Hobbes and Hume may be correct, but they are telling only half the story, and not the best half.

We can see from a variety of authors and scholars like Sapolsky (a scientist), Cox Richardson (a historian), Rauch (a political scientist and journalist), and Haidt (a social psychologist) that there are undoubtedly biological, historical/political, and philosophical underpinnings to the divisions we experience among ourselves. Through their scholarship we can better name and understand these divisions, and then, from this vantage point, we can begin to do something about them.

As Catholics, though, we can add to this biological, historical, and philosophical sizing up of the roots of human discord the concept of original sin. It is clear from the first chapters of Genesis, written by those who wished to explain in some fashion the origin of things, including good and evil, that conflict comes along almost immediately in our life as ensouled beings on this earth. Whether it is the circle of blame demonstrated by Adam and Eve after eating of the fruit of the tree of knowledge or the jealous fratricide of Cain killing Abel, scapegoating and violence seem to be a part of our "spiritual DNA," as well as our biological DNA.

In a homily on creation and the fall, Joseph Cardinal Ratzinger commented that at the root of this is a forgetting of our fundamental relationship to God as creatures:

> At the very heart of sin lies human beings' denial of their creatureliness. . . . They do not want to be creatures, do not want to be subject to a standard, do not want to be dependent. They consider their dependence on God's creative love to be an

---

12. Haidt, *Righteous Mind*, 57.
13. Rauch, *Constitution of Knowledge*, 25.

imposition from without. But that is what slavery is and from slavery one must free oneself. Thus human beings themselves want to be God. When they try this, everything is thrown topsy-turvy. The relationship with the other becomes one of mutual recrimination and struggle.[14]

With this, we can now add the much-needed perspective of the "queen of the sciences," theology. Pope Benedict speaks to the theological anthropological core of our rivalry with one another. It is a rivalry rooted first in our seeing God as a threat to our freedom, rather than its author and guarantor, and our subsequent rejection of his loving rule.

As with the earlier premises proposed by Hobbes, Hume, Sapolsky, Rauch, and Haidt, we need to admit and accept this reality. At the same time, we need not succumb to it. Rather, this is the unfortunate starting point, but not the endpoint for humanity from the Christian anthropological perspective. Not to admit of original sin would be naïve, but to let it have the final say would be hopeless, and we are a people of hope.

What theology can add even more than the other sciences we have mentioned to this point is precisely this virtue of hope. It is a hope that has as its solid foundation not only the redemption won for us by Christ, the "New Adam," but also the original and fundamental goodness of human beings, made in the image and likeness of God. As with Hobbes' and Hume's gloomy assessments, the story of humanity's rejection of God and fall from grace is only half the story and not nearly the best half. Remembering this will be essential as we look to craft a realistic, yet hopeful pastoral response to the deep divisions of our own time and circumstances.

The secular, Enlightenment philosophers as well as the more contemporary scholars we have considered to this point do not expose the origins of human conflict in order to lead us to despair. They are not working their way toward the existentialist or nihilistic solution that life is ultimately absurd or meaningless. Rather, they do this to give us a starting point from which we can build a more just society. Their stark observations are in service to a hope that we can collectively overcome our divisions. Still, apart from faith and the eternal perspective that it grants us, they can bring us only so far, at best to a secular, scientific, worldly utopia. Theology grants us something much more.

---

14. Ratzinger, *In the Beginning*, 70.

Before considering some possible directions for a response from the perspective of pastoral leadership within the church, I would like in the next section to offer a personal reflection based on my own experiences in ministry. This will hopefully provide some timely and relevant context.

Personal Reflection

It seems like a lot has changed in the world in the almost twenty years since I was ordained in 2004. In some ways, the early 2000s seems now like a simpler time. And yet, this time had its own highly polarized political scene and its own contentious election. It saw a horrific attack on American soil, a new world of precautions in a different kind of global lockdown, and the ensuing war on terror, which we all thought would be over quickly. It had its own uneasy sense of the place of America on the world stage. And then, of course, there was the clergy sexual abuse crisis that shook the Catholic Church to its core, particularly in the United States. But for all of that, it seems like it was a very different world and a very different church than today, so what changed?

The world is likely much as it has ever been. It may be that human beings are changing in a significant way in how we navigate the world, and so also within the church. Are we now more susceptible to our historic/evolved biases, for example to conformity bias (going with crowd) in an age when a sense of belonging is all more necessary to counteract the feeling of distance and isolation that can come with modern technology? Similarly, are we more susceptible to confirmation bias in an age when we can each "fact check" ourselves by selecting our sources on the internet or when they are selected for us by algorithms?

Jonathan Rauch asks, "What happens when individual biases, especially confirmation bias, interact with through group dynamics of conformity bias? The result is epistemic tribalism."[15] Perhaps this is the biggest change from the early 2000s to the present day: the spread and degree of this "epistemic tribalism." In other words, we now "know" according to our "tribe." We believe what we believe based on sources we have carefully cultivated (confirmation bias) and those identities we take to ourselves (conformity bias). Muddying the waters further is the fact that this confluence of biases only further blinds us to our biases in a

---

15. Rauch, *Constitution of Knowledge*, 34.

kind of overarching "meta-bias."[16] As Rauch explains, "Often we think we are most rational and feel we can be most certain when we are in fact most mistaken and most deceived."[17] We are blind and we do not know that we are blind.

Added to this general assessment of how far down the path of epistemic tribalism we have gone in just the past twenty years, I would offer three examples from my own ministry that illustrate the challenges of our time. They represent three related but distinct threats, as I see them, namely: (1) a deepening sense of moral relativism, (2) a declining respect for the concept of the common good, and (3) an unwillingness to dialogue about difficult topics. All three examples relate to the biases and tribalism we have previously discussed.

The first example comes from when I was teaching a high school moral theology course sometime in 2015. That day we were discussing the Catholic Church's teaching on abortion. I assumed that my students knew what the church's teaching was, but not really why the church teaches as it does on this issue. I was trying to build a philosophical foundation, rather than just explaining this as a matter of belief in the "sanctity of human life" beginning at conception. I explained that when we try to determine any time after conception (e.g., implantation or birth) as the beginning of life the lines start to become very blurry and arbitrary. I talked about the amazing process of self-organization that begins to unfold at conception and the biological and genetic uniqueness of this newly created zygote. I further tried to explain that it seems illogical that this "thing" would be considered a human being in one place (outside the womb), but not a human being in another place just moments before (inside the womb, if even only partially, as in the case of partial birth abortion). Similarly, I explained that the humanity of this "thing" could not be based simply on whether or not the mother desired to bring the child to full term. My point in all this was that the church's position on life was not merely a position of faith, but that we could reason our way to a pro-life position. I fully recognized that many of my students, even at a Catholic school, might otherwise dismiss this idea as a preference of religious faith.

I thought I was doing well, until one student blurted out: "It's a baby if you want it to be a baby and it's not a baby if you don't want it to be a

---

16. Rauch, *Constitution of Knowledge*, 27.
17. Rauch, *Constitution of Knowledge*, 27.

baby." I was dumbstruck. No one had put it that starkly. This young man had just articulated in a single breath the essence and logical conclusion of pure, unadulterated moral relativism. In other words: something is true if I want it to be true and it is not true if I do not want it to be true.

As I thought of this later, I wanted to believe that he was saying this just to be provocative, but the more I replayed this in my head, I think this student really believed what he said, and that was both sad and frightening to me. It is precisely the kind of thinking that leads to the gas chamber. I recalled the famous line of Cardinal Ratzinger about the "tyranny of relativism" in his homily before the conclave in which he was elected pope. It struck a powerful chord with me, as it did with many in the church, and yet I am not sure I fully understood it until this experience. Sadly, this deep sense of relativism has not left us, but may be even more ingrained, at least in the West.

The second example is from the summer of 2021, just as the wave of the Delta variant of SARS-CoV-2 was making its sweep of the country and "pandemic fatigue" was reaching fever pitch. In my work as vicar general for the diocese this was also a time when demand for religious exemptions from vaccination was sharply on the rise (in part due to local employer mandates), and the bishop and diocese were being asked to issue some guidance. We issued a letter along the same lines as several other dioceses stating that we could not offer a "religious exemption," given that the Holy Father, the Congregation for the Doctrine of the Faith, and the United States Conference of Catholic Bishops, backed by a host of reputable moral theologians (among them, many respected conservatives), had all said that the vaccine was morally acceptable, particularly under the circumstances of a global pandemic, and that being vaccinated was, in fact, a loving thing to do for our fellow human being and in service to the common good.

I decided that as pastor of the cathedral parish and vicar general I could not duck under my desk on this one. I needed to address this head on in a Sunday homily. I did so in what I thought was a very reasoned and gentle way, and it was generally well received. I had a number of parishioners and others who made affirming comments after Mass or sent me kind emails in support, but I also had a few who were less than happy with me, and possibly one that left the parish over it.

A conservative and very pro-life parishioner arranged to meet with me to discuss her issues with what I said in my homily. I was grateful that she was willing to meet with me in person. We had a pleasant and charitable conversation and walked away with some better understanding of each other, but still really "agreeing to disagree" on the core issue, namely, the acceptability of the vaccine. What struck me in this conversation and really about this whole issue, though, was that it had become less about the medical merits or moral liceity of vaccination and more about the individual choice or "right" of the individual over and above the common good. Ironically, when it came to the issue of vaccination, some of the most "pro-life" voices in the church were now saying things like, "My body, my choice!" It was one of several moments for me in the recent past when the world suddenly felt "upside down." Above all, what this incident taught me is that any *sensus fidelium* about the concept of the "common good" has significantly eroded and will require a lot shoring up if we are going to overcome the present polarization within the church, much less civil society.

The research on religious and party affiliation and vaccination rates is also worth mentioning here. According to the Public Religion Research Institute's June 2021 study, 79 percent of white Catholics and 80 percent of Hispanic Catholics were vaccine accepters.[18] Still, that leaves a not insignificant 20 percent, or one in five Catholics within those populations, who at the time of the study were either vaccine hesitant or outright refusers.

What is as or more interesting in this study was to see how this tracked compared to other religions, along political party lines, and depending on what media sources one consumes. The highest vaccine refusal rate was among white evangelical Protestants.[19] Fox News-watching Republicans were also more like to be vaccine hesitant or vaccine refusers.[20] It would not be a stretch to say that the person I had this conversation with would probably align in these ways. It would seem that a significant minority of Catholics are more likely to go along with their Evangelical friends, Fox News, and the Republican party on this issue than with the pope and the bishops, which raises another interesting aspect of this discussion.

In regard to respect for the teaching authority of the Catholic Church, especially the pope, there seems to have been a reversal within Catholic "tribes." Catholics who fifteen or twenty years ago during the pontificates of John Paul II and Benedict XVI would have said, "We may

18. Public Religious Research Institute, "Religious Identities," 11.
19. Public Religious Research Institute, "Religious Identities," 11.
20. Public Religious Research Institute, "Religious Identities," 14.

not question the pope," have become today's questioners-in-chief during the pontificate of Francis. And those Catholics who fifteen or twenty years ago would have said, "The pope is just one man, one bishop; take him or leave him," are now hanging on Francis' every word. To put it somewhat simplistically, yesterday's Ultramontanists have become today's Gallicans and vice versa. Each "side" vigorously supports the pope and the bishops, so long as the pope and the bishops support their views.

Before moving on from this more personal reflection based on my ministry experiences to the beginnings of a pastoral response, I would like to offer a third and final example of what we are up against. In the struggle against tribalism and polarization, we are facing an unprecedented unwillingness to dialogue, especially when it comes to those difficult subjects that most require it.

In January 2021, our bishop formed an ad hoc committee to look carefully at the "transgender issue." We had a choice: we could either stick our heads in the sand on this issue or enter the fray and really examine it. At the outset, our work was intended to prepare for the increasingly likely situation of a transgender child presenting in a Catholic school or parish faith formation program. We began studying the issue with the idea of drafting a cut and dry policy within a matter of months, to be issued possibly before the start of the 2021–22 school year. We started signing up for webinars, we reached out to those doing ministry for transgender people and to a few transgender Catholics (or former Catholics) and their families. We read a number of books and articles on the subject. We did a lot of listening in what I would now all a very "synodal" process, and we learned a lot. We quickly abandoned the idea of a policy and turned instead to the idea of issuing a statement and possibly some guidelines for pastoral care. More than two years later and we are still at it.

What I have discovered after more than a year of looking at this issue from as many angles as possible is that both sides of this debate have their own set of questions which, it seems, may not be asked. For those who would like to see a more robust welcoming of the LGBTQ+ community within the church (if not an actual change in church teaching in certain areas), the following seem to be on the index of banned topics: the actual data of the body; the relationship between sex and gender; Christian anthropology/"Theology of the Body"; sports; bathrooms; and questions about the therapeutic merits and long-term effects of "gender affirming" treatments. To venture into these topics can be dismissed as simplistic or reductive, if not offensive and transphobic.

For those who want a more black and white approach to this issue, these are the areas of discussion that seem to be off limits: questions about the finer points of neurobiology; discussion of when sexual differentiation occurs; pronouns; exploring the possibility of even modest accommodations in schools and parishes; giving any credence to the actual experience of transgender persons or their loved ones; and any pastoral response other than some version of "tough love." We have a serious problem if we cannot ask questions without automatically being pigeon-holed into one camp and summarily dismissed by the other. This issue perhaps more than any other in the church that I have seen at present has caused good Catholics to put up the intellectual barricades and retreat to their epistemological tribes.

These are real issues and attitudes that I am facing as a pastoral leader, and I know that I am by no means alone. The question then becomes what we do with this. How do we respond to these issues and many others in light of this "epistemic tribalism" and the deepening divides we are seeing even among Catholics? The options before the church seem to be: (1) run away in hopes of waiting this out, (2) brazenly charge in as the "culture warrior" and deal with the aftermath later, or (3) actually try to develop a pastoral response that is at once charitable, brave, practical, and wise. Between cowardice and recklessness, can we not find that virtuous mean of true courage in the face of these challenges? That is what we will begin to consider in the final section of this paper.

Towards a Solution

As we turn now to some pastoral starting points in dealing with the divisions we face as a church and in society, there are three ways in which I believe we can make some progress toward our goal. Each of these build on what has already been presented.

First, following the lead of scientists and scholars like Robert Sapolsky and Jonathan Haidt, we need to embrace and work with, not against, the science behind our biases. Reminding ourselves of this biological and sociological reality frequently, yet without falling into a kind existential despair, is itself already a powerful check against tribalism. But also, by acknowledging and redirecting both the process and the power of our biases, perhaps we can actually begin to reverse them.

For example, recognizing our innate tendency to group people as either "us" or "them," there are things we can do to expand our sense of who belongs to this in-group, in other words, who counts as "us." As Sapolsky explains, "Although human biology makes the rapid, implicit formation of us-them dichotomies virtually inevitable, who counts as an outsider is not fixed. In fact, it can change in an instant."[21] He gives the example of an experiment in which the subjects were shown a series of pictures of people, some who looked like them and others who did not. As predicted, they began to sort people into these us-them categories. The subjects were then shown the same people a second time, only now with some of them wearing the colored jerseys of their favorite sports team. Suddenly, "them" became "us," as subjects "automatically began to categorize the people by their uniforms instead, paying far less attention to race."[22]

If these kinds of ingrained biases can begin to be undone based on something as ultimately unimportant as sports team affiliation, then surely Catholicism, a worldwide religion that embraces every race, ethnicity, culture, and language, already possesses a distinct advantage in breaking down many of our social barriers. If we can "trick" our brains into widening the circle of those we consider to be in-group people (and with real effect), then maybe we can use this same principle in bringing Catholics back together, while also addressing other biases. For example, introduce a white, suburban Catholic to a black, inner city Catholic and maybe their common Catholicity will enable them to understand each other better, to see each other as "us," and to break down other biases.

Along these lines, in his review of *The Righteous Mind*, William Saletan gleans from Jonathan Haidt's work some guidelines "to organize society so that reason and intuition interact in healthy ways," the first of which is "to help citizens develop sympathetic relationships so that they seek to understand one another instead of using reason to parry opposing views."[23] Does this not sound a lot like the repeated calls of Pope Francis to build a culture of "encounter?"

Jonathan Rauch also addresses this idea of the inevitably of human bias, but without being totally resigned to it and even calling on our ability to find ways around it. He writes: "Humans are inherently biased and tribal, but we are also capable of outwitting our biases and tribes and thinking well. We do it a lot of the time. We are not doomed

21. Sapolsky, "This Is Your Brain," para. 13.
22. Sapolsky, "This Is Your Brain," para. 14.
23. Saletan, "Why Won't They Listen?," para. 18.

to be gullible, easily brainwashed suckers who are likely to believe whatever people tell us."[24]

Rauch ultimately calls for the renewal of those basic moral, social, and intellectual institutions that make it possible to "think well." He writes, "The most interesting question is not how often human beings get reality right or wrong in a laboratory . . . it is how we can create a social environment which increases rightness and reduces wrongness."[25]

Lastly, returning once more to Sapolsky, we see that we may be stuck with a certain amount of human divisiveness, but that it "would perhaps be more productive to harness these dynamics rather than fight or condemn them."[26] He adds that, therefore, "leaders should appeal to peoples innate in-group tendencies in ways that incentivize cooperation, accountability, and care for one's fellow humans."[27] While Sapolsky is writing specifically in regard to the phenomenon of nationalism and therefore calling for political leaders to do this, a cross-application to pastoral leadership seems more than appropriate, especially given religious leaders disproportionate ability to influence those who listen to them.

Related to this, a second important way in which we can begin to bridge our many divides, particularly within the church, is by simply admitting more fully the reality of original sin and the structural and personal sin that come in its wake. Just as at a biological and sociological level we need, as we have seen, to admit our biases and tribalistic tendencies, in the same way spiritually we need to admit our brokenness before we can begin to heal. First, we deny our creatureliness, as Cardinal Ratzinger noted in his homily, then we deny our sinfulness. We see this played out in the story of the fall in Genesis, as Adam quickly blames his wife, Eve, who in turn quickly absolves herself by pointing to the serpent. Ever since we have been sinning, we have been denying our sinfulness, and thereby only preventing the wound from healing and allowing it to fester. The way out is to start by admitting the wound.

One might assume that the less we focus on the negative reality of sin, the more loving, free, and understanding we would become. This seems to have been the tack of many within the church in the past fifty or so years. But paradoxically, sin turns out to be a great "equalizer." By acknowledging the reality of sin (original, personal, and structural) there

---

24. Rauch, *Constitution of Knowledge*, 42.
25. Rauch, *Constitution of Knowledge*, 42.
26. Sapolsky, "This Is Your Brain," para. 23.
27. Sapolsky, "This Is Your Brain," para. 23.

is a sense that, despite our many differences, we are "all in the same boat" and in need of a savior. The "other" then becomes one like me, a brother or sister, striving to live according to our truest and original nature. As strange as it sounds, we are united in our sin, but still more powerfully united in the grace of our redemption. We certainly do not need to go back to the days of browbeating and overinflated "Catholic guilt," but this hardly seems the dominant error of our time, especially among the young. Still, if we would heal, then we must face openly and honestly our illness and then turn to the Divine Physician.

The third and final way that we might begin to heal the divisions in the church and society is by bringing everything that we have to offer from nearly two millennia, the best of our Catholic social tradition, and placing it at the service of this task. In many cases, we do not have to reinvent the wheel, but to draw from this deep well, to build on these good foundations, even if that means new, creative, and yet faithful applications of these concepts and practices. I would offer just a few of them here.

The first and most foundational is our unbending insistence on the goodness and dignity of the human person. We can find many expressions of this, but perhaps the *Catechism of the Catholic Church* summarizes it best in speaking of the human person as *imago Dei* and *capax Dei* and when it states:

> Being in the image of God the human individual possesses the dignity of a person, who is not just something but someone. He is capable of self-knowledge, of self-possession and of freely giving himself and entering into communion with other persons. And he is called by grace to a covenant with his Creator, to offer him a response of faith and love that no other creature can give in his stead.[28]

We find in this a much-needed positive corrective to that gloomier vision of the human person and of sin presented earlier, but of which we must also not lose sight. As the *Compendium of the Social Doctrine of the Church* reminds us: "This marvelous vision of man's creation by God is inseparable from the tragic appearance of original sin."[29] What is presented in the *Catechism* and the social doctrine of the church is a much fuller and hopeful vision of the human person, one rooted in our fundamental relationship with God and with each other.

---

28. *Catechism of the Catholic Church*, no. 357.

29. Pontifical Council for Justice and Peace, *Compendium of the Social Doctrine of the Church*, no. 115.

It follows that a second core concept we bring to the table from our tradition is our insistence on the social nature of the human person. Drawing on *Gaudium et Spes* from the Second Vatican Council and the teaching of two previous popes, the *Compendium* states: "The human person is essentially a social being because God, who created humanity, willed it so,"[30] and, "All social life is an expression of its unmistakable protagonist: the human person."[31] Again, this lends a powerful corrective to the notion that we are isolated ("islands" unto ourselves) and doomed to conflict. In fact, one could argue that even our conflicts point to our inherently social nature. We fight precisely because we are in relationship with each other and have an equally deeply ingrained desire for harmony, for communion. The point is: if we do not acknowledge and embrace this social nature of our being from the outset, then there is little chance of us finding a path to any meaningful communion or social harmony.

A third and final central concept that will need to drive any response to growing polarization and tribalism in our time is our belief in the common good. We have not and must not give up on this ideal, even if it may never be perfectly realized "this side of heaven." Our commitment to that "sum total of social conditions which allow people, either as groups or individuals, to reach their fulfillment more fully and easily,"[32] as defined in *Gaudium et Spes* and the *Catechism* is essential. And this, in turn, "depends on a healthy *social pluralism*."[33] As the *Compendium* explains: "The different components of society are called to build a unified and harmonious whole, within which it is possible for each element to preserve and develop its own characteristics and autonomy."[34]

We could add to these core beliefs many others, such as the concepts of solidarity, subsidiarity, the universal destination of goods, the preferential option for the poor, as well as our general commitment to the ideals of authentic freedom, truth, and justice. The concept of synodality, much more in our vocabulary in recent years, is another powerful tool, if used well, the church can apply to the issues we face.

---

30. Pontifical Council for Justice and Peace, *Compendium of the Social Doctrine of the Church*, no. 149.

31. Pontifical Council for Justice and Peace, *Compendium of the Social Doctrine of the Church*, no. 106.

32. *Catechism of the Catholic Church*, no. 1906.

33. Pontifical Council for Justice and Peace, *Compendium of the Social Doctrine of the Church*, no. 151.

34. Pontifical Council for Justice and Peace, *Compendium of the Social Doctrine of the Church*, no. 151.

We could further add to these concepts and beliefs the very ways or institutions in which they are formed, articulated, and practiced, namely, our robust intellectual and spiritual traditions, our willingness and learned habit of taking time for careful study and prayerful discernment. If as Jonathan Haidt says, "we need to create time for contemplation,"[35] appealing to "a power capable of circumspection, reflection and reform,"[36] then, again, the church already has a distinct advantage here. We come already well equipped to build, to rebuild, or to renew those social, moral, and intellectual institutions that those like Rauch and Haidt see as keys to our common flourishing.

Jonathan Rauch concludes his chapter on "The State of Nature: Tribal truth" in *The Constitution of Knowledge* on a hopeful note. He writes:

> *Something* has made it possible not only to defeat the Hobbesian paradigm but to reverse it, creating a virtuous cycle linking more and more people into a reality-based community. . . . *Something* allowed us to surmount the myriad biases and impulses and group dynamics which deceive and distort. *Something* made it possible for humans to learn not just individually but on a species-wide scale. That *something* did not arise naturally, of its own accord. . . . [I]t was founded by visionaries and born of struggle.[37]

While this "something" may not have arisen naturally, as Rauch says, but had to be carved out and fought for by brave visionaries, could it be that the very capacity to do this is in fact supernatural, and that it is written into the being of every human person? I firmly believe so. The Catholic Church, with its rich anthropology and social teaching, its intellectual and moral traditions, its diversity, and worldwide presence has its finger firmly on the pulse of this "something." It is poised perhaps better than any other institution in the world to bridge the divides the exist between us.

Conclusion

I would like to conclude briefly where I began, with the church in Corinth. After pointing out the various divisions among the Corinthians in the earlier part of his epistle, St. Paul later speaks eloquently about the unity and harmony of the church. He writes: "God has so constructed the

---

35. Saletan, "Why Won't They Listen?," para. 18.
36. Saletan, "Why Won't They Listen?," para. 23.
37. Rauch, *Constitution of Knowledge*, 42.

body . . . so that there may be no division in the body, but that the parts may have the same concern for one another. If one part suffers, all the parts suffer with it; if one part is honored, all the parts share its joy. Now you are Christ's body" (1 Cor 12:24b–26).

This is the vision to which we must hold, first as the church, the Body of Christ, but also in a wider sense as a human race, as brothers and sisters, children of God, until it is realized as far as possible on earth and fully in heaven. The pastoral leadership, lay and ordained, of the Catholic Church in the coming years and decades will be absolutely indispensable in making this hope a reality.

Bibliography

Catechism of the Catholic Church. 2nd ed. Vatican City: Libreria Editrice Vaticana, 2000.

Cox Richardson, Heather. *How the South Won the Civil War: Oligarchy, Democracy, and the Continuing Fight for the Soul of America*. New York: Oxford University Press, 2020.

Francis. *Fratelli Tutti: On Fraternity and Social Friendship*. Vatican City: Libreria Editrice Vaticana, 2020.

George, Francis. *A Godly Humanism: Clarifying the Hope That Lies Within*. Washington, DC: The Catholic University of America Press, 2015.

Haidt, Jonathan. *The Righteous Mind: Why Good People Are Divided by Politics and Religion*. New York: Vintage, 2013.

Pontifical Council for Justice and Peace. *Compendium of the Social Doctrine of the Church*. Washington, DC: United States Conference of Catholic Bishops, 2005.

Public Religion Research Institute. "Religious Identities and the Race against the Virus: Successes and Opportunities for Engaging Faith Communities on COVID-19 Vaccination." July 28, 2021. https://www.prri.org/research/religious-vaccines-covid-vaccination.

Ratzinger, Joseph. *In the Beginning: A Catholic Understanding of the Story of Creation and the Fall*. Translated by Boniface Ramsey. Grand Rapids: William B. Eerdman's Publishing Company, 1995.

Rauch, Jonathan. *The Constitution of Knowledge: A Defense of Truth*. Washington, DC: Brookings Institution Press, 2021.

Saletan, William. "Why Won't They Listen?" *The New York Times*, March 23, 2012. https://www.nytimes.com/2012/03/25/books/review/the-righteous-mind-by-jonathan-haidt.html.

Sapolsky, Robert M. "This Is Your Brain on Nationalism: The Biology of Us and Them." *Foreign Affairs*, March/April 2019. https://www.foreignaffairs.com/articles/2019-12-12/your-brain-nationalism.

29

The Future of Catholic Social Teaching

John A. Coleman, SJ, Institute for Advanced Catholic Studies

Abstract: This essay considers the future of Catholic Social Teaching given the vastly different shape of global Catholicism in our century as compared to the preceding one. These differences begin with the radical shift of the majority of Christians from Europe—where postwar social democracy aligned well with CST—to a more global distribution. Much of this new global Catholicism is also deeply wounded by the sexual abuse crisis and the declining mass participation following the COVID-19 pandemic. It is further marked by deepening polarities between more traditionalist or conservative Catholics, on the one hand, who often dislike Pope Francis and post conciliar social teaching. On the other hand, are more progressive Catholics who support CST but are less likely to emphasize Catholic sexual and life ethics. The consensus expectation is that this global Church will be largely non-Western, non-white, non-affluent, younger, more conservative on many sexual issues, more liberal on questions of social justice, more suspicious of free-market capitalism, largely anti-war and pro-United Nations, and motivated to work aggressively to address climate change. The social teaching of Pope Francis is presented as a major resource to address the challenges facing this evolving Church, including ecology, inter-religious dialogue, and broad discernment and conversation about how to address the evolving signs of the times. For this, a more a synodal Church of disciples walking together with Jesus must emerge. The ability of this social doctrine to bear its fruits of justice, peace, friendship and renewal will depend on its embodiment in broad movements of Catholics witnessing to God's love through work for the common good.

Introduction

THE TOPIC I WAS asked to address in this chapter is "The Future of Catholic Social Teaching." Because I wrote a rather extensive chapter for a book published by Georgetown University Press on the same topic several years ago,[1] I will try to write a different kind of chapter for this book. I will do so in three steps, considering first the vastly different shape of global Catholicism in the twenty-first century. In the second, I will survey three works that articulate the hope Pope Francis interprets and develops the Catholic social tradition to address this new situation. In the third, I will offer some very brief remarks on how the Catholics social tradition must be embedded in social movements if it is to bear fruit, which points to the theme of this project, namely "Social Catholicism for the Twenty-First Century?"

The Vastly Changed Situation of Global Catholicism in the Twenty-First Century

Catholic social teaching in the twenty-first century will be quite different than it was in the twentieth century because global Catholicism in the twenty-first century is vastly different than global Catholicism in the twentieth century.

In 1920, the English Catholic, Hilaire Belloc could acclaim that "The Church is Europe: and Europe is the Church."[2] But today the majority of the Christian population shifts from Europe and North America to the Global South, Africa and Latin America. In 1910 Europe was home to roughly two-thirds of the world's Christians (66.6 percent) but by 2010 that number had dropped to 25.5 percent and is projected to drop to 15.6

---

1. Coleman, "Future of Catholic Social Thought," 610–36.
2. Belloc, *Europe and the Faith*, ix.

percent by 2050. One reason is diminishing fertility. Europe now has the lowest fertility rate of any global region.

Another factor is religious switching, or people ceasing to practice religion. In twelve out of twenty-one European countries studied, most young people said they have no religion. The percentage of practicing Catholics has diminished strongly in the Netherlands. Also, largely because of the sex abuse scandal, mass attendance in Ireland which was once around 90 percent of the Catholic population has dropped to about 30 percent.[3] While in the early 1990s, 80 percent of the French called themselves Catholic, by 2007 that number had fallen to 51 percent.

Much of Catholic Social Teaching and social Catholicism in the twentieth century was deeply influenced by Christian Democratic Parties in Germany, Italy, the Netherlands. Few of those parties remain robust. In North America, both in the United States and Canada, the percentage of the population which is Catholic has fallen. The same is true for Australia but in Africa, Latin America and Asia the number of Catholics has grown, especially in Africa where the Christian population is expected to grow by 2050 to 2.2 billion, making its Christian population twice that of Latin America and Europe combined.

I highly recommend Thomas Rausch's recent book on global Catholicism and the ways it will have impact on Catholic Social Teaching and social Catholicism.[4] Rausch goes across the world, continent by continent, and most continents also by country, to present data on the state of Catholicism. He recounts the impact on Catholic practice by the clergy sexual abuse crisis, by the shortage of priests internationally (and also a merging of parishes which can sometimes be too big and cut off from a deep sense of community belonging, as well as an often-diminished number of masses etc. in parishes), by increasing cultural and religious pluralism in the Church, leading to the polarities he talks about in the title to his book. Global Catholicism involves not just an enlargement of boundaries but also a deepening of polarities which split the Church. Traditionalist Catholics and more conservative ones tend not to appreciate Pope Francis. Many social justice activists Catholics, often enough, neglect the centrality of prayer. Many Catholics do not accept Church teaching on abortion, euthanasia, homosexuality or sexual mores. Rausch also wonders what the effect of the COVID-19 pandemic

---

3. For Ireland, see Scally, *Best Catholics in the World*.
4. Rausch, *Global Catholicism*.

will have on Catholic parishes, with masses restricted to only zoomed versions and with deep cuts in the money coming in to support parishes.

Rausch then turns to Pope Francis' efforts to renew the Catholic Church and also to present new versions of Catholic Social Teaching appropriate for the twenty-first century. Pope Francis has called the Church to a pastoral conversion. Christians are called to be missionary disciples, to bring the good news to the peripheries, to all the excluded—the poor, the suffering, the migrants. The Church should be described by what it is for, not what it is against, building bridges instead of walls. It needs to rediscover the grace and mercy of God.

Pope Francis has sought to reimagine the Church as a synodal Church (a point I will take up again when I go through Francis' contributions to Catholic Social Teaching). A synodal Church grants more authority to national and regional conferences to make decisions concerning their lives, liturgy and mission. This gives them both voice and agency. This move will be welcome especially to the Catholics of Africa who are stressing more inculturation. A number of commentators see tomorrow's Catholics as largely non-Western, non-White and non-affluent.

They will be more conservative on many sexual issues, more liberal on questions of social justice. They will be largely anti-War, pro-United Nations and sometimes suspicious of free-market capitalism. They may also be more biblical and evangelical in engaging with cultural issues; more concerned with a strong Catholic identity in the face of religious pluralism; younger and more optimistic; also, more open to indigenous religious practice than Catholics in Europe and North America. Africans want to develop a more authentically African theology. Asians stress a threefold dialogue with the poor, with culture and with other religions.

Pope Francis has stressed a more synodal Church, where the bishops listen to one another and speak about what is in their hearts, not simply repeat what they thought the pope wanted them to say. As a Jesuit, Francis has stressed discernment and for genuine discernment honesty is essential. At the synod for the Amazon, the bishops voted for the ordination of married men who are already recognized as religious leaders in the many communities without priests. They voted 128 yes to this proposal versus 41 no votes. On the question of women deacons, they voted 137 yes votes to 30 no votes.

There is a drastic shortage of priests. In Africa, Asia and Latin America, pastoral leadership is often in the hands of lay catechists. In those areas, lay catechists and lay missionaries number in the hundreds of thousands. But in Africa and Latin America, catechists do more than just catechesis. In many countries they are congregational leaders and perform many of the ministries reserved to priests and deacons in the United States and Europe. In Latin America women also frequently serve as leaders of communities, catechists, ministers of the Word and extraordinary ministers of baptism and giving communion.

In much of the global south, there is a multiplication and flourishing of new churches: Evangelical, neo-Pentecostal and the African Instituted Churches. The more established churches cannot simply ignore these new churches of the Southern hemisphere, but relating to them will require a new, more inclusive ecumenism. These churches and communities are not so much interested in theological dialogue and consensus statements which have so characterized the ecumenical movement since the end of Vatican II, nor are they prepared for them. More important to them is personal testimony, sharing stories about life in the spirit and a sense of mission based on gospel values. This is also an approach favored by Pope Francis who favors walking, working and praying together. He also often speaks of a need to move toward the peripheries in the Church.[5]

Three Examples of Pope Francis' Social Teaching

In this section, I will survey three examples of Pope Francis's social teaching as potential indications of the future of Catholic Social Teaching. These three examples include *Laudato Si'*, *Fratelli Tutti*, and *Let Us Dream*. Let us begin with *Laudato Si'*.[6]

Laudato Si'

Although both John Paul II and Benedict XVI each had written documents dealing with ecology and climate change, they did not do so in dedicated encyclicals. By writing *Laudato Si'* as an encyclical, Catholic social teaching now also includes teaching on the environment. Against those who argue that a papal writing on the environment has no real authority, Francis explicitly states that *Laudato Si'* is now added to the body

---

5. Cf. Faggioli, *Liminal Papacy of Francis*.
6. Cf. for *Laudato Si'*, Martin, "Ten Takeaways"; Dorr, *Creed for Today*. See also Dahl, "Encyclical on Environment and Poverty."

of Catholic social teaching.[7] An encyclical is a type of teaching which enjoys the highest level of authority in the Church, second only to the Gospels and Church Councils such as Vatican II. As such, it continues the kind of reflection on modern social problems that began with Leo XIII's 1891 encyclical *Rerum Novarum* on capital and labor. Francis calls upon some of traditional Catholic social teaching, such as an appeal to the common good to frame his discussion.

Written just before the 2015 United Nations Climate Change Conference held near Paris, a spiritual dimension is now part of the discussion on the environment, as in Francis' systematic overview on environmental issues. Previous to Francis, discussion of ecology and climate change was done mainly with political, scientific and economic language. Now the language of faith also enters the discussion. Francis did not impose his faith on those concerned with the environment. He says: "I am well aware that not all are believers."[8] *Laudato Si'* grounds its discussion of ecology on a spiritual view and invites others to listen to a religious point of view and understand creation as a holy and precious gift from God to be reverenced by all. The pope also hopes to offer ample motivation for Christians to take up action to limit climate change and to care for nature seriously.[9] Yet, Francis also insists that science must also be respected.

The poor are disproportionately affected by climate change. This disparate effect on the poor and on the developing world is highlighted in almost every section of the encyclical. Francis provides many examples of the harmful effects of climate change whose worse impacts are felt by those living in developing countries. This is not to imply that the richest and most powerful never take the poor into account but because the poor themselves have fewer financial resources to enable them to adapt to climate change. Additionally, the natural resources of these poorer countries "fuel the development of the rich countries" at the cost of their own and poorer countries own present and future.[10] Francis appeals to the Book of Genesis, to Catholic social teaching and to statements of recent popes to critique the exclusion of anyone from benefiting from the goods of creation. Overall, in decisions regarding the environment and

---

7. Francis, *Laudato Si'*, no. 15.
8. Francis, *Laudato Si'*, no. 52.
9. Francis, *Laudato Si'*, no. 41.
10. Francis, *Laudato Si'*, no. 52.

the use of the earth's common resources, Francis repeatedly calls for an appreciation of the extreme detriment felt by the poor.[11]

In saying that "less is more," Francis takes aim at what he calls the "technocratic mindset" in which technology is seen as a principal key to human existence.[12] He critiques an unthinking reliance on market forces in which every technological advancement is embraced, before or without considering the harm it can do to the environment and without concern for its potential impact on human beings.[13] This is not to take the view of a Luddite. In fact, Francis goes out of his way to praise technological advances. But he resists the belief that every increase in technology is good for the earth and for humanity. *Laudato Si'* also points out a society of extreme consumerism in which people are unable to resist when the market places a new change before them, while the earth is despoiled, and billions left impoverished.[14] It is time to accept growth in some parts of the world in order to provide recourse to the poorest places to experience some healthy growth.[15] Christian spirituality stresses a growth which embraces moderation and creates a capacity to be happy with less,[16] In fact, Francis calls for a redefinition of our current notion of progress.

Everything is connected—including the economy. Francis links all of creation: "We are part of nature, included in it and thus in constant interaction with it."[17] But our actions, particularly about consumption and production, have an inevitable impact on the environment. Francis links a "magical conception of the market" which privileges profit over the market's impact on the poor or the environment.[18] A heedless pursuit of money which sets aside the interest of the marginalized and leads to ruination of the planet are connected. He evokes Francis of Assisi's work for nature, his efforts toward justice for the poor, his commitment to society and to interior peace.[19] Far from offering a naïve condemnation of capitalism, Francis provides an intelligent critique about the limits of the

11. Francis, *Laudato Si'*, no. 58.
12. Francis, *Laudato Si'*, no. 104.
13. Francis, *Laudato Si'*, no. 109.
14. Francis, *Laudato Si'*, no. 203.
15. Francis, *Laudato Si'*, no. 103.
16. Francis, *Laudato Si'*, no. 222.
17. Francis, *Laudato Si'*, no. 139.
18. Francis, *Laudato Si'*, no. 190.
19. Francis, *Laudato Si'*, no. 10.

market, especially where it fails to provide for the poor. "Profit cannot be the sole criterion of our decisions."[20]

Scientific research on the environment is to be praised and used. Francis does not try to avoid science. He accepts the "best scientific research available today and builds on it rather than entering into a specialist's debate."[21] Speaking of the great forests of the Amazon and Congo, of glaciers and aquifers, he simply says "We know how important they are for the earth."[22] Widespread indifference and selfishness worsen our environmental problems. Francis reserves his strongest criticism for the wealthy who ignore the problem of climate change and its effect on the poor. "Many of those who possess more resources seem mostly to be concerned with masking the problems or concealing their symptoms.[23] Why, he asks, are so many of the wealthy turning away from the poor? Not only because some view themselves as more worthy than others but also because frequently decision makers are "far removed from the poor" physically, with no real contact with their brothers and sisters.[24] Selfishness leads to a refusal to confront the notion of the common good. These effects are not simply found in the underdeveloped and developing world but also in the inner cities of our developed countries. Francis calls for what might be termed an "urban ecology." One does not care for the rest of nature if our hearts lack tenderness, compassion and concern for our fellow humans.

More than any other encyclical, Francis draws from the experience of people from around the world (somewhat like his insistence on synodality in later documents). He uses the insights of bishops' conferences from Brazil, New Zealand, Southern Africa, Bolivia, Portugal, Germany, Argentina, The Dominican Republic, The Philippines, Australia and the United States among other places. In this way, he embodies the Catholic principle of subsidiarity which, in part, looks to local experience and local solutions. Moreover, the new dialogue and honest debate he calls for is not simply one within the Catholic Church.[25] Patriarch Bartholomew, the leader of the Eastern Orthodox Church enters into the encyclical, as does a Sufi poet. In fact, the pope calls for an inter-religious dialogue with

---

20. Francis, *Laudato Si'*, no. 187.
21. Francis, *Laudato Si'*, no. 15.
22. Francis, *Laudato Si'*, no. 38.
23. Francis, *Laudato Si'*, no. 26.
24. Francis, *Laudato Si'*, no. 90.
25. Francis, *Laudato Si'*, nos. 14, 16.

all people about our common home.[26] A global dialogue is also needed because there are no uniform recipes. What works in one region may not in another.[27] The encyclical's worldwide scope, as opposed to a narrower Eurocentric one, makes it a vital invitation for a worldwide community.

While both John Paul II and Benedict XVI each spoke about climate change, they did not fully address the way other creatures, besides humans, mirror God and thus if they are lost, we lose something of God. They each tended to emphasize in a somewhat one-sided manner, the human hegemony over other creatures. Francis does not do so. Finally, he emphasizes the need for a change of heart. Dealing with climate change demands really a true conversion. Thus, after *Laudato Si'*, future Catholic social teaching must involve a true dialogue with science, while also calling to attention what other religious groups or other episcopal authors say about a particular issue.

Fratelli Tutti

Fratelli Tutti (2020) is a second important social encyclical by Francis. Earlier, Francis co-authored with the Moslem Ahmed Al-Tayyeb from Abu Dhabi a document in which they wrote that "God has created all human beings equal in rights, duties and dignity and has called them to live together as brothers and sisters." Yet, in the present day there are many attempts to eliminate or ignore the other as such. *Fratelli Tutti* addresses that issue. There are eight chapters in the encyclical, beginning with "Dark Clouds over a Closed World."[28]

Myopic, extremist and aggressive nationalisms are on the rise. Globalized cultures unite the world but divide persons and nations and turn individuals into mere consumers. There is a loss of a sense of history that gives rise to limitless consumption, empty individualism and cultural colonization. Too many offer slick marketing techniques instead of long-term plans to improve people's lives and advance the common good. We live also in a throwaway world where there is a waste of food and a downplaying of the elderly, unborn and disabled. Too many contemporaries treat people as objects or means to the end. A growing culture

---

26. Francis, *Laudato Si'*, no. 62.
27. Francis, *Laudato Si'*, no. 180.
28. I was inspired by an essay by Fredricks, "*Fratelli Tutti*," 376–83, and by an unpublished YouTube presentation about *Fratelli Tutti* by Bishop Robert McElroy, given Feb. 27, 2021 to alumni at Saint Patrick's Seminary, Archdiocese of San Francisco.

of walls has emerged, creating an "us versus them" mentality. Much of what was thought of as "communication" is a misnomer: hindrance to true dialogue and digital campaigns are fueled by hatred and destruction of the "other." A true globalization should help each country to grow in their own way and not just be like the present prosperous countries. The Coronavirus shows how we are connected to each other's calamities and the pandemic shows how our lives are interwoven. No one is saved alone.

Chapter 2, "A Stranger on the Road," presents a profound meditation on the parable of the "Good Samaritan." It reminds us that love and care for the other includes foreigners. Love cannot be indifferent to suffering or allow anyone to go through life as an outcast. In our own world the story of the Good Samaritan is constantly relived. We have all experienced it. Some of us have been robbers, many of us are like the passers-by who neglect the wounded victim the Good Samaritan cares for. Some of us have been the wounded one. Some, like the Good Samaritan, care for those who are suffering. The parable reminds us that we are neighbors without borders. We are not just called to care for our social group. Note how the passers-by were all religious but did not do good deeds for the wounded man. In fact, in our world, sometimes unbelievers may be more like the Good Samaritan and do good more than those who call themselves religious.

Chapter 3 is called "Envisioning an Open World." It reminds us that we need to move beyond ourselves or only relate to our small groups. We seek a love that is ever more open which helps us transcend our own limitations. We need to work for open societies that integrate everyone: the foreigner, the disabled, the elderly. The famous triad, "Liberty, Equality, Fraternity" is not just something abstract. We have to fight against a false individualism which forgets that we are all socially connected. Solidarity is a prime Christian and moral virtue. It depends on a real conversion. It finds its concrete expression in service and care for our common home. True solidarity will mean we need to re-envision the social role of property. There is a fundamental right of peoples to subsistence and some kind of progress. False individualism denies that we are all social and need to find ways to welcome the strangers, the outcasts, the disabled and those who did not get born with all the advantages of richer people.

Chapter 4 is called "A Heart Open to the Whole World." Our response to migrants should be to welcome, protect, promote and integrate. Borders do also have limits. Nor should we demand migrants to give up their own respective cultural and religious identities. Each will be enriched by the other's culture through fruitful exchange and dialogue. There needs to be a fruitful exchange where poorer nations have an effective voice in matters of shared decision. The local also needs to be embraced. Local flavor is important since there is no real dialogue without a sense of identity.

Chapter 5 is entitled, "A Better Kind of Politics." Populism has a problem in that it tends to disregard people. Society is not a mere aggregate of individuals. Closed, populist groups distort the word, People. They also make too much of short-term advantages. Francis emphasizes the right to work. Employment is an essential dimension of social life. There are some benefits but also limits to liberal approaches. We need to remember that there is no one solution, no single acceptable methodology, no economic recipe that can be applied indiscriminately to all. Liberalism too often ignores selfishness and weakness. Not everything can be resolved by a mere appeal to market freedom. We also must pay attention to the weakening of the power of nation states. But sometimes effective civil society groups can help compensate for international weaknesses. We cannot expect economics alone to solve our problems.

Francis then speaks about Political Love. He notes that the Church's social doctrine derived from charity or love. But love is also civic and political. There are no real "peoples" without respect for the individuality of each person. "People" and person are and must be correlative terms. Charity is also closely related to truth. There is no place for sheer relativism in a healthy politics. Moreover, the exercise of political love is not just an individual thing. It can have political implications.

Chapter 6 is entitled "Dialogue and Friendship in Society." It advises against confusing social dialogue for a new culture with the feverish exchange of opinion on social networks. These often exclaim: "We are right and everyone else is wrong." Reality is one but it can be approached from various angles and with different methodologies. The solution is not relativism. We seek consensus, to be sure, but we also seek to link consensus with truth. Catholics believe that some enduring truth is accessible to the human intellect (this conviction underlies appeals to 'natural law'). In a renewed culture we need to be passionate about building bridges, recovering kindness and learning how to truly listen to each other.

Chapter 7, "Paths of Renewing Encounter" deals with legitimate conflict but also forgiveness. It asks about the best ways to move on and forgive (but not necessarily forget). Francis insists truth should not lead to revenge. One part of the path forward is to begin with the least. Vast inequalities and lack of human development make peace impossible. In discussing the value and meaning of forgiveness, Francis does think there can be legitimate conflict. Forgiveness does not involve renouncing our rights or refusing to confront evils, but it does not think harms done should be allowed mainly to fuel our anger. We may need to move on from past injustices but we can't move on without remembering and addressing our past.

Forgiving is not the same as forgetting. Francis then addresses two key issues: war and the death penalty. About war, Francis notes the many injustices it occasions. He says: "We can no longer think of war as a solution because its risks (think of massive so-called collateral damage to innocent civilians)—will be greater than its supposed benefits." The just war theory supported coming to the aid of others who suffer the oppression of a bad dynasty. But even it carried the presupposition that such aid would actually improve their lot and that of peace. Francis cast doubts on how many wars can really follow the "just war" theory. He also calls for the need to bring about the total elimination of nuclear weapons. How to do so in a way that is justified and good is another obvious issue.

About the death penalty, Francis says: "The death penalty is inadmissible and the Church is firmly committed to calling for its abolition worldwide." Again, he notes: "It is impossible to imagine that states today have no other means than capital punishment to protect the lives of other people from the unjust aggressor." We need to protect the lives of the innocent and oppose and punish crimes, to be sure, but capital punishment is not the best means of doing so.

Chapter 8, "Religion at the Service of Fraternity in Our World," enunciates the proper role of religion in politics. The Church cannot restrict its mission just to the private sector. Francis does not support the Church engaging in party politics but instead should address the political and just dimensions of institutions and organizations in our society and world. He notes that the Church demands freedom even when it is a minority but promises to give it to others when it is in the majority.

Francis ends with citing the powerful document he and Ahmed al-Tayyeb wrote on opposing any use of religion for violence. It and some other prayers at the end of the document are worth reading and reflecting on. As *Laudato Si'* brought together Catholic Social Teaching and the environment, *Fratelli Tutti* brings together inter-religious dialogue with Catholic Social Teaching. As Father James Fredericks put it: "The fact that Pope Francis has chosen to reflect on interreligious dialogue in a social encyclical is of enormous significance. Francis is saying that our work of dialogue must not be separated from the Church's mission of proclaiming the Gospel by building social solidarity, promoting justice and accompanying the marginalized. If the promotion of justice and the common good constitutes a starting point for the ministry of interreligious dialogue, then our work with those who follow other religious paths constitutes a concrete praxis for the promotion of justice and the common good." This means that the future of Catholic Social Teaching will entail a more active attention to interreligious dialogue than Catholic Social Teaching always did in the twentieth century.

Let Us Dream

Although not an encyclical, Pope Francis' book, *Let Us Dream*, espouses Catholic Social Teaching and gives us a clue as to its future. The book contains three chapters and an epilogue. In the prologue, Francis reflects on COVID-19 and remarks that we are going through a crisis during the pandemic which is shattering our categories. We don't come out of a crisis the same as we were before. We have to choose and our choices show where our hearts are. In a crisis we experience both good and bad things. The choices we face include either making care for people a priority or continuing to prioritize the financial system. There is always a temptation to retreat away from needed choices. Besides COVID-19 and the lockdown we have gone through, there are other crises: a growth in weapons; refugees fleeing poverty or persecution; climate change; the problems of hunger and violence in our world.

Francis asks us to dare to dream: to dream about another kind of economics which stresses basic human need, for land, for adequate lodging and for food and labor; to dream also about another form of politics which stresses fraternity and equality but not rugged individualism.

Chapter one is called "A Time to See." In his three chapters, Francis takes his lead from the famous triad of Catholic Action: See, Judge, Act. In this first chapter, Francis notes that we often get discouraged by the vastness of world problems we see and maybe want to retreat. He suggests instead that we focus on concrete situations and people we can actually see or imagine. There are many persecuted others, such as the Rohinga but Francis noted how the people of Bangladesh, even though themselves poor, gave them food and a place to live. We need antibodies to the virus of indifference. The Lord asks that we choose a culture of service, not a throwaway culture. We may feel powerless, even afraid, but we need not let that keep us from seeing what is and what needs to be done.

The pandemic made visible our throwaway culture. Many do not have housing that allows social distancing or even clean water to wash themselves. Slums show us how many have been denied elemental rights to hygiene, food and a dignified life. Children go without schooling or go hungry every day. The virus of indifference blocks discernment. Francis suggests we start by seeing new possibilities in the little things that surround us or in what we do every day. The pandemic also showed us sins of entitlement: people who refused to wear masks, who avoided social distancing and who embody racism. We do need a new consensus building but by debate and dialogue, not acts of force. We also need to not just focus on the technical or become intolerant of inherent limits (among other things by climate change). As Francis notes, the green and the social go together. Much sickness has come from waste, pesticides and the enormous amount of plastic thrown into the sea.

Francis refers to three COVID-like (or lockdown) experiences in his own life. The first was when he was a teenager and very sick, perhaps in danger of losing his lungs. He refers to two nurses who took care of him and gave him even more medicine to fight his disease than the doctors had ordered. His second COVID-like experience was when he spent time in Germany, working on his doctoral dissertation. He felt adrift and away from the people he knew. He speaks of it as a kind of COVID of displacement. The third was the time he was sent into a kind of exile in Cordoba. He says that when he had been provincial and rector he could be very harsh. He admits he deserved his exile, but it led him to prayer, reflection and a genuine conversion.

Francis ends chapter one by saying: "Today we have to avoid falling back into individual and institutional patterns that have led to COVID and the various other crises that surround it: the hyper-inflation of the individual combined with weak institutions and the despotic control of the economy by a very few." Again, he notes: "Without the we of a people, of a family, of institutions of a society that transcends the I of individual interests, life quickly fractures and becomes violent, a battle for supremacy between factions and interests; and if the state is no longer capable of managing violence for the sake of social peace, it can end up fomenting violence to defends its interests. We need to feel again that we need each other."

The second chapter in Francis' book, "A Time to Choose" (rather than judge as in the Catholic Action formula of see, judge, act) allows the Jesuit pope to evoke the Ignatian formula of discernment. For this second challenge, we need not just an openness to reality but a set of criteria to guide us. We also need a healthy capacity for silent reflection. Some of the values we bring to discernment include the Beatitudes and some principles of Catholic Social Teaching: The preferential option for the poor; the universal destination of the goods of the earth (reminding us that the goods of life—land, lodging, labor—should be made available to all). Add solidarity which acknowledges our inter-connections and includes welcoming the stranger, forgiving debts, giving a home to the disabled and allowing other people's dreams and hopes for a better life to become our own. Another principle is subsidiarity—we let local actions deal first with needed changes.

We are living in a change of an era and the categories and assumptions that we used before to navigate our world no longer are effective. Things we never imagined would take place—the environmental collapse; a global pandemic, the return of populism—mean that what we once considered normal will increasingly no longer be. It is an illusion to think we can just go back to where we were before.

Discernment asks us to look also at new truths: the signs of the times the Church speaks about. Francis goes through Ignatian discernment about what comes from the evil spirit and what comes from God. He says of these spirits:

> They speak different languages; they use different ways to reach our hearts. The voice of God never imposes but proposes, whereas the enemy is strident, insistent and even monotonous. The voice of God might correct us, but gently, always encouraging, consoling, giving us hope. The bad spirit on the other hand offers us dazzling illusions and tempting sensations, but they are fleeting. It exploits our fears and suspicions and seduces us with wealth and prestige. If we ignore it, it responds with contempt and accusation, telling us: "You're worthless!" The voice of the enemy distracts us from the present by getting us to focus on our fears for the future or the sadness of our past. The voice of God, on the other hand, speaks to the present, helping us to move ahead in the here and now. What comes from God asks: "What is good for me? What is good for us?"

Francis sees hope and a sign of the times in new roles for women in society, the economy and the Church. He says the Church and society must avoid tribal division and polarizations which divide us into two simply opposing camps. Sometimes we need to see seeming opposites as contra-positions rather than contradictions. We need to look at the horizon of possibilities but also the limits on them; we need to focus on the local and yet connect it with the global. We need to see what is the whole and what is the part, but this is not giving in to simple relativism.

Francis then talks about his desire to re-invigorate the practice of synodality and talks about it involving not only open discussion, listening to one another but also times of quiet silence and prayer. As he insists, the Church that teaches must also listen. He also affirms that "what effects all should be discussed by all." Clericalism involves not listening or giving voice to the laity. He then discusses what he learned from the three synods he has held: first, on the family as reflected in the 2016 *Amoris Laetitia* with a discussion of pastoral outreach to the divorced-remarried; second, on youth as reflected in the 2018 *Christus Vivit*; third, on Amazonia as reflected in the 2020 *Querida Amazonia*.

Chapter 2, "A Time to Act," reminds us that we are a people, invoking solidarity and shared vulnerability. A people is not the same as a country, a nation and state. A people calls forth unity in diversity—*e pluribus unum* (with a need to stress both unity and diversity). The dignity of a people comes from its closeness to God. A people also has many faces. As he did in the synod on Amazonia So, Francis says that we must speak in the dialect of each place. The Church must try to stay close to the people, in their sorrows and hopes. Once again, Francis lifts the danger of rugged individualism and populism. Market forces are not enough. They do not often include the human needs for land, lodging, labor, education and health care.

Many structural reforms are called for: against human trafficking; dealing with migration as a global issue. There can be no slavery nor capital punishment. We must stand against and refute the Neo-Darwinian ideology of the survival of the fittest. As Francis puts it: "The Neo-Darwinist ideology of the survival of the fittest, underpinned by an unfettered market obsessed with profit and individual sovereignty, has penetrated our culture and hardened our hearts. The successful growth of the technocratic so often demands the sacrifice of innocent lives: the child abandoned on the streets; the underage sweatshop worker who rarely sees the light of day; the worker dismissed because his company has been asset-stripped to generate dividends for shareholders; the refugees denied a chance to work; the elderly abandoned to their fate in underfunded rest homes." We also need an ecological conversion.

Francis has also tried to dialogue with popular movements who see the issues in our present society as inequality, unfair access to land, lodging and labor. He thinks we need a new form of Jubilee to address these issues. He also says that he has learned that the health of any society can be judged by its periphery. Francis goes, therefore, to the periphery by visiting Iraq, for example, and raises bishops and cardinals from the periphery. This does not mean any true attack on the role of business. As Francis notes, the very etymology of the word company is found in the Latin—*cum panis*—which means a sharing of bread. A company, therefore, refers to people working and serving together.

In summary then, Francis's social teaching insists that the future of Catholic social teaching will be linked to issues of ecology, inter-religious dialogue, a discernment about the new signs of the times and a care for synodality and true dialogue with groups in the Church.

A Brief Addendum on the Embodiment of Catholic Social Teaching in Social Movements

The future of Catholic social teaching will also deeply depend on the continued vigor of Catholic social movements such as *Pax Christi*, Community Organizing groups (many of which were founded by or deeply influenced by Catholics), The Catholic Worker, The Jesuit Refugee Service, The Jesuit Volunteer Corps, The Community of Sant Egidio, the Catholic Climate Covenant, Catholic Charities, The Saint Vincent DePaul Society, Network and many other social groups and movements. Such movements, of course, bring to a local action or area the basic principles of Catholic Social Teaching and make that teaching available so it becomes practicable. As I noted in my chapter on "The Future of Catholic Social Thought" in the Georgetown University book cited in footnote 1, however, a great deal of papal Social Thinking (and that found in bishops' letters) actually came from earlier teachings and actions of Catholic Social Movements. In that chapter, I noted how much of *Quadragesimo Anno* came from its principal author, Oswald von Nell Breuning's connection to German Catholic labor unions and the socioeconomic thought of the Munchen-Gladbach school. The idea for "socialization" in *Mater et*

Magistra, furthermore, seems to have originated in a *Semaine Sociale*—a study week of French social Catholics—held in Grenoble in 1960. A great part of John XXIII's famous opening to the left and cooperation with socialism found in *Pacem in Terris* , moreover, was closely aligned with moves by the Italian Christian Democratic Party to find new support from Italian socialist groupings.[29] In a similar way, many of the new elements in Pope Francis' social encyclicals, such as his new treatment of "Just War" theory and his total condemnation of Capital Punishment in *Fratelli Tutti* came from his incorporating of what he had learned from the teaching of *Pax Christi* about Just War and from the teaching of The Community of Sant Egidio about capital punishment.[30] So clearly the future of Catholic social teaching will entail also new ideas and positions being espoused by Catholic social movements as they get taken up by and incorporated into papal and episcopal encyclicals and letters.

Bibliography

Belloc, Hilaire. *Europe and the Faith*. New York: Paulist, 1920.

Coleman, John A. "The Future of Catholic Social Thought." In *Modern Catholic Social Teaching: Commentaries and Interpretations*, edited by Kenneth Himes et al., 610–36. Washington, DC: Georgetown University Press, 2018.

Dahl, Arthur Lyon. "Summary and Commentary on *Laudato Si'*, the Pope's Encyclical on Environment and Poverty." *International Environmental Forum*, June 2015. https://iefworld.org/ddahl15d.

Dorr, Donal. *A Creed for Today: Faith and Commitment for Our New Earth Awareness*. Maryknoll, NY: Orbis, 2020.

Faggioli, Massimo. *The Liminal Papacy of Francis: Moving Toward a Global Catholicity*. Maryknoll, NY: Orbis, 2020.

Francis. *Fratelli Tutti: On Fraternity and Social Friendship*. Vatican City State: Libreria Editrice Vaticana, 2020. https://www.vatican.va/content/francesco/en/encyclicals/documents/papa-francesco_20201003_enciclica-fratelli-tutti.html.

———*Laudato Si': On Care for Our Common Home*. Vatican City State: Libreria Editrice Vaticana, 2015. https://www.vatican.va/content/francesco/en/encyclicals/documents/papa-francesco_20150524_enciclica-laudato-si.html.

Francis, and Austen Ivereigh. *Let Us Dream: The Path to a Better Future*. New York: Simon and Schuster, 2020.

---

29. See Coleman, "Future of Catholic Social Thought," 612–13.

30. For the role of the Community of Sant Egidio in opposing capital punishment, see the Wikipedia, s.v. "Community of Sant Egidio," https://en.wikipedia.org/wiki/Community_of_Sant%27Egidio. For the role of PAX Christi in raising objections to the just war theory, see Wikipedia, s.v. "PAX Christi," https://en.wikipedia.org/wiki/Pax_Christi.

Fredricks, James L. "*Fratelli Tutti*: An Interreligious Perspective." *Pro Dialogo* 166 (2020) 376–83.
Martin, James. "Ten Takeaways from *Laudato Si'*." *America Magazine*, June 18, 2015.
Rausch, Thomas. *Global Catholicism: Profiles and Polarities*. Maryknoll, NY: Orbis, 2021.
Scally, Derek. *The Best Catholics in the World: The Church and the End of a Special Relationship*. Westminster: Penguin, 2021.

30

Epilogue
After Populism and Polarization— A Better Kind of Politics

Paul Vallely

Abstract: A new populism has arisen in many Western democracies as a backlash to the growth of twentieth century economic globalization which has promoted increasing inequality within nations and left large swathes of the population feeling alienated, dispossessed, or "left behind." This new populism has its roots in a mix of economic, philosophical, social and cultural factors. It feeds on a discontent which has found articulation initially outside mainstream politics in the US through movements like the Tea Party and in the UK by anti-European movements like UKIP. But it has spread into mainstream politics all over the world under Donald Trump, Boris Johnson, Viktor Orbán, Matteo Salvini, Giorgia Meloni, Recep Tayyip Erdoğan, Jair Bolsonaro and Narendra Modi. Its discontents manifest themselves in divisive debates on national identity and immigration.

Epilogue—Vallely

Pope Francis—with his one-time sympathies to Peronism and his advocacy of a *teología del pueblo*—is seen by many as a populist pope. But in *Fratelli Tutti* he takes care to distinguish between the populist and the popular. Populists, he warns, play on fear of economic insecurity, of losing old traditions and values, of losing national sovereignty, and of the Other. They feed a growing intolerance with easy slogans and ready scapegoats, using culture wars to reinforce a sense of "us and them." This chapter scrutinizes the parallels Francis draws between today's populists and Adolf Hitler in the deployment of one-sided truth and the Big Lie. It explores why voters don't care when politicians lie to them. And it examines the suggestion that the antidote to populism is solidarity and what Francis calls "a politics of fraternity."

> *The development of a global community of fraternity based on the practice of social friendship on the part of peoples and nations calls for a better kind of politics, one truly at the service of the common good.*[1]

Western democracy is at a cross-roads. The old order is under threat. The great international institutions created in the decades after the Second World War—the United Nations, the Universal Declaration of Human Rights, the World Bank, the World Trade Organization, the European Union, the International Criminal Court—all of which constituted the most rule-based structure for political and economic relations in modern history—were informed by an understanding of the mutuality of our interests. They were undergirded by a sense of the common good and a common purpose. But today everywhere we are seeing this broken down and replaced by a new more volatile politics. Our old political institutions are creaking under a new set of polarizing forces. This shift was addressed by Pope Francis in his 2020 encyclical on fraternity and social friendship *Fratelli Tutti*. He wrote:

> Ancient conflicts thought long buried are breaking out anew, while instances of a myopic, extremist, resentful and aggressive nationalism are on the rise. In some countries, a concept of popular and national unity influenced by various ideologies is creating new forms of selfishness and a loss of the social sense under the guise of defending national interests.[2]

---

1. Francis, *Fratelli Tutti*, no. 154.
2. Francis, *Fratelli Tutti*, no. 11.

This nationalist populism is, Pope Francis says, a "regression" and "another source of polarization in an already divided society."[3] Sadly, he adds, "politics today often takes forms that hinder progress towards a different world."[4] Our old politics has been weakened; some would even say it is broken.

It is not hard to think of who and what Pope Francis has in mind. At the start of the third decade of the twenty-first century the political successes of Donald Trump in the United States, Vladimir Putin in Russia, Boris Johnson in the United Kingdom, Viktor Orbán in Hungary, Matteo Salvini and Giorgia Meloni in Italy, Recep Tayyip Erdoğan in Turkey, Jair Bolsonaro in Brazil and Narendra Modi in India, testified to the potency of a renewed belligerent chauvinist populism all across the globe. It grows from a perfect storm of broken politics and estranged economics mixed with a new nationalism of culture and identity. It purports to speak for "the people" who have been abandoned by the political elite. And it offers simple solutions to complex problems.

How Did We Get Here? Economic, Philosophical, Social and Cultural Factors

How did we get here? This new populism has its roots in a mix of economic, philosophical, social and cultural factors. Let us begin with the economy. Of course, the world has always seen economic differences in its societies—rich and poor, north and south, town and country. Marx saw it as about class. But since the Second World War industrial capitalism has found ways of maintaining the privilege of the elite whilst also improving the lives of the vast majority of the population. So what brought about the current "gear change"? Two things: the great deregulation of finance which occurred during the 1980s under Ronald Reagan and Margaret Thatcher; and the rise of a global economy which was embraced as inevitable by almost every politician until the arrival of this new populism.

Deregulation brought a great rise in global wealth—but also a great rise in inequality. Globalization took that inequality outside individual nations and spread it around the world. In every country there was a wealthy elite—which often had more in common with the elites of other

---

3. Francis, *Fratelli Tutti*, no. 156.
4. Francis, *Fratelli Tutti*, no. 154.

nations than with its own people. In every nation there were groups of people who felt their economic security was undermined by globalization. In the US these people were given names like "Rust Belt rejects." In the UK they were described as "the Left Behind." In France, Marine Le Pen—who garnered ten million votes, more than a third of the electorate, in the 2017 presidential election[5]—spoke of "forgotten France."[6] These groups became the breeding ground for the new populism which has so increased social polarization.

In the Western world, society is today the most unequal it has been since the First World War. From the 1930s until around 1980 inequality was steadily reduced. The rich still took a greater share of national income than everyone else but the bottom 90 percent of the population earned 72 percent of the nation's take-home pay. But with financial deregulation that trend went into reverse. Inequality began to rise and has risen steadily ever since.[7] With deregulation the financial sector expanded hugely. The integration of the world economy accelerated. Low-paid jobs migrated abroad. Trade unions lost influence and membership, which reduced their bargaining power, and lowered wages in real terms. Those "left behind" felt an increasing sense of economic insecurity. As Pope Francis has put it "behind the rise of populist politics in recent years is a genuine anguish: many feel thrust aside by the ruthless juggernaut of globalized technocracy."[8]

Meanwhile the income of the wealthy increased. Globally, the richest 1 percent have never held a greater share of world wealth than they do today. In the US the bottom half of the population earn only half of what they did in 1980—as a percentage of national income. By contrast, the top 1 percent earn double. "Today, the United States has less equality of opportunity than almost any other advanced industrial country," says the Nobel Prize-winning economist Joseph Stiglitz.[9] The typical chief executive in a top US company, would have earned twenty times more than their average worker in 1965; today he or she earns 312 times more. By contrast the wages of ordinary workers have barely increased.[10] Some forty million people in the US—one-third of them children—live

5. Conseil Constitutionnel of France, "Décision n° 2017–171 PDR du 10 mai 2017."
6. Willsher, "Le Pen's Young Backers."
7. Dorling, *Injustice*; Singleton, "Gap between Rich and Poor."
8. Francis and Ivereigh, *Let Us Dream*, 117.
9. Stiglitz, "Equal Opportunity Myth."
10. Mishel and Schieder, "CEO Compensation Surged in 2017."

in poverty. One person in eight depends on food stamps. Five million Americans live in the kind of abject deprivation normally associated with developing countries.[11]

The picture in Britain is depressingly similar. In 2007 the bottom 90 percent of the population earned only 57.4 percent of the nation's income—the least pay they had taken home since 1929, the year of the Wall Street Crash that began the Great Depression.[12] Income inequality has now reached a new maximum, according to Danny Dorling, the Professor of Human Geography at the University of Oxford. Since 2015 infant mortality has risen across Britain. Food banks—which had not been seen since the 1930s—are back. In 2022–23 some 2.9 million emergency food parcels were given out in the UK.[13] Worldwide progress in reducing poverty has essentially come to a halt, according to the World Bank.[14] The problem has been exacerbated by the COVID-19 pandemic which hit the poorests and most vulnerable hardest.[15] We are now witnessing "the sharpest increase in global inequality since the Second World War."[16] The words of Pope Benedict XVI in his 2009 encyclical *Caritas in Veritate* have proved prophetic—"as society becomes ever more globalized, it makes us neighbors, but does not make us brothers."[17] Rather, in the words of Pope Francis, "the global economy . . . unifies the world, but divides persons and nations."[18]

But the discrediting of traditional politics is about more than economics. There was a significant cultural and philosophical shift at the heart of the changes ushered in by the Reaganite/Thatcherite vision of the primacy of efficiency and freedom. It promoted a new individualism which spoke persuasively to one source of human motivation—economic self-advancement. But the Reagan and Thatcher revolution had a psychological as well as an economic impact. Margaret Thatcher famously said in an interview in 1987: "There's no such thing as society. There are individual men and women and there are families. And no

---

11. Guardian Staff, "Poverty and inequality under Trump."

12. Dorling, "Peak Inequality."

13. This represents a 37% increase on the previous year. The Trussell Trust, "End of Year Statistics."

14. World Bank, "Global Progress Grinds to a Halt."

15. Joi, "COVID-19 Has Worsened Global Inequality."

16. Elliott, 'Top Economists Call for Action."

17. Benedict XVI, *Caritas in Veritate*, no. 19.

18. Francis, *Fratelli Tutti*, no. 12.

government can do anything except through people, and people must look after themselves first. It is our duty to look after ourselves and then, also, to look after our neighbors."[19]

The assumption was that individuals driving themselves would become the motor for a successful national economy. For some that worked, but for many it did not. The subversive dynamism of market forces has inexorably dissolved the social fabric of extended families and communities—and the rules, rituals and traditions which sustain them and give meaning to life. Pope John Paul II was alert to this as early as 1995 when in *Evangelium Vitae* he observed that "the criterion of personal dignity—which demands respect, generosity and service" has been "replaced by the criterion of efficiency, functionality and usefulness."[20] Others are considered not for what they "are," but for what they "have, do and produce." These "powerful cultural, economic and political currents" effectively constitute "a war of the powerful against the weak."[21]

But what the Reaganite/Thatcher revolution also did for everyone was to shift the balance between the individual and the community. Individualism has replaced the collective as the primary driver of modern behavior. It produced increased aspiration and the dream of social mobility. But also had malign consequences which reached their *reductio ad absurdum* in a philosophy summed up in Gordon Gekko's notorious epithet that "Greed is Good." In the last homily he gave before becoming Pope Benedict XVI, Cardinal Joseph Ratzinger described modern life as ruled by a "dictatorship of relativism which does not recognize anything as definitive and whose ultimate goal consists solely" of satisfying "the desires of one's own ego."[22] The former UK Chief Rabbi, Jonathan Sacks, saw this at the root of the fragmentation of culture, the collapse of the family, the ghettoization of cities, the loss of a sense of continuity with the past, and a growth of a mindset in which individuals have no larger loyalties than personal choice and provisional contracts.[23] This emphasis upon individual self-interest, says Pope Francis, has deformed *homo sapiens* into *homo œconomicus*—men and women so obsessed with the creation of wealth that they have become oblivious to the atomizing effect

---

19. Thatcher, "Interview for *Woman's Own*."
20. John Paul, II, *Evangelium Vitae*, no. 23.
21. John Paul, II, *Evangelium Vitae*, no. 12.
22. Ratzinger, "Homily for Mass '*Pro Eligendo Romano Pontifice*,'" para. 11.
23. Sacks, *Faith in the Future*, 62–68.

this had on society.[24] The philosophical shift to the individual means that celebrity is now the greatest currency of personal achievement. A recent survey of American and British school kids asked them what they wanted to be when they left school: the most common answer was to be famous.[25] We live in an increasingly fragmented world. A handful of television channels have given way to thousands of digital outlets. Personal headphones are the symbol of how our individualism has turned to solipsism.

In the West globalization brought the death of the old heavy industries like steel making, coal mining, automobile manufacture and shipbuilding. With them died the spirit of many of the communities which had been sustained by that traditional work. In the UK the brass bands died and so did social solidarity; in the US the political scientist Robert D. Putnam coined the metaphor of *Bowling Alone* in a work which charted the decline of social capital in the US at the end of the twentieth century. Putnam examined the decline in all the forms of in-person social intercourse which enrich the fabric of our social lives. This decline, he suggested, also undermined the active civil engagement which undergirds a strong democracy.

There is more to this than relative economic deprivation and a dislocation of the old sense of community. For many people the changes are profoundly psychologically disturbing. Roger Eatwell and Matthew Goodwin—in their study of the rise of this new phenomenon, *National Populism: The Revolt against Liberal Democracy*—have observed, in comparing this new politics across the United States and Europe, two other factors at work. They speak of distrust and de-alignment. This new distrust is rooted in the growing sense of certain sections of society that traditional politics have failed them. Central to this were those groups who felt left behind as inequalities of income and wealth rose and who feel that they no longer have a voice in their national conversation. But the discontent goes further than that. Eatwell and Goodwin show that many of the voters attracted to populist politicians have average, or above average, incomes but also have a fear they are losing out relative to others. And this has become entwined with issues of identity fueled by the

---

24. Francis, "Universal Destination of Goods and Hope."

25. A Harris Poll of schoolchildren in the US, UK, and China in July 2019 showed that schoolchildren in the US and UK were three times more likely to want to be a YouTuber than an Astronaut. In China the figures were the other way round. Harris Poll, "Group Kicks Off Global Program."

sense that global trade and finance—abetted by the mainstream politicians who favor this liberal economics—were eroding the power of the nation state.

This created what the political psychologist and behavioral economist Karen Stenner calls "classic normative threats."[26] The feeling of having been let down by politicians, institutions, and influential sections of their fellow citizens, creates a "feeling like 'no-one agrees on anything anymore' [and] 'we've lost the things that once made us great.'"[27] This political distrust has become embroiled in questions of national identity and has coalesced around the totemic issue of immigration. The free movement of money and goods around the world has been paralleled by a free movement of people. Thus, the disenfranchised claim, globalization is doing more than robbing sections of the population of their economic security; it is eroding their sense of the nation and national identity. A globalized economy which has encouraged mass migration to serve new open labor markets is seen as allowing immigrants to steal the jobs of the settled population—and be given preferential treatment over the relatives and friends of local people. These concerns, as Eatwell and Goodwin point out, are not always grounded in objective reality—which is why immigration is a prominent issue in countries like Hungary and Poland, where actual levels of immigration are low. Immigration is nonetheless an issue there because national identity and a traditional way of life are perceived as under threat from the global forces of liberal economics. Issues of race and religion further entrench these fears. Many of the 1.2 million applications for asylum made in Europe in the great migrant influx in 2015 came from Muslims fleeing war in Syria, Iraq and Afghanistan. At the same time large numbers of Africans arrived after the collapse of border controls during Libya's 2014–20 civil war. All this seemed to open an untrammeled route for migrants.[28]

This discontent found articulation initially outside mainstream politics. In the United States, in the second decade of the twenty-first century, activists formed the Tea Party movement—a loose affiliation of national and local groups with conservative, libertarian, and originalist agendas—to give voice to their discontent with the agenda of mainstream politics. In the UK discontent crystalized around a marginal organization which called itself the United Kingdom Independence Party (UKIP)

26. Stenner, *Authoritarian Dynamic*.
27. Stenner, "Authoritarianism and the Future of Democracy."
28. Eurostate News Release, "Record Number of Asylum Seekers."

set up to campaign for Britain to leave the European Union. But the concerns of these fringe movements were readily exploited by populist politicians who subsequently rode to power on the coattails of this popular disgruntlement. The 2016 Brexit referendum which determined that the UK should leave the EU took place only months after the peak of the European refugee crisis. One of the two main groups campaigning for Brexit focused its campaign on the immigration issue portraying the European Union as inept and unable to control its borders. The politician who subsequently became British prime minister, Boris Johnson, shamelessly conflated the refugee crisis with unease over the prospect of Turkey applying to join the EU even though very few of the refugees came from Turkey.[29] In America the topic of US border security and illegal immigration became a prominent issue in the 2016 presidential election campaign of Donald Trump. The future President's figures on the subject were questioned by experts, as was his contention that immigrants are responsible for higher levels of violent and drug-related crime. But the strategy proved electorally effective—as did his frequent proposals to issue a ban on Muslims entering the United States.[30]

The result of all this in the US and UK, as in many other countries across the world, was that the old era of liberal democracy—characterized by relatively stable politics, strong mainstream parties and loyal voters—has been called into question. What Eatwell and Goodwin call "de-alignment" has occurred between large sections of the electorate and mainstream politicians. All across the world, politics are far more volatile, fragmented, chaotic and unpredictable than in the past. Large sections of the electorate find the polarizing rhetoric of populist politicians more plausible than the certainties of the old order. Some have said that this new confrontational nationalist populism is merely "one last howl of rage" from a dinosaur generation yearning for some a return to a mythical golden age. But others fear that trust in traditional politics has been smashed. It is in this sense that Western democracy appears to be at a cross-roads.

---

29. Menjívar et al., *Oxford Handbook of Migration Crises*.
30. Green, "Trump Hypothesis," 506–24.

Francis's Distinction between Popular and Populist

In *Fratelli Tutti* Pope Francis takes care to make a distinction between the popular and the populist. Populists frequently couch their approach in terms of an appeal to the will of the people but their approach "disregards the legitimate meaning of the word 'people,'" Francis suggests.[31] He continues:

> To be part of a people is to be part of a shared identity arising from social and cultural bonds. And that is not something automatic, but rather a slow, difficult process . . . of advancing towards a common project.[32]

"Popular" leaders can nurture such an approach, he says, and then adds:

> But this can degenerate into an unhealthy "populism" when individuals are able to exploit politically a people's culture, under whatever ideological banner, for their own personal advantage or continuing grip on power. Or when, at other times, they seek popularity by appealing to the basest and most selfish inclinations of certain sectors of the population. This becomes all the more serious when, whether in cruder or more subtle forms, it leads to the usurpation of institutions and laws.[33]

What he calls "irresponsible populism" distorts the notion of the "people." In those circumstances a "lack of concern for the vulnerable can hide behind a populism that exploits them demagogically for its own purposes" or to serve "the economic interests of the powerful."[34] The concept of "the people" of which Pope Francis approves is, by contrast, that of "a living and dynamic people, a people with a future . . . one constantly open to a new synthesis through its ability to welcome differences . . . open to being mobilized, challenged, broadened and enriched by others."[35] In this Francis is firmly in the tradition of earlier popes. Pope John Paul II, in *Centesimus Annus*, his 1991 encyclical to mark one hundred years of Catholic Social Teaching, had warned: "If there is no ultimate truth to guide and direct political activity, then ideas and convictions can easily be manipulated for reasons of power. As history demonstrates,

---

31. Francis, *Fratelli Tutti*, no. 157.
32. Francis, *Fratelli Tutti*, no. 158.
33. Francis, *Fratelli Tutti*, no. 159.
34. Francis, *Fratelli Tutti*, no. 155.
35. Francis, *Fratelli Tutti*, no. 160.

a democracy without values easily turns into open or thinly disguised totalitarianism."[36]

How then does contemporary nationalist populism measure up against this papal template? There is precious little evidence of a shared identity or a common project in most of the contemporary populism stretching from the United States and Britain to Brazil or India. Rather division seems to be the order of the day. The 2020 US presidential election saw the populist, protectionist, isolationist and nationalist Donald Trump forced from the White House but his successful rival, President Joe Biden, secured only 51.3 percent of the vote compared to Trump's 46.8 percent[37] leaving the nation still rift in twain—with a majority of Republicans still believing that Trump had been cheated of the election a full six month after the vote.[38] Britain was split by a remarkably similar percentage by the Brexit vote which saw the nation 52 percent in favor of leaving Europe and 48 percent against. Pro-Brexit politicians triumphally proclaimed the Leave vote to be the "overwhelmingly" decisive view of the British people. It is a very odd kind of mathematics which regards just over half as an overwhelming number—especially when the large number of people who did not vote are taken into account. Overall only 37 percent of the total British electorate voted to leave. Politics not arithmetic sets the vocabulary here. The inescapable reality is that majority politics is now often governed by minority votes. The government of Boris Johnson forced through the most severe of the range of options on the extent to which the UK should disengage from Europe, taking no account of the narrowness of the vote. A sense of common purpose has given way to a corrosive winner-takes-all mentality.

This culture of division is creating new fault lines within as well as between tribes. In the United States the staunchly conservative Congresswoman Liz Cheney was expelled from her post as Republican leader in the House of Representatives by her fellow Republicans after refusing to accept Trump's "big lie" that the election had been stolen from him and then criticizing the outgoing President for inciting the storming of the US Capitol by a mob of his supporters intent on preventing the recognition of Biden as President. Republicans who spoke out against Trump

---

36. John Paul II, *Centesimus Annus*, no. 46.

37. Biden won the election receiving 81.3 million votes (51.3 percent) to Trump's 74.2 million (46.8 percent) and winning the Electoral College by 306 to 232. *New York Times*, "Presidential Election Results."

38. Ipsos/Reuters Poll, "Big Lie."

found themselves ostracized by many of their party colleagues. The division between constitutional loyalists and Trump partisans looks set to split the party for years to come. In the UK the main opposition party is also divided, though in a different way. For decades Britain's Labour Party was a *de facto* coalition between working people and university-educated progressive professionals. But the forces which engendered populism have broken that apart. Brexit has severed the umbilical cord between the Labour leadership and many of its former supporters. Voters have deserted it in a series of elections including, archetypally, the northern former industrial town of Hartlepool which was formerly a working-class stronghold where once they weighed Labour votes rather than counting them. But it was also the most pro-Brexit town in the UK. Decades of loyalty to Labour, and the trade unions which supported that party, were unable to prevent the closure of the old heavy industries or protect the voters from losing their once well-paid industrial jobs. The defeated Labour candidate in Hartlepool said afterwards that voters had told him they felt betrayed by decades of loss.

The same pattern can be seen across Britain's once-industrial north. Those who have been disenfranchised economically are making their presence felt electorally. Where once voters divided along class lines of poor versus rich a different divide has opened up between "the ordinary people" and the "metropolitan elite"—the younger university-educated voters who left the towns for the cities. Thanks to globalization the two sides have increasingly separate interests and values which find expression in a whole range of attitudes—to the family, sexuality, political correctness, the royal family, foreign aid, free speech, the flag, the military, and much else. Tribal loyalties are in decline. The old political dispensation cannot reflect the changed nuances of a society polarized on entirely different lines.

There is more to this than an unbridgeable chasm in values. There is a sense of growing intolerance of the other. When Left Behind voters express concerns about immigration they are branded racists by their more cosmopolitan fellows. The second most senior bishop in the Church of England, Stephen Cottrell, Archbishop of York, sees this as a theological issue: "Many English people feel left behind by metropolitan elites in London and the South East, and by devolved governments and strengthened regional identities in Scotland and Wales. Their heartfelt cry to be heard is often disregarded, willfully misunderstood or patronized as backwardly xenophobic." There is little sense of loving your neighbor as yourself, he observed, despite the Church being "one of the only institutions left in our nation with a local branch in virtually every community" which remains committed to a common vision for the nation.[39] In such circumstances at least a third of the population—those predisposed to authoritarian solutions—turn to populist leaders, according to the political psychologist Karen Stenner, formerly of Princeton University, who has made a study of political temperaments in Western democracies:[40]

> When you exclude certain kinds of discussions from mainstream political processes you basically push those people who want to have those conversations out to the extremes or underground. People feel like the boundaries are drawn too strictly around what's allowed to be said. So you hear all the complaints about political correctness and "No one will let me say this." And this is why people have such weird glee when someone like Donald Trump comes out and says stuff that's unspeakable normally. They feel a sense of relief that somebody saying those things out loud.[41]

Political correctness, she adds, mistakenly prohibits discussions we should be able to have in the open in a mature democracy. A veto is placed on questions like: How much immigration can we absorb? What's the appropriate extent and pace of immigration? Does it matter from which parts of the world immigrants are coming? Do they need to have a strong cultural match with the settled population for this to work? What kind of resources should be allocated to support immigrants to become assimilated? "We must allow people to engage in honest discussions about race and immigration in a multicultural society," Stenner writes.[42] Branding such questions as implicitly racist, as progressives have done, she suggests, pushes many ordinary voters into the embrace of populist politicians.

Those Pope Francis describes as unhealthy or irresponsible populists seek to exacerbate this discontent rather than striving to reduce it. One technique often used by such politicians, in pursuit of personal advantage or consolidating their grip on power, is the framing of simple solutions to complex problems. They coin easy slogans like Make America Great Again, Drain the Swamp, Take Back Control, For All French People, Let's go forward, not backward! Get Brexit Done or Italy and

---

39. Cottrell, "Courageous and Compassionate," para. 14.
40. Stenner, *Authoritarian Dynamic*.
41. Stenner, "Hope Not Hate."
42. Stenner, "Authoritarianism," para. 105.

Italians first! Another common technique is the revival of a tendency to look for scapegoats particularly among marginalized groups. All across the Western world migrants are the prime target. Immigrants are "taking our jobs," "jumping the housing queue," "overcrowding our classrooms" and "overburdening our hospitals." This is the clearest example of what Pope Francis has in mind when he speaks of populists "appealing to the basest and most selfish inclinations of certain sectors of the population." Populists play on fear: fear of economic insecurity, fear of losing old traditions and values, fear of losing national sovereignty, fear of the Other. Citizens already resentful at economic inequality, and disillusioned with the promises of government, are easy prey to additional threats, real or perceived, from those with a different skin color, religion, or language. Populists in the US, UK, the Netherlands, Denmark, Poland, Sweden and Switzerland peddle fear of Islam. In Britain, Hungary, Greece and Italy they warn of a threat to national identity. In Poland, Romania, Bulgaria, Ukraine and Russia the threat is seen as being to conservative Christian culture.[43] Anti-Semitism is once again on the rise along with other forms of cultivated xenophobia. Donald Trump labelled COVID-19 "the China virus." Boris Johnson blamed all manner of Britain's woes upon the European Union. Messages are promoted through hyperbolic vocabularies, exaggerated statistics, dog-whistle messaging and the oblique endorsement of conspiracy theories. Pluralism is disparaged by the construction of narrowly defined versions of national identity which promote a sense of intolerance.

Central to this is the promotion of "culture wars" which reinforce a sense of "us and them." Populist politicians, who are frequently media-savvy and strategically provocative, have set up confrontational polarities on a wide range of issues: from race, gender and sexuality; abortion and gay marriage; climate change and healthcare; to vaccination and mask-wearing. At one point the single greatest predictor of whether an American had been vaccinated or not was whether they voted for Biden or

---

43. Pope Francis notes that the "defense of 'Christian civilization' from perceived enemies, whether Islam, Jews, the European Union, or the United Nations," often appeals "to those who are often no longer religious but who regard their nation's inheritance as a kind of identity." He writes: "Their fears and loss of identity have increased at the same time as attendance at churches has declined." And he adds: "Irreligious or superficially religious people vote for populists to protect their religious identity, unconcerned that fear and hatred of the other cannot be reconciled with the Gospel." "To reject a struggling migrant, whatever his or her religious belief, out of fear of diluting a 'Christian' culture is grotesquely to mispresent both Christianity and culture. Migration is not a threat to Christianity." Francis, *Let Us Dream*, 118–19.

Trump.[44] The focus on culture wars is seen by many political commentators as a willful attempt by populists not simply to consolidate their support base but also to distract public attention from the leader's failures or the real causes of economic or social problems. In the UK the prime minister Boris Johnson even has a name for this, the Dead Cat Tactic. If you throw a dead cat on the dining room table, he has said, people will stop "talking about the issue that has been causing you so much grief" and start talking about the dead cat.[45] Pope Francis has levelled a similar accusation against the Church. In his speech in the pre-conclave meeting before he was elected Pope, he spoke of the delusion of "self-referential" obsessions and the tendency to focus attention and indignation on internal issues rather than those of the wider world. He called it a "kind of theological narcissism."[46] Populists don't just fall into that same trap; they deliberately set it for voters.

Drawing from an Old Playbook to Usurp Contemporary Institutions

But it is the "usurpation of institutions and laws" by populists—whether "in cruder or more subtle forms"—which most disturbs Pope Francis in *Fratelli Tutti*.[47] In an interview with the Spanish newspaper *El País*, given on the same day that Donald Trump was sworn in as President in Washington, the Pope spelled out explicitly what he has in mind here. The great example of populist leadership, he suggested, is to be found in Adolf Hitler. The German people, crushed by the victors in the First World War, in 1933 looked for a charismatic leader who could give them back their identity. "Hitler did not steal power, he was voted in by his people, and then he destroyed his people. That is the danger," the Pope said. In times of crisis people look for "a savior who will give us back our identity" and who would defend that people with walls, or barbed wire or some other means. But the identity which the charismatic leader who was Adolf Hitler offered was "a distorted identity and we know what happened."[48]

---

44. Polling suggested 86 percent of Democrats had received at least one shot compared to just 45 percent among Republicans. *Washington Post*, "June 27–30, 2021, poll."
45. Delaney, "How Lynton Crosby Won," para. 8.
46. Vallely, *Struggle* 151–52.
47. Francis, *Fratelli Tutti*, no. 159.
48. Francis, "Danger."

It might seem an exercise in rhetorical hyperbole for Pope Francis to compare today's populist politicians with Adolf Hitler. But a reading of chapter 6 of Hitler's 1925 autobiographical manifesto *Mein Kampf* reveals a significant number of points of comparison. "Propaganda must always address itself to the broad masses of the people," Hitler begins.[49] "It must appeal to the feelings of the public rather than to their reasoning powers."[50] He continues:

> The great majority of a nation is so feminine in its character and outlook that its thought and conduct are ruled by sentiment rather than by sober reasoning. This sentiment, however, is not complex, but simple and consistent. It is not highly differentiated, but has only the negative and positive notions of love and hatred, right and wrong, truth and falsehood.[51]

Therefore the rhetoric of the populist must be directed to "the lowest mental common denominator among the public it is desired to reach."[52] Hitler continues:

> The receptive powers of the masses are very restricted, and their understanding is feeble. On the other hand, they quickly forget. Such being the case, all effective propaganda must be confined to a few bare essentials and those must be expressed as far as possible in stereotyped formulas. These slogans should be persistently repeated until the very last individual has come to grasp the idea that has been put forward.[53]

Propaganda, Hitler continued, "must not investigate the truth objectively" rather "it must present only that aspect of the truth which is favorable to its own side".[54] Those Hitler repeatedly calls "the broad masses" are "a vacillating crowd of human children who are constantly wavering between one idea and another." Therefore "propaganda must be limited to a few simple themes and these must be represented again and again."[55]

---

49. Hitler, *Mein Kampf*, 155.
50. Hitler, *Mein Kampf*, 156.
51. Hitler, *Mein Kampf*, 156.
52. Hitler, *Mein Kampf*, 156.
53. Hitler, *Mein Kampf*, 156.
54. Hitler, *Mein Kampf*, 158.
55. Hitler, *Mein Kampf*, 159.

Only constant repetition will "succeed in imprinting an idea on the memory of the crowd."[56]

All these techniques are easily identifiable in the rhetorical lexicon of today's populist leaders. So, too, is the understanding of the importance of neutering the mainstream media. One of the tactics of Hitler's propaganda chief, Joseph Goebbels was, early on, to launch a systematic assault on the independence of newspapers. His technique was to single out a particular "enemy" for special vilification. For Goebbels it was *The Munich Post*, which was eventually closed with many of its journalists disappearing or being sent to Dachau. The attacks by Trump cronies on the *New York Times* had sobering echoes—as does his branding of anything inconvenient as "fake news." In Britain attacks on the BBC by Conservative politicians are routine, especially in the run-up to negotiations over the public license fee which funds BBC broadcasting. An independent press is vital to an effective democracy scrutinizing the actions of the executive and holding it to account. Populists routinely seek to undermine this.

But today's populists go beyond adopting Hitler's propaganda techniques of stereotypes and simplifications. In chapter 10 of *Mein Kampf* the man who bluffed his way into power via the ballot box writes of the importance of lying to populist propaganda. Donald Trump—whose ex-wife Ivana disclosed during their divorce that her husband read from a book of Hitler's collected speeches, *My New Order*, which he kept in his bedside cabinet[57]—was a master of lies of all sizes. Trump's ghost writer, Tony Schwartz, later told *The New Yorker* that lying was "second nature" to the President. He added: "More than anyone else I have ever met, Trump has the ability to convince himself that whatever he is saying at any given moment is true, or sort of true, or at least ought to be true." He "lied strategically" and "had a complete lack of conscience about it."[58] White House correspondents kept a catalogue of the President's untruths. After he left the White House in 2020 the *Washington Post* reported that he had made no fewer than 30,573 false or misleading claims over his four years as President. In the first year he told an average of six falsehoods a day. In the second year that rose to sixteen. In his third year that increased to twenty-two a day. And by his last year as President he was telling an average of thirty-nine lies a day—with an all-time record of 503 in one

---

56. Hitler, *Mein Kampf*, 160.
57. Brenner, "After the Gold Rush."
58. Mayer, "Donald Trump's Ghostwriter Tells All."

single day, the day before the vote, "as he barnstormed across the country in a desperate effort to win re-election."[59]

But such behavior is not the aberration of a single outlandish individual. Many of today's populist politicians demonstrate an elastic relationship with the truth. In France, Marine Le Pen has lied about how her party spends public money yet ten million people voted for her.[60] In Hungary, prime minister Viktor Orbán lies gigantically and systematically about immigration to his country and has used those lies to extend his already authoritarian powers.[61] In India, a website subtitled *The Most Accurate List Of PM Modi's Many Lies*—declares "the Modi government has made lying an art form."[62] In Brazil President Bolsonaro lied and insulted minorities throughout his election campaign and then went on to run the country in the same morally corrupt manner.[63] In Italy they had a song about Matteo Salvini's alternative version of reality which insisted "if his lips are moving, he's lying."[64] In Britain the Conservative political commentator, Peter Oborne, a former friend and colleague of Prime Minister Boris Johnson, published a book called *The Assault on Truth* which sets out to examine "how, under Boris Johnson and his soulmate Donald Trump, lying has become endemic in political culture." Oborne wrote: "I have been a political reporter for almost three decades and I have never encountered a senior British politician who lies and fabricates so regularly, so shamelessly and so systematically as Boris Johnson."[65]

Often it is assumed that the populists' persistent blurring of the line between fact and fiction, or their preference for ideological opinion over empirical truth, is unintelligent or careless. It is not. It is a deliberate and a constant feature of populist politics. Again there is precedent in Adolf Hitler. In chapter 10 of *Mein Kampf* he sets out the strategy of the Big Lie. This involves the telling of untruths so "colossal" that few would believe anyone "could have the impudence to distort the truth so infamously."

59. Kessler et al., "Trump's False or Misleading Claims," para. 1.

60. Fieschi, "Why Europe's New Populists Tell So Many Lies." See also Fieschi, *Populocracy*.

61. Balogh, "Orbán's 100 Lies"; Kington, "Orban 'Spent €100 Million of State Cash'"; Enyedi and Krekó, "Orbán's Laboratory of Illiberalism," 39–51.

62. *Modi Lies*'s website was recently shut down. His information is now found on Facebook: https://www.facebook.com/ModiLiesOfficial/.

63. Survival International, "Brazil's Indigenous Peoples."

64. Fieschi, "Why Europe's New Populists Tell So Many Lies," para. 2.

65. Davies, "Boris Johnson's Lies," para. 4.

The Big Lie, which initially appears to be "idiotic in its impudent assertiveness," next comes to be "looked upon as disturbing" and then, finally it is believed.[66] "The broad masses," Hitler asserted, "in the primitive simplicity of their minds," always "more readily fall victims to the big lie than the small lie."[67] Examples of this abound among populists across the political world but none is more glaring than the attempt by Donald Trump to assert that the 2020 presidential election was stolen from him by electoral fraud. Trump convinced millions of his followers, in the face of all the evidence to the contrary, that he was the victim of a Big Steal when in fact they have been the victims of his Big Lie.[68] Trump's followers then set about actively purging the Republican Party of conservatives who reject his populism and embarked upon maneuvers to manipulate the electoral system in favor of Trump or a candidate in his image. The peril of populism remains as alive in the United States as it is in other parts of the world.

All this raises a deeper problem. So many of the statements made by these populists are obviously and verifiably false. The crowds they claim aren't there. The numbers they quote are transparently made up. The lies they deny are there on film. The blatant dishonesty leaves reporters speechless. Yet the populist politicians do not care—because they know that the voters do not care. Studies by academics show why. Research by cognitive psychologists in the UK show that voters make a distinction between honesty and "authenticity." Honesty is about factual accuracy, but authenticity is about the extent to which there is an alignment between the public and the perceived persona of a politician.[69] Populist authenticity is not so much about being as good as you claim to be but about being as shamelessly bad as people might imagine you could be. Populist politicians articulate sordid views which many voters share but which, in previous times, they did not dare articulate for fear of being ostracized. But today, shamelessness is populism's debased form of authenticity—which is why racist and sexist comments by these politicians serve only to enhance their image among their supporters. Research in

66. Hitler, *Mein Kampf*, 160.
67. Hitler, *Mein Kampf*, 196.
68. According to Ipsos/Reuters, "Big Lie," over half of Republicans believe Donald Trump is the actual President of the United States. According to a CNN poll on September 15, 2021, 78 percent of Republicans say that Biden did not win. Agiesta and Edwards-Levy, "CNN Poll."
69. Stephan Lewandowsky, Chair of Cognitive Psychology at the University of Bristol discusses this in Lewandowsky, "Why People Vote for Liars."

the United States has shown that people will accept politicians who lie if those voters feel disenfranchised and excluded from the political system; they are perfectly happy to accept lies from a politician who presents himself as a champion of "the people" against the "establishment" or "elite."[70] Where the false claims of such populists are exposed they frequently portray themselves as victims of conspiracies and campaigns. If they cast themselves as modern Robin Hood figures, then populist politicians cannot fail; they can only be sabotaged.

But Isn't Pope Francis Himself a Populist?

Is Pope Francis a populist? A number of commentators, both academic and political, have suggested that the thinking and *modus operandi* of Francis himself is populist. He is a leader with considerable personal charisma which he deploys to advance his agenda for reform and he places "the people" at the center of his theological and political analysis, seeing the poor as excluded or oppressed by the affluent mainstream.[71] Indeed Pope Francis recognizes that there are some "who criticize him for being a populist in his own way."[72] It is not hard to see why unsympathetic critics leap to this conclusion.

Long before he was Pope, in the time when he was leader of the Jesuits in Argentina, Jorge Mario Bergoglio was deeply influenced by a school of Argentinian thought known as *teología del pueblo*, the Theology of the People. The approach was, according to one of its central proponents, Juan Carlos Scannone, another Argentinian Jesuit, one of four strands of Liberation Theology—though some critics saw it in contradistinction to the Theology of Liberation. Scannone and his peers developed the Theology of the People as a revolt against a worldview handed down from Argentina's colonial masters which saw local culture as "barbaric" in contrast to European culture, which it presented as "civilization." The hierarchy of the Argentinian church largely held to the disdainful dismissal of indigenous culture which they had inherited from the Spanish colonial authorities. So much so that the history of the

70. Hahl et al., "Appeal of the Lying Demagogue," 1–33.

71. McCormick, "Populist Pope?"; Gregg, "Understanding Pope Francis," 361–74.

72. Anna Rowlands, professor of Catholic Social Thought and Practice at the University of Durham, speaking at the Vatican press conference for the release *Fratelli Tutti* in the Synod Hall at the Vatican on Oct. 4, 2020, quoted in O'Connell, "Francis Identifies the Paradox of Populism," para. 5.

Jesuit *reducciónes*—the missionary settlements in Latin America in the seventeenth and eighteenth centuries which allowed the Gospel to speak through the culture of the local people—was then not even taught in Argentina's Catholic schools.[73] All of this resonated deeply for Bergoglio for it offered an intellectual underpinning to his sympathy for the forms of "popular religiosity" with which he had been brought up by his grandmother—the shrines, statues, processions, medals and the rest of what many of his fellow Jesuits dismissed as "folk religion."[74] In his essay *Meditaciones para religiosos* (Meditations for the Religious), written in 1982, when he was Rector of the Jesuit seminary in Buenos Aires, Bergoglio spoke of how "the faithful people are infallible in believing." The experts of the Vatican could teach who the Virgin Mary was but only the ordinary faithful people could "teach you how to love her."[75] Thus, in Scannone's own words: "Argentine People's Theology does not use Marxist analysis, but a historical and cultural one. It pays attention to social structures, but it does not consider class struggle as the main principle."[76] Where Liberation Theology wanted to help the poor use politics to gain control over their own destiny, the Theology of the People focused on cultural rather than economic change. Scannone wrote:

> In Latin America, the poor are those who, at least in practice, retain the very culture of their people as a structuring principle for everyday life and common life. Likewise, they hold on to the historical memory of the people—and ensure that the interests of the people coincide with a common historical project of justice and peace, given that they may live in an oppressive situation of structural injustice and institutionalized violence. Therefore, in Latin America, at least *de facto*, the option for the poor coincides with the option for culture.[77]

Thus, though the Theology of the People did not ignore the pressing social conflicts in Latin America, its understanding of the concept of "the people" privileges unity over conflict, Scannone insists—a priority which Pope Francis emphasizes in *Evangelii Gaudium*.[78] Bergoglio at that

73. Vallely, *Struggle*, 133–35.
74. Vallely, *Struggle*, 18–27.
75. Bergoglio, *Meditaciones para religiosos*, 46. See also Pope Francis, *Evangelii Gaudium*, no. 124.
76. In correspondence with the author. See Vallely, *Struggle*, 134.
77. Scannone, "Francis and the Theology of the People," 121.
78. Scannone, "Francis and the Theology of the People," 122.

point thought that Liberation Theology imposed a European ideological straitjacket which patronized the faith and culture of the Argentine people.

The Theology of the People also resonated with Bergoglio's long-standing affinity to Peronism—a political movement distinct to Argentina which involved a curious amalgam of forces not elsewhere associated with one another: the military, the trade unions and the Church. Peronism was a form of populism which saw itself in contradistinction to a business or land-owning elite. It was enormously popular in Bergoglio's youth under its founder General Juan Domingo Perón and his wife Evita (whom Pope Francis has boasted of once having met).[79] The couple, both immensely skilled populist politicians, rooted their thinking, in part, in one of the major documents in the history of Catholic Social Teaching—the encyclical *Quadragesimo Anno*. This was issued by Pope Pius XI in 1931 to mark the fortieth anniversary of the first Catholic social encyclical, *Rerum Novarum*, in which Pope Leo XIII in 1891 had set out to discover a third way between capitalism and communism. By 1931 Pope Pius XI had come to the conclusion that there was no alternative to capitalism; Pius gave it, implicitly, his blessing and exhorted it to behave more responsibly. But two years before *Quadragesimo Anno* was published there had been a worldwide collapse of money markets after the 1929 Wall Street crash. So Pope Pius proposed a grand corporate plan for the reconstruction of the social order which would do away with class struggle between bosses and workers—and promote harmonious cooperation within industries and professions in its place. The regulator of all this was to be the State, a notion which was discredited by the fact that the obvious vehicles for this in the 1930s were the fascist movements of Italy, Germany and Spain. Enthusiasts for the Theology of the People in Argentina tended to insist on a great deal of government intervention. Right-wing critics of Pope Francis claim that he has never thrown off this statist bias while on the left the argument against *teología del pueblo* has been, as the leading liberation theologian Juan Luis Segundo argued, that it is not just incapable of fostering real change but was actually an obstacle to it.[80]

The notion of the infallibility of the ordinary "holy, faithful people of God" which Bergoglio draws from the Theology of the People is clearly

---

79. Camara and Pfaffen, *Aquel Francesco*, quoted in Vallely, *Struggle*, 114.
80. Vallely, *Struggle*, 137.

susceptible to the accusation of theological populism. This is reinforced in *Evangelii Gaudium* where Francis writes:

> God furnishes the totality of the faithful with an instinct of faith—*sensus fidei*—which helps them to discern what is truly of God. The presence of the Spirit gives Christians a certain connaturality with divine realities, and a wisdom which enables them to grasp those realities intuitively, even when they lack the wherewithal to give them precise expression.[81]

But Pope Francis makes a distinction between populism and what he calls *popularism*. In his interview with *El País* he describes populism as a misleading word. "In Latin America populism has another meaning. There it means the protagonism of the peoples, for example the popular movements. They organize among themselves . . . it's something else."[82] Popular movements, in various forms, have consistently been supported by Francis, as a priest and bishop in Argentina, and as Pope, hosting meetings of hundreds of leaders of popular movements in 2014, 2015, 2016 and also writing to encourage them during lockdown.[83] In 2017, in a speech to EU leaders, the Pope had said that the antidote to populism was solidarity.[84] Solidarity, he said in *Fratelli Tutti*, "finds concrete expression in service, which can take a variety of forms in an effort to care for others":[85]

> Solidarity means much more than engaging in sporadic acts of generosity. It means thinking and acting in terms of community. It means that the lives of all are prior to the appropriation of goods by a few. It also means combatting the structural causes of poverty, inequality, the lack of work, land and housing, the denial of social and labor rights. It means confronting the destructive effects of the empire of money. . . . Solidarity, understood in its most profound meaning, is a way of making history, and this is what popular movements are doing.[86]

But he went further in a message to grassroots community organizers at an event run by the Centre for Theology and Community in the UK

81. Francis, *Evangelii Gaudium*, no. 119.
82. Francis, "We Look for a Savior."
83. Francis, "Letter to the Popular Movements," 35–40.
84. Francis, "Address for the Celebration of the Treaty of Rome."
85. Francis, *Fratelli Tutti*, no. 115.
86. Francis, *Fratelli Tutti*, no. 116.

a year later. There in 2021 the Pope set out his alternative to populism. "I like to use the term *popularism*. . . . [I]t is about finding the means to guarantee a life for all people that is worthy of being called human, a life capable of cultivating virtue and forging new bonds," he said.[87] In his address, Francis cited the notion of "inclusive populism" put forward by the Anglican priest, Angus Ritchie, who is the leader of the hosting center.[88] Inclusive populism, Ritchie writes, is about finding ways to engage grassroots communities in the public square so as to combat both the exploitative populism of the far-right and the failure of liberal politics to engage a broad cross-section of groups in decision making.[89] Many of the conference's participants, Francis noted, had long been working in the peripheries, "walking with the people's movements." The key difference between solidarity and inclusive populism, Francis suggested, was that the new politics must open new paths for the people to organize and express themselves. It has to be politics, the Pope says, not "just *for* the people, but *with* the people, rooted in their communities and in their values." It was about assisting people to take control of their own lives, to give them voice, to give them agency.

This subverts several of the qualities which make populism attractive to voters who feel excluded from the political, economic and social conversation. Direct involvement in the activities of popular movements allows the Left Behind to gain experience on the ground which reveals the inadequacy of the quick-fix simple solutions which populists like to offer to complex problems. When those who feel alienated can take control of something in their lives this can help dispel the sense of impotence and fear on which populists trade. Populist politicians are then exposed as just another elite group bent upon seeking personal advantage or consolidating their grip of power. It can also have another beneficial impact. If progressive liberals offer their skills to work with ordinary people in popular movements that can improve relations between the Left Behind and the metropolitan liberals who previously formed a progressive alliance. Working together enables the two groups to increase their understanding of one another's cultural and social values, ensuring, in the words of *Evangelli Gaudium*, that "unity prevails over conflict."[90] Without that, those who ought to be working together are doomed to allow

87. Francis, "Politics of Fraternity," para. 4.
88. Ritchie, *Inclusive Populism*.
89. Lamb, "Pope Takes People's Path against Populism."
90. Francis, *Evangelli Gaudium*, nos. 226–30.

populism to triumph. "A politics that turns its back on the peripheries will never be able to understand the center, and will confuse the future with a self-projection, as if in a mirror," Pope Francis told the community organizers at the Centre for Theology and Community.[91] But if the Left Behind become agents of their own destiny they will be far less prone to accept the blatant lies of politicians who speciously present themselves as the champions of the powerless and voiceless.

Francis continued: "When people are cast aside, they are denied not just material wellbeing but the dignity of acting, of being a protagonist of their own destiny and history, of expressing themselves with their values and culture, their creativity and fruitfulness." For this reason, the Pope added, "it is impossible for the Church to separate the promotion of social justice from the recognition of the culture and values of the people, which include the spiritual values that are the source of their sense of dignity."[92] The restoration of this dignity is at the heart of Francis's popularism, as he explains towards the end of *Let Us Dream*:

> To recover the dignity of the people we need to go to the margins of our societies to meet all those who live there. Hidden there are ways of looking at the world that can give us all a fresh start. We cannot dream of the future while continuing to ignore the lives of practically a third of the world's population rather than seeing them as a resource. I mean those who lack regular work living on the margins of the market economy. They are landless peasants and smallholders, subsistence fishermen and sweatshop workers, garbage pickers and street vendors, sidewalk artisans, slum dwellers and squatters. In developed countries, they are the ones who live from odd jobs, often on the move, poorly housed, with poor access to drinking water and healthy food: both they and their families suffer all kinds of vulnerability. Yet if we manage to come close and put aside our stereotypes we discover that many of them are far from being merely passive victims. Organized in a global archipelago of associations and movements, they represent the hope of solidarity in an age of exclusion and indifference. On the margins I have discovered so many social movements with roots in parishes or schools that bring people together to make them become protagonists of their own histories, to set in motion dynamics that smacked of dignity. Taking life as it comes, they do not sit

---

91. Francis, "Politics of Fraternity," para. 11.
92. Francis, "Politics of Fraternity," para. 6.

around resigned or complaining but come together to convert injustice into new possibilities.[93]

Pope Francis sees in these movements which mobilize for change and search for human dignity "a source of moral energy, a reserve of civic passion, capable of revitalizing our democracy and reorienting the economy." Today's national populism can never achieve this. A politics which promotes polarization is incapable of promoting the common good. Seeking common purpose is the hallmark of Pope Francis's inclusive populism, in contrast to exclusive populism. In this way Catholic Social Teaching can ride upon the same currents in global politics to create something far more constructive—not an alternative to populism but a transcending of it:

> The true response to the rise of populism is precisely not more individualism but quite the opposite: a politics of fraternity, rooted in the life of the people.[94]

The challenge now is to work out how use this politics of fraternity to formulate an alternative to culture wars and irresponsible populism and instead renew our institutions and inform our policy debates, guided by the principles of Catholic social teaching, to re-invigorate our public life with this spirit of fraternity.

Bibliography

Agiesta, Jennifer, and Ariel Edwards-Levy. "CNN Poll: Most Americans Feel Democracy Us Under Attack in the US." *CNN Politics*, September 15, 2021. https://edition.cnn.com/2021/09/15/politics/cnn-poll-most-americans-democracy-under-attack/index.html.

Balogh, Eva S. "Viktor Orbán's 100 Lies." *Hungarian Spectrum*. https://webarchive.loc.gov/all/20191009074212/http://hungarianspectrum.org/2018/06/01/observer-viktor-orbans-100-lies/.

Benedict XVI. *Caritas in Veritate*. June 29, 2009. https://www.vatican.va/content/benedict-xvi/en/encyclicals/documents/hf_ben-xvi_enc_20090629_caritas-in-veritate.html#.

Bergoglio, Jorge Mario. *Meditaciones para religiosos*. Edited by Diego de Torres. Buenos Aires: San Miguel, 1982.

Brenner, Marie. "After the Gold Rush." *Vanity Fair*, September 1990. https://archive.vanityfair.com/article/share/e515a2cd-a51b-4f83-8d61-6ebb9a104e0a.

---

93. Francis and Ivereigh, *Let Us Dream*, 120.
94. Francis, "Politics of Fraternity," para. 4.

Camara, Javier, and Sebastian Pfaffen. *Aquel Francisco: Narrativa argentina*. Buenos Aires: Raíz de Dos, 2014.
Conseil Constitutionnel of France. "Décision n° 2017-171 PDR du 10 mai 2017." https://www.conseil-constitutionnel.fr/decision/2017/2017171PDR.htm. Accessed August 25, 2023.
Cottrell, Stephen. "Courageous and Compassionate: In Search of the English." August 7, 2021. https://www.archbishopofyork.org/news/latest-news/courageous-and-compassionate-search-english.
Davies, William. "The Assault on Truth by Peter Oborne Review—Boris Johnson's Lies." *Guardian*, February 3, 2021. https://www.theguardian.com/books/2021/feb/03/the-assault-on-truth-by-peter-oborne-review-boris-johnsons-lies. Accessed Sept 18, 2021.
Delaney, Sam. "How Lynton Crosby and a Dead Cat Won the Election." *Guardian*, January 20, 2016. https://www.theguardian.com/politics/2016/jan/20/lynton-crosby-and-dead-cat-won-election-conservatives-labour-intellectually-lazy.
Dorling, Danny. *Injustice: Why Inequality Still Persists*. Bristol: Policy, 2015.
———. "Peak Inequality." *New Statesman*, July 4, 2018.
Eatwell, Roger, and Matthew Goodwin. *National Populism: The Revolt Against Liberal Democracy*. London: Pelican, 2018.
Elliott, Larry. 'Top Economists Call for Action on Runaway Global Inequality." *Guardian*, July 17, 2023. https://www.theguardian.com/inequality/2023/jul/17/top-economists-call-for-action-global-inequality-rich-poor-poverty-climate-breakdown-un-world-bank.
Enyedi, Zsolt, and Péter Krekó. "Explaining Eastern Europe: Orbán's Laboratory of Illiberalism." *Journal of Democracy* 29 (2018) 39–51. https://www.journalofdemocracy.org/articles/explaining-eastern-europe-orbans-laboratory-of-illiberalism/#f11-text.
Eurostate News Release. "Record Number of Over 1.2 Million First Time Asylum Seekers Registered in 2015." March 4, 2016. https://ec.europa.eu/eurostat/documents/2995521/7203832/3-4032016-AP-EN.pdf/.
Fieschi, Catherine. *Populocracy: The Tyranny of Authenticity and the Rise of Populism*. Newcastle: Agenda, 2019.
———. "Why Europe's New Populists Tell So Many Lies—And Do It So Shamelessly." *Guardian*, September 30 2019. https://www.theguardian.com/commentisfree/2019/sep/30/europe-populist-lie-shamelessly-salvini-johnson.
Francis. "Address of His Holiness Pope Francis to the Heads of State and Government of the European Union in Italy for the Celebration of the 60th Anniversary of the Treaty of Rome." March 24, 2017. https://www.vatican.va/content/francesco/en/speeches/2017/march/documents/papa-francesco_20170324_capi-unione-europea.html. Accessed Sept 1, 2023.
———. "The Danger Is That in Times of Crisis We Look for a Savior." *El País*, January 22, 2017. https://english.elpais.com/elpais/2017/01/21/inenglish/1485026427_223988.html.
———. *Evangelli Gaudium: On the Proclamation of the Gospel in Today's World*. Vatican City State: Libreria Editrice Vaticana, 2013. https://www.vatican.va/content/francesco/en/apost_exhortations/documents/papa-francesco_esortazione-ap_20131124_evangelii-gaudium.html.

———. *Fratelli Tutti: On Fraternity and Social Friendship*. Vatican City State: Libreria Editrice Vaticana, 2020. https://www.vatican.va/content/francesco/en/encyclicals/documents/papa-francesco_20201003_enciclica-fratelli-tutti.html.

———. "A Politics of Fraternity Is the True Response to the Rise of Populism." *Osservatore Romano*, April 22, 2021. https://www.osservatoreromano.va/en/news/2021-24/ing-017/a-politics-of-fraternity-is-the-true-response-to-the-rise-of-pop.html. Accessed Sept 1, 2023.

———. "To an Invisible Army: Letter to the Popular Movements 12 April 2020." In *Life after the Pandemic*, 35–40. Vatican City State: Libreria Editrice Vaticana, 2020.

———. "The Universal Destination of Goods and the Virtue of Hope." August 26, 2020. https://www.humandevelopment.va/en/news/2020/the-universal-destination-of-goods-and-the-virtue-of-hope.html.

Francis, and Austen Ivereigh. *Let Us Dream*. London: Simon & Schuster, 2020.

Green, David. "The Trump Hypothesis: Testing Immigrant Populations as a Determinant of Violent and Drug-Related Crime in the United States." *Social Science Quarterly* 97 (2016) 506–24.

Gregg, Samuel. "Understanding Pope Francis: Argentina, Economic Failure, and the *Teología del Pueblo*." *Independent Review* 21 (2016/2017) 361–74.

Guardian Staff. "Poverty and Inequality under Trump: Human Rights under Threat." *Guardian*, June 26, 2018. https://www.theguardian.com/world/2018/jun/22/poverty-and-inequality-under-trump-human-rights-under-threat.

Hahl, Oliver, et al. "The Authentic Appeal of the Lying Demagogue: Proclaiming the Deeper Truth about Political Illegitimacy." *American Sociological Review* 831 (2018) 1–33. doi:10.1177/0003122417749632.

Harris Poll. "LEGO Group Kicks Off Global Program to Inspire the Next Generation of Space Explorers as NASA Celebrates 50 Years Of Moon Landing." July 16, 2019. https://theharrispoll.com/briefs/lego-group-kicks-off-global-program-to-inspire-the-next-generation-of-space-explorers-as-nasa-celebrates-50-years-of-moon-landing/.

Hitler, Adolf. *Mein Kampf*. Translated by James Murphy. https://greatwar.nl/books/meinkampf/meinkampf.pdf.

Ipsos/Reuters Poll. "The Big Lie—Over Half of Republicans Believe Donald Trump Is the Actual President of the United States." May 21, 2021. https://www.ipsos.com/en-us/news_and_polls/over-half-republicans-believe-donald-trump-actual-president-united-states.

John Paul II. *Evangelium Vitae*. March 25, 1995. https://www.vatican.va/content/john-paul-ii/en/encyclicals/documents/hf_jp-ii_enc_25031995_evangelium-vitae.html.

Joi, Priya. "The Stark Reality of How COVID-19 Has Worsened Global Inequality." *GAVI: The Vaccine Alliance*, June 29, 2022. https://www.gavi.org/vaccineswork/stark-reality-how-covid-19-has-worsened-global-inequality.

Kessler, Glenn, et al. "Trump's False or Misleading Claims Total 30,573 over 4 Years." *Washington Post*, January 24, 2021. https://www.washingtonpost.com/politics/2021/01/24/trumps-false-or-misleading-claims-total-30573-over-four-years/.

Kington, Tom. "Viktor Orban 'Spent €100 Million of State Cash on Lies about George Soros.'" *Times*, May 15, 2018. https://www.thetimes.co.uk/article/george-soros-charity-damns-viktor-orban-for-100m-spent-on-lies-gpspdk2rz.

Lamb, Christopher. "Pope Takes People's Path against Populism in London." *The Tablet*, April 16, 2021. https://www.thetablet.co.uk/news/14058/pope-takes-people-s-path-against-populism-in-london.

Lewandowsky, Stephan. "Why People Vote for Politicians They Know Are Liars." *The Conversation*, December 19, 2019. https://theconversation.com/why-people-vote-for-politicians-they-know-are-liars-128953.

Mayer, Jane. "Donald Trump's Ghostwriter Tells All." *New Yorker*, July 18, 2016. https://www.newyorker.com/magazine/2016/07/25/donald-trumps-ghostwriter-tells-all.

McCormick, William. "The Populist Pope? Politics, Religion, and Pope Francis." *Politics and Religion* 14 (2020) 159–81.

Menjívar, C., et al., eds. *Oxford Handbook of Migration Crises*. Oxford: Oxford University Press, 2019.

Mishel, Lawrence, and Jessica Schieder. "CEO Compensation Surged in 2017." *Economic Policy Institute*, August 16, 2018. https://www.epi.org/press/top-ceos-compensation-increased-17-16-percent-in-2017.

New York Times. "Presidential Election Results: Biden Wins." December 11, 2020. https://www.nytimes.com/interactive/2020/11/03/us/elections/results-president.html.

O'Connell, Gerard. "In *Fratelli Tutti* Pope Francis Identifies the Paradox of Populism." *America*, October 8, 2020. https://www.americamagazine.org/faith/2020/10/08/fratelli-tutti-pope-francis-paradox-populism-catholic.

Putnam, Robert D. *Bowling Alone*. New York: Simon & Schuster, 2000.

Ratzinger, Joseph. "Homily of His Eminence Cardinal Joseph Ratzinger Dean of the College of Cardinals for Mass '*Pro Eligendo Romano Pontifice*.'" April 18, 2005. https://www.vatican.va/gpII/documents/homily-pro-eligendo-pontifice_20050418_en.html.

Ritchie, Angus. *Inclusive Populism: Creating Citizens in the Global Age*. Notre Dame: University of Notre Dame Press, 2019.

Sacks, Jonathan. *Faith in the Future*. London: DLT, 1995.

Scannone, Juan Carlos. "Pope Francis and the Theology of the People." *Theological Studies* 77 (2016) 118–35.

Singleton, Laura. "Gap between Rich and Poor Has Increased More Quickly in the US Than in Europe." *Imperial College Business School*, January 25, 2023. https://www.imperial.ac.uk/news/242756/gap-between-rich-poor-increased-more/.

Stenner, Karen. *The Authoritarian Dynamic*. Cambridge: Cambridge University Press, 2005.

———. "Authoritarianism and the Future of Liberal Democracy." *Hope Not Hate*, January 11, 2020. https://www.hopenothate.org.uk/2020/11/01/authoritarianism/.

———. "Hope Not Hate: Karen Stenner and the Authoritarian Predisposition." *The Spark*, July 30, 2021. Radio interview. https://www.bbc.co.uk/sounds/play/m000y7sq.

Stiglitz, Joseph E. "Equal Opportunity, Our National Myth." *New York Times*, February 16, 2013. https://archive.nytimes.com/opinionator.blogs.nytimes.com/2013/02/16/equal-opportunity-our-national-myth/.

———. *The Price of Inequality*. New York: Norton, 2012.

Survival International. "What Brazil's President, Jair Bolsonaro, Has Said about Brazil's Indigenous Peoples." https://www.survivalinternational.org/articles/3540-Bolsonaro.

Epilogue—VALLELY

Thatcher, Margaret. "Interview for Woman's Own ('No Such Thing [as Society]')." https://www.margaretthatcher.org/document/106689.

Trussell Trust. "End of Year Statistics." https://www.trusselltrust.org/news-and-blog/latest-stats/end-year-stats/.

Vallely, Paul. *The New Politics—Catholic Social Teaching for the Twenty-First Century*. London: SCM, 1999.

———. *Philanthropy—From Aristotle to Zuckerberg*. New York: Bloomsbury, 2020.

———. *Pope Francis—The Struggle for the Soul of Catholicism*. New York: Bloomsbury, 2015.

———. *Pope Francis–Untying the Knots*. London: Bloomsbury, 2013.

Washington Post. "June 27–30, 2021, Washington Post-ABC News poll." https://www.washingtonpost.com/context/june-27-30-2021-washington-post-abc-news-poll/9f67b281-b289-4e67-a9e1-9515018d7e90/?itid=lk_interstitial_manual_8.

Willsher, Kim. "In 'Forgotten France', Le Pen's Young Backers Say Only She Cares for Them." *Guardian*, April 9, 2017. https://www.theguardian.com/world/2017/apr/09/forgotten-france-marine-le-pen-president.

World Bank. "Global Progress in Reducing Extreme Poverty Grinds to a Halt." *World Bank Press Release*, October 5, 2022. https://www.worldbank.org/en/news/press-release/2022/10/05/global-progress-in-reducing-extreme-poverty-grinds-to-a-halt.

Subject Index

Abernathy, Ralph, 178
abortion, 68, 310–11, 323, 353
ACTU (Association of Catholic Trade Unionists), 120
Adenauer, Konrad, 96, 152
Afghanistan, 347
AFL-CIO, 119
Africa, 322, 323, 324, 325, 328, 347
African Americans, 57, 171, 174
    Catholic, 182–90
    in Charleston, 183–86
    in Chicago, 186–90
    economic problems of, 175
African Instituted Churches, 325
agency
    human, 24, 103, 128n47, 135
    of workers, 240, 245
Ahmann, Matthew, 178, 180–81
AI. *See* artificial intelligence (AI)
Albania, 148, 159
algorithms, 17
Alter, Karl J., 171n9, 173n14
American Federation of Labor, 119
American paradox, 305
Amnesty International, 44
Amoris Laetitia, 226, 336
Anglican church, 205
Annunciation, 73
anthropocentrism, 23
anthropology
    Augustinian, 66
    Christian, 308

    destructive, 24
    naturalistic, 23
    philosophical, 66
    theological, 54, 308
anthropomorphism, 33
anti-authoritarianism, 47
anti-clericalism, 75
antiliberalism, 2
anti-Semitism, 353
anti-speciesism, 28
Arab Spring, 274
Archdiocesan Catholic Hospital Council, 188
Argentina, 119, 328, 359–61, 362
artificial intelligence (AI), 17, 24, 31–32, 33, 36, 84, 109, 224
Asia, 323, 324
assisted reproduction, 68
Association of Catholic Laymen, 182, 183
Association of Catholic Trade Unionists (ACTU), 120
atheism, 19, 49
Augustine of Hippo, Saint, 26, 65, 70, 71, 75
Australia, 323, 328
authoritarianism, 3, 357
autocracy, 7, 11
automation, 225
Ave Maria Press, 191
Axial Age, 20–21

Subject Index

Babette's Feast (film), 232n33
Balkan states, 160
Baltic states, 148
Bangladesh, 333
Baptists, 179
Bartholomew, Orthodox Patriarch, 293, 328
Begin, Floyd, 176
Belgium, 117–18
Benedict IX, Pope, 289
Benedict XVI, Pope
    Caritas in Veritate, 115, 130, 136–37, 231, 243, 259, 344
    on digital networking, 261, 269
    on economics, 116
    on the environment, 325, 329
    in Europe, 147
    on relativism 345
    Spe Salvi, 233
    support for new ecclesial movements, 207
    theology of, 247n78, 307–8
    World Communication Day message, 263
Benedictine movement, 203
Bergoglio, Mario, 147, 151, 296, 359–62
    see also Francis, Pope
Berrigan, Daniel, 209–10
Berrigan, Philip, 209–10
Bertrand, Joseph, 176
Bezou, Henry, 183
biases, 309–10, 314–15
Biden, Joe, 114, 350, 353
Binz, Leo, 173n14
biopolitics, 57
birth control, 53
Bishops of South Korea, 299
Bishops' Program for Social Reconstruction, 120
Black Lives Matter movement, 197, 199–200
Black Lives Matter Network, 200
Black Power movement, 193
Blair, Tony, 7, 83
Bolivia, 328
Bolsonaro, Jair, 340, 342, 357
Bosnia and Herzegovina, 148, 159
Brady, William O., 173n14

Brazil, 119, 292, 328, 342, 350, 357
Brotherhood of Sleeping Car Porters, 174
Brothers of the Christian Schools, 203, 204
Brown v. Topeka, 2, 172, 175, 181, 192
Buddhists, 285
Bulgaria, 148, 353
Burke, Tarana, 271
business enterprises, 136–39

Cabirac, Henry, 183
Canada, 323
Cantwell, Dan, 177, 189
capax Dei, 317
capital punishment, 332, 338
capitalism, 96, 117, 131–32, 142, 234, 236, 236n49, 237n50, 361
    free-market, 321, 324
    global, 134, 295
    industrial, 342
    limitations of, 327–28
    opposition to, 57
    progressive, 83, 84–85
    and redistribution, 238–39
    social, 118
    surveillance, 245–46n76
    wellness, 32
carbon emissions, 87, 90–91, 109–10
Cardijn, Joseph, 118, 206, 215
caritas. *See* charity
Caritas in Veritate, 115, 130, 136–37, 231, 243, 259, 344
Caritas Internationalis, 289
Carter Administration, 57
Catechism of the Catholic Church, 317, 318
Catholic Action, 117, 141, 173, 333, 335
Catholic Campaign for Human Development (CCHD), 201, 218
Catholic Charities, 337
Catholic Church
    in Africa, 324, 325
    in Asia, 323, 324
    authority of, 55, 312–13
    as bearer of Christ, 79, 80
    Bishops of South Korea, 299
    as Body of Christ, 320

Subject Index

challenges for, 304
desegregation of, 181–82
diplomatic corps, 287
duties and role of, 5, 255–56
as embodied community, 274–76
in Europe, 146–58, 322–23, 324
in France, 338
"hidden life" of, 76–78, 80
institutional infrastructure of, 4
in Latin America, 323, 325
Marian path of, 71–78
missionary work, 295, 324, 360
and modernity, 48, 66, 71
in the peripheries, 159–64, 324–25, 337, 364–65
and politics, 62–65
reform movements, 208
relationship with the state, 287–93
religious life, 203–6
renewal of, 294, 324
as "salt and light," 5
sex abuse scandals, 13, 293, 309, 323
shortage of priests, 323, 324–25
social movements, 202–3, 337
sovereignty of, 289–90
in the U.S., 120, 169, 173–90, 193
virtual Mass experience, 275, 324
in the Western world, 75–76
Catholic Climate Covenant, 337
Catholic Committee of the South, 175, 192
Catholic Council on Human Relations in the Archdiocese of New Orleans, 183
Catholic guilt, 317
Catholic Interracial Councils, 177–78, 187, 188, 189, 192
   Diocese of Raleigh, 182
   New York (CICNY), 173–77, 191
Catholic Nonviolence Initiative (CNI), 215
Catholic organizations, 124–25, 141–42, 184, 192
   associations, 122
   and civil rights, 175
   religious orders, 289
Catholic Relief Services, 218

Catholic Social Doctrine (CSD), 1
   and conservatism, 2–3
   and integral humanism, 16
   and liberalism, 2–3
Catholic Social Movements, 202–3, 337
Catholic Social Teaching (CST), 11, 225, 361, 365
   as alternative to neoliberalism, 113, 115–16
   in dialogue with culture, 276
   ecological vision of, 135–36
   on the economy, 115, 130–31
   future of, 12–13, 321–38
   global perspective, 12, 283–300
   and human rights, 41–43, 59
   and inequality, 107
   and integral human development, 101
   and interracial justice, 174
   and inter-religious dialogue, 332–33
   key concepts on social communication, 254–59
   and labor, 105
   in Latin America, 119
   vs. neoclassical economics, 98–102
   non-magisterial sources, 218
   on racism, 170–73
   and recent social media trends, 269–72
   and *Spe Salvi*, 233
   and social democracy, 94–96
   and social media, 259–72
   social movements and, 196–97, 337–38
   theological framework of, 134
   in the U.S., 168
   and work, 231, 244
Catholic social tradition, 5–15, 214, 303, 317
Catholic Worker Movement, 209–10, 337
Catholic Youth Organization (CYO), 188
Catholicism
   fraternal vs. paternal, 96
   global presence of, 12–13, 285–87, 315, 321, 322–25
   and modernity, 53–56

Subject Index

Catholics
  African American, 182–90
  American, 53, 119–23, 169–70, 192–93, 323
  in American politics, 120
  attitude toward vaccination, 312
  as bearers of light, 256
  in Charleston, 183–86
  in Chicago, 186–90, 192
  conservative, 3, 58, 321, 323
  distributists, 244
  global demographics, 323
  global family of, 285–87
  as immigrants, 123
  at the March on Washington, 181
  Polish, 47
  social, 6, 168
  social justice activists, 323
  subcultures of, 122–23
  traditionalist, 203, 323
CCHD (Catholic Campaign for Human Development), 201, 218
Centesimus Annus, 115, 130, 132, 134–36, 227n12, 349
Centre for Theology and Community, 362–64
charity, 12, 17, 137, 277, 331
  social, 168
Chávez, César, 209
Cheney, Liz, 350
child labor, 90
Chile, 119
China, 7
chlorofluorocarbon emissions, 87
Christ. *See* Jesus Christ
Christendom
  birth and death of, 5n1, 62, 65–70
  historical interpretations of, 62–63
  "new," 66–67
  remnants of, 76
Christian Democratic parties, 122, 323, 338
  in Europe, 117, 118–19
  in Latin America, 119
Christian discipleship, 131, 137
Christianity
  Constantinian, 74
  dualism of, 68, 69
  and European civilization, 157
  global scope of, 285–87
  and human dignity, 76
  and modernity, 69
  roles of women in, 77
  secularization of, 20
  and social movements, 202–3
  social nature of, 64
  in the Western world, 73–74
  see also Catholicism; Protestantism
Christians
  in the digital world, 261
  and the digital world, 269
  persecution of, 75
  role of witness, 70
  see also Catholics
Christus Vivit, 336
Church. *See* Catholic Church
Church and Internet, The, 259
Church of England, 351–52
Cicognani, Amleto, 181
CIJOC (International Coordination of Young Christian Workers), 206
Cistercians, 203
City of God, 231
civic friendship, 27
Civil Rights Act, 185
Civil Rights movement, 10, 168, 169, 172, 180, 181, 199
civil rights organizations, 174–75
civil society, 7, 27, 83, 116, 127, 137, 147, 150, 153, 287, 288–90, 312, 331
clericalism, 336
climate change, 94, 109, 110, 321, 325, 329, 353
climate disasters, 300
Clinton, William J. "Bill," 7, 83
CNI (Catholic Nonviolence Initiative), 215
Cody, John, 177, 181
Cohen, Seymour, 179
Cold War, 209, 292
collectivism, 52, 102
colonization, cultural, 329
Commission of the Bishops' Conferences of the European Community, 147, 150, 155–56

Subject Index

Commission of the Bishops' Conferences of the European Union, 150
Commission of the Episcopates of the European Union (COMECE), 152
common good, 7, 80, 94, 96, 98–102, 326
    belief in, 318
    business and, 103
    declining respect for, 310–11, 312
    and economics, 103
    and inequality, 107
    labor and, 105
    and *Pacem in Terris*, 292–93
    rights and, 99
    work for, 12
communication
    Jesus as example, 255
    See also social media
Communio et Progresso, 254, 254n5, 257, 258, 266, 276, 277
communion, 18, 19, 26–27, 34, 35, 218, 247, 262
    see also Eucharist
communism, 42, 44, 45, 48, 49, 57, 95, 103, 122, 132, 134
    integration as, 190, 191
communitarianism, 52, 97
Community of Sant'Egidio, 207, 337, 338
compassion, 30, 212, 276, 328
Compendium of the Social Doctrine of the Church, 2, 3, 4, 214, 282, 284, 285, 287, 289, 317, 318
Conference of the Franciscan Family, 205
confirmation bias, 309
conformity bias, 309
Confraternity of Christian Doctrine, 184
Confucius, 20
Congregation for the Doctrine of the Faith, 311
Congress of Industrial Organizations, 119
conscience, 53, 68, 265
    media, 256
conservatism, 347
    hard right, 3
    and human rights, 43
conspiracy theories, 353
consumerism, 223, 234, 236–37, 239, 242–43, 246, 327

contemplation, 262, 319
contraception, 53
Cordier, Andrew, 292
corporate social responsibility, 137
corporatism, 66
cosmotheism, 69
Council for Inclusive Capitalism, 138
Council of Europe, 147, 149
Councils of Catholic Men, Women, and Youth, 184
COVID-19 pandemic, 114, 200, 270–71, 293, 311, 323–24, 333, 334, 344, 353
Crusades, 289, 296
CSD. *See* Catholic Social Doctrine (CSD)
CST. *See* Catholic Social Teaching (CST)
Cuban Missile Crisis, 291, 292, 299
Cullors, Patrisse, 200
culture wars, 3, 353–54
Cuomo, Andrew, 272
Cyprus, 148

Damiano, Alessandro, 149
Darwinism, 34
de Sales, Francis, Saint, 21
death penalty, 332, 338
Declaration of Independence, 169, 305
decolonialization, 289
deep carbonization, 110
deepfakes, 17
democracy
    American, 3, 171
    under assault, 111
    Catholic notion of, 45
    Christian, 96, 117
    and Christian human rights, 59
    constitutional, 3, 14
    liberal, 43, 55–56, 348
    mature, 352
    multiracial, 2
    pluralistic, 37
    protection of, 3
    social, 9, 94–96, 110–11
    and the threat of populism, 13
    weak, 32
    Western, 341, 346, 348, 352
Denmark, 353

Subject Index

Department of Health, Welfare, and
    Education (HEW), 185
deregulation, 83, 106, 342
desegregation
    of the Archdiocese of Chicago,
        186–90
    of Catholic churches, 181–84
    of Catholic hospitals, 185, 187–88
    of Catholic organizations, 176–77
    of Catholic schools, 181–86, 187,
        192
    of the defense industries, 174
    of the Diocese of Charleston,
        183–86
    of education, 172, 180, 181
    of federal programs, public
        accommodations, and
        employment, 180
    of housing, 188–90
    of the military and federal
        employment, 171
    of public transportation, 172
Dicastery for Integral Human
    Development, 137
digital divides, 268
digitalization, 30–35, 36
dignity
    of work, 105, 226–27
    see also human dignity
discernment, 324, 334, 335
disinformation, 11, 266, 270
distributism, 244, 245
diversity, 57, 127, 155, 179, 208, 286,
    299, 319, 336
divestment, 214
division
    biological, 305, 307, 315
    historical/political, 305–6, 307
    philosophical, 305, 306–7
divorce, 68, 336
Doctors Without Borders, 290, 291
dog-whistle messaging, 353
Dominican Republic, 328
Duffy, John A., 171n9

Eastern Orthodox Church, 293, 328
ecclesiology, integral, 212

ecology
    cultural, 127
    of daily life, 127
    economic, 127–28
    integral, 9, 98–99, 113, 126–28
    social, 127
economics
    biophilic markets, 7–8, 86–91
    capitalist, 234
    Catholic approach to, 124
    Christian, 136
    and the common good, 94, 96, 103
    evolution of, 89
    Francis's view of, 327–28
    free-market, 82, 96, 114, 116, 125
    global, 344
    and human rights, 60
    Keynsian, 95, 235–38
    liberal, 347
    and market fitness, 89–90
    and market inequity, 34–35
    mixed economies, 95, 103
    modern, 233–34
    neoclassical, 9, 94, 98–102, 107,
        110, 234
    neoliberal, 57, 242
    and the power of the market, 7, 84
    and religion, 50
    and the rule of law, 83
    scarcity, 238
    social market, 96
    traditional, 243–44
    virtue, 111
economy
    civil, 103, 243, 245
    as closed system, 129
    as complex system, 131–32
    as nonlinear system, 132–35
    as open system, 129–31
Economy of Communion movement,
    137, 208
Economy of Francesco, 139
ecosystems, 127–28
ecumenical movement, 325
Egan, John, 189
Egypt, 293, 297
El Salvador, 58, 205–6

376

Subject Index

Elementary Catechism on the Morality of Segregation and Discrimination, An, 184
Enlightenment, 4, 41, 69, 308
environmental crisis, 83, 94, 106, 109–10, 283, 325–27
environmental sustainability, 138
environmentalism, 199, 246
epistemology, 305
Epistle to Diognetus, 64, 77
Epstein, Jeffrey, 272
Equal Rights Amendment, 272
equality, 57, 305, 330, 333
   economic, 171
   political, 171
   for women, 272
   see also inequality/inequity
Erdoğan, Recep Tayyip, 340, 342
eschatology, 55, 233
   anti-work, 233–39
   Christian, 134, 226
   consumerist, 234, 236, 239, 242–43, 246
   economic, 236
Essentials of a Good Peace, 171
Estonia, 155
eternal life, 233
ethics
   Catholic, 228
   life, 4, 6, 13, 225, 321
   sexual, 4, 6, 13, 225, 321
   social, 251
   theological, 225
   Thomistic, 227
   of the university, 241
   virtue, 227
   of work, 233, 234, 240
Ethics in Advertising, 258
Ethics in Internet, 259
Eucharist, 77, 275
   see also communion
Europe
   Catholic movements in, 117–18, 240
   Christian Democratic parties in, 117, 118–19
   Christian heritage of, 9–10
   Church in, 322
   declining fertility in, 323
   Francis's vision of, 146–58
   human rights in, 55
   lay social movements, 206–7
   post-war, 96
   rising prosperity in, 95
   secularization of, 54–55
   social Catholicism in, 120, 252
   soul of, 156–58
   see also Belgium; European Union; France; Germany; Italy; Spain; United Kingdom
European Parliament, 149, 151, 154
European Union, 147, 149, 150, 157, 158, 291, 341, 348, 353
   see also Europe
euthanasia, 323
Evangelii Gaudium, 125, 159, 163, 360, 362, 363
Evangelium Vitae, 345
evangelization, 2
Evers, Medgar, 180
evil, 11, 22, 31, 134, 204, 258, 264, 307, 332
   of racism, 169, 179, 193
existentialism, 308
Extinction Rebellion, 84
extractivism, 102

Fair Employment Practices Commission, 174–75
fake news, 256, 356
Familiaris Consortio, 226
family unit, 116, 119, 124, 158, 345
   see also marriage
fascism, 42, 43, 45, 48, 66, 96, 361
   critique of, 54
   and human rights, 48
   integration as, 190
   neo-, 3, 6
Filipino community, 162
financialization, 83, 108, 110, 245–46n76
Fletcher, Albert, 184
Floyd, George, 168, 169, 199, 200
Focolare, 137, 207–8
Foley, John, 258
forgiveness, 149, 179, 331–32
Fossil Fuel Divestment Toolkit, 214
fossil fuels, 109–10

Subject Index

Fourth National Missionary
Conference, 162
France, 96, 117, 131, 150, 151–52, 154,
159, 208, 323, 338
  populism in, 357
  worker priest movement in, 122
  see also Europe
Francis, Pope
  at Abu Dhabi, 296
  addressing the World Meeting of
    Popular Movements, 139–40,
    197, 201–2
  addressing US Congress, 296
  Amoris Laetitia, 226, 336
  on a "better kind of politics," 13–14,
    331
  call to evangelism, 9
  Centesimus Annus, 115, 130, 134,
    134–36, 227n12, 349
  at the Centre for Theology and
    Community, 362–64
  and Christian discipleship, 137
  Christus Vivit, 336
  commitment to the peripheries,
    148–49, 155, 159–64
  Council for Inclusive Capitalism,
    138–39
  criticism of, 295, 296, 321
  on "culture of encounter," 315
  on "culture of narcissism," 33
  on "dark clouds," 329
  Day of Grandparents and the
    Elderly, 151–52
  on disinformation, 12
  ecological vision of, 117, 125–26,
    130, 136, 142
  Economy of Francesco, 139
  environmental teachings of, 212,
    247n78, 321, 325–27, 328
  Evangelii Gaudium, 125, 159, 163,
    360, 362, 363
  family background, 147–48
  Francis of Assisi as inspiration,
    296–98
  Fratelli Tutti, 12, 212, 215, 216, 218,
    239, 260, 265, 282, 283, 284,
    285, 293–94, 298–99, 329–33,
    338, 341, 349, 354, 362, 396–97

  global outreach of, 295–99
  on human dignity, 6, 200
  on human rights, 60
  humanism of, 3, 16
  on integral ecology, 9, 113, 126–28
  on the Internet, 271
  in Iraq, 286–87
  as Jesuit, 298, 324, 335
  Laudato Si,' 8, 17, 109, 125–26, 150,
    210, 212, 213, 218, 260, 264,
    268, 282, 284, 285, 293–94, 296,
    325–29
  Let Us Dream, 333–37, 364
  opposition to, 13
  popularism of, 14–15, 349–54
  on populism, 349–55, 359–65
  priorities of, 12
  Querida Amazonia, 336
  on religious movements, 204
  on signs of the times, 322, 336, 337
  social teaching of, 6, 13, 146–64,
    217, 212, 321–22, 324, 325–37
  on solidarity, 111
  support for, 312–13
  support for ICAN, 199
  on synodality, 217
  on technology, 241, 245
  on "theology of the people," 13, 14
  World Day of Peace Message, 216
Francis of Assisi, Saint, 283, 296–98,
  327
Franciscan order, 205, 298
Franciscans International (FI), 205, 214
Fratelli Tutti, 12, 212, 215, 216, 218, 239,
  260, 265, 282, 283, 284, 285,
  293–94, 298–99, 329–33, 338,
  341, 349, 354, 362, 396–97
fraternity, 341
free will, 28, 258, 305
freedom, 35, 134, 171, 318, 332
Freedom House, 290
Frei, Eduardo, 119
French Revolution, 43, 44, 50–51
Fribourg Union, 206, 252
futurism, utopian, 66

Gamaliel Foundation, 201
Garza, Alicia, 200

Subject Index

Gasperi, Alcide De, 96, 152, 157
Gaudium et Spes, 134, 214, 291, 318
Gautama, 20
GCCM (Global Catholic Climate Movement), 210, 213
gender issues, 5, 71, 313–14, 353
Genesis, 307, 316, 326
genocide, 284, 289, 290, 291
Germany, 96, 117, 118, 131, 208, 323, 328, 334, 354
 fascism in, 361
 industrial relations in, 105, 111
 see also Europe
ghettoization, 345
Gilmore, Joseph M., 173n14
Glennon, John Mark, 171n9
Global Catholic Climate Movement (GCCM), 210, 213
global governance, 49
globalism, 49, 56, 242
globalization, 83, 106, 110, 113, 148, 330, 342
 and the death of heavy industry, 346
 economic, 123, 138, 340, 347
 and employment, 108
Goebbels, Joseph, 356
Good Samaritan parable, 27, 200, 260, 298, 330
government
 and the economy, 114
 role of, 102–3, 119
grace, 55, 130, 134, 159, 193, 300, 317, 324
 fall from, 308
gratuitousness, 99, 100, 130–31
gray pragmatism, 164
Great Depression, 95, 96, 105, 209, 344
Greece, 148, 353
Greek tragedy, 28, 29
Green New Deal, 84
Greenpeace, 199
Guatemala, 58

Hallinan, Paul, 179, 184–85
Hart, Luke, 176
healthcare, 353
Hebrew prophets, 20
hedonism, 130n50

Herod, 74–75, 78, 80
heuristics, 305
Hickey, James Aloysius, 295
Hindus, 285
Hitler, Adolf, 13–14, 341, 354–56, 357–58
Holocaust, 284, 289
Holy Roman Empire, 289
homosexuality, 68, 323
hope, 9, 29, 30, 37, 146, 151, 157, 201, 233, 247, 255, 308, 336
hubris, 34
Huerta, Dolores, 209
human capital, 129–30
human development, integral, 98, 101, 103, 156, 201, 247
human dignity, 3, 23, 27, 28, 42, 48, 54, 59, 95, 118, 169, 170, 256, 295, 317, 345
 and the BLM movement, 200
 and Christianity, 76
 in Europe, 146
 and the Franciscan movement, 205
 and human rights, 58
 and humanism, 157
 at the margins, 364–65
 and racism, 191
 and social media, 274
 see also dignity
human flourishing, 17, 22, 99, 105, 109, 110, 224, 252
human nature, 24–30, 55
human paradox, 24, 31
human rights
 Catholic approaches to, 44–51, 55, 57, 59–60, 288, 289
 Christian, 41, 50, 53, 54, 55, 56, 59
 and fascism, 42, 43
 Francis's commitment to, 158
 and globalism, 56
 and human dignity, 58
 in Latin America, 57–58
 and Maritain, 45–46
 of Moyn, 41–46
 and natural law, 51–52
 and Pax Christi, 209
 and pluralism, 56
 politics of, 54, 57–58, 60

Subject Index

human rights (cont.)
  protection of, 284
  scholarship on, 4–5, 40–60
  and segregation, 172–73
  and social Catholicism, 1, 3–6, 285
  and Thomism, 45–46
  violation of, 54
human trafficking, 208, 336
humanism
  anthropocentric, 19
  atheist, 19
  Christian, 1, 3–4, 18–19, 22–23, 30–35
  European, 150
  exclusive, 19–20
  and human dignity, 157
  integral, 16, 17–18, 19
  new/full-bodied, 17, 19
  non-Promethean, 28
  ontological underpinnings of, 19–24
  of Pope Francis, 3, 16
  and religion, 19–20
  roots of, 20–21
  secular, 22
  and social Catholicism, 3–6
  solidary, 12
  trans-, 34
humanitarian aid, 285
humanitarianism, 68, 69, 76
Hungarian Reformed Church, 179
Hungary, 150, 153, 342, 347, 353, 357
Hunton, George, 174, 175, 176, 177
Hyland, Francis, 184
hyperbole, 13–14, 353, 355

ICAN (International Campaign to Abolish Nuclear Weapons), 199
Ignatian Family Teach-In for Justice, 205
Ignatian movement, 205
Ignatian Solidarity Network (ISN), 205–6
Ignatius of Loyola, Saint, 205–6, 298, 335
illiberalism, 4, 5
imago Dei, 18, 24–30, 34, 287, 300, 308, 317
IMCS-Pax Romana (International Movement of Catholic Students), 207, 212
IMF (International Monetary Fund), 107, 133
Immaculate Conception, 73
immanence, 18, 21, 22, 23
immigrants and immigration, 83, 123, 148, 193, 201, 246, 295, 324, 330–31, 336, 340, 347
  assimilation of, 352
  in Europe, 347–48
  sanctuary for, 208
  as scapegoats, 353
  in the U.S., 348
inclusion, 286
Inclusive Capitalism Platform, 138
India, 342, 350, 357
indifference, 334
indigenous peoples, 288, 359–60
individualism, 52, 97, 121, 138, 329, 330, 336, 345–46
Industrial Revolution, 88, 108–9
  second, 206
industrialization, 160
inequality/inequity, 83, 84, 85, 94, 95, 97–98, 106–7, 109, 125, 337, 340, 342, 343–44, 362
  economic, 84, 115, 353
  of education, 111
  and injustice, 160, 161, 164
  in the market, 34–35
  racial, 171
  and social dysfunction, 107
  see also equality
infanticide, 68
injustice
  economic, 18
  environmental, 18
  racial, 173
  social, 18
  see also justice
Institution of the Synod of Bishops, 217
instrumentalism, 258, 265
integralism, 63, 66
  postliberal, 2–3, 4, 5
Inter Mirifica, 255–56, 266
interfaith networks, 140–41
intermediate associations, 115–16, 124
International Association of Lasallian Universities, 205

Subject Index

International Campaign to Abolish Nuclear Weapons (ICAN), 199
International Campaign to Ban Landmines, 199
International Coordination of Young Christian Workers (CIJOC), 206
International Criminal Court, 341
International Monetary Fund (IMF), 107, 133
International Movement of Catholic Students (IMCS-Pax Romana), 207, 212
International Young Catholic Workers, 121
International Young Christian Workers (IYCW), 206–7
Interracial Review, 174, 175, 191
inter-religious dialogue, 321–22, 328, 332, 337
Iraq, 286–87, 337, 347
Ireland, 323
ISIS, 286
Islam, 285, 353
ISN (Ignatian Solidarity Network), 205–6
Italy, 96, 147, 159, 289, 323, 338, 342, 353, 357, 361
  see also Europe
IYCW (International Young Christian Workers), 206–7

James the Apostle, Saint, 78
Japan, 95
Jesuit order, 205, 209, 298, 324, 335, 359–60
Jesuit Refugee Service, 337
Jesuit Volunteer Corps, 337
Jesus Christ
  Beatitudes, 335
  birth of, 74
  Body of, 54, 55, 65, 74, 191, 320
  Incarnation of, 22, 121, 258
  ministry of, 77, 78, 80–81, 284
  as "New Adam," 308
Real Presence of, 275
  Redemption of, 258
  Sermon on the Mount, 209
  as Word made flesh, 254–55

Jeunesse Ouvrière Catholique (JOC), 117–18, 120, 121, 206
John Paul II, Pope, 247n78, 312
  on business enterprise, 137
  Centesimus Annus, 115, 132, 134–36, 227n12, 349
  on the economy, 116, 130, 235
  on the environment, 325, 329
  in Europe, 147
  Evangelium Vitae, 345
  Familiaris Consortio, 226
  on human rights, 47
  on the Internet, 268–69
  Laborem Exercens, 229, 239
  Redemptoris Mater, 71–72, 73
  social teachings of, 212
  Sollicitudo Rei Socialis, 132, 211
  support for new ecclesial movements, 207
  on work, 230, 236
  World Communication Day message, 260
John XXIII, Pope/Saint
  on the common good, 283
  Mater et Magistra, 215, 337–38
  Pacem in Terris, 284, 289, 292–93, 338
  and Vatican II, 289
Johnson, Boris, 14, 340, 342, 348, 350, 353, 354, 357
Josephites, 187, 209
Jubilee, 336
Judaism, 28, 68–69, 286, 298
Judeo-Christian dialogue, 289
just peace, 215, 285, 298, 299
just wages, 44, 57, 105, 228, 230, 241, 272–73
just war theory, 332, 338
justice, 27, 35, 57, 95, 168–69, 272, 318
  Catholic notions of, 100
  climate, 210
  commutative, 100, 102
  economic, 18
  environmental, 18, 205
  interracial, 168, 170, 181
  labor, 208
  and law, 18
  and Pax Christi, 209

381

Subject Index

justice (cont.)
  racial, 10, 168, 169, 173–90, 179–80, 190–93
  social, 18
  and transcendence, 22
  work for, 12, 274
  see also injustice; social justice
Justice and Peace institutions, 293

Kelly, Steve, 210
Kennedy, John F., 180, 292
Kennedy, Robert F., 292
Keogh, Francis P., 173n14
Ketteler, Wilhelm von, 252
Khrushchev, Nikita, 292
King, Martin Luther Jr., 178, 179, 180, 190
Kingdom of God, 77, 78, 134
kleptocracy, 7
Knights of Columbus, 176–77
Knights of Labor, 119
Korfanty, Wojciech, 47

labor
  and the common good, 105
  dignified employment, 108–9
  history of, 224
  see also work
labor unions, 57, 95, 103, 105, 106, 116, 199, 201, 209, 343, 351
  Catholic, 118
  German Catholic, 337
  secular, 118
  social role of, 119
  in the U.S., 119–20
Laborem Exercens, 229, 239
Lampedusa, 148–49, 159
landless farmers, 201, 202
Lasallian Brothers, 203, 204
Last Dance, The (documentary), 229
Latin America, 119, 322, 323, 325, 359–60
  church organizations in, 141
  economics in, 160
  in human rights scholarship, 57–58
  populism in, 362
  social Catholicism in, 120
  Young Catholic Workers in, 121

Latvia, 155
Laudato Si', 8, 17, 109, 125–26, 150, 210, 212, 213, 218, 260, 264, 268, 282, 284, 285, 293–94, 296, 325–29
Laudato Si' movement, 210
law
  constitution, 55
  human rights, 56
  international, 55
  justice and, 18
  of nature, 51
  obedience to, 53
  rule of, 7, 83
Le Pen, Marine, 343, 357
Le Sillion, 206
Leadership Conference on Civil Rights, 175
Left Behind, 14, 340, 343, 346, 351, 363–64
leisure consumption, 235
leisure studies, 232n31
Leo XIII, Pope, 65, 127, 228
  Rerum Novarum, 51, 105, 120, 170, 211, 215, 237n50, 326
Lesbos Island, 159, 160
Let Us Dream (Pope Frances), 333–37, 364
LGBTQ+ community, 313–14
liberalism
  anti-, 2
  and human dignity, 42
  metropolitan, 14
  progressive, 7, 14, 83, 363
  see also neoliberalism
liberation theology, 40, 57, 58, 59–60, 359, 361
libertarianism, 6, 102, 347
Libya, 347
Liquori Press, 191
Lithuania, 155
love
  Church's culture of, 37
  divine, 2, 30, 34, 79, 254, 294
  for God, 21
  God as, 26, 30
  political, 331
  preferential, 79–80, 99
  primacy of, 27

Subject Index

and racial reconciliation, 179
self-, 79
and transcendence, 22
Lubich, Chiara, 207
Luddites, 244
Lutheran Church, 179, 205

Magi, 74, 75, 80
Magnificat, 5, 78–81
Malta, 148
March on Washington, 180–81
marginalized persons, 2, 6, 15, 201, 268, 295, 299, 327, 353
market fitness function, 8
marriage
    Catholic view of, 225, 227
    debates about, 225
    and divorce, 6, 68, 336
    interracial, 191
    nature of, 5, 71
    remarriage, 6, 336
    same-sex, 353
Martin, Trayvon, 199
Marxism, 132–33, 134, 237
Mary (Virgin Mother)
    as example, 71–78
    and the Magnificat, 78–81
Maryknoll nuns, 58
mask-wearing, 353
mass extinction, 8, 86–87
Mater et Magistra, 215, 337–38
materialism, 22, 138
    bourgeois, 35
    naturalistic, 18, 36
Maurin, Peter, 209
McAlister, Elizabeth, 210
McDevitt, John, 176–77
McDonough, Thomas, 184
McIntyre, James Francis Cardinal, 173n14
McNicholas, John T., 171n9
media
    advertising, 256, 266, 268
    Catholic, 173, 193
    independent press, 356
    journalism and news, 266–67
    social communication on, 253n2
    truth in, 257
    warnings about, 270–71
    see also social media
Meloni, Giorgia, 340, 342
meritocracy, 111
metaphysics, 22, 51–52
#MeToo movement, 200, 271–72
Meyer, Albert G., 173n14, 179, 189
migration. *See* immigrants and immigration
Milano, Alyssa, 271–72
military conscription, 53, 209
minimum wage, 240–42
    see also just wage
Miranda Prorsus, 258
misinformation, 270
    see also disinformation
Mittelstand, 131
Mitty, John J., 171n9
modernism
    fraternal, 48–49, 53
    paternal, 48, 53
modernity, 48, 66
    Catholicism and, 53–56
    and Christianity, 69
    religion and, 50, 71
modernization theory, 133
Modi, Narendra, 340, 342, 357
monopolies, 95, 245
monotheism, 68–69
Mooney, Edward, 171n9
moral autonomy, 28
moral capital, 110
moral luck, 240
moral machines, 31
moral neutrality, 264
moral relativism, 310–11
Movement for Black Lives, 200
multipolarity, 154
multi-track diplomacy, 207
Munchen-Gladbach school, 337
Muslims, 285, 296, 298, 347, 348
Myanmar, 212

narcissism, 33, 107, 354
Nassar, Larry, 272
National Association for the Advancement of Colored People (NAACP), 174, 180, 185

Subject Index

National Catholic Conference for Interracial Justice (NCCIJ), 178–80
National Catholic Rural Life Conference (NCRLC), 120
National Catholic Welfare Conference (NCWC), 170–71, 178
    Social Action Department (SAD), 175
National Conference of Catholic Bishops. *See* United States Conference of Catholic Bishops (USCCB)
National Conference on Religion and Race (1963), 178–79
National Council for a Permanent Fair Employment Practices Committee, 174n19
National Domestic Workers Alliance, 201
National Farm Workers Association, 199
National Urban League, 174
nationalism, 47, 284, 287, 316, 329, 341, 348, 350
    far-right, 7, 83
natural law tradition, 40, 45–46, 51–52, 54, 59, 288
naturalism, 23
Naziism, 96
NCCIJ (National Catholic Conference for Interracial Justice), 178–80
NCRLC (National Catholic Rural Life Conference), 120
NCWC (National Catholic Welfare Conference), 170–71, 175, 178
neighborhood association, 116
Neo-Darwinism, 336
neofascism, 3, 6
    see also fascism
neoliberalism, 44, 82–91, 104
    decline of, 114
    economic, 57, 114
    and the environment, 110
    failures of, 1, 7, 9
    globalist, 242
    and neoclassical economics, 94
    in the U.S., 82
    see also liberalism

neo-paganism, 76
neo-stoicism, 27
Netherlands, 117, 323, 353
Network, 337
network theories, 211–12
New Deal, 96, 120
New Zealand, 328
Nicaragua, 58
nihilism, 24, 308
Noll, John F., 171n9
nongovernmental organizations (NGOs), 290
nonprofits, 116, 138
nonviolence, 209
"Nonviolence and Just Peace" conference, 215
North America, 95, 322
    see also Canada; United States
North American EoC Association, 208
Nostra Aetate: Declaration on the Relation of the Church to Non-Christian Religions, 170, 294–95
nouvelle théologie, 40, 54, 55, 59
nuclear weapons, 199, 202, 210, 283, 284, 285, 291, 292, 299

Obama administration, 114
O'Boyle, Patrick A., 173n14
Occupy Wall Street movement, 114–15
Octogesima Adveniens, 217
Oeuvre des Cercles Catholiques d'Ouvriers (Society of Catholic Worker Circles), 206
oligarchy, 245
ontology, 23
    destructive, 24
    of digitalization, 31
    of humanism, 19–24
Orbán, Viktor, 340, 342, 357
Organization of Catholic Parents, 184–85
original sin, 316
originalism, 347

Pacem in Terris, 284, 289, 292–93, 338
pacifism, 215–16
    see also peace activism
paganism, 67, 68, 69
Papal states, 289

Subject Index

Pareto efficiency, 101
Paris Agreement, 87, 110
paritirisme, 131
Parks, Rosa, 172
pastoral leadership, 2, 12, 303–20
Paul of Tarsus, Saint, 12, 64, 227, 269, 304, 319–20
Paul VI, Pope/Saint
   Gaudium et Spes, 134, 214, 291, 318
   Inter Mirifica, 255–56, 266
   Nostra Aetate, 170, 294–95
   Octogesima Adveniens, 217
      Populorum Progressio, 16, 17, 123, 156, 211, 247
Pax Christi International, 208, 215, 216, 289, 337
PCSC. *See* Pontifical Council for Social Communications (PCSC)
peace activism, 208–9, 213, 215–16
peacebuilding, 289, 298–99, 332
Pentecost, 78
Perón, Evita, 361
Perón, Juan Domingo, 361
Peronism, 341, 361
phenomenology, 21, 30, 31
Philippines, 328
philosophy
   Christian humanism as, 18
   of human nature, 24
   humanistic political, 18
   moral, 4
   political, 46, 102
PICO National Network, 201
Pius VII, Pope, 50–51
Pius XI, Pope, 45, 47, 127, 137
   Quadragesimo Anno, 120, 170, 228, 337, 361
   Vigilanti Cura, 254
Pius XII, Pope, 42, 45, 255
   Miranda Prorsus, 258
Plauche, Charles, 183
Plowshares actions, 210, 213
pluralism, 1, 37, 353
   cultural, 323
   human rights and, 56
   religious, 43, 323
Poland, 46, 347, 353
polarization, 12, 13, 15, 111, 284, 313, 318, 336, 342, 343, 348, 351

politics
   and the Church, 62–65, 78
   of human rights, 54, 57–58, 60
   humane, 9
   and inequality, 106–7
   of the Magnificat, 78–81
   populist, 356–58
   and religion, 50
   traditional, 344, 346, 348
pollution, 87, 109
Pontifical Council for Justice and Peace, 137, 293
   Compendium of the Social Doctrine of the Church, 2, 3, 4, 214, 282, 284, 285, 287, 289, 317, 318
Pontifical Council for Social Communications (PCSC), 254, 254n5, 255–56, 275, 276
   The Church and Internet, 259
   Communio et Progresso, 254, 254n5, 257, 258, 266, 276, 277
   Ethics in Advertising, 258
   Ethics in Internet, 259
popular movements, 200–202
popularism, 362–63
populism, 5, 13–14, 15, 115, 284, 287, 331, 335, 336, 340, 341, 342, 346, 348, 351
   contemporary, 2
   exclusive, 365
   inclusive, 15, 363
   irresponsible, 349
   nationalist, 114, 115, 342, 348, 350
   vs. popularism, 349–54
   prairie, 244
   progressive, 114
   theological, 362
Populorum Progressio, 16, 17, 123, 156, 211, 247
Portugal, 147, 151, 328
positivism, 23, 32
poverty, 14, 32, 110, 126, 239, 296–97, 333, 344, 362
   and climate change, 326–27
   reducing, 287
   spirit of, 247
   vows of, 204, 208
Presidential Commission on Civil Rights, 171, 189

Subject Index

Principle to Protect, 291
privatization, 121, 122
progress, 20–21, 35–36, 68, 256, 263, 327
progressivism, 70
propaganda, 355–56
property rights, 102
prophets, 20–21
proprietorship, 245
Protestantism, 49, 179
    Anglican, 205
    Baptist, 179
    in Europe, 118
    Evangelical, 312, 325
    and the Franciscan movement, 205
    liberal, 56–57
    neo-Pentecostal, 325
psychology, moral, 306–7
psychotherapy, 25
public good, 76
Public Religion Research Institute, 312
Putin, Vladimir, 342

Quadragesimo Anno, 120, 170, 228, 337, 361
Quakers, 179
Queen's Work, The, 191
Querida Amazonia, 336

racism, 2, 168, 169, 170, 201, 284, 358
    Catholic Social Teaching on, 170–73
    denouncement of, 169, 179, 191–92, 193
Randolph, A. Philip, 174, 174n19, 180
rationalism, 17
Reagan, Ronald, 7, 8, 342, 344, 345
Reagan administration, 58
reason, 17, 20, 21, 25, 26, 28, 30, 31, 306–7, 315
Rebora, Clemente, 152
reciprocity, 99, 100, 101, 243–44
reconciliation, 10, 209, 299
redemption, 233, 258, 317
Redemptoris Mater, 71–72, 73
redistribution, 103, 238–39, 246
reformism, center-left, 7, 83
refugees, 295
    see also immigrants

Reh, Francis, 185
relationality, embodied, 30
relativism, 310, 311, 336, 345
religion
    folk, 360
    and humanism, 19–20
    and modernity, 50
    privatization of, 121, 122
    and social movements, 202–3
    see also Catholicism; Christianity; Protestantism
religious freedom, 295
religious pluralism, 324
religious switching, 323
Rerum Novarum, 51, 105, 120, 170, 211, 215, 237n50, 326
ressourcement, 19
revelation, 11
Review of Life, 206, 215
rights
    of African Americans, 171
    Catholic notions of, 99
    civil, 169
    and common good, 99
    economic, 95, 96
    of man, 41
    see also human rights
Ritter, Joseph E., 173n14, 181
robotics, 224
robotization, 84
Rohinga people, 333
Rom community, 149
Roman Empire, 67–68, 74, 162
Romania, 148, 149, 353
Romanian Orthodox Church, 179
Roosevelt, Franklin D., 96, 174
rule of law, 7, 83
Rummel, Joseph F., 171n9, 183
rural cooperatives, 120
Ruskin, Bayard, 180
Russell, John, 184
Russia, 291, 342, 353
Rwanda, 284, 290

Sabbath, 232, 291
Saint Frances Xavier hospital, 185
Saint Vincent DePaul Society, 337

Subject Index

salvation, 26, 77, 79, 233, 254–56, 258, 264
Salvini, Matteo, 340, 342, 357
Scali, John, 292
School of Salamanca, 288
School of the Americas, 206
Schuman, Robert, 96, 152
Schwartz, Tony, 356
Second Vatican Council
   authority of, 325
   critical views of, 294
   on evangelization, 206
   Gaudium et Spes, 134, 214, 291, 318
   goals of, 289, 293
   and human rights, 47
   rejection of, 203
   themes of, 294–95
   Universal Call to Holiness, 2, 11, 223, 226, 227
secularism, 23
secularity, 54, 67
secularization, 20, 54–55, 67, 121, 122, 148
"see-judge-act" method, 206, 215, 333
segregation, 10, 169, 171, 172–73, 180, 184
self-determination, 58
self-interest, 241
self-preservation, 51
Semaine Sociale, 338
Sensus Fidelium, 217
Service Employees International Union, 201
sexism, 358
sexual abuse scandals, 13, 293, 309, 323
sexual minorities, 6
sexuality, 5, 50, 71, 227, 353
Shean, Maurice, 184
Sheil, Bernard, 188
Shuttlesworth, Fred, 178
signs of the times, 2, 3, 6, 294, 322, 335, 337
Sivori, Regina Maria, 147
skepticism, 28
slavery, 10, 169
small and middle-sized enterprises (SMEs), 131

social capital, 107, 346
social Catholicism
   as alternative to neoliberalism, 124, 142
   "better politics" of, 2
   challenges for, 36–37
   and the common good, 80
   coordination of efforts, 218
   decline of, 113, 121–25, 138
   ecology of, 10, 211–17
   and economics, 6–15
   in Europe, 252
   high point of, 117–20
   and human rights, 3–6
   and humanism, 3–6
   insights on social media, 272–77
   lay social movements, 206–7
   new context of, 17–19
   post-Christendom, 5, 71
   and race, 10
   renewal of, 125–42
   Review of Life method, 215
   and social media, 251–77
   in the U.S., 116–17, 252
   and work, 226, 240
   see also social movements
social Darwinism, 336
social friendship, 1, 4, 15, 341
social justice, 168, 323, 324, 364
   Let Us Dream, 364
social media
   and the #MeToo movement, 271–72
   and Catholic Social Teaching, 254–69
   creating solidarity and liberation, 271–72, 274
   data harvesting, 273–74
   defined, 253n3
   divisive potential of, 11–12
   platforms, 252, 273
   positive use of, 11
   and social Catholicism, 2, 251–53
   and social fragmentation, 267
   and social movements, 200, 210, 213
social movement organizations (SMOs), 198–99, 204–5, 218

Subject Index

social movements, 124–25, 139–41
   Catholic, 202–3, 212–13
   and the Catholic Church, 197–202, 217–19
   Catholic Social Teaching in, 337–38
   function of, 198
   issue based, 208–10
   as mediators, 212–14, 218–19
   new ecclesial, 207–8
   political influence of, 214
   popular movements, 200–202
   religious life, 203–6
   and social Catholicism, 196–97
   specialized Catholic action, 206–7
social organizations, 124–25
social pluralism, 318
social theory, 218
socialism, 44, 48, 95, 338
socialization, 337
Society of Christian Ethics, 225
Society of the Divine Word Fathers, 187
sociology, critical realist, 11
Socrates, 20
solidarity, 99, 100, 101, 102, 110, 111, 115, 169, 212–13, 247n78, 288, 289, 290, 318, 330, 335, 336, 341, 362, 364
solipsism, 346
Sollicitudo Rei Socialis, 132, 211
Sophocles, 28, 76
Southern Christian Leadership Conference, 178, 199
sovereignty, 288–91, 341
Soviet Union, 292
Spain, 334, 361
   see also Europe
Spe Salvi, 233
Spellman, Francis Cardinal, 171n9, 173n14
spirituality, 20, 70, 141, 205–7, 231, 275, 327
stagflation, 97
Stritch, Samuel A., 171n9, 187–88, 189
subsidiarity, 99, 102, 103, 244, 288, 289, 290, 318, 328, 335
suffering, 29, 30, 63, 271, 276, 330
suicide, 68
supernatural, 21, 54, 56, 59, 247

supernaturalism, 59
Supreme Court, 172, 175, 181, 192
sustainable development, 104
Sweden, 353
Switzerland, 353
synodality, 217, 286, 318, 328, 336, 337
Syria, 347
systems thinking, 128–35

Tea Party movement, 114, 340, 347
technocracy, 343
technological paradigm, 265
technology
   and carbon emissions, 110
   communication, 138, 254, 258
   critical use of, 16, 264
   digital, 16, 17, 18–19
   labor-enabling, 108
   labor-replacing, 109
   limitations of, 32
   misuse of, 11–12, 264
   use by power, 245, 264
theoconservatism, 240
theology, 308
   African, 324
   Christian, 77
   Marian, 72
   moral, 310
   pre-Vatican II, 228
   sacramental, 275
Theology of the People, 13, 14, 359, 360–61, 361
theosis, 25
Thérèse de Lisieux, Saint, 26
Thomism, 45
Tometi, Opal, 200
totalitarianism, 48, 55–56, 190, 350
trade unions. *See* labor unions
tradition, 43, 52, 53, 59
tragedy, 29–30
transcendence, 18, 20–24
transgenderism, 313–14
transhumanism, 34
transphobia, 313
transversality, 151
Trappists, 80, 203
Treaty of Detroit, 235n44
Treaty of Lisbon, 151

Subject Index

Treaty of Rome, 149, 157
Treaty of the Prohibition of Nuclear Weapons, 199
Treaty of Westphalia, 287, 290–91
tribalism, 12, 309–10, 313, 314, 318, 336, 351
Truman, Harry S., 171
Trump, Donald, 13–14, 83, 84, 114, 340, 342, 348, 350–51, 353, 354, 356–57, 357
Trump, Ivana, 356
trust, 95, 284, 300
　decline of, 98, 107, 108
truth, 35, 277, 318, 331
　in the media, 257
　sharing, 262
　in social media, 270
　and transcendence, 22
Turkey, 159, 342, 348

UDHR (Universal Declaration of Human Rights), 95, 288, 292, 341
Ukraine, 291, 300, 353
United Farm Workers, 209
United Kingdom, 84, 340, 342, 343, 346, 354
　Brexit referendum, 348, 350
　inequality in, 344
　political division in, 351
　populism in, 350, 351, 353
United Kingdom Independence Party (UKIP), 347–48
United Nations (UN), 199, 214, 283, 296, 299–300, 321, 341
　Climate Change Conference (2015), 326
　Economic Commission for Latin America, 160
　General Assembly, 291, 300
　Human Rights Council, 214
United States, 328, 340, 342, 346
　Capitol insurrection, 350–51
　Catholics in, 53, 119–23, 169–70, 183–90, 192–93, 323
　and the Cold War, 292
　decline of religion in, 122–23
　inequality in, 343–44

nonviolence and peace movements, 209
populism in, 350, 353, 358–59
social Catholicism in, 120–21, 252
work conditions in, 230
United States Conference of Catholic Bishops (USCCB), 120, 170–71, 180, 218, 270, 311
　Discrimination and Christian Conscience, 172
　and interracial justice, 181
　"Open Wide Our Hearts," 10, 168, 169
　Social Action Department (SAD), 120
Universal Call to Holiness, 2, 11, 223, 226, 227
Universal Declaration of Human Rights (UDHR), 95, 288, 292, 341
universal destination of goods, 99, 101, 103, 105, 223, 238–39, 242, 318, 335
University of Alabama, 180
Unterkoefler, Ernest, 185–86
urban ecology, 328
urbanization, 160
USCCB. *See* United States Conference of Catholic Bishops (USCCB)
US Federation of Worker Cooperatives, 201
US Women's National Soccer Team, 272
utopianism, 66

vaccinations, 311–12, 353
values, cultural, 33
Vatican
　Department for Integral Human Development, 201
　on social communication, 252, 253
Vatican II. *See* Second Vatican Council
Vietnam War, 53, 209
Vigilanti Cura, 254
virtue ethics, 227
Vocation of the Business Leader: A Reflection, 104, 137–38

Wall Street Crash, 344, 361
Wallace, George, 180

Subject Index

Walsh, Emmet M., 173n14
Washington Consensus, 133
Waters, Vincent, 179, 181–82
Weinstein, Harvey, 271, 272
welfare state, 96, 106, 108
West Papua, 214
wisdom, 16, 22, 26, 28–31, 37, 252, 262, 362
work
    anti-work eschatologies, 233–39
    dignified, 105, 108, 274–75
    ethical reflection on, 226–33
    future of, 240–47
    good, 223, 228, 230, 240, 241, 243
    good-enough, 228, 229–30, 231, 246
    goodness of, 227
    and leisure, 232
    meaningful, 229, 231
    nature of, 226n11
    objective dimensions of, 229
    refusal of, 227–28n13
    and the Sabbath, 232
    sacramental, 228, 231–33, 240, 241
    and social Catholicism, 223–26
    and social life, 331
    workplace issues, 229–30
    see also just wages; labor
Work of Mary, 207
worker ownership, 245n74
worker priest movement, 122
World Bank, 133, 341, 344
World Communication Day, 254, 259, 260, 263
World Congresses of Ecclesial Movements and New Communities, 207, 218
World Inequality Report, 97
World Meeting of Popular Movements, 139–40, 197, 201–2, 218
World Trade Organization, 341
World War I, 206, 343
World War II, 42, 52, 95, 118, 341

xenophobia, 115, 351, 353

Young Catholic Worker (YCW) movement, 120, 206, 215, 216
Young Christian workers, 203n22
Young Men's Christian Association (YMCA), 179
Young Women's Christian Association (YWCA), 179

Zarathustra, 20
Zimmerman, George, 199
Zuroweste, Albert R., 173n14

Author Index

Accetti, Carlo Invernizzi, 60
Adler, Alfred, 25, 37
Agiesta, Jennifer, 365
Ahern, Kevin, 142, 219
Akin, Jimmy, 164
Allman, Mark J., 219
Anderson, Monica, 277
Anderson, R. Bentley, 194
Annett, Anthony M., 112, 142
Appelbaum, Binyamin, 98, 112
Aquinas. *See* Thomas Aquinas, Saint
Aristotle, 63, 64, 76, 77
Armondi, Simonetta, 164
Asad, Talal, 56
Ash, Roberta, 222
Auxier, Brooke, 277
Avella, Steven M., 194

Balogh, Eva S., 365
Barbato, Mariano P., 164
Bartoli, Andrea, 219
Bednar, Jenna, 92
Beinhocker, Eric D., 92
Bell, Daniel, 142
Bell, Karissa, 277
Belloc, Hilaire, 322, 338
Ben-Ami, Daniel, 248
Benedict XVI, Pope, 37, 142, 248, 277–78, 300, 365
Benestad, Brian, 248
Berger, Peter L., 219
Bergoglio, Jorge Mario, 360, 365
Berrios, Fernando, 142

Berry, Wendell, 229, 237
Beser, Ari, 219
Bethke Elshtain, Jean, 27, 37
Betz, John, 164
Bokenkotter, Thomas S., 219
Borjas, George, 235, 248
Bourdieu, Pierre, 37
Bourg, Julian, 52, 53, 60
Bovée, David S., 143
Bowles, Samuel, 248
Bradley, Gerard, 248
Brady, Bernard, 248
Breidenbach, Michael, 60
Brenner, Marie, 365
Brown, Wendy, 56
Bruegger, Christian, 248
Bruni, Luigino, 248
Buchanan, Larry, 219
Buechler, Steven M., 219
Buttigieg, Joseph A., 144

Caccamo, James F., 278
Caccia, Gabriele, 301
Cahill, Edward, 219
Cajka, Peter, 60
Camara, Javier, 366
Cantalamessa, Raniero, 164
Carboni, Chiara, 38
Casanova, José, 219
Cass, Oren, 242–46, 248
Castronova, Edward, 248
Catholic Nonviolence Initiative, 220
Cavanaugh, William T., 116, 143

Author Index

Ceballos, Gerardo, 92
Chaillet, Pierre, 54
Chamedes, Giuliana, 60
Chappel, James, 48–49, 53, 56, 60, 96, 112
Clark, Charles M. A., 248
Clark, Meghan J., 112
Climate Action Tracker, 92
Cloutier, David, 248
Cobbler, Jason, 278
Cockerell, Isobel, 278
Coeckelbergh, Mark, 31–32, 36, 37, 38
Coleman, John A., 338
Congar, Yves, 54, 56
Congregation for Catholic Education, 278
Connelly, John, 60
Conseil Constitutionnel of France, 366
Cook, Scott, 248
Cooper, Harold, 192
Costanza, Robert, 143
Cottrell, Stephen, 351, 366
Cowen, Tyler, 248
Cox, Joseph, 278
Cox Richardson, Heather, 305–6, 307, 320
Cressler, Matthew J., 190, 194

Dabla-Norris, Era, 112
Dahl, Arthur Lyon, 338
Daly, Daniel, 240
Dante Alighieri, 29
D'Antonio, William V., 143
Davies, William, 366
Dawson, Andrew, 143
Day, Dorothy, 209, 210, 220
Deane-Drummond, Celia, 34, 38
DeChant, Tim, 278
Deiana, Claudio, 164
Delaney, Sam, 366
Delsol, Chantal, 62, 65–71, 76, 80, 81
Diamond, Louise, 220
Dias, Darren, 164
Dicastery for Promoting Integral Human Development, 112
Dodson, Christopher, 248
Dorling, Danny, 344, 366
Dorr, Donal, 248, 338

Drutman, Lee, 92
Du Bois, W. E. B., 169, 194
Dubois, Alexandre, 167
Dupuis, Jacques, 301
Duranti, Marco, 60
Duriez, Bruno, 143
Dutton, J. E., 250

Eatwell, Roger, 346–48, 366
Eckholt, Margit, 164
Economy of Communion, 220
Edelstein, Daniel, 50, 51, 60
Edwards-Levy, Ariel, 365
Ehrman, Terrence P., 143
Ejiowhor, M., 165
Ellali, Ahmed, 278
Ellen MacArthur Foundation, 92
Elliott, Larry, 366
Engels, Friedrich, 145
Enyedi, Zsolt, 366
Escriva, Josemaria, 248
Esping-Andersen, Gøsta, 143
Evans, Tony Tekaroniake, 248

Faggioli, Massimo, 338
Farley, Margaret, 225
Farmer, J. Doyne, 92
Fessard, Gaston, 54
Fieschi, Catherine, 366
Finn, Daniel K., 143, 240, 248
Finnis, John, 51, 52, 60
Flannery, Austin, 194
Fleet, Michael, 143
Flores d'Arcais, Paolo, 38
Focolare Movement, 220
Foucault, Michel, 42, 56
Francis, Pope, 15, 112, 143, 165–66, 220, 249, 278–79, 283, 297, 301, 320, 338, 366–67
Franciscans International, 220
Frank, Robert, 249
Fredricks, James L., 339
Frenkel, Sheera, 279
Frey, Carl Benedikt, 108–9, 112, 249
Fukuyama, Francis, 143

Galbraith, John Kenneth, 103
Gallup, 249

Author Index

George, Francis, 320
Gérard, Dom, 81
Gill, Lesley, 220
Giovagnoli, Agostino, 166
Gobry, Pascal-Emmanuel, 81
Gold, Lorna, 143, 220
Goodman-Thau, Eveline, 29
Goodwin, Matthew, 346–48, 366
Gordon, Robert J., 97, 112, 249
Gowler, David B., 166
Graeber, David, 92, 246
Gray, John, 20, 29, 38
Greeley, Andrew, 249
Green, David, 367
Greenberg, Udi, 49, 59, 60
Gregg, Samuel, 367
Griffiths, Richard T., 143
Guterres, António, 283, 301

Hahl, Oliver, 367
Haidt, Jonathan, 306–8, 314, 315, 319, 320
Hall, Lauren, 81
Hall, Peter A., 143
Hanauer, Nick, 92
Hanebrink, Paul, 60
Hanley, David, 144
Hannigan, John A., 220
Harris Poll, 367
Harter, Jim, 249
Hartwick, Elaine, 145
Harvey, David, 144
Hecht, Robert, 194
Heilbroner, Robert, 249
Henderson, Rebecca, 92
Hennessy, Martha, 210, 213, 220
Henry, A.-M., 81
Heschel, Abraham, 37, 38, 179
Hikota, Riyako Cecilia, 166
Hill, Kashmir, 279
Hinze, Bradford E., 220
Hinze, Christine Firer, 228–29, 249
Hirsch, Fred, 249
Hitler, Adolf, 367
Hittinger, Russell, 244, 249
Hobbes, Thomas, 306–8, 319
Hobsbawm, Eric, 43, 60
Hodgson, Geoffrey M., 144

Holland, Joe, 144
Hollenbach, David, 112, 144, 198, 220
Hubbard, Glenn, 243
Hubbard, R. Glenn, 249
Hughes, John, 232, 249
Hume, David, 306, 307, 308
Hütter, Reinhard, 81

Ignatian Solidarity Network, 220
Institute of the Brothers of the Christian Schools, 221
Intergovernmental Science-Policy Platform on Biodiversity and Ecosystem Services, 92
International Raoul Wallenberg Foundation, 301
Ipsos/Reuters Poll, 367
Iskander, Natasha, 86–88, 92
Ivereigh, Austen, 220, 338, 367

Jaspers, Karl, 20
Jesuit Networking, 221
John Paul II, 81, 112, 144, 221, 249, 279, 367
John XXIII, 283, 301
Joi, Priya, 367
Jones, Jefferey, 280
Jordan, Michael, 229, 237
Judt, Tony, 96–97, 112
Jungmann, Josef, 81

Kalyvas, Stathis N., 144
Kant, Immanuel, 27
Kauffman, Christopher J., 194
Keck, Margaret E., 221
Keeley, Theresa, 58, 60
Keenan, James, 241, 249
Kelly, Conor, 249
Kemper, Donald J., 194
Kersbergen, Kees van, 118, 144
Kessler, Glenn, 367
Ketteler, Wilhelm von, 65
Keynes, John Maynard, 105–6, 112, 236, 238, 250
Khomami, Nadia, 280
Kierkegaard, Søren, 70
Kincaid, Elizabeth Rain, 250
Kington, Tom, 367

Author Index

Klimczuk, Andrzej, 166
Klimczuk-Kochańska, Magdalena, 166
Korgen, Jeffry Odell, 221
Kosicki, Piotr, 46, 47, 53, 60–61
Kozerska, Ewa, 167
Krekó, Péter, 366
Krier Mich, Marvin L., 221
Kselman, Thomas, 144

LaFarge, John, 170, 173–77, 181, 191, 194
Laffin, Arthur J., 221
Lamb, Christopher, 368
Lant, Thilo, 167
Lantigua, David, 52, 57, 58, 61
Lasch, Christopher, 33, 38
Law, Stephen, 19–20, 38
Lawson, Tony, 144
Leahy, Brendan, 221
Lee, Bernard J., 144
LeGoff, Jacques, 150, 167
Leo XIII, Pope, 144, 194, 250
Levin, Yuval, 250
Lewandowsky, Stephan, 368
Lindhart, Robert, 48
Lipovetsky, Gilles, 33, 38
LiveLaudatoSi, 221
Livingston, James, 224, 250
Llorente, Bernarda, 163, 167
Locke, John, 102
Love, Maryann Cusimano, 301–2
Lowe, Nichola, 86–88, 92
Lowrey, Annie, 250
Lubac, Henri de, 22, 24, 38, 54, 55, 56
Luxmoore, Jonathan, 302

Mac, Ryan, 280
MacIntyre, Alasdair, 4, 66
Mahmood, Saba, 56
Maiberg, Emanuel, 278
Maillard, Sébastien, 167
Mainwaring, Scott, 144–45
Mankiw, N. Gregory, 235, 250
Marcel, Gabriel, 33, 37, 38
Marion, Jean-Luc, 66, 81
Maritain, Jacques, 3, 4, 17–19, 30, 35, 37, 38, 45–49, 51, 54–56, 58, 59, 68, 81

Martensen, Katherine, 194
Martin, James, 339
Marx, Karl, 132, 145, 236, 342
Massis, Henri, 48
Matsa, Katerina Eva, 281
Matz, Brian, 250
Maurras, Charles, 66
Mayer, Colin, 104, 112
Mayer, Jane, 368
McCormick, William, 368
McDonald, John, 220
McGreevy, John T., 56, 61, 144, 194
McLeod, Hugh, 144
McShane, Joseph M., 144
Meckler, Laura, 280
Medaille, John, 250
Melloni, Alberto, 221
Menjívar, C., 368
Metz, Johann Baptist, 29, 38
Mich, Marvin Krier, 280
Midgley, Mary, 38
Milanovic, Branko, 106, 112
Mishel, Lawrence, 368
Misner, Paul, 145
Mitchell, Amy, 280
Molla, Rani, 280
Moltmann, Jürgen, 29
Montaigne, 28
Montgomery, Anne, 221
Mounier, Emmanuel, 48, 54
Moyn, Samuel, 4, 5, 40–48, 50, 52, 53, 55–58, 61
Musto, Ronald G., 208, 221

Natanson, Hannah, 280
National Renewable Energy Laboratory, 92
Naughton, Michael, 232, 250
Neary, Timothy B., 194
Nell Breuning, Oswald von, 337
Nepstad, Sharon Erickson, 221
Neuhaus, Richard John, 219
Newman, Mark, 186, 194
Nietzsche, Friedrich, 42
Nolan, Hugh, 194

Oborne, Peter, 357
Ochs, Stephen J., 194

Author Index

O'Connell, Gerard, 368
O'Connor, Flannery, 69
O'Donovan, Oliver, 250
O'Grady, Siobhán, 278
O'Neill, Daniel W., 92
Osheim, Amanda, 211, 221
Ossewaarde-Lowtoo, Roshnee, 4
Ostry, Jonathan D., 112

Pardes, Arielle, 280
Pattison, Mark, 280
Paul VI, Pope, 145, 167, 194, 221, 250, 280, 302
Pax Christi International, 221
Peet, Richard, 145
Pepper, Stephen, 145
Peters, Tiemo Rainer, 38
Pfaffen, Sebastian, 366
Pickett, Kate, 107, 112
Piehl, Mel, 194
Pigou, Arthur C., 92
Piketty, Thomas, 111, 112
Pimentel, Álvaro Mendonça, 167
Pius XI, Pope, 145, 250, 280
Pius XII, Pope, 280
Plato, 76
Poche, Justin D., 195
Polanyi, Karl, 103
Pontifical Council for Justice and Peace, 15, 145, 221, 302, 320
Pontifical Council for Social Communications, 280–81
Posadas, Jeremy, 225, 250
Pozza, Marco, 167
Prebisch, Raul, 160, 167
Prentiss, Craig R., 145
Przywara, Erich, 153, 156
Public Religion Research Institute, 320
Pugh, Rhiannon, 167
Putnam, Robert D., 346, 368

Ranger, Terence, 43, 60
Ratzinger, Joseph, 4, 16, 18, 22, 24–27, 29–31, 34, 38, 250, 307, 311, 316, 320, 345, 368
Rauch, Jonathan, 305–9, 315–16, 319, 320
Rausch, Thomas, 323–24, 339

Rawls, John, 57
Rebala, Pratheek, 281
Riccardi, Andrea, 207, 221
Riley, Frank, 191
Ritchie, Angus, 363, 368
Robinson, Kali, 281
Rogers, Kim Lacy, 195
Rostow, W. W., 133, 145
Rushkoff, Douglas, 245, 246, 250
Ryan, John A., 120, 228, 229, 240, 252, 281

Sacks, Jonathan, 345, 368
Sahlins, Marshall, 250
Saletan, William, 315, 320
Sapolsky, Robert M., 305, 307, 308, 314, 315, 316, 320
Scally, Derek, 339
Scannone, Juan Carlos, 359, 360, 368
Scheeben, Matthias, 72, 81
Schieder, Jessica, 368
Schneiders, Sandra, 222
Schuman, Michael, 93
Schwartz, Barry, 224, 227, 229, 237, 250
Scott, Timothy, 167
Scully, Timothy R., 145
Seaton, Douglas P., 145
Seaton, Paul, 81
Sedmak, Clemens, 167
Segundo, Juan Luis, 361
Sepúlveda, Juan Ginés de, 80
Shadle, Matthew A., 145, 240
Shortall, Sarah, 53, 54, 55, 56, 57, 61
Siemaszko, Corky, 281
Sikkink, Kathryn, 221
Singer, Peter, 28, 38
Sinyai, Clayton, 145
Sisters of Mercy, 222
Smith, Adam, 100, 243
Smith, Gavin J. D., 36, 38
Smith, Jackie, 222
Smith, Janet, 225–26
Smith-Spark, Laura, 281
Snape, Robert, 250
Snow, David A., 222
Soskice, David, 143
Southern, David W., 195
Spadaro, Antonio, 163, 167

Author Index

Speigel, Henry, 250
Springsteen, Bruce, 224
Stanger, Anya, 222
Steinmetz-Jenkins, Daniel, 49, 56, 59, 60, 61
Stenner, Karen, 347, 352, 368
Stiglitz, Joseph E., 85, 343, 368
Strauss, Leo, 4, 46, 52
Suarez, Francisco, 51
Survival International, 368
Susskind, Daniel, 250
Suzman, James, 224, 227, 250
Synod of Bishops, 281

Tachibanaki, Toshiaki, 143
Tacitus, 68
Taylor, Charles, 4, 16, 18–19, 21–27, 30, 32, 34, 36, 38
Al-Tayyeb, Ahmad, 293, 299, 301, 329, 332
Terkel, Studs, 224, 250
Thatcher, Margaret, 342, 344, 345, 369
Thomas Aquinas, Saint, 46, 51, 211, 276
Tibken, Shara, 281
Tierney, Brian, 52
Trussell Trust, 369
Turkle, Sherry, 281
Turkson, Peter A., 167

UN Security Council, 302
United States Catholic Conference of Bishops, 195
US Department of Health and Human Services, 145

Valadier, Paul, 4, 16, 18, 22, 25–30, 32, 34, 37–39
Vallely, Paul, 369

Van Stichel, Ellen, 216, 222
Vanderklippe, Nathan, 281
Verstraeten, Johan, 145, 222
Vidler, Alexander Roper, 222
Vitoria, Francisco de, 51
Vogel, Jefim, 93
Vonthethoff, Ben, 36, 38

Waldstein, Edmund, 81
Walker, Mason, 281
Ward, Kate, 240
Weber, Max, 234
Weck, Guillaume de, 222
Wengrow, David, 92
Wijsen, Franx Jozef Servaas, 222
Wilken, Robert Louis, 81
Wilkinson, Richard, 107, 112
Williams, Daniel, 61
Willliamson, M. Daigle, 164
Willsher, Kim, 369
Winright, Tobias, 219
Wittberg, Patricia, 202, 222
Wittgenstein, Ludwig, 23
World Bank, 93, 369
World Meeting of Popular Movements, 222
Wrzesniewski, Amy, 250

Yoder, John Howard, 81

Zahn, Gordon C., 197, 216, 222
Zald, Mayer N., 222
Zamagni, Stefano, 245, 248
Zielinski, Martin A., 195
Zsupan-Jerome, Daniella, 281
Zuboff, Shoshana, 250
Zubovich, Gene, 61

www.ingramcontent.com/pod-product-compliance
Lightning Source LLC
Chambersburg PA
CBHW071229290426
44108CB00013B/1340